NEW IBERIA

NEW IBERIA

*Essays on the Town
and Its People*

Compiled by

Glenn R. Conrad

Second Edition

Center for Louisiana Studies
University of Southwestern Louisiana
Lafayette, Louisiana

Library of Congress Catalog Number: 86-070808
ISBN: 978-1-935754-59-6

Copyright 1979, 1986 by the University of Southwestern Louisiana
Published 1979. Second Edition 1986

University of Louisiana at Lafayette Press
P.O. Box 40831
Lafayette, LA 70504-0831
http://ulpress.org

For Five Special Stars in My Firmament
Margaret Anne Stewart, Christopher Eugene Conrad, Alan James Stewart
Sarah Adele Nigreville, and Stephen Andrew Conrad

Contents

I	New Iberia: The Spanish Years	1
II	Some Facts and Traditions about New Iberia	15
III	A Narrative of Events Connected with the Early Settlement of New Iberia	73
IV	The Obituary of William F. Weeks	114
V	The Reflections of John M. Weeks	137
VI	Reminiscences of the '60s and '70s	153
VII	New Iberia and Yellow Fever: Epidemic and Quarantine	173
VIII	New Iberia Becomes the Parish Seat	188
IX	The Centennial Celebration at New Iberia, 1876	201
X	The Iron Horse Comes to New Iberia	209
XI	The New Iberia Conflagration of 1899	217
XII	New Iberia Gets a Post Office	229
XIII	The Electric Railway	246
XIV	New Iberia's Steamboat Days	264
XV	The United Confederate Veterans of New Iberia	276
XVI	A Brief Look at the Industry and Commerce of New Iberia	285
XVII	An Historical Sketch of New Iberia's Banks	316
XVIII	The Discovery of Oil in Iberia Parish: Little Bayou, 1917	332
XIX	1920	339

XX	The Teche Country in the Flood of 1927	356
XXI	Reminiscences of the Teens and Twenties	363
XXII	The Story of Education in New Iberia, 1848-1983	378
XXIII	Retrospections on New Iberia in the Twenties and Thirties	406
XXIV	An Historical Overview of Afro-Americans in New Iberia 1865-1960	429
XXV	A History of the New Iberia Library	454
XXVI	Entertainment, Sports, and Recreation in New Iberia 1830-1978	462
XXVII	Some Recollections of New Iberia	497
APPENDIX		509
INDEX		517

Preface

As I wrote in the first edition of this work, published in 1979, the idea of writing a history of New Iberia has always fascinated me, but I had hesitated to do so because of the realization that in the history of a community there are often long periods of routine which when translated into historical narrative prove to be dull and dreary. Hoping to avoid these depressions along the high road of our town's history, I decided on a topical approach which I used in the first edition and which I employ to a greater extent in this edition.

The idea of the topical format was not original with me. My inspiration was drawn from earlier work done by Edward T. Weeks, Sr., his brothers, and friends. Apparently their idea was to tell the story of New Iberia through reminiscences, an admirable approach to the subject because the average person tends to recall the exciting or inspiring moments of a lifetime. Nevertheless, a written account based upon memory alone can omit certain information necessary for a later generation of readers who, not contemporary with an event, may fail to understand the historical sequence. I therefore took the liberty in the first edition to edit and annotate these reminiscences which were recorded between 1895 and 1935. In this edition I have expanded upon many of those annotations.

To this concept of history through recollection, I addended the reminiscences of several individuals who were able to pick up the story where the earlier raconteurs had left off. I am indebted to Miss Alice Gates, Mrs. Yvonne Southwell, Mrs. Gertrude Taylor, and Mr. Johnny Holbrook for their contributions to the first edition which now appear in this edition.

I am equally grateful to Ruth Lefkovits, Carla Klapper, and Carl Brasseaux for their contributions to the essays which, for this edition, they have revised and updated.

When I was preparing the first edition of *New Iberia* for publication, I hurried along in order to have the book available in time for the town's bicentennial celebration. The work thus went forward even though I was fully conscious of the fact that it omitted a large segment of New Iberia's history--the story of the Afro-American community. That lacuna is now filled because of the energy and talent of Sandra Egland who generously agreed to research and write an overview of the black experience in New Iberia between 1865 and 1960. I am deeply appreciative of Ms. England's contribution to this work. My fondest hope is that she will pursue her research toward the end result of producing a monograph on the subject of the black experience in New Iberia.

Also added to this edition is an essay on the formation and early politics of Iberia Parish and an essay entitled "1920" which tells the story of New Iberia on the morrow of World War I. Finally, the present edition contains significantly more illustrations than its predecessor. In light of the additional text and illustrations, I reluctantly decided to forego an updated version of the biographical section which appeared in the first edition.

No work such as this can be accomplished without the cooperation of many individuals, particularly those who provide information, illustrations, and advice. I express appreciation to everyone who has contributed in this way. I also thank Carl Brasseaux and Flossie Montgomery for long hours spent in proofreading.

Finally, I am beholden to my wife Sylvia who, in addition to offering consolation and encouragement whenever I have slipped into one of those depressions which pit the high road of life, has never failed to lend an ear when I have still another story to tell about New Iberia.

New Iberia, Louisiana
May 19, 1986

NEW IBERIA

I

New Iberia: The Spanish Years

by
Glenn R. Conrad

In April 1979, New Iberia celebrated the bicentennial of its founding. Not only is the town's age noteworthy among the towns of the state, but of greater significance is the fact that New Iberia is one of a small number of towns in the Mississippi Valley founded during the years of Spanish domination. Indeed, it is today the only remaining town in the state of Louisiana to have been founded by the Spaniards. What is even more fascinating is the fact that after more than two hundred years the descendants of many of the founding families remain residents of the town or its immediate environs.

The Teche country was largely unknown to the French during their years in the Mississippi Valley. By the time that France ceded Louisiana to Spain only a few adventurers, a few Indian traders, had trekked into the region of the upper Teche--that is today the area of Opelousas--but the region of the lower Teche would not be penetrated until the end of the French era.[1]

In 1765 Louis Andry, a civil engineer, led 231 Acadian refugees from Santo Domingo into the Teche Valley where they established the Poste des Attakapas--

---

1. For further discussion of the settlement pattern along the Teche, see the following essay.

or St. Martinville--and thus the vast coastal plain stretching from the Atchafalaya Basin to the remote Mermentau River was designated the Attakapas District--the name being taken from a handful of Indians who still lived along the region's bayous and coastal plain.

Before the French finally ceded Louisiana to Spain in the late 1760's, a number of enterprising Frenchmen entered the Attakapas District and secured large land grants. Most of these people were former officers of the French army who had elected to remain in the colony after its cession to Spain. Many of their names are familiar today: Fuselier de la Claire, Prevost, Boutte, Grevemberg, Etier, Berard, DeClouet, DeBlanc, and others. The activities of these settlers between 1765 and 1770, however, are little known to us, for these were years of transition from French to Spanish administration. To compound the administrative confusion of the times, these were also the hectic years of rebellion along the Mississippi River and lawlessness on the plains of the Attakapas.

It was not until shortly after the arrival of General Alejandro O'Reilly that order was restored and an administrative system for the colony was established.[2] According to the new plan, which was an expanded version of the old French administrative system, each district was presided over by an official possessing civil and military authority. The official was called a commandant and his place of residence was termed a post. The area over which he presided was referred to as a district; hence, the Teche country came to be included in the Attakapas District. The first commandant of this district was Gabriel Fuselier de la Claire who was appointed by Governor O'Reilly in February, 1770. Shortly after the new administration came to the colony, a general census was taken and revealed (in 1774) that the Attakapas District had a total population of 323, scattered mainly along the banks of the Teche.

---

2. After the rebellion of 1768 succeeded in driving out the first Spanish governor of Louisiana, fully ten months passed before his successor, Alejandro O'Reilly, arrived with sufficient troops to overawe the Louisiana rebels. O'Reilly, however, easily succeeded in assuming control of the colony and, shortly thereafter, in establishing the necessary administrative machinery for the colony's day-to-day operation. After dealing with the leaders of the rebellion, O'Reilly left no stone unturned in his efforts to smooth the transition from French to Spanish control of Louisiana. So rewarding were his efforts, O'Reilly was able to leave Louisiana early in 1770. The reins of government then passed into the hands of Luis de Unzaga, a man of peace and reconciliation, who paved the way for the popular response to Louisiana's next Spanish governor, Bernardo de Gálvez. For a detailed analysis of the 1768 Louisiana rebellion and its aftermath, see John Preston Moore, *Revolt in Louisiana: The Spanish Occupation, 1766-1770* (Baton Rouge, 1976), and David Ker Texada, *Alejandro O'Reilly and the New Orleans Rebels* (Lafayette, La., 1970).

The Spanish Years

We know that shortly after the Spanish acquisition of Louisiana official action was taken to plant Spanish settlers among the predominantly French population of the colony. Traditionally, the reasons given for this strategy have been the need to supplement the colony's scant population and to augment defenses, especially against the British occupying the east side of the Mississippi. There are certain indications, however, that this traditional reasoning provides only the obvious segments of the overall Spanish strategy for Louisiana--at least during the first decade of Spanish domination. There may well be a facet of this strategy which has remained obscure and which might, even now, depend almost entirely upon deductive reasoning for proof of its existence. Let us for a moment investigate this theory.

The Spanish crown, if not shaken by the Louisiana rebellion of 1768, was indeed troubled by it. Without doubt, that event provoked suspicion among the Spaniards concerning the willingness of Frenchmen in Louisiana to live under the strict administration of the dons. Thus, if French loyalty was questionable, would it not behoove the Spanish administrators of Louisiana to establish settlements of their own people in key areas across the colony? Then, should some unfortunate incident occur, for example rebellion or invasion, these Spanish settlers acting as a citizens' militia could easily serve to augment the small Spanish military force in the colony. Thus, would it not behoove Spanish officials to quietly establish Spanish communities at strategic locations in the lower colony: at Terre aux Boeufs, just below New Orleans; at Gálvez Town, where the Spanish and British empires met on the high road between Baton Rouge and New Orleans; at Valenzuela, where Bayou Lafourche flows away from the Mississippi to the Gulf of Mexico; and, finally, at some point along Bayou Teche, also flowing into the gulf and the main avenue of approach to the Attakapas and Opelousas districts.

Thus, it would appear that this covert policy coupled to the acknowledged policy of reconciliation sponsored by O'Reilly's successor, Governor Luis de Unzaga, prevailed in the colony for a decade. Such a theory might also go far toward explaining the rapid rise and fall of the several Spanish communities planted in Louisiana prior to 1780. The strategic settlement aspect of Spanish policy was apparently abandoned after the events of August 1779 led to Spain's involvement in the American War for Independence. The overwhelming response of Louisiana French, German, and Acadian settlers to Governor Gálvez's march on British-held Baton Rouge proved conclusively to the Spaniards that the loyalty of Louisianians was no longer questionable. Therefore the entire program of Spanish emigration, a costly program in every respect, was

Don Francisco Bouligny

brought to an abrupt end. Nevertheless, it was this program which gave birth to New Iberia, and the midwife of that event was Don Francisco Bouligny.

Bouligny was born in Alicante, Spain, and arrived in Louisiana with General O'Reilly in 1769.[3] Then, in 1775, supposedly for personal reasons, he returned home. Concerning his activities in Spain, we know little, but we do know that in 1776 he presented an emigration plan to the minister of the Indies. In this memoir, which is extant, he argued that increased population would mean a more productive Louisiana. He did not refer directly to the possible strategy mentioned above, but he did conclude the proposal by recommending that the Spanish emigrants be established in communities of fifty families throughout the colony.

Another year passed before the crown authorized Governor Bernardo de Gálvez to promote Spanish emigration to Louisiana. Only after considerable bargaining and many official promises, was a group of Canary Islanders finally persuaded to emigrate, and they were settled at Terre aux Boeufs. Meanwhile, a group of Spanish refugees from British occupied Florida crossed into Louisiana, and Gálvez established them on the Mississippi at the place they would call Gálvez Town in his honor.

In the meantime, Bouligny was recruiting emigrants in southern Spain, particularly in the port town and province of Malaga. Thus, between July, 1777, and June, 1778, he succeeded in convincing sixteen families, constituting eighty-two people, to emigrate to Louisiana. To encourage this emigration, the crown agreed to subsidize the settlers until their first crop was harvested. With these promises made and all arrangements completed, the Malagueños sailed out of Malaga on the *San Josef.* When the ship put in at Cadiz, sixteen of the would-be settlers disembarked because of illness, and, after the Atlantic crossing, a few more emigrants debarked in Puerto Rico. In the end, only forty members of the original party arrived in New Orleans. Eventually, however, those from Cadiz and a few more Malagueños, totalling about sixty people in all, arrived in New Orleans on the *Princesa de Asturias.*

Bouligny, meanwhile, had returned to Louisiana, and Gálvez placed him in charge of settling the Malagueños. Now realizing that there would be so few Spanish emigrants, the two men debated the most strategic location to settle

---

3. For a detailed discussion of Bouligny's role in establishing New Iberia, see Gilbert Din, "Lieutenant Colonel Francisco Bouligny and the Malagueño Settlement at New Iberia, 1779," *Louisiana History,* XVII (1976), 187-202.

the Malagueños. Bouligny favored a spot on the Ouachita River; Gálvez objected, contending that the Ouachita was too remote. In the end, the two men agreed to a compromise location on Bayou Teche. It is interesting to note that when informed of this decision, the commandant of the Attakapas District, Alexandre DeClouet, expressed opposition to the plan and suggested that the settlers be sent elsewhere.

DeClouet's objection was probably based upon the knowledge that the New Iberia settlement would, like the other established Spanish settlements, constitute a completely separate administrative entity within a larger district. In establishing these strategic communities, Spanish officials provided for leadership and administration which was unquestionably loyal to the crown and completely independent of the local commandant, who, because of a shortage of Spanish administrators, was usually a Frenchman.[4]

After extensive preparations, Bouligny and the Malagueños, accompanied by a group of leased slaves and a handful of soldiers left New Orleans in mid-January, 1779. On February 7 the little cavalcade of boats entered Bayou Plaquemine and thence crossed the Atchafalaya Basin. Four days later, the group entered the Teche. Ascending the bayou, Bouligny scrutinized potential sites and finally selected what to him was the most strategic: a spot where a large bend in the bayou brought the stream to within a mile of the Atchafalaya lake system. We call the spot Charenton--he called it Nueva Iberia.

In the neighborhood were a few French settlers and a tribe of Indians. Winning the friendship of the Indians, Bouligny marked off the boundaries of the settlement. Each farmer would receive a parcel of land six arpents wide facing the bayou and forty arpents deep. From DeClouet, Bouligny purchased thirty-two pair of oxen, twenty cows, and twelve horses. The oxen would be used to till the fields that would be planted with crops of wheat, barley, flax, and hemp. Meanwhile, the slaves cut trees and sawed planks for house construction.

All went well until April when disaster struck suddenly. Incessant rain caused the bayou to rise rapidly and the tiny settlement was inundated by six feet of water. Discouraged, but not despairing, Bouligny and his little group gathered up what was left and started up the Teche in search of higher ground.

---

4. DeClouet's letter is found in Spain, Archivo General de Indias, Papeles procedentes de Cuba, legajo (bundle) 192. The archival documents found in legajos 186 to 221 have been arranged by post and microfilmed by the Center for Louisiana Studies of the University of Southwestern Louisiana. References hereafter will be to that microfilmed collection and will be cited as Cuba papers, followed by legajo and page numbers.

Route taken by the Malagueno Settlers
from New Orleans to New Iberia

Just before reaching the next bend of the bayou, about twenty miles above the abandoned site, the group came upon a slight bluff and decided that there they would settle. To everyone's surprise, however, they discovered that the land selected had already been granted to Francois Prévost, called Colet. Undaunted, Bouligny struck a deal with Prévost and purchased a parcel of land thirty arpents wide by eight arpents deep for four hundred pesos.[5] The purchased land was located on the west side of the Teche at the spot where it turns from a

---

5. Concerning the purchase arrangement with Francois Prévost, Bouligny stated, "In this predicament, finding all desirable locations on the Teche established or settled, I was forced to buy land from Mr. Colet. . . . I paid him 400 pesos and promised to grant him, subject to Your Lordship's good pleasure, two islands near the same place . . . ." The two "islands" that Bouligny refers to was Jefferson Island and a tract of land on Bayou Parcperdue subsequently acquired by Prévost. For Bouligny's account of the settlement of New Iberia, see Mathé Allain, ed. and trans., "Bouligny's Account of the Founding of New Iberia," *Attakapas Gazette*, XIV (1979), 124-131.

westerly course toward the southeast.[6] The area was locally known as Petite Fausse Pointe.

Here the Spanish settlement of New Iberia was established, and in June nine more Malagueños joined the group. By July some local Acadians were brought in to assist with the construction. The settlers' homes all measured fifteen by twenty-eight feet and were raised nine feet off the ground in anticipation of future flooding. It was while this work was proceeding that Bouligny received word of the event which would soon make projects like New Iberia no longer necessary. In August, news arrived that Spain had declared war on Britain in the American colonies' war of independence. Aware for some time that this event was inevitable, Bouligny immediately left New Iberia to assume a command along the Mississippi. He took fifteen Malagueños with him; those remaining continued the work of construction. Bouligny would never again return to New Iberia, even though he continued to live in Louisiana until his death in November, 1800.

In the fall of 1779 Nicolas Forstall was named by Governor Gálvez to be the first commandant of New Iberia. But no longer was the attention of the New Orleans officials focused on these small Spanish communities. Thus, with growing governmental neglect, the Malagueños at New Iberia began to assume an attitude of indifference toward the establishment of the town. Moreover, some of those families originally destined for New Iberia, but who had been delayed for various reasons, were reluctant to leave New Orleans for so remote a place. Such was the case, for example, of the Gabriel Lopez family.

By the fall of 1780, the dilatory attitude of the New Iberians was so great that Forstall reported to New Orleans that while he was continuing to push them, they were, nevertheless, "insufferable and impertinent."[7] In November of that year, he reported having to hire bricklayers to complete some of the construction at New Iberia. Farm production was similarly lagging.

The problems which early visited New Iberia would persist for the next fifteen years and would result not only in the ultimate collapse of the Spanish plan for the settlement, but would also result in an end to the Spanish phase of New Iberia's history. There were many problems.

First, the Malagueño settlers had virtually been bribed to come to Louisiana

---

6. The center of the Spanish settlement would be approximately the location of the present-day Iberia Sugar Co-op.

7. Nicolas Forstall to Pedro Piernas, Cuba papers, 193:563 verso.

The Spanish Years

The Segura House, built (1836) by Raphael Segura

The reconstructed Segura House as it appeared in 1979

There had been many government promises of subsidies, promises which were kept, so that, in turn, the crown expected to be repaid for its investment.[8] What occurred, however, was that the settlers, suspicioning that they were quasi-government agents, expected the subsidies to continue in large measure and gave little thought to repayment. An indication of this fact is, of course, the reluctance of the colonists to work because their labors would be essentially for the crown and not for themselves. In 1782, Governor Gálvez questioned Bouligny as to why the establishment of New Iberia was costing so much per year. Bouligny offered flimsy excuses, but he probably knew well the cause of the problem.

Second, assuming that the Malegueños were farmers, and not seamen or shopkeepers, it was planned that they would grow wheat, barley, flax, and hemp on the lands of the New Iberia District, but these crops will not grow in South Louisiana. Thus, ten years after their establishment, the Spanish settlers were only growing small plots of corn.

Third, the New Iberia District proved to be too small for the number of families residing in it. The pressure of population on the land had become so acute that in March, 1791, the then commandant, Jean-Baptiste St-Marc Darby, reported that the district had exhausted its supply of wood for building, for fences, and for heating. He therefore asked for an additional grant of woodland for the community. There was apparently no response to this request.

The economic circumstances in which the Malagueños found themselves continued to be an ongoing problem. Unable or unwilling to produce commodities for sale or barter, they begged, borrowed, and bought on time all of their necessities. Thus, not only the government hounded them for payment of debt, but also local merchants and tradesmen. Indeed, one of the first things which Darby, the second commandant of New Iberia,[9] reported was that the Malagueño families owed considerable debts and had no way to pay the merchants.[10] This situation persisted until June, 1787, when Governor Miro ordered the commandant of the Attakapas District to circulate notices that no one was to buy

---

8. For the agreements between the crown and the colonists, see Maurine Bergerie, *They Tasted Bayou Water, A Brief History of Iberia Parish* (New Orleans, 1962), pp. 106-126.

9. Jean-Baptiste St-Marc Darby received his commission as commandant of New Iberia in September, 1787. See Jean-Baptiste St-Marc Darby to Miro, September 15, 1787, Cuba papers, 200:641.

10. Jean-Baptiste St-Marc Darby to Miro, *ibid.*, 268.

The tomb of Salvador Migues, a Malagueño settler -
St. Peter's Cemetery

from or sell to the Malagueño families until they had first paid off their debt to the government.[11]

Caught in this economic stranglehold, Iberians, the following year, proposed to the governor that he allow them to sell some of their cattle and with the money hire slaves to plant and cultivate indigo.[12] The plan was apparently unacceptable to Governor Miro, but for some reason he did relent his commercial interdiction, and in March, 1789, announced that the Malagueños could henceforth buy and sell at will; however, they could not leave the district without his permission.[13]

Obviously Miro had come to realize that, regardless of government pressure, the New Iberia District would never be profitable because it was overpopulated. Thus, gradually he began to permit a few Malagueño families to leave New Iberia. Rafael Vidal, for example, was permitted to leave for Pensacola in November, 1786.[14] Josef Artacho and his family were permitted to resettle in New Orleans in November, 1788,[15] Gonsalo de Prados and his family were given permission to resettle on the Mississippi so long as Prados recognized his debt to the crown.[16]

Governor Miro's successor, the Baron de Carondelet, was not so lenient. When, in August, 1793, Darby requested permission for four families to leave this district,[17] Carondelet responded emphatically that they would not be granted permission to leave under any circumstances.[18] He reminded Darby that the residents of New Iberia had "cost the crown an immense sum of money to transport them from Malaga to New Iberia and to establish them there." He noted that the king had not received so much as a penny in return.[19]

11. Proclamation of Alexandre DeClouet, May 30, 1787, *ibid.*, 625.

12. Jean-Baptiste St-Marc Darby to Miro, August 23, 1788, *ibid.*, 201:772-772 verso.

13. Governor Miro to Darby, March 4, 1789, *ibid.*, 202:429.

14. Darby to Miro, November 4, 1786, *ibid.*, 199:738.

15. Darby to Miro, November 19, 1788, *ibid.*, 201:776.

16. Darby to Miro, September 2, 1789, *ibid.*, 202:447.

17. Darby to the Baron de Carondelet, August 26, 1793, *ibid.*, 208:364.

18. Carondelet to Darby, September 23, 1793, *ibid.*, 208:365.

19. *Ibid.*

The Spanish Years

Thus, we can only conclude that the planned community of New Iberia was nothing short of a complete failure. This fact is best reflected in the population figures for the district during the fifteen years of the Spanish phase. The settlement had begun with about 125 people of whom seventy were Malagueños. Ten years later the population numbered 122 with about the same number of original Spanish settlers. But with the coming of Governor Miro's relaxed policy of letting some settlers leave, the Malagueño population fell to fifty-nine in December, 1792. There were, in addition, fourteen Creoles living in the district, making a total white population of 74. There were nineteen blacks.

The end of Spanish New Iberia came quickly thereafter. For reasons which are still unclear, but perhaps having to do with the death of Darby,[20] Carondelet in 1795 took several important steps. First, he rescinded the decree preventing the Malagueños from leaving the New Iberia District. Second, he abolished the district and apparently the outstanding debts of the residents. Finally, he confirmed to the residents of the district the land on which they lived.

As these events unfolded, most of the remaining Malagueño families moved away from the original area of settlement and secured tracts of virgin land, particularly in the area of Lake Flammand, which now came to be known as Spanish Lake. Here eight to ten Malagueño families settled down to ranching on the Prairie Vermilion, the broad grassland that flowed away from the lake. They were few in number now, but their numbers would increase quickly as the years passed. Moreover, their names would be forever linked with the founding of New Iberia. They were the Seguras, the Pradoses, the Garidos, the Lopezes, the Fernandezes, the Romeros, the Villatoros (Viators), the Apontes, and the Ortizs. One family did not sell its land in the old district and continued to live on it until the new, essentially Anglo-American, town of New Iberia came into existence. This was, of course, the Miguez family.

Thus ended the first phase, the Spanish phase, of New Iberia's history. The Louisiana Purchase soon followed and, with the influx of Anglo-Americans and refugees from Santo Domingo, the next phase of New Iberia's history would be played out by such families and the Smiths, the Duperiers, the Weekses, and others. But the area of the "Little False Point" which the band of Malagueños selected in April 1779 to establish their town of New Iberia has continued to bear that name as a proud reminder of its simple beginnings.

---

20. Jean-Baptiste St-Marc Darby died July 14, 1795, at age 50. See St. Martin of Tours Church Records, vol. 4, no. 83.

GENERAL CENSUS OF THE MALAGUENOS AND OTHERS ESTABLISHED AT NEW IBERIA, 1792*

	Age		
		Joseph Fernandez	32
Gonsalo de Prados	57	Francisca Lopez Fernandez	32
Aumada de Prados	47	Maria Fernandez	8
Salbador de Prados	12	Joseph Fernandez	4
		Marie Lopez	1
Manuel de Prados	28		
Pepa Lopez de Prados	22	Feliz Lopez	28
Rosalia de Prados	6	Antonio Lopez	29
Joseph de Prados	3	Juan Lopez	4
Ignes Garido	50	Francisco Segura	31
Juan Garido	14	Maria de Prados Segura	38
Joseph Garido	12	Maria Segura	9
		Joseph Segura	5
Gabriel Lopez	50		
Catalina Lopez	24	Maria Grano Romero	53
Juan Lopez	7	Joseph Romero	27
Ignes Lopez	6	Juan Romero	15
		Antonio Romero	13
Marie Ruis Lopez	50	Bernardo Romero	8
Bernardo Lopez	10		
Antonio Lopez	7	Juan Miguez	53
		Salbadora Guerrero Miguez	48
		Salbador Miguez	15
		Bernardo Miguez	10

*Spain. Archivo General de Indias, Papeles Procedentes de Cuba, legajo 208:355.

II

Some Facts and Traditions about New Iberia

by
Edward T. Weeks, Sr.*

edited, annotated, and expanded
by
Glenn R. Conrad

To a native-born Iberian, our people afford a delightful topic. They are kindly, charitable, and courteous. They are self-respecting and law abiding; ordinarily, they are patient and tolerant of differing views. Because of the pleasing character of the subject, some of us feel the urge to set down in writing some facts concerning our town which may assist a more ambitious person to write the history of New Iberia and vicinity. Naturally, there are some matters worthy of inclusion in such a story which are dry and lacking in human interest. Such, for instance, is an account of the original acquisitions of the land and of its subsequent ownerships. Appreciating that a discussion of land titles is about as dull and unengaging as is a discussion of an algebraic equation, yet, upon recalling other facts, it is the purpose of this essay to tell of the lands which now comprise New Iberia and of the people who owned them, for to do so will give completeness to the story of the town.

It is generally agreed that the efforts of the French to colonize Louisiana were chiefly confined to their military posts and to the region near New Orleans,

---

*This essay was originally written by Mr. Weeks about 1934. This version of his manuscript has been edited and expanded.

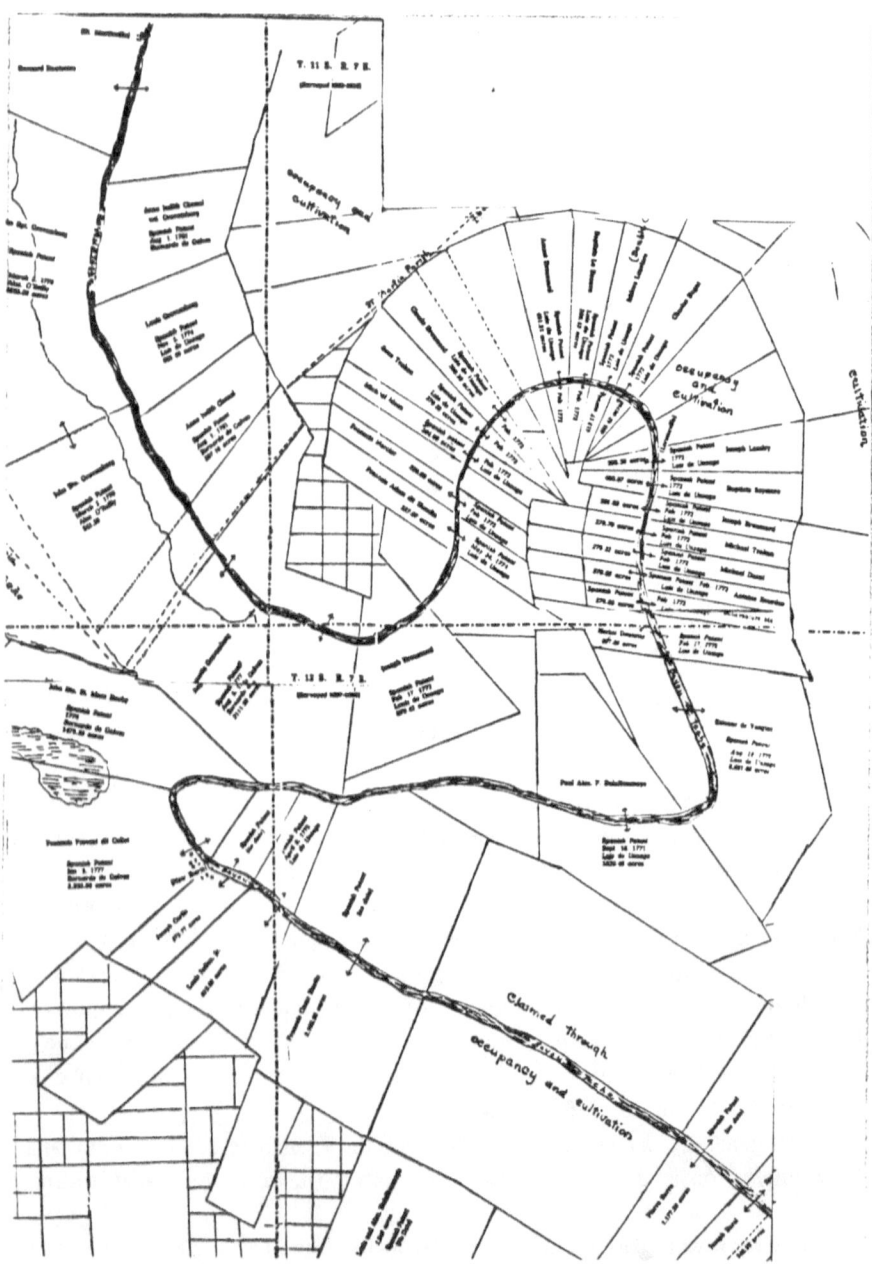

French and Spanish land grants in the New Iberia area
(from "Land Grants Along the Teche," *Attakapas Gazette*)

and that little or no effort was made to develop the country along the Teche until shortly prior to the coming of the Acadians. The Spanish judicial records for a later period indicate that an Edward Masse was in the Teche area as early as 1747. Masse had gathered to himself large and valuable possessions at different places in the province. The *American State Papers* show that in November, 1760, on one day, the commandant (probably Gabriel Fuselier de la Claire) passed four sales of lands from the Indians to white purchasers. The tracts of land conveyed in such sales were of almost incredible extent. For instance, one of these four tracts, the one bought by Gabriel Fuselier de la Claire, extended from Bayou Fuselier to the Vermilion, its northern and southern limits being somewhat vague. But this claim was not allowed by the American land commissioners, except for a small fraction of the land. This land had been "bought" by Fuselier de la Claire in November of 1760 "from Kinemo, chief of the Indian village called in French Lamourier." Possibly the commissioners, in confirming the purchase for the lesser quantity, felt that the grantee was even then getting a wonderful bargain.[1] The Edward Masse mentioned above, together with Jean Antoine Bernard d'Hauterive, seems to have owned and operated a *vacherie* before the coming of the Acadians. This ranch was on the east side of the Teche, in the area of Bayou Portage, in what is now Iberia Parish. The story of this *vacherie* and of its exchange is told in the case of the U. S. vs. *D'Hauterive* in 10 Howard, page 690. The evidence presented in this case states in part that Masse and D'Hauterive had for a long time owned these lands, but that when the Acadians came, cattle from the *vacherie* trespassed on the lands of the newcomers with disturbing results. The evidence further indicates that to avoid trouble Masse and D'Hauterive surrendered these lands to the Acadians and in return received from the French governor, in 1764, a grant of lands of princely dimensions.[2] It extended from Lake Tasse and Bayou

---

1. In November, 1760, Gabriel Fuselier de la Claire bought from Kinemo, chief of the Attakapas village, a tract of land five miles wide stretching from Bayou Vermilion to Bayou Teche (not Bayou Fuselier, as stated above), a distance of approximately fifteen miles. This extraordinary purchase was later confirmed by Governor Kerlérec. See Henry P. Dart,"Louisiana Land Titles Derived from Indian Tribes," *Louisiana Historical Quarterly*, IV (1921), 133-44. See also, *American State Papers*, 1789-1838, V, 20th Congress 1st and 2nd sessions, December 4, 1827 - February 25, 1829, 737.

After Spanish governor O'Reilly's arrival in Louisiana in 1769, he ordered that no landholding could exceed one league square (about two-and-one-half miles square). Fuselier de la Claire then petitioned Governor O'Reilly to confirm to him a tract of land on Bayou Teche which was one league square. *Ibid.*

2. The reasons for surrendering these lands to the Acadians were more complicated

Tortue to the Bayou Vermilion and from the Mauvais Bois to the coastal marsh. The *vacherie* was moved to these lands and D'Hauterive bought out Masse, who had prospered and owned much property in different parts of the province. D'Hauterive died soon thereafter; his widow Elisabeth Monteau de Monberault, married a second time to Jean-Baptiste DeGruÿ and they moved to St. Charles Parish. In a suit filed by the D'Hauterive heirs many years later (on June 16, 1846), the U. S. Supreme Court entirely disallowed the claim and held that, because Louisiana had been secretly transferred to Spain before the grant was made, the French governor (acting governor, Charles-Philippe Aubry) was without authority to alienate the Spanish domain. But D'Hauterive seems to have had a goodly supply of other lands, and Judge Félix Voorhies states that in 1765 he donated the lands on which was built the Catholic church in St. Martinville.[3]

---

than Mr. Weeks' presentation indicates.

The first group of 231 Acadian refugees from Santo Domingo arrived in New Orleans in early February 1765. In the litigation referred to by Mr. Weeks, evidence presented indicates that the new grant to D'Hauterive and Masse was dated March 2, 1765 (not 1764 and thus a significant difference). The opening lines of the first paragraph are particularly significant:

> Upon the demand made by Messrs. D'Auterive and Masse, partners, to grant them a parcel of land named La Prairie du Vermilion, bounded east by the River des Tortues and the Lake du Tasse, north by the Mauvais Bois, west by the River Vermilion, and south by the muddy prairie, considering their petition above, and in other part, and for consideration of the cession made by them to the Acadian families, recently arrived in the province.

Now, it is possible to conclude that the Acadians were already in the Attakapas, but leaders signed an agreement in New Orleans with D'Hauterive to raise cattle on shares, and, on April 17, 1765, French officials in New Orleans issued instructions to Louis Andry, the royal surveyor, to lead the Acadians to their new home in the Attakapas country. Thus, one must arrive at the conclusion that D'Hauterive not only signed an agreement with the Acadians to raise cattle on shares, but that he also supplied them with the land to do so. For the full text of the March 2, 1765, grant, see *The United States* vs. *Jean-Baptiste Dauterive et al*, in Stephen K. Williams, ed., *Reports of Cases Argued and Decided in the Supreme Court of the United States* (Newark, N. Y., 1883), Book XIII, 609-27. For the agreement between Dauterive and the Acadians, see Grover Rees, trans., "The Dauterive Compact: The Foundation of the Acadian Cattle Industry," *Attakapas Gazette*, XI (1976), 91. For the text of Andry's instructions, see Jacqueline K. Voorhies, trans., "The Attakaps Post: The First Acadian Settlement," *Louisiana History*, XVII (1976), 91-96.

3. This statement, attributed to Judge Felix Voorhies, coincides with the facts pre-

Among the few others who settled along the Teche prior to the Acadian migrations were probably the families of Pellerin, Courtableau, Grevemberg, and Fuselier de la Claire.[4] Nearly all these early settlers founded families that have remained in the land of their heritage and have been faithful to its development.

While mentioning these early settlers, it may be informative to recall the grantees of the lands now forming the town site of New Iberia, and to trace these grants a bit into the old subdivsion of the town, with some reference to later owners. There were four persons to whom lands were granted within the present-day city limits. All the land grants were made during the Spanish domination and were of varying frontages on the bayou, but each had a depth of at least forty arpents. On the west side of the bayou (the highest of the two banks of the bayou at New Iberia), these grants from north to south were made to François Prévost, Joseph Carlin, Louis Judice, Jr., and André-Claude Boutté.[5]

---

sented in the foregoing footnote. The land ceded by D'Hauterive and Masse to the Acadians ran from present-day St. Martinville eastward to the mouth of Bayou Portage.

4. For a census of the Attakapas and Opelousas districts before the coming of the Acadians, see Jacqueline K. Voorhies, comp., *Some Late Eighteenth-century Louisianians* (Lafayette, La., 1973), pp. 126-27.

5. One should be careful not to confuse an American land claim for a French or Spanish land grant.

A land grant normally involved a lengthy process which began when a colonist requested that he be issued a patent for the land he occupied. A patent was simply official recognition of the colonist's uncontested ownership of a given piece of land. If the local authorities, usually the commandant, felt that the colonist was worthy of a land grant, they would forward his request to the governor. If the request was approved by the governor, a survey was ordered to establish the precise limits of the land to be granted. Once that was done, the colonial governor would issue a patent. The colonist was then free to use, or to dispose of, the land at will. The process of granting land from the time of the colonist's request to the granting of the patent could take years and might be interrupted at any point along the way to the issuance of the land grant.

After the Louisiana Purchase, the American government required that all landowners should demonstrate proof of ownership through one of several means. If, for example, the landowner was a French or Spanish grantee and could produce the patent or evidence of the colonial government's intentions to issue a patent to him, the American land commissioners examining the evidence immediately confirmed the colonist's ownership and declared him eligible for an American patent. If the landowner was not the original grantee, he could offer proof of ownership through a chain of conveyances from the original grantee to himself. Thus, while he was the owner of the land, the land had originally been a land grant

The two most extensive of these grants were those at what would be opposite ends of the town. These were the Prévost and Boutté grants. François Prévost[6] may well be considered the father of the modern town of New Iberia, for it was from the lands of his grant that succeeding subdivisions came to compose the nucleus of the nineteenth-century and twentieth-century town.

The Prévost grant stretched along Bayou Teche from the old Spanish town of New Iberia; that is, from about where present-day Hopkins Street meets the bayou, southeastward to about 200 feet east of present-day Center Street (see Fig. 1). This grant was awarded to Prévost on January 5, 1777. A few years later, he acquired by grant the lands on the east side of the Teche, that is those in the large bend of the bayou.[7] Later, he purchased from Joseph Carlin six arpents wide of the ten arpents width that had been granted to Carlin (see Fig. 2).[8] The Prévost lands on the west side of the Teche extended back from the stream for a distance of fifty arpents; the land which Prévost purchased from Carlin had a depth of forty arpents.[9]

If Prévost had acquired these lands for agricultural purposes, he soon changed his mind and decided to sell them for a profit. The Prévost grant was at that point along the Teche which was the head of navigation for the merchant schooners of the day. Land at that point along the stream was being sought by merchants wanting to construct storage facilities for products being exchanged with nearby residents. There was, however, another reason which made the

---

to someone else, but the owner traced his right of ownership back to the original grantee for the sake of the American land commissioners. In this way many land claims have come to be confused with land grants. For the French and Spanish grantees along Bayou Teche, see the three maps in the series by Gertrude C. Taylor entitled *Land Grants Along the Teche*, published by the Attakapas Historical Association.

6. François Prévost was the son of Joseph Prévost of Illinois and Magdelaine Mayeux of Pointe Coupée. He was born in Pointe Coupée in 1752. On December 29, 1774, he married Geneviève Bonin of Attakapas. *Diocese of Baton Rouge Catholic Church Records, Vol. 1, 1707-1769* (Baton Rouge, 1978), 209; St Martin Parish Original Acts, Book 1, no. 13, hereafter cited as SMOA.

7. The grants to François Prévost are recorded in *American State Papers*, III, 187.

8. The Carlin sale to Prévost is found in SMOA, Bk. ll, no. 50.

9. New Iberia developed mostly on the west bank of the Teche; therefore, all future sites or locations mentioned will be on that bank unless otherwise noted. The probable reason for the early development of the west bank is that it is higher than the east bank and therefore less prone to flooding.

Facts and Traditions

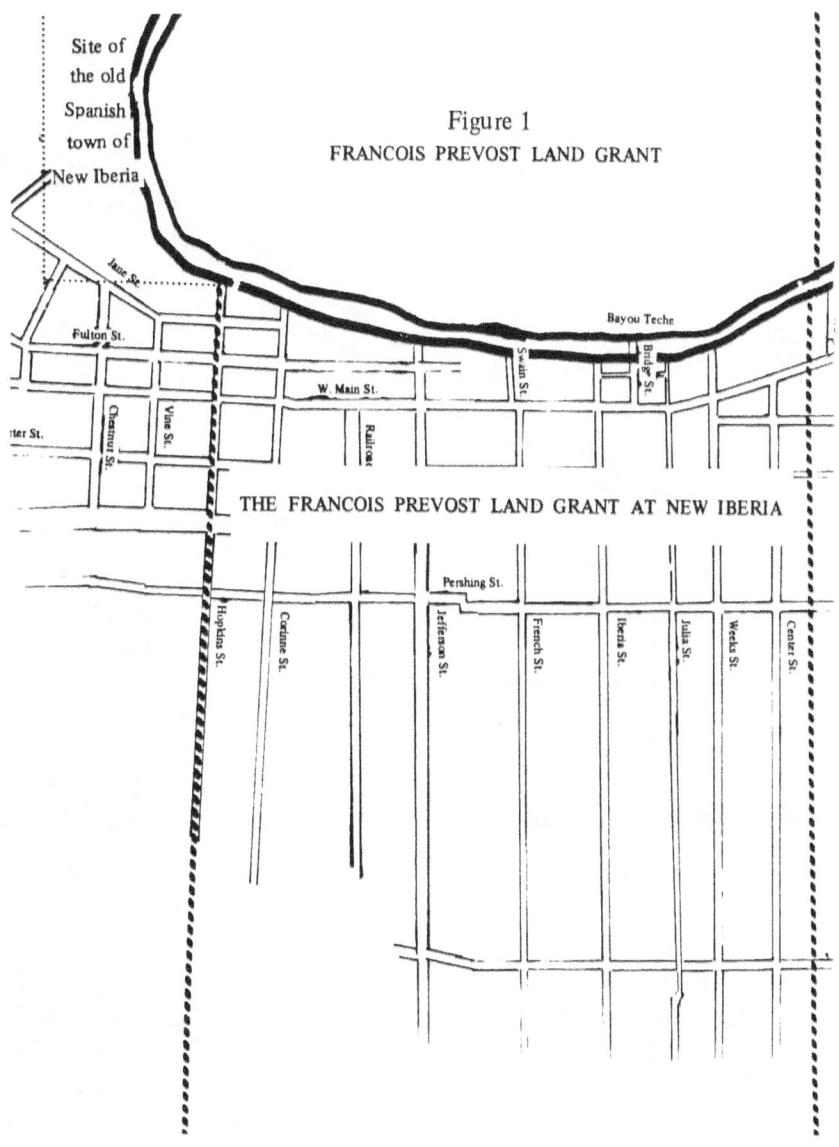

Figure 1
FRANCOIS PREVOST LAND GRANT

THE FRANCOIS PREVOST LAND GRANT AT NEW IBERIA

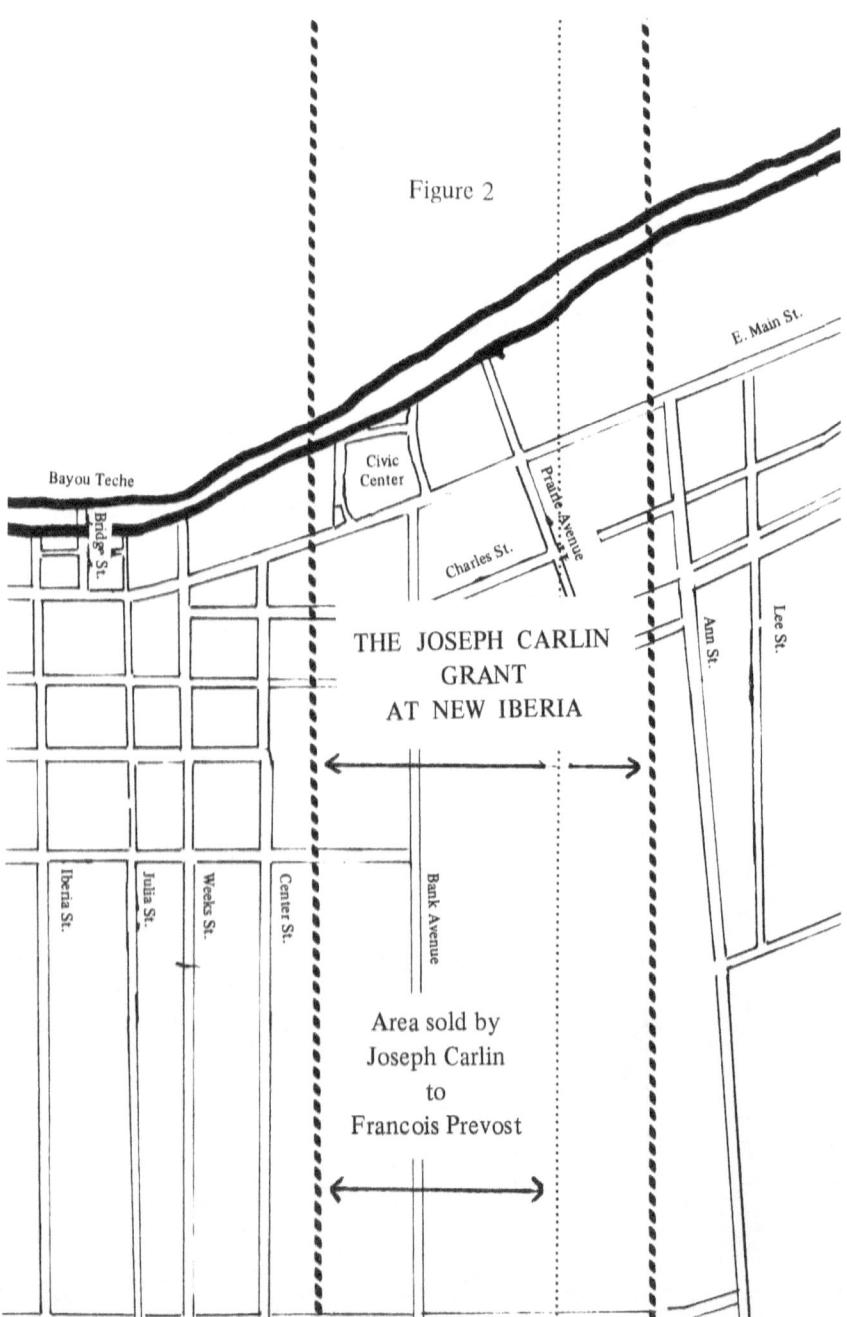

Facts and Traditions   23

Prévost lands desirable. The Spanish settlers of old New Iberia had exhausted the resources of their original settlement, especially the wood supply. They therefore sought to acquire some of the nearby Prévost land. Thus, barely three years after acquiring his grant, François Prévost began to sell parcels of it to various individuals. The area between Hopkins Street and Julia Street was sold to Spaniards moving out of the old New Iberia site. Among the purchasers were Bernard Aponte, Felix Lopez, Juan Migues, Francisco Ortiz, and Joseph Artacho.[10] The last-named individual purchased the area between present-day Julia and Fisher streets.[11] The land between Julia Street and to a spot about 200 feet east of Center Street was given by Prévost as a wedding present to his daughter Julie and her husband, Nicolas Hébert.[12] Finally, the land which Prévost acquired from Carlin (six arpents wide), was sold to the merchant John Kershaw (see Fig. 3).[13]

The area of the former Prévost grant from just east of Jefferson Street westward to beyond the present-day city limits passed through the hands of several individuals before it was consolidated again under the ownership of members of the De Blanc family in the years shortly before 1800.

Louis-Charles de Blanc was a Frenchman in the service of the Spanish government of Louisiana. He had served as commandant of Natchitoches before being transferred to the Attakapas Post in the 1790s. The large plantation which De Blanc acquired (see Fig. 4) was derived by purchase from many of the original Spanish settlers. By far the largest component of the De Blanc tract was the land he acquired from Joseph Borel on August 18, 1797. Borel had acquired this tract from Josef de Porra in 1789.[14] Other De Blanc lands were subsequently acquired from other Spanish settlers. An interesting sale was that made by Juan Migues to De Blanc. This conveyance involved a piece of land four ar-

---

10. The sales to the Spaniards are recorded in SMOA. None of these original purchasers from Prévost held his land for very long. The tracts therefore changed hands several times before 1800.

11. The Artacho purchase is recorded in SMOA, Bk. 2, no. 6.

12. The donation is found in the marriage contract of Nicolas Hébert and Julie Prévost, recorded in SMOA, Bk. 16, no. 22.

13. The Prévost sale to Kershaw is recorded in SMOA, Bk. 21, no. 110.

14. These transactions are recorded in SMOA, Bk. 7, no. 18, and SMOA, Bk. 18, no. 43. The chain of title is also developed in *American State Papers*, III, 187.

pents square, bordering the old Spanish town of New Iberia. Migues had bought it from Joseph Prévost, François' father, a few months after the Spaniards founded New Iberia. The four arpents represented what remained of the elder

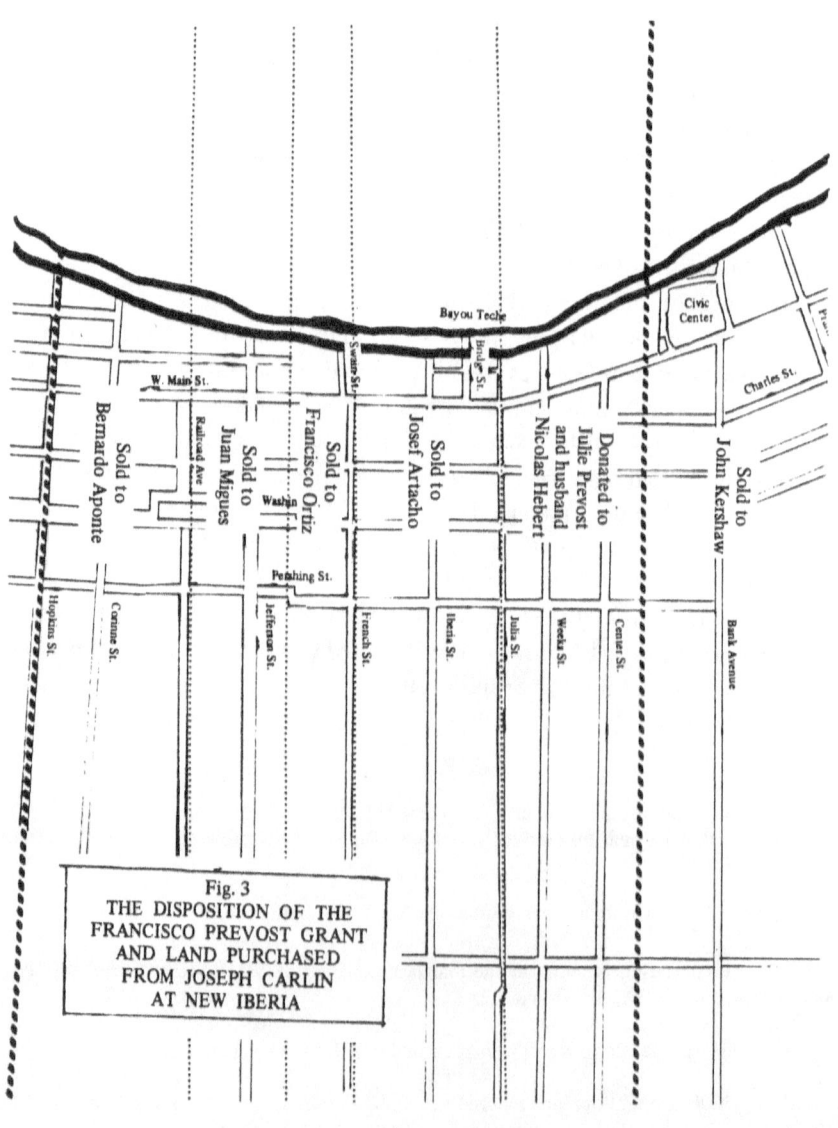

Fig. 3
THE DISPOSITION OF THE
FRANCISCO PREVOST GRANT
AND LAND PURCHASED
FROM JOSEPH CARLIN
AT NEW IBERIA

Facts and Traditions 25

Prévost's holdings after his sale to Francisco Bouligny.[15]

Another member of the De Blanc family to acquire land in the immediate New Iberia area was the commandant's son, Joseph. In 1800 he purchased from Juan Puche y Solis a tract of land measuring two-and-one-half-arpents wide by forty arpents deep. This tract would later be designated Section 44 of Township 12 South, Range 6 East (see Fig. 4).[16]

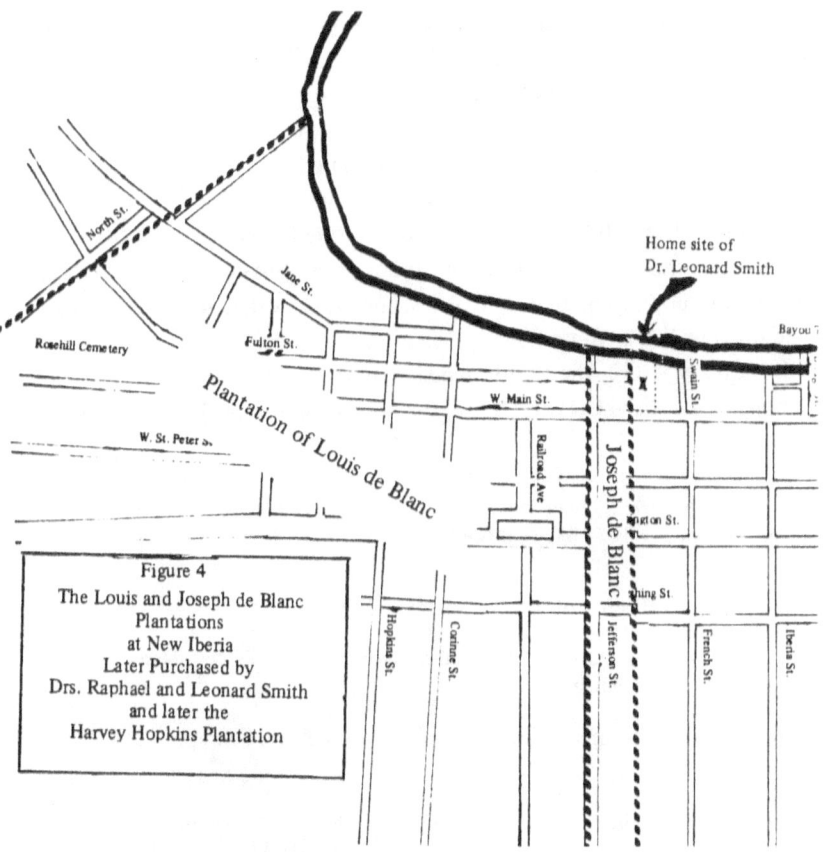

Figure 4
The Louis and Joseph de Blanc
Plantations
at New Iberia
Later Purchased by
Drs. Raphael and Leonard Smith
and later the
Harvey Hopkins Plantation

15. For the sale from Prévost to Migues, see SMOA, Bk. 2, no. 2. The sale from Migues to Louis-Charles de Blanc is recorded in SMOA, Bk. 18, no. 69.

16. This land had been part of the Francois Prévost grant and had passed from him to

A short time after the death of Louis-Charles de Blanc in 1826, his heirs placed in public sale their father's plantation nearest New Iberia.[17] This sale occurred on January 29, 1827, and the vendee was Dr. Raphael Smith, a native of Maryland but then a resident of Opelousas. Two months later, Dr. Smith purchased Joseph de Blanc's plantation from his widow, Marie Colin Lacour.[18]

Upon the death of Dr. Smith in 1829, his estate passed (by means described elsewhere) to a nephew, Dr. Leonard Smith (see Fig. 4). Leonard Smith was then married to Marie Ladoiska Darby, the daughter of François St-Marc Darby and Constance de Blanc. Mrs. Smith was the granddaughter of Louis-Charles de Blanc.[19]

Dr. Leonard Smith was the builder of what later generations knew as the Alma House, or the Elks Apartments, or the Olivier Building. This antebellum home, a landmark in the 200 block of West Main Street until it was demolished about 1965, was not built on Dr. Smith's plantation. For his home site, Dr. Smith acquired two lots immediately below the plantation (see Fig. 4). One was acquired from Louis Segura; the other from Josiah French.[20] Here the house was built and completed in 1834, the same year that David Weeks completed his New Iberia home.[21]

In January, 1852, the Smith mansion and plantation were sold. The house was bought by Marie Celeste Darby, the widow of Joseph Dauterive Dubuclet,

---

Juan Migues and then to Juan Puche y Solis. The sale from Puche y Solis to Joseph de Blanc is recorded in SMOA, Bk. 20, no. 43.

17. De Blanc died on April 6, 1826. His heirs were Joseph Marie Charles, Louis Marie Cesaire, Maximillien Derneville, George Thomas Cesaire, the two children of the deceased Jean-Baptiste Dorsinos, Marie Louise Marthe, Marie Aspasie, Elisabeth Marcelite and Marie Constance. St. Martin Parish Estate 551.

18. These Smith purchases are found in St. Martin Parish Conveyance Book (hereafter SMCB) 3, pp. 3, 73.

19. Leonard Smith and Ladoiska Darby were married on March 6, 1828. They had two children who survived to adulthood, Leopold and Mary Ladoiska. Mrs. Smith died in March, 1858; Dr. Smith died on February 9, 1869. Donald J. Hebert, comp., Southwest Louisiana Records, 29 vols. (privately printed, 1974-1982), II, 230; IX, 371, hereafter cited as *Southwest Louisiana Records*; St. Martin Parish Estate 1606.

20. Smith's purchase from Louis Segura occurred on July 10, 1832; the sale by Josiah French was on June 29, 1833. These sales are described in SMCB 16, p. 194.

21. The completion date for the Smith house is found in St. Martin Parish Estate 632.

who converted the place into a hotel.[22] The plantation was sold to Harvey Hopkins of Plaquemines Parish.[23]

After these sales and the subsequent death of his wife, Dr. Smith, in ill health, returned to his native Maryland to recuperate.[24] He returned to New Iberia in 1856, and in January 1859 he purchased the large plantation formerly owned by John D. Wilkins, located about three miles southeast of New Iberia.[25] Dr. Smith died on his plantation in 1869.

Mrs. Dubuclet continued to own the old mansion throughout the Civil War. On December 2, 1866, it was sold to Dr. Robert C. Hilliard, a North Carolinian who had moved to Louisiana in 1847.[26] Dr. Hilliard was a victim of the yellow-fever epidemic of 1867, and, after his death, his widow operated a hotel in the old house. For a long time it was known as the Live Oak Hotel.

In the early 1850s, when a railroad was being planned from New Orleans to Houston through New Iberia, the entire section along the Teche was much interested in procuring the rights-of-way for the expected railway. In New Iberia, these were secured along what is the present course of the Southern Pacific Railroad, but the railroad did not come to New Iberia until 1879.[27]

In 1854, Harvey Hopkins, having donated to the railroad the lands for the right-of-way through his plantation and also the depot site, switch, tracks, wharves and the like, created out of the lower part of his plantation the Hopkins

---

22. The sale of the house to Mrs. Dubuclet is recorded in SMCB 20½, p. 116.

23. For the sale to Harvey Hopkins, see SMCB 24, p. 256.

24. Dr. Smith's sojourn in Maryland is recorded in St. Martin Parish Civil Suit 4709.

25. This purchase is recorded in St. Mary Parish Conveyance Book M, p. 652. For the story of the Wilkins and Peebles families in the New Iberia area, see the essay entitled "A Narrative of Events Connected with the Early Settlement of New Iberia."

26. The Dubuclet-Hilliard conveyance is found in SMCB 31, p. 71.

Dr. Hilliard was married to Mary Rebecca Harrison Walker, the daughter of John Mumford Walker and Lucy Cargill Jones of Virginia. She married Dr. Hilliard on December 20, 1837. For more on the Hilliards, see *William and Mary Quarterly*, Series 1, XI, 264; Gertrude C. Taylor, "Virginians in the Teche Country, Part V, The Tie that Binds," *Attakapas Gazette*, XVII (1982), 162.

27. For events leading to the construction of the railroad to and through New Iberia, see the essay entitled "The Iron Horse Comes to New Iberia."

Addition to New Iberia.[28] This addition commenced at a point just east of the old Hopkins Plantation drain, which crossed Main Street to the Teche. In other words, the southern boundary of the addition was then the northern limits of the town and was along a line crossing Main Street 250 feet east of Jefferson Street. This addition divided into lots the property from the Hopkins Plantation drain to Corinne Street. It thus opened quite a number of new streets, including Jefferson, Washington, Madison, Railroad, Fulton, and Corinne. Main Street and St. Peter Street were then extended.[29]

Two of the first industrial plants to be located in this part of the town were sawmills, both on the immediate west bank of the Teche. One of these, built by Gall and Riggs, will be mentioned again.[30] The other sawmill belonged to Ulger Decuir and Dominique Ulger Broussard.[31] Ulger Decuir was the older and was then a man of substance--a successful merchant--thus, the partnership left the sawmill mainly under the management of D. U. Broussard.[32] It pros-

---

28. Hopkins' first donation to the New Orleans, Opelousas and Great Western Railroad was made on May 17, 1853, and was for a plot of land for a depot and right-of-way from the depot to the bayou. That right-of-way corresponds to the present-day Railroad Avenue between Main Street and the depot and the parallel siding which still extends beyond Main Street toward the Teche. The reason for the right-of-way was to allow the trains to make direct connections with steamboats on the bayou, primarily for freight purposes. Although the railroad was not actually built for another 26 years, the idea of the link between overland and waterborne traffic persisted.

On August 9, 1859, Hopkins made still another donation to the N. O. O. & G. W. This time he gave the company a right-of-way across his plantation along an extension of Graveyard Street, which he subsequently renamed Washington Street. Twenty-six years later, Morgan's Texas and Louisiana Railroad finally laid track and New Orleans and Houston were linked by rail. For Hopkins' donations to the N. O. O. & G. W., see SMCB 20½, p. 477, and Bk. 27, p. 392.

29. The lands included in the Hopkins Addition were surveyed and laid out in town lots in early February 1854. See SMCB 30, p. 88 (dated August 4, 1865).

30. Jasper Gall of St. Mary Parish bought three lots on the northeast corner of Jefferson and Main streets on December 2, 1856. See SMCB 25, p. 106.

31. Dominique Ulger Broussard was the son of Don Louis Broussard and Felonise Broussard. He was born in the New Iberia area on August 4, 1838, and died in New Iberia in June, 1885. *Southwest Louisiana Records*, III, 102; XVII, 89.

32. The partnership had previously existed between Ulger Decuir and his brother Frejus. After the death of Frejus, Ulger, on January 22, 1868, formed the partnership with Broussard by letting Broussard buy one half of Frejus' interest in the business. The partner-

pered, but soon came the Civil War, and regardless of his business interests, D. U. Broussard early answered the call of the Confederacy and was a gallant defender of the South.

The sawmill, like all other business concerns in this section, suffered heavily. Ulger Decuir, whose financial affairs in general had declined severely during the war, died on May 15, 1871, and it was only after D. U. Broussard formed a partnership with Albert J. Decuir that the sawmill was again at its best.

It is due to his memory to say that there were few men in New Iberia who more deservedly enjoyed the confidence of her people or whose leadership was so excellent as was that of D. U. Broussard. He was recognized as unselfish and as a man of high integrity. He was mayor, or president of the board of trustees, of the town soon after 1868 and again in 1884. He was later president of the police jury that erected the old courthouse.[33]

After the death of Harvey Hopkins (September 9, 1867), his widow, Jane Hopkins, in February, 1868, subdivided a much larger portion of her plantation into town lots so that practically all of the town northwest of Jefferson Street stands on what formerly were the cane and corn fields of the Hopkins Plantation.[34]

The Hopkins home was a long, low, one-story frame house and, even in the 1870s, it showed that it was of long standing. It was situated back from Jane Street (named for Mrs. Hopkins) on a tract of ten acres or more, just south of North Street and extending from Jane Street to the bayou. It continued to be the residence of Mrs. Hopkins following her husband's death. Later it was the

---

ship was therefore actually composed of Decuir, Broussard, and the estate of Frejus Decuir, represented by J. Alcide Decuir. For the partnership arrangements, see SMCB 32, p. 223.

33. "On December 2, 1882, Police Jury President D. U. Broussard announced that the parish legislature had purchased a lot from the firm of Taylor and DeValcourt for $4,000." Iberia Parish's first courthouse was completed in the spring of 1884. For further information on the creation of Iberia Parish and the building of the courthouses, see the essay entitled "New Iberia Becomes the Parish Seat."

34. According to the inventory of community property taken at the time of Hopkins' death, there were 222 unsold lots. He also possessed 200 shares of stock in the N. O. O. & G. W. Railroad which were appraised as worthless. See St. Martin Parish Estate 2023. The sale mentioned above occurred in February, 1868, a few months after Hopkins' succession was probated. See SMCB 32, p. 238.

home of the William Lourd family. Mrs. Hopkins died childless (December 9, 1879), and for a time differences among heirs threatened to involve in litigation the very considerable portion of the lands of the town which were included in her estate, but these differences were settled in compromise.

Among other structures erected about 1855 within the Hopkins Addition were the two section houses of the then-proposed railroad. They faced each other as two empty, yellow, ill-kept structures east of Main Street and facing Railroad Avenue for nearly a generation of time awaiting the building of the railroad. One of these still stands.

Ralph's Floor Center, Inc. (1985)
Originally erected 1855 as a railroad section house

From this addition, Harvey Hopkins, on August 15, 1857, donated to the Episcopal church, the hundred-foot lot on the southwest corner of Main and Jefferson streets, where the church and rectory now stand. He also gave the land for Rosehill Cemetery.[35] But the cemetery area has been greatly enlarged since then. The Episcopal church was built in 1857. Numbered among others of its congregation were the following families and their branches: Hopkins, Marsh, Avery, DeValcourt, Miller, McGill, Robertson, Ker, Mealey, Stubinger, Lewis, Weeks, Cade, Taylor, Smedes, and Miss Fanny Hunter. The last named lady, a Virginian, and a sister of Mrs. Alfred C. Weeks, is generally credited with being an active worker for its construction. To these, either then or as of early date thereafter, should be added the families of Emmer, Bauman, Rose, Koch, Sonneman, Fuller, King, and others.

The lots in that portion of the Hopkins Addition sold rapidly and were built upon. Among new structures was the store of Alcide Babin on the lower corner of Railroad Avenue and Main Street and his adjoining residence. He was the first assessor of Iberia Parish.

Gall and Riggs Sawmill, which was soon acquired solely by Jasper Gall, was built on the bayou immediately below Jefferson Street. Facing Main Street, on the corner of Jefferson (diagonally from the Episcopal church), Gall built three homes. The Temperance Hall, constructed later, was between these and Dr. Smith's house. In the upper one of these homes (the one on the corner of Jefferson and Main streets), Mr. Gall resided for many years. It was from the front gallery of this home that Mrs. Gall is said to have watched the skirmish between the Confederate troops under General Taylor and the Union army under General Banks. The fighting took place within and above this same Hopkins Addition. The Confederate breastworks were apparent for years thereafter.[36]

---

35. On August 15, 1857, Harvey Hopkins donated to the vestry of the Church of the Epiphany, represented by the Reverend J. S. Hutchinson, rector of the church, who accepted as per vestry authorization dated April 9, 1857, a lot of ground "near the town of New Iberia." The lot had a frontal width of one hundred feet on the west side of Main Street by a depth of 198 feet. The said depth extending one half the distance from Main to St. Peter Street, the lot fronting on Jefferson Street.

At the same time Hopkins donated "a burying ground about five arpents west of the road from New Iberia to St. Martinville." The size of the donation was one-and-one-half arpents square. For these donations, see SMCB 25, p. 495.

The cornerstone of the Church of the Epiphany was laid in October, 1857.

36. The breastworks may actually have been the work of Union forces. There is no mention in official records of the Confederate forces building defenses on the north side of

Jasper Gall was a man of great charity. Though he had prospered in the sawmill business and acquired extensive tracts of land in Iberia Parish, he gave to his less-fortunate brothers lumber and shingles so freely in the lean years that followed the Civil War that his fortune became much impaired. He lived to be more than ninety, and in earlier days served the town as mayor.[37]

Across from the Gall property, fronting two hundred feet on the southeast corner of Main and Jefferson streets, was the two-story home of Dr. Henry Stubinger.[38] Dr. Stubinger was a native of Canada who practiced medicine in New Iberia from the early 1830s until 1875.[39] He was highly esteemed, and his son George was an early sheriff of Iberia Parish. Sheriff Stubinger was shot and killed by a man whom he was endeavoring to arrest. The killer was disposed of summarily, "without benefit of clergy."[40]

New Iberia. Indeed, to have done so would appear to have been a waste of time because any Union assault on the town, in all probability, would come from the southeast. This, in fact, was the way in which Union forces did approach and eventually occupy New Iberia.

It is possible that the breastworks mentioned by Mr. Weeks, and years later spoken of to this writer by Mr. Edwin Bernard, who also remembered them as a child, were actually those of the Union occupiers of New Iberia. Throughout November, 1863, the Union commander at New Iberia repeatedly reported that he feared Confederate guerilla attacks on the town. Then, in December, 1863, General S. G. Burbridge reported that workers were finishing the defensive works around the town. Since the Confederate guerillas were located to the north and west of New Iberia, it seems perfectly plausible that Gen. Burbridge would construct breastworks on the north side of town. For Burbridge's report, see *Official Records of the War of the Rebellion* . . . (Washington, D. C., 1889), Series 1, XXVI, part 1, p. 363.

37. Jasper Xavier Gall was a native of Germany. Although little is known about his early life, it is a fact that he lived in Patterson before coming to New Iberia, apparently in the mid-1850s. He married Frances Riggs of New Iberia and the couple had several daughters and one son, Slyvanus. Mrs. Gall died in 1888. Mr. Gall survived until April 18, 1907. He was 91 at the time of his death.

38. Dr. Stubinger's presence in New Iberia is first documented in a sale to him in 1845. St. Martin Parish Mortgage Book 1, p. 408. For a long time the Stubingers lived in the block between Swain Street and Jefferson Street. They then built the house (now located at 115 Jefferson Street) before actually purchasing the property. This is pointed out in the sale of the property to Mrs. Stubinger (Martha Cecil) on March 5, 1869. See Iberia Parish Conveyance Book (hereafter IPCB) 1, p. 121.

39. Dr. Stubinger left New Iberia in 1875 in order to reside with a daughter in Maryland. He died there the following year.

40. From the creation of Iberia Parish in October, 1868, until April, 1869, James Griswell was sheriff. In the spring of 1869, Governor Henry Clay Warmoth appointed

Facts and Traditions   33

The Wattigny Home -- Built by Dr. Henry Stubinger, 1856
Originally facing Main Street, now facing Jefferson Street

Near the lower limits of the Hopkins Plantation, long before the property was subdivided, there had been dug a large plantation canal used to drain the back lands to the Bayou Teche.[41] This canal crossed Main Street along the

---

George Stubinger to the position. After Stubinger's murder in late November of that year, Clermont Young became sheriff and served until 1872. For an account of the murder of Sheriff Stubinger, see *Attakapas Gazette*, XIV (1979), 43-44.

41. Canals dug for this purpose were numerous in the New Iberia area. In 1873, the town of New Iberia had a similar canal dug along the right-of-way of Weeks Street to drain the area south of St. Peter Street. The canal was six-feet deep when it crossed St. Peter Street, nine feet deep when it crossed Main Street, and twelve feet deep when it flowed into the Teche. To prevent caving in, the sides were bulkheaded. The digging of this canal was under the supervision of William Burke. The project cost $2,500. See the *Louisiana Sugar Bowl*, July 3, 1873.

One of these well-known drainage canals just outside New Iberia city limits is the Nelson Canal.

southern boundary line of the Stubinger property and was a major drain for the town after its incorporation. The Stubinger property was later the home of Judge Robert S. Perry of the court of appeals. Judge Perry was one of the ablest lawyers that ever practiced at the Iberia bar.[42]

Judge Robert S. Perry

---

42. After Dr. Stubinger's death, his heirs sold the house to Mrs. Harvey Hopkins on November 24, 1879 (IPCB 7, p. 313). Judge Perry acquired the house in the 1880s and lived there until his death in 1900. The house then passed to Perry's son J. Robert, who owned it until 1903 (see IPCB 44, p. 197, and Bk. 50, p. 235). On September 8, 1903, J. Robert Perry sold the house to Dr. Henry A. King, and the King family owned the place until it was sold to Gerard B. Wattigny in 1977.

Facts and Traditions 35

Next below the Stubinger property was the boys' school conducted by J. R. Freeman around the year 1873.[43] Within two or three years, however, the school was moved to Iberia Street, just off Main, and was then conducted by Mollie Hartman, who later married Ira Knight. To gauge the size of these schools, students were taught in one room by one teacher.[44]

The former site of the Frederic Hotel and present-day site of the François Building was eventually sold to William Robertson, one of the town's early mayors.[45] Robertson was a native of Tennessee (born in 1819) and a graduate of West Point. He came to New Iberia in the 1840s, married Eliza Marsh, and resided there until his death on February 17, 1890. His home was a large, two-story structure which stood well back from the street among beautiful oaks. The lot later became the site of the Frederic Hotel.[46] Mr. Robertson was broad gauged and kindly and for more than forty years carried on the Robertson Insurance Agency.

On the northwest corner of Main and Swain streets there stood until 1927 one of the oldest and one of the most interesting dwellings in New Iberia. It

---

43. This would have been in the present-day area of 233 West Main Street. Freeman was not the only person to open a school in 1873. Between May and August of that year a Miss Colgin, Pierre Lagarde, and Mrs. T. F. Delacroix also opened private schools in New Iberia. One reason for the proliferation of private schools is the fact that funds for the operation of public schools were always lacking; thus, the public school operated on an abbreviated school year. The private schools usually opened after the public schools closed in order to complete the students' academic year. See the *Louisiana Sugar Bowl*, May 22, May 29, and August 4, 1873.

44. For more information on education in New Iberia, see the essay entitled "The Story of Education in New Iberia, 1848-1985."

45. The site of the Frederic Hotel, and subsequently the Francois Office Building, had been part of the Stine subdivision and the land had passed through several hands before Robertson acquired it. Robertson purchased it from Constance de Blanc, the widow of Francois St-Marc Darby, on July 30, 1852 (St. Martin Parish Mortgage Book N, p. 143). Constance Darby had acquired the tract from her son-in-law, Dr. Leonard Smith, in May, 1846 (SMCB 15½, p. 7). Smith had purchased the land in 1833 from Josiah French, who had acquired it from Philip Stine. Stine had acquired it from his brother-in-law, Nelson Johnson. Johnson had acquired the property from the estate of John Stine, Sr. These transactions are found in SMCB 8, p. 171.

William Robertson was mayor of New Iberia in 1859. SMCB 27, p. 431.

46. Mary A. Robertson and Kate Robertson sold this property to Felix Patout on August 24, 1912 (see IPCB 74, pp. 251-52). The hotel was built in 1913 and was largely demolished in 1976. A wing of the hotel was converted into the Francois Office Building.

had been built and occupied for many years by Louis Segura, a son of one of the Spanish colonists. It was a one-story house on quite high brick pillars, with a basement of brick.[47]

John D. Swaim's residence was on the northwest corner of French and Main streets (if one regards Main Street as being oriented east and west).[48] As late as the 1870s he carried on a warehouse business at the foot of Swain Street (formerly known as New Street) on the bank of the bayou.[49] He was a tall, spare, silent man, dignified and dressed usually in a black Prince Albert suit.

The Robertson and Swaim properties were the northernmost part of the lands owned by John Stine in the early days of the nineteenth century. The Stine tract fronted on the bayou and its southern boundary was approximately the upper line of what is now Iberia Street. The Stine lands fronting on the west side of Main Street (roughly speaking, the area between Iberia Street to about 230 feet east of Jefferson Street) were mainly residential lots measuring about one-half arpent wide. The area remained mainly residential until well after 1870.

---

47. For a further discussion of this house, see footnote 5 of the essay entitled "A Narrative of Events Connected with the Early Settlement of New Iberia."

48. The town lot which John D. Swaim acquired on the corner of French and West Main streets was purchased from Mary E. Reynolds Riggs on February 12, 1853 (SMCB 20½, p. 329). The lot ran back from Main Street a distance of three-and-one-half arpents, or to a lot owned by the Methodist church on the corner of French and Graveyard (Washington) streets (*ibid.*). At the time of the purchase and until 1870 St. Peter Street was a dead end at French Street. That year, however, Marion Swaim, John Swaim's son, sold sufficient land to the town of New Iberia in order that St. Peter Street might be extended westward. D. U. Broussard, mayor of New Iberia at the time, acted for the city (IPCB 2, p. 224).

Ely Riggs had acquired the parcel of land sold to John Swaim at the succession sale of Elizabeth Clark, widow of John Stine, Sr., on March 20, 1832 (see St. Martin Parish Estate 687).

49. On November 23, 1850, Dr. Henry Stubinger and John D. Swaim formed a partnership in the warehouse and lumber businesses. The firm was known as "John D. Swaim & Co." Stubinger supplied the land for the warehouses and lumber yard, which were located on both sides of New (later Swain) Street. The company was managed by Swaim. SMCB, 19, p. 411. Swaim sold the warehouses to Auguste Erath in May, 1883 (IPCB 11, p. 168). Mr. Swaim probably died shortly thereafter. No record of his death has been found.

John Stine, a staunch Methodist, is said to have come to Louisiana about 1790.[50] He acquired his property in New Iberia in two separate purchases, both being two and one-half arpents wide by forty arpents deep. The chain of title for the first purchase, from the grantee to Stine, is

Spanish Grant to
FRANCOIS PREVOST
January 5, 1777

5 Arpents sold to
JOSEPH ARTACHO
April 25, 1780
(SMOA,* Bk. 2, no. 6)

5 Arpents sold to
JOSEPH PREVOST, JR.
March 24, 1789
(SMOA, Bk. 7, no. 89)

5 Arpents sold to
NICOLAS HEBERT
January 10, 1794
(SMOA, Bk. 16, no. 72)

---

50. John Stine's presence in New Iberia is documented beginning in 1796. At that time he was 26 years old and was living on the property of, and working for, François Prévost. See SMOA Bk. 17, no. 35.

John Stine, the son of John, senior, and Barbara Kruger, married Elizabeth Clark (January 15, 1792), the daughter of Patrick Francis Clark, a native of Ireland, and Rachel Malone, a native of Carolina (SMOA, Bk. 1, no. 132). John Stine was from Pennsylvania according to his marriage record (cited in Donald J. Hebert, comp., *Southwest Louisiana Records*, 32 vols (Eunice and Cecilia, La., 1976-85), I, 526.) Patrick Clark and John Stine may have been among the refugees from Fort Pitt mentioned in Glenn R. Conrad, "Friend or Foe? Religious Exiles at the Opelousas Post in the American Revolution," (*Attakapas Gazette*, XII (1977), 137-40). Clark is certainly on the list of "foreigners" in the District of Opelousas and Attakapas compiled on May 15, 1781 (*ibid.*).

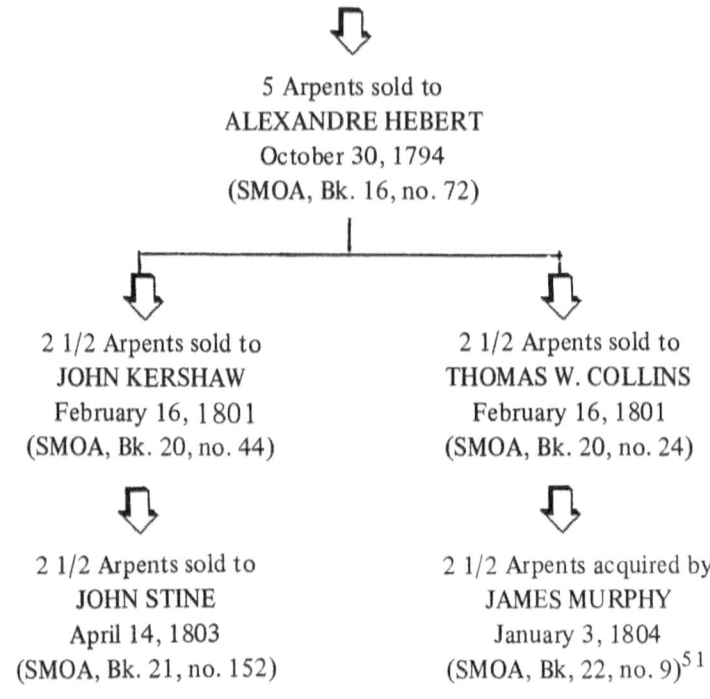

⇩

5 Arpents sold to
ALEXANDRE HEBERT
October 30, 1794
(SMOA, Bk. 16, no. 72)

⇩ ⇩

2 1/2 Arpents sold to   2 1/2 Arpents sold to
JOHN KERSHAW   THOMAS W. COLLINS
February 16, 1801   February 16, 1801
(SMOA, Bk. 20, no. 44)   (SMOA, Bk. 20, no. 24)

⇩ ⇩

2 1/2 Arpents sold to   2 1/2 Arpents acquired by
JOHN STINE   JAMES MURPHY
April 14, 1803   January 3, 1804
(SMOA, Bk. 21, no. 152)   (SMOA, Bk. 22, no. 9)[51]

In addition, John Stine acquired through purchase another tract of land being 2 1/2 arpents wide by 40 arpents deep adjoining his purchase from John Kershaw. Documentation for this chain of title is fragmentary, but it is clear that in July, 1804, Thomas W. Collins, a merchant, sold the tract of land to Thomas Urquhart of New Orleans. Then, in October, 1818, Urquhart sold the tract to John Stine.[52]

---

51. James Murphy leased these two-and-one-half arpents from Thomas Collins in January, 1804, for a period of six years. No formal sale from Collins to Murphy has been found in the St. Martin Parish records. Nevertheless, when Murphy died some years later this tract of land was listed in the inventory of his estate. Murphy therefore acquired it by private sale or by sale recorded outside St. Martin Parish.

52. These sales are recorded in SMOA, Bk. 22, no. 130, and SMCB 1B, p. 434. Fragmentary evidence would indicate that this tract of land, originally a part of the Francois Prevost Spanish land grant, was conveyed to Francisco Ortiz and then by him to Juan Migues. Migues sold it to Juan Puche y Solis on September 9, 1800 (SMOA, Bk. 19, no. 136), and apparently Puche y Solis sold it to Thomas Collins.

When the American survey system was introduced in 1805, and Stine had properly

Facts and Traditions 39

When John Stine, Sr., died in 1829, much of his property in the immediate vicinity of Bayou Teche and today's Main Street was platted into lots measuring one-half arpent wide facing the street.[53] This subdivision created by the Stine

Figure 5
THE STINE LANDS
AT NEW IBERIA
LATER ACQUIRED BY
JOSIAH FRENCH
AND
OTHER STINE HEIRS

claimed title to these lands, the two-and-one-half acres he had purchased from Kershaw was designated Section 42 of Township 12 South, Range 6 East. The property he purchased from Urquhart was designated Section 43 of the same township and range.

53. For further discussion of this subdivision of the Stine lands, see footnote 21 of the essay entitled "A Narrative of Events Connected with the Early Settlement of New Iberia."

family actually marked the beginning of New Iberia as an urban center. Residences built in this new subdivision stood back in the yards, some of them among trees and shrubbery, even down to the end of the century.

The old Stine residence was a large, single-story, frame house occupying the sites of the old courthouse and old city hall (an area presently incorporated into Bouligny Plaza). The house was demolished in 1884 to make way for the courthouse. The homesite had been acquired by John DeValcourt and John Taylor in 1837, but was later owned solely by DeValcourt.[54]

In 1860 the town bought the southern part of this property for the town market building.[55] This was quite a large structure built mainly of latticed sides with a high, shingled roof. The market stalls ranged facing a wide center space with earthen floor. In front of the market were the tables of the market gardeners from which their produce was sold. There was a coffee shop in conjunction.

The lot on the southeast corner of Main and French streets (the present site of Radio Station KDEA) was for many years the homesite of Abner Decker Minor, a surveyor. Next below that was the residence of Dr. Jacob Schreiner, a dentist, who also had a drug store.[56] He married a second time, on April 5,

---

54. Upon the death of Elizabeth Clark, Widow Stine, in early 1832, the Stine property was further subdivided. According to the succession sale (St. Martin Parish Estate 687), the lot measuring one-half arpent wide from the road to the bayou next above the corner lot (Main and Iberia streets) which then belonged to Cornelius Guyon was sold to Theodore Shute. The lot next above that (where the old city hall and old courthouse stood until 1975), containing the Stine family home, was sold to John Stine, Jr., for $1,710. The next lot above (between the old courthouse and Fisher Street) was sold to Thomas Johnson.

John Stine, Jr., sold the family home site to DeValcourt and Taylor on August 29, 1837. SMCB 10, p. 214.

55. The instrument reads in part:

> John DeValcourt . . . of the firm of Taylor and DeValcourt, in liquidation, sells to the trustees of New Iberia, namely William Robertson, president [mayor], Joseph D. Etie, Ulger Decuir, John Swaim, and John DeValcourt, a lot on the east side of Main Street having a front of 48 feet by a depth to the bayou.

For this transaction, see SMCB 28, p. 2, dated March 15, 1860.

56. On December 19, 1851, Mary Stine, wife of Josiah French, leased to Dr. Schreiner for five years a town lot measuring 84 feet wide and extending back to St. Peter

1853, to Mary E. Cobb. It was the custom of the country in those days that such a marriage should be followed by a *charivari*; which meant that the friends of the newlyweds gathered in front of the residence with pans, tin horns, and every possible instrument of noise and discord, and would sound them at their loudest, continually, until the bridegroom would capitulate, invite them in, and extend to them befitting hospitality. The crowd would then leave satisfied. But, occasionally, this was not so, as, for instance, in the case of Dr. Schreiner. When he was charivaried, tradition says that he became angered and stubbornly refused to yield and to invite the crowd to refreshments. But the young men on the outside were equally determined that surrender he must. And so the *charivari* continued by night and by day unceasingly for several days. As it continued more noise-making appliances were conveyed to the scene. Even large pots, and finally boilers were brought and were hammered upon. The crowd and the din increased until finally the incensed old gentleman gave in and invited the crowd into the house, according to the custom. Dr. Schreiner continued his drug store at that locality until after 1880.[57]

Included in the former Stine property was the lot owned by John DeValcourt and located next to the Schreiner home. The house on this lot was known in the 1870s as the "Dayton House," it being then used by Dayton DeValcourt as a hotel.

The next lot down had been acquired by Dr. Leonard Smith from the Stine estate, but it was purchased from him by Augustin Bergerie in 1858.[58] Mr. Bergerie's home stood about opposite the old courthouse.[59]

Street (SMCB 20½, p. 19). It was not until March 14, 1863, that Dr. Schreiner bought the lot from George Vest who had earlier purchased it from Mrs. French (SMCB 29, p. 446).

57. Dr. Schreiner died in 1887. See Iberia Parish Probate Book 10, folio 313.

58. Leonard Smith had purchased a lot 96 feet wide by a depth to St. Peter Street. From this he sold a lot 48 feet wide to Bergerie and the other half of his lot he sold to Marguerite Clelie Migues, wife of Joseph Bienvenue. The sales to Bergerie and Migues are recorded in SMCB 25, pp. 660, 669.

At the time that Bergerie purchased this property, it was being occupied by the Bienvenues who operated a bakery on the site. Bergerie then purchased from the Bienvenues all the baking equipment (SMCB 26, p. 46). The Bienvenues then moved to the lot they had purchased from Dr. Smith, located between Bergerie and DeValcourt.

59. Augustin Louis Bergerie (1816-1897), the son of Jean Bergerie and Catherine

Next below, on the southwest corner of Iberia and Main streets, was the property owned in the 1850s by Leontine Migues, wife of Jean Fontelieu. They were the parents of Judge Theodore Fontelieu, Laodice Fontelieu, Paulin and Pauline Fontelieu (who married Augustin Bergerie, Jr.), Zulmé Fontelieu, who married Alphé Cestia, and Alphé Fontelieu, who married Florence Ledger. Of these, Theodore Fontelieu was for years the leader of the Republican party in Iberia. He was first elected parish judge in 1872 and later became district judge, but was finally defeated for reelection by Fred L. Gates in 1884. Laodice Fontelieu kept a saloon and was a trusted political lieutenant of his brother. The story of the politics of Iberia Parish in those days of Reconstruction would fill a volume.

On June 7, 1874, Paulin Fontelieu fell victim of the custom of duelling. Fontelieu was in Abbeville, attending a dance at the Veranda Hotel and was drinking with his close friend Granville Shaw.[60] Both men were crack shots, but Shaw as much the better, having a national reputation as such. They became involved in a dispute, and it was suggested that they shoot it out. The duel occurred immediately and just in front of the hotel. Fontelieu shot first and, in the darkness, missed his man. He had a cigarette in his mouth, and as he drew upon it the bright head of the cigarette furnished a perfect target. Shaw fired and Fontelieu fell dead.

There was a brick and frame, two-story building on the southwest corner of Main and Iberia streets, the lower floor used at times as a store and at other times as a saloon. A wooden staircase against the outside of the Iberia Street

---

Fourteau, was a native of Bordeaux, France. He arrived in Louisiana as a result of a shipwreck in 1832. He was found lying exhausted at the corner of Main and Iberia streets on his way to a boat at the foot of Iberia Street. A member of the Migues family found him, took him home, and nursed him back to health.

Augustin worked on the Migues farm for several years. Although sometimes homesick, he decided to remain in Louisiana and, in 1838, became a U. S. citizen. In 1839, he married Anna Carmelite Migues, the daughter of Bernardo Gorge Migues and Maria Bernarda Romero. Carmelite was the grand-daughter of original settlers of New Iberia, Juan Migues and Salvadora de Quero.

Augustin established a bakery and store in New Iberia on the south side of West Main Street in the 100 block. He returned for a visit to France in 1878, but the familiar faces were gone and the country seemed strange. In 1888 he retired to live a quiet life in New Iberia. He died in 1897.

60. Granville Shaw was probably sheriff of Vermilion Parish at this time. A biographical sketch of Shaw can be found in Vermilion Historical Society, comp., *History of Vermilion Parish, Louisiana* (Abbeville, La., 1983), pp. 275-76.

wall led to a hall which ran along the rear of the upper story, and into this opened the doors to three rooms. Over the sidewalk extended a wide upper gallery upon which these rooms faced. So far as all present recollections go, this building "was always old." The three rooms had doubtless seen various uses. The one nearest Iberia Street (if the writer may here interject a personal remark) was the first office of the law firm of Weeks and Weeks when they commenced practicing law on June 11, 1887.

One incident concerning this building deserves mention. The Lottery campaign of 1890 to 1893 was nearing its close and the election was at hand. The Antis, under the excellent leadership of Judges Robert S. Perry and Joseph A. Breaux, Robert F. Broussard, Hipolyte Bayard, John M. Avery, Joseph A. Provost, James A. Lee, Walter J. Burke, and others, were woefully in the minority, having polled in the first test of strength less than 350 votes in the parish. But before the day for voting on the "Lottery Amendment" to the constitution, a bit more headway had been made. There were then in New Iberia a large number of individuals called "floaters," that is, voters who were suspected of lending a too attentive ear to the argument expressed in greenbacks. Some of the young men among the Antis adopted a novel plan for dealing with floaters. In twos and threes, the night before the election, the floaters were invited to the upper rooms of this building to partake of refreshments, and were so frequently "refreshed" and successfully entertained that by morning more than forty of such voters were "on hand." The only polling place for the town was across the street in the courthouse. The Antis were up early, and immediately upon the opening of the polls, these thoroughly "refreshed" voters, with Antis flanking them, were marched across the street and were voted. This action may be subject to criticism, but its use seemed to us fully justifiable then. At this election, Robert F. Broussard, a candidate for district attorney, made his first bid for political office. Though the entire Anti-Lottery ticket in this parish was overwhelmingly defeated, Broussard's personal popularity and merits elected him to office.

At this point we will reverse the sequential order of the land grants and proprietorships and will commence with the southernmost of the grants within the present city limits, thus coming upstream on the west side of Bayou Teche. This will permit better consideration of the business center of town.

The large grant requested by André-Claude Boutté in 1771, and awarded after his death to his son, François Cézar Boutté, in 1792, extended from a line about 125 feet east of Evangeline Street to a point about one-quarter mile east of the Nelson Canal (see Fig. 6).[61] Tradition has it that François Boutté was one of two brothers of French descent living and possessing much property

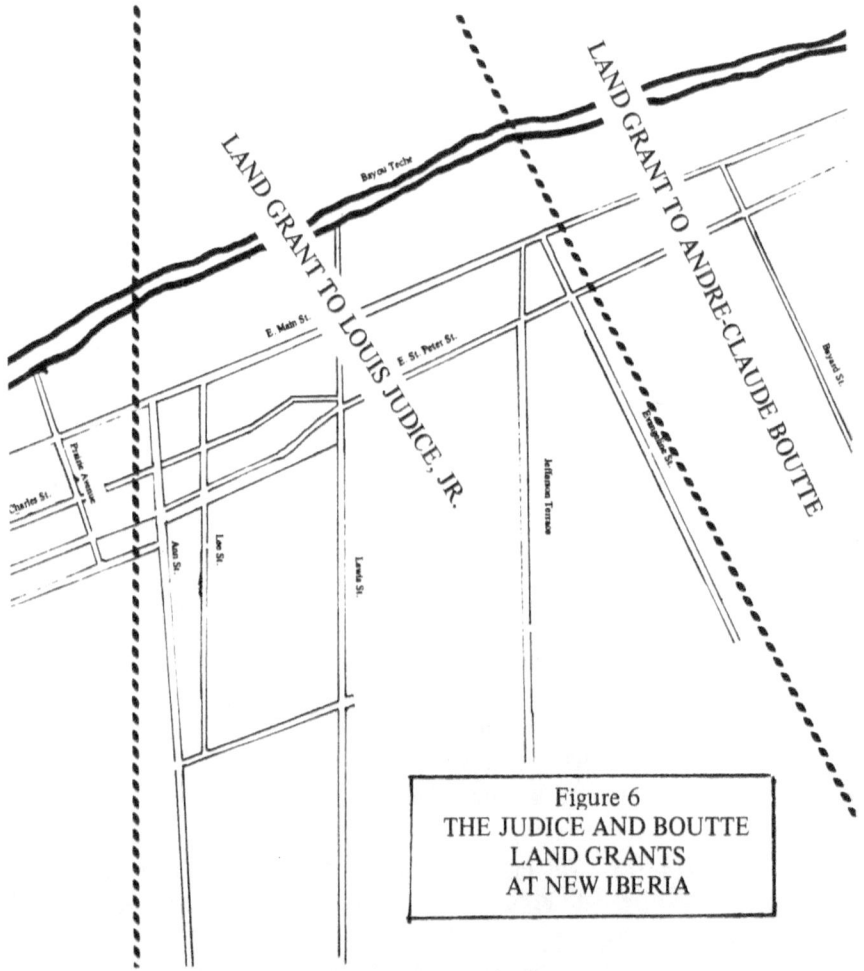

Figure 6
THE JUDICE AND BOUTTE
LAND GRANTS
AT NEW IBERIA

61. The dates for the request and for the grant are found in SMOA, Bk. 19, no. 26. The grant was for forty arpents square on both banks of Bayou Teche. On the south side of the Teche this grant later comprised Section 38 of Township 12 South, Range 7 East, and Section 77 of Township 12 South, Range 6 East. The western boundary line of this grant later became the boundary line between St. Martin and St. Mary parishes until Iberia Parish was created in 1868.

around New Orleans, as well as tracts in other parts of the province. Tradition also has it that after the cession of Louisiana to Spain, and after Governor O'Reilly's arrival in the colony in 1769, Boutté refused to salute the Spanish governor as required and was thrown into jail; finally, it is said that when he was released his financial matters were seriously impaired. Probably he, in later years moved to the Teche.[62]

At any rate, on July 7, 1806, one of his daughters, Marie-Thérèse, married Samuel Charles Meyer, a young man born in France in 1781 and educated in Paris, whose political views differed from those of the then government of France. As a consequence, he emigrated to New Orleans in his early twenties. Two children were born of this marriage, Euphémie Ida Meyer (b. June 1, 1807), who married François Mestayer at Plaquemine, and Emelie Léocade (b. September 5, 1809) who was first married to Ursin Gonsoulin and, after his death, to Dr. Jean-Baptiste Hacker.[63] Another daughter of François Cézar Boutté, Hortense, was first married (July 2, 1806) to Achille Berard, and after his death on March 2, 1816, to Baron Bayard (December 20, 1819). He died in 1852. His widow continued to live in the two-story brick house on their property through the disastrous years of the war and until she died in 1868. Long before her death, on February 16, 1859, Mrs. Bayard informally partitioned her plantation of twenty-one arpents width by forty arpents depth among her seven children by her two marriages (see Fig. 7). This partition was formalized ten years later when each heir received a tract of land three arpents wide by forty arpents deep. The heirs were Hortense Berard, then widow of Frederick Henry Duperier; Baron Bayard, Jr.; Ernest and Mathilde Bérard (jointly heirs of Jean-Baptiste Bérard; Alfred Bayard; Hipolyte Bayard; Achille Bérard; and Camille Bérard. Most of this property has remained in the hands of the heirs of the Bérard and Bayard families.

---

62. The Bouttes were among those French families in the Mobile area that left their homes when the territory became British in 1763. Although they were in New Orleans for a brief time, it would appear that Francois' father, Andre-Claude, moved to the Attakapas country in the mid-to-late 1760s. In 1770 Francois Cezar and his brothers were listed as being in the New Orleans militia (which would tend to discredit the tradition about Boutte's altercation with Governor O'Reilly). Andre-Claude and his family are recorded in the 1774 census of the Attakapas. Francois Cezar and his brother, Antoine, married on the same day, July 12, 1778, to two sisters. Francois Cezar's wife was Marie-Therese DeGruy.

63. The Meyers had a third child, Charles Christian, born on September 1, 1818. The child's mother died the following day. The child's father survived until 1828. See *Southwest Louisiana* Records, II, 114, 648; St. Mary Parish Estate 166.

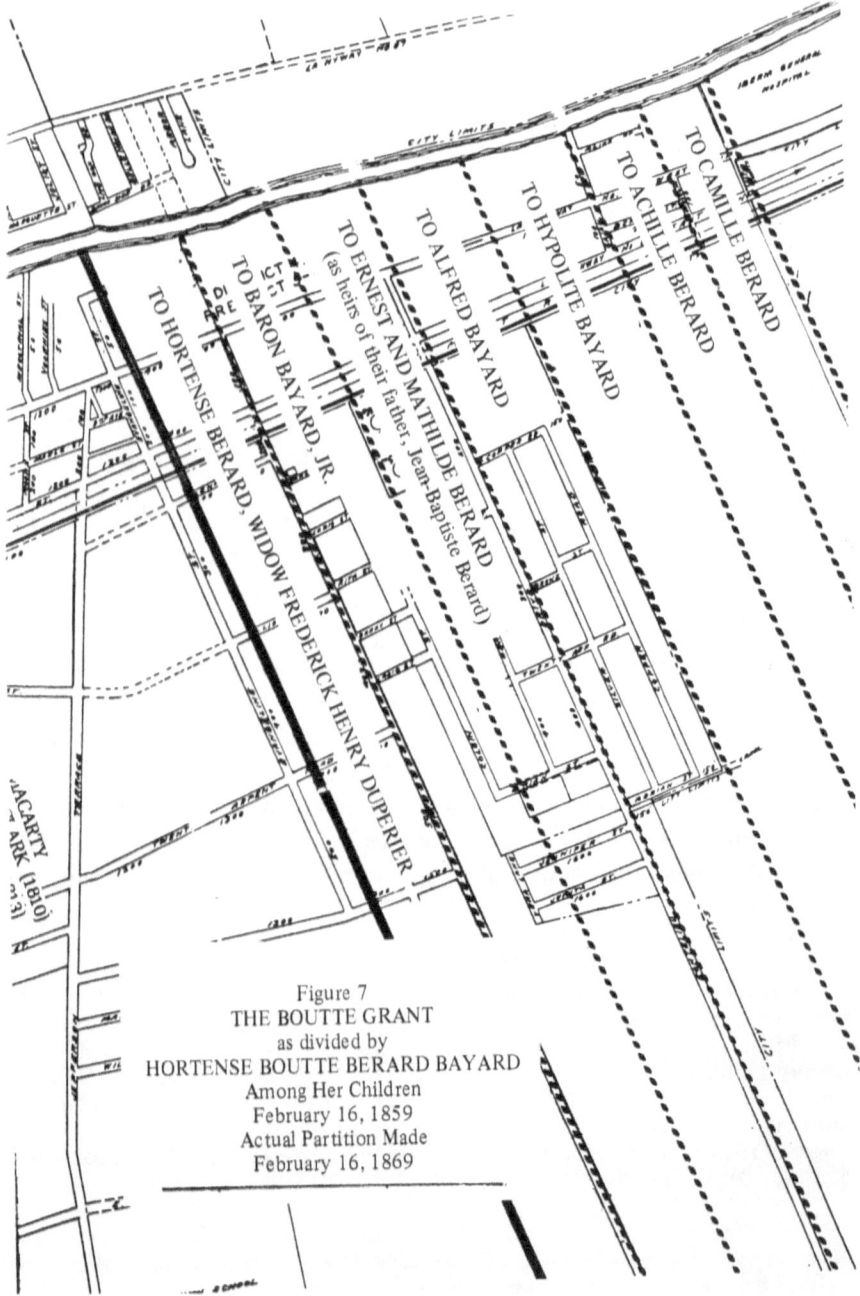

Figure 7
THE BOUTTE GRANT
as divided by
HORTENSE BOUTTE BERARD BAYARD
Among Her Children
February 16, 1859
Actual Partition Made
February 16, 1869

The Odd Fellows' Hall
circa 1859
(Present-day site of the Old Post Office)

The land donated by Mrs. Bayard to her daughter Hortense was sold, long before Mrs. Bayard's death, to Stanley C. and Millington M. Hartman. It may be recalled at this time that the western boundary of this tract (which lies about 125 feet east of, and parallel to, Evangeline Street) was the boundary line between the parishes of St. Mary and St. Martin until the creation of Iberia Parish in 1868. The Hartmans built the house now known as "Mintmere" and sold it to E. B. Smedes shortly before the Civil War.[64] Smedes did not long survive his purchase of the property, but his widow, the former Sarah Cade, outlived him by many years.[65]

The lands next above the Boutté tract were granted to Louis Judice, Jr., by Governor Luis de Unzaga, April 8, 1775, and were claimed by Jean-Baptiste Macarty after the Louisiana Purchase (see Fig. 6).[66] His heirs in 1810 sold this tract of twenty arpents front along the bayou to what is now the dividing line between Sections 38 and 39 of Township 12 South, Range 6 East (approximately one hundred feet west of Ann Street) to Daniel Clark, who died in 1813. This land was, therefore, involved in the famous Myra Clark Gaines litigation, which is one of the most celebrated of private litigations in the history of the United States. A history of the matter would provide all the thrills of a novel.[67] There was the vast estate at issue, as a motive for the alleged wrongdoing. There was romance, "the affair," and the birth of Myra. The alleged

64. For additional information on the Hartmans, Smedes, and other owners of Mintmere Plantation, see "Return to Mintmere," *Attakapas Gazette*, XV (1980), 24-29.

65. Sarah Cade Smedes died May 12, 1904. Louisiana Society NSDAR, comp., *Louisiana Tombstone Inscriptions*, 11 vols. (n.p., 1957-60), XI, 20.

66. The Judice grant is recorded in the map series by Gertrude C. Taylor entitled *Land Grants Along the Teche*. The grant is found in *Part 2, St Martinville to Sorrel*.

Jean-Baptiste Macarty, scion of a French family that arrived in Louisiana in 1732, was born in New Orleans on March 7, 1750, the son of Barthelemy Daniel Macarty and Francoise Helen Pellerin. He married Heloise Charlotte Fazende, member of a distinguished Creole family, and they had three children: Barthelemy (who never married); Edmond (or Edward), who married Marie-Eleonore Destrehan; and Marie-Celeste, who married Paul Lanusse. Jean-Baptiste Macarty died November 10, 1808. For additional information on this family, see Stanley Clisby Arthur, *Old Families of Louisiana* (New Orleans, 1931), pp. 330-33.

The Judice grant in the area of East Main Street ran from just east of Evangeline Street to just west of Ann Street.

67. The best account of the Clark-Gaines story is that of Nolan B. Harmon, Jr., *The Famous Case of Myra Clark Gaines* (Baton Rouge, 1946).

secret marriage of the parents which was so secret that it was not known even to the child for more than twenty-five years after the death of her parents. The suppression and destruction of the will to the child (if it was really ever made) and this only asserted after an equally long lapse of time. Then followed the fiercest of legal battles. Nothing is lacking in the story for material for a best seller. The executors under the will of Daniel Clark sold the above-mentioned tract regularly in his succession and it passed into the ownership of John F. Miller and his mother Mrs. Sarah Canby (see Fig. 8).[68]

Myra Clark Gaines ascertained nearly twenty-five years after Daniel Clark's death that she was his daughter, and she claimed that under a will made by him subsequent in date to that under which the estate property was sold, but which will she urged to be utterly destroyed, she was his heir. Surely, her case seemed flimsy.

Nevertheless, in 1836 or 1837, she began the litigation for the recovery of extensive and valuable tracts of land, including the Macarty tract sold to John F. Miller. What is even more remarkable, she produced evidence that convinced the courts of the merits of her story and obtained judgments recognizing her rights. Due to this litigation, and to the cloud thus cast upon the title, practically no permanent improvements were placed on the Macarty tract, except the property now owned by Mrs. J. Patout Burns, and which was occupied by James A. Lee

---

The tract of land referred to throughout this paragraph is Section 38 of Township 12 South, Range 6 East, and Section 44 of Township 12 South, Range 7 East. Louis Judice, Jr., was put into possession of the land in 1775, as a result of an order of survey from Governor Unzaga. Macarty purchased the property from Judice as is set out in *American State Papers*, III, 410.

For details of the sale from the Macarty heirs to Daniel Clark, see footnote 71 of this essay.

68. The statement concerning the manner in which the Clark lands came to be sold is essentially correct, except for the Clark lands at New Iberia. According to the deposition of Daniel Coxe of Philadelphia, given in connection with the litigation brought by Myra Clark Gaines, he received the Clark lands at New Iberia in the following manner:

> I took from Messrs. Chew and Relf [the executors of Clark's estate], in part payment of debt due to me as per the settlement of our co-partnership accounts, the lands debited to me in their account current. I also took in part payment of a debt due Edward Burd, my father-in-law, a tract of land at New Iberia, of about twelve arpents [wide].

For the entire deposition of Daniel W. Coxe, see Harmon, *Myra Clark Gaines*, pp. 290-95.

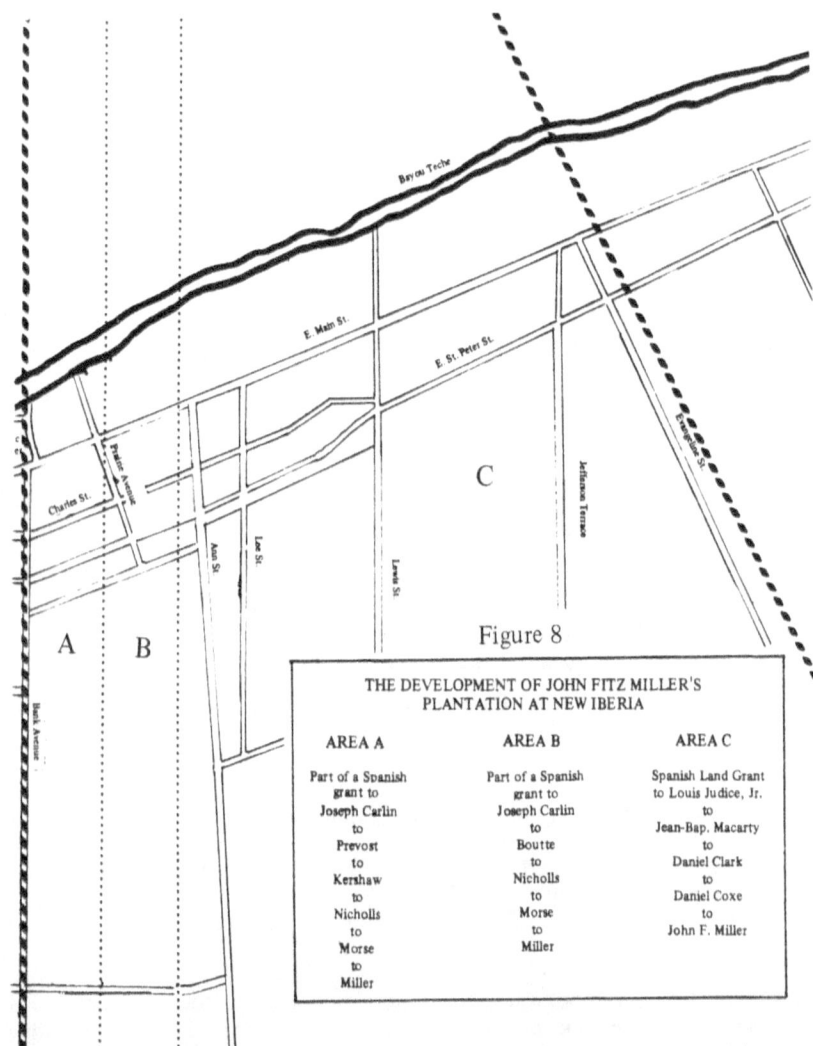

Figure 8

THE DEVELOPMENT OF JOHN FITZ MILLER'S
PLANTATION AT NEW IBERIA

AREA A	AREA B	AREA C
Part of a Spanish grant to Joseph Carlin to Prevost to Kershaw to Nicholls to Morse to Miller	Part of a Spanish grant to Joseph Carlin to Boutte to Nicholls to Morse to Miller	Spanish Land Grant to Louis Judice, Jr. to Jean-Bap. Macarty to Daniel Clark to Daniel Coxe to John F. Miller

as a residence between 1856 and 1870.[69] It was probably built before the suits were filed by Myra Clark Gaines. The plantation home of John F. Miller, the

---

69. Miller, however, had not acquired the property when the litigation began. The fact that he would purchase this property seems to indicate that there was, at least at the time of purchase, no question about title. At any rate, on April 23, 1839, Joshua Baker, acting for Daniel Coxe, sold to Miller the tract of land which was 20 arpents wide by 80 arpents deep. Part of this tract had been acquired by Coxe in the manner described in the

sugarhouse, overseer's house, and the quarters were all built on the upper part of the plantation, that is, on the seven-arpent tract above the Macarty lands.[70]

In 1869, the litigation brought against Mrs. Cordelia D. Lewis, the heir to the Miller estate, by Myra Clark Gaines was compromised and the title of this tract was transferred to Mrs. Lewis.[71] She then had the property surveyed and opened streets, these being Peebles Avenue, Lewis Avenue, and Ann Street.[72] Within a few months she sold the greater part of this Macarty strip. The tract adjoining Peebles Avenue, twenty arpents deep, was sold to Dudley T. Peebles and later to C. C. Weeks. On part of this tract, between the Teche and Main Street, is now located the Charles Boldt Paper Mill.[73] The Gebert brothers later purchased the next adjoining tract for sawmill purposes.[74]

In 1871 Charles Clerc and Louis Delcambre, two cattlemen, purchased the two arpents front, above where the Geberts afterwards bought, this being

---

foregoing footnote. The property was bounded above by that of the vendee and that belonging to Eli Riggs; below it was bounded by the property of Baron Bayard. Miller paid $10,700 for this tract of land. SMCB 11, p. 344.

70. For further discussion of the seven-arpent tract above the Macarty lands, which Miller also acquired, see footnote 89 below.

71. On October 28, 1868, Myra Clark Gaines, of New York, sold to Cordelia D. Lewis, nee Wheeler, of St. Martin Parish, a tract of land purchased by Daniel Clark on June 30, 1810, from the heirs of Jean-Baptiste Macarty, namely, Edward and Barthelemy Macarty and Paul Lanusse (this transaction was recorded by Pierre Pedesclaux, a New Orleans notary). The land measured 20 arpents wide along the west bank of Bayou Teche by 40 arpents deep. It was the same tract of land for which Myra Clark Gaines instituted a suit against Cordelia Lewis in Circuit Court of the United States for the Eastern District of Louisiana (Docket no. 5057) in 1866. See IPCB 1, p. 23.

The case was closed with the sale (the compromise) to Cordelia Lewis in October, 1869. Sale price was $2,000.

72. The naming of Lewis Avenue is obvious. Ann Street was probably named for Ann Lewis, wife of Mathew Lewis, Cordelia's brother-in-law. Cordelia apparently had great regard for Ann, for the first provision of Cordelia's will concerns Ann. Peebles Avenue was named for Dudley Peebles who purchased from Cordelia Lewis a tract of land between parallel lines measured eastward from Lewis Avenue. On the eastern boundary he developed the thoroughfare known as Peebles Ave. It was later renamed Jefferson Terrace.

73. The sale to Peebles occurred on May 17, 1869, and is recorded in IPCB 1, p. 261.

74. The sale to the Gebert brothers occurred in May, 1888, and is recorded in IPCB 16, p. 411.

bounded by Lewis Avenue.[75] A tract of land two arpents wide and twenty arpents deep above (i. e., west of) Lewis Avenue was purchased by James L. Burke. The land then went through several conveyances until it belonged to Mrs. E. T. King. The Kings then established a brickyard on the property.[76] The two arpents frontage west of the King property were sold to Emanuel J. Etié, the parish judge. On the same day, May 8, 1869, James A. Lee purchased the adjoining front of two arpents of land.[77]

The Lewis family continued to own much of the remaining property up to, and including, the Burns property for a number of years, but during the 1880s and 1890s, and later, it was sold in lots to many different purchasers. Included among these were Paul Suberbielle, Walter Burke, Grayson Morrell, Miss Nannie Peebles, and M. W. Fisher.[78]

The tract of ten arpents front by forty arpents deep granted by the Spanish government to Joseph Carlin embraces the lands between the west boundary of the Burns property and a point about seventy feet west of the west line of the Civic Center, or Section 39 of Township 12 South, Range 6 East. Carlin retained the land only a short time before he sold four arpents width by forty arpents depth to Philippe Boutté and six arpents width by forty arpents depth to François Prévost.[79]

---

75. On September 16, 1871, James A. Lee, acting for Cordelia D. Wheeler, widow of John Lloyd Lewis, sold to Charles Clerc and Louis Delcambre a tract of land located below the town of New Iberia, containing 40 superficial arpents (being 2 arpents wide by 20 arpents deep), fronting on Bayou Teche and bounded above by the road known as Lewis Avenue. IPCB 3, p. 262.

76. James L. Burke bought the land from Cordelia Lewis on May 8, 1869 (IPCB 1, p. 237). He then sold the property to R. Hamilton Marsh on December 28, 1869 (IPCB 1, p. 619). Then, on July 28, 1873, Mrs. R. Hamilton Marsh sold the property to Elizabeth Morse, wife of Jonas Marsh (IPCB 4, p. 274). Finally, on August 12, 1874, Mrs. Jonas Marsh sold the property to Margaret A. Marsh, wife of E. Thomas King (IPCB 4, p. 523).

77. The Etie transaction is recorded in IPCB 1, p. 237. The Lee transaction is found in IPCB 1, p. 241. Lee's western boundary would be present-day Lee Street. The street, of course, was named for this Lee family. Philip Street, running from Main Street to Bayou Teche and located approximately at mid-point of the Lee purchase, was named for James A. Lee's son.

78. This tract of land, running from Lee Street westward to approximately one hundred feet west of Ann Street was specifically reserved for the Lewis family by Cordelia Lewis as is described in IPCB 1, p. 241.

79. These sales, occurring in February 1791, are recorded in SMOA, Bk. 11, nos. 44 and 50.

Facts and Traditions   53

Boutté held his portion of the Carlin tract until September 17, 1805, when he sold it to Edward Church Nicholls.[80] François Prévost sold his segment of the Carlin tract to John Kershaw on December 14, 1802.[81] Kershaw, in turn, sold half of this property, the eastern half to Nicholls on August 9, 1805.[82] Thus, by September, 1805, Edward C. Nicholls had come to own all of Section 39 of Township 12 South, Range 6 East, except the western-most three arpents which Kershaw had previously sold to Mongault and Myer.[83] Nicholls' property extended, then, from near Ann Street westward to approximately the eastern line of Bank Avenue (see Fig. 8).

This Edward Church Nicholls was the grandfather of Governor Francis T. Nicholls. The elder Nicholls held high office for some years by recognition of President Thomas Jefferson and appointment by Governor Claiborne.[84] He was a Marylander, a friend of Thomas Jefferson, but apparently much inclined to spend beyond his means. He was in Louisiana about a year before sending for his family; they reached the state in 1805.[85] The story of their trip by sea and then up the Mississippi and across to Butte La Rose and thence by wagon to New Iberia, and also their life in New Iberia, is well told by Edward's son, Thomas C. Nicholls. Part of his narrative was published by Lyle Saxon in *Old Louisiana*.

The newcomers fared famously with the French and Acadian inhabitants but apparently found little in common with those of the English-speaking people whom they met. Nicholls eventually lost his position through dissipation.[86] Meanwhile, Nathan Morse, then a young lawyer from New Jersey, settled in New

---

80. SMOA, Bk. 24, no. 80.

81. SMOA, Bk. 21, no. 10.

82. SMOA, Bk. 24, no. 5.

83. SMOA, Bk. 22, no. 120.

84. Nicholls was appointed judge of Attakapas on May 5, 1805.

85. Nicholls, according to his son's account, arrived in Louisiana in early 1804. His family followed a year later, leaving Baltimore in December, 1804.

86. For more information on Edward C. Nicholls, see footnote 27 of the essay entitled "The Obituary of William Weeks."

Iberia and soon afterward married one of Judge Nicholls' daughters.[87] It was their son Isaac who, in later years, was the frequent Democratic opponent of Judge John Moore, a Whig, for a seat in Congress from the local congressional district. During the 1830s and 1850s the two alternated in Congress as the wishes of the voters decided.[88] The district then included all the western part of Louisiana as far north as De Soto Parish.

The Nicholls family moved from New Iberia to Lafourche, and their property was purchased by John F. Miller. Ownership of this plantation alternated between himself and his mother Mrs. Canby, until Miller's death in 1857, when the property was willed to Miller's niece Cordelia W. Lewis.[89]

87. Nathan Morse married Martha Craufurd Nicholls. For more on the Nicholls and Morse families, see footnote 27 of the essay entitled "The Obituary of William Weeks."

88. John Moore, a native of Berkeley County, Virginia (now West Virginia), was the son of Lewis Moore and Rebecca Henshaw. He was born in 1788. The Moore family moved to Louisiana about the time of the Purchase and settled in St. Mary Parish. In 1810 John Moore married Adelaide Demaret, and the couple had two children, Adelaide and Evelina.

Moore, a planter, was also active in politics. He served in the state legislature from 1825 to 1834. In 1833 he became judge of St. Mary Parish, and in 1840 was elected to the national House of Representatives as a Whig. He served until 1843, after losing a bid for reelection to Pierre Bossier. Bossier died in office and was replaced by Isaac Morse on December 2, 1844. Morse, a Democrat, served as the district's representative in Washington until March, 1851, having lost his bid for reelection to Moore, who then served one term in Congress.

Moore married Mary Clara Conrad, widow of David Weeks, on April 15, 1841. They had no children.

In 1861 Moore was active in the Secession Convention and signed the resolution dissolving the union between the United States and Louisiana. During the Civil War years, Moore served in the Confederate legislature of Louisiana. After the war he returned to New Iberia and died at The Shadows on June 17, 1867. He is buried in the family graveyard on the grounds of the mansion.

For additional information on John Moore, see *Biographical Directory of the American Congress, 1774-1949* (Washington, D. C., 1950), p. 1581; and Gertrude C. Taylor, "John Moore: Planter, Politician, Husband, and Father," *Attakapas Gazette*, XIX (1984), 146-151.

89. John F. Miller purchased the Nicholls property from Martha Craufurd Nicholls, widow of Nathan Morse, on April 6, 1835. This was a tract of land seven arpents wide (the Bank Avenue to near Ann Street property) and forty arpents deep. SMCB 9, p. 360. To this tract Miller added the land purchased from Daniel Coxe on April 23, 1839 (see footnote 69 above). Thus, Miller owned the land from just east of Evangeline Street westward to Bank Avenue, being forty arpents deep from the bayou.

Cordelia Wheeler Lewis was the daughter of Nathan Wheeler and Mary Ann Jane Miller, the sister of John Fitz Miller. The Wheelers lived in Cincinnati. Their daughter Cordelia married John Lloyd Lewis of Kentucky. When her bachelor uncle died, Cor-

The Burns Home
This house, originally built (c. 1846) by John F. Miller as a residence for his mother Sarah Canby, was later the home of the Lewis family.

Mrs. Canby and her son came to Louisiana from South Carolina where, it was the often repeated story of Mrs. Canby, she had seen George Washington on

---

delia inherited his Louisiana properties. Although Cordelia, then a widow, spent some years in New Iberia, she eventually returned to Kentucky where she died in 1883. Being childless, her estate passed to her brother-in-law and his wife, Mathew and Ann Lewis, who then came to New Iberia to make their home. Mr. Lewis died at his New Iberia residence on the corner of East Main and Ann streets (the present-day Burns home) on November 22, 1901. For additional details on this family, see Gertrude C. Taylor, "How Do I Love Thee: The Life and Writings of John Lloyd Lewis," *Attakapas Gazette*, XV (1980), 134-139.

his historic trip through the Southern states.[90] The old lady lived well over one hundred years of age. Her son was a colorful character. In addition to his town plantation and lands in the Loreauville area, he acquired and owned until his death what is now called Jefferson Island, which was known before that as Orange Island and before that as Miller's Island.[91]

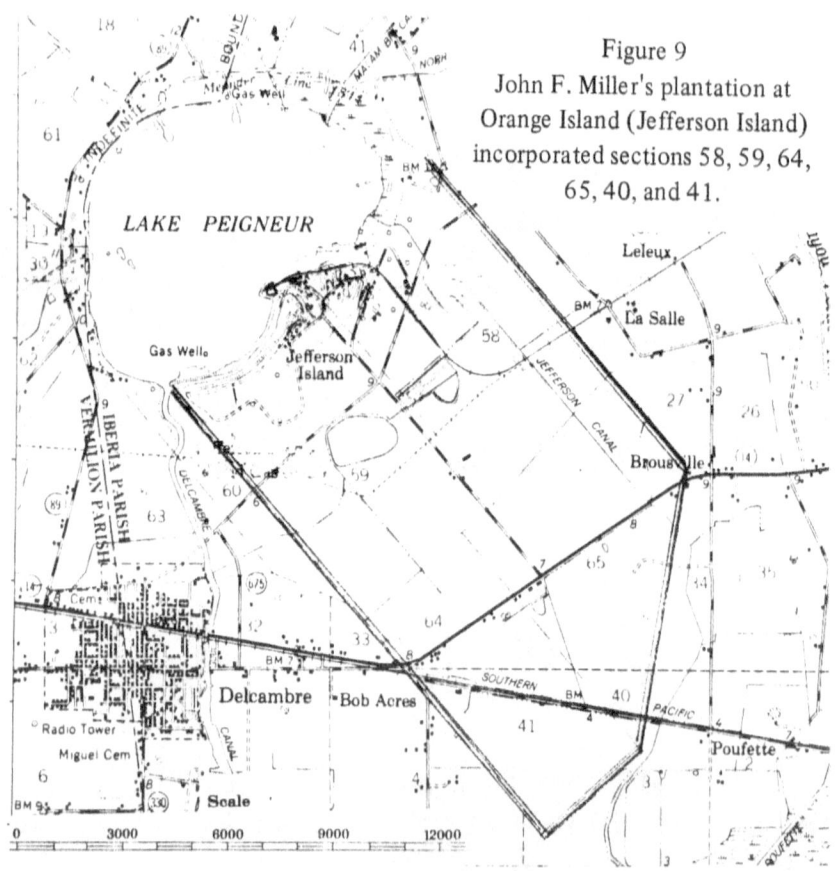

Figure 9
John F. Miller's plantation at Orange Island (Jefferson Island) incorporated sections 58, 59, 64, 65, 40, and 41.

90. Mrs. Canby was Sarah Wessels, who married first John Fitz Miller, Sr., of Philadelphia, and second Joseph Canby. Mrs. Canby and her son and daughter may have come to Louisiana from South Carolina, but John Fitz Miller, Jr., always recorded himself as a native of Philadelphia. There may be little coincidence, therefore, between this fact and the fact that he purchased land from Daniel Coxe, a Philadelphia merchant.

91. On February 6, 1778, Governor Bernardo de Galvez signed an "order of survey" as a further step toward granting Francois Prevost a tract of land that contained the north-

Miller's home was a large, two-story brick building on the tract of land between the bayou and Main Street. It was located about 400 feet below Bank Avenue and occupied the site upon which later stood the Russell home.[92] The homesite and the seven-acre front on Bayou Teche had been mortgaged to the Citizens' Bank of New Orleans before the Civil War. After the war, Miller's heirs could not cancel the mortgage and the property was seized by court order on January 21, 1869. Placed on the auction block, the purchaser was the Citizens' Bank which, in July, 1869, sold the tract of land to Brainerd T. Smith of Chicago. Smith's intentions were to subdivide a large portion of the property, particularly the block between Bank and Prairie avenues and running back to Washington Street (now Lafayette Street).[93]

---

east half of Butte à Peigneur. When land claims were filed with the American land commissioners after the Louisiana Purchase, no final Spanish grant (or patent) could be produced for the land. Hence, the American commissioners confirmed the land to Prevost as a Second Class Claim; that is, one based on documented proof of an order of survey (which amounted to a Spanish intent to grant). For additional details on this and other matters connected with Jefferson Island, see Glenn R. Conrad, "Wilderness Paradise: A Glimpse of Jefferson Island and Its Owners for the Past Two Centuries," *Attakapas Gazette*, XIV (1979), 52-63; *American State Papers*, III, 181.

It has often been said that Miller bought Jefferson Island and nearby lands from Isaac Randolph. This is incorrect. Randolph's properties were seized by order of the court for debt and were sold at sheriff's sale on June 15, 1833. The purchasers were John Brownson and his wife Caroline Stelle. They paid $11,500 for the Randolph lands, which included the southwest half of the "island" then known as Butte a Peigneur. Then, in October, 1833, the Brownsons sold this land to John Fitz Miller for $19,500. SMCB 8, p. 236; St. Martin Parish Sheriff's Book A, p. 283.

Meanwhile, on August 25, 1883, Miller bought the northeast half of Butte à Peigneur or Pine (or Miller, or Orange, or Jefferson) Island and adjoining lands from Eliza Provost (the daughter of Joseph Provost and Madeleine Prevost), wife of Andrew Wilson Dismukes of St. Mary Parish. The property sold was described as being the "undivided seventh part of a tract which she inherited from the estate of her grandfather, Francois Prevost." See SMCB 8, p. 200.

It is not known when Miller and family arrived in New Iberia. At the time of this purchase and the purchases described above, Miller was recorded as being a resident of New Orleans.

Isaac Randolph was the husband of Eliza McCall, the daughter of Jesse McCall, the owner and operator of a salt evaporation works on Avery (then McCall or Petite Anse) Island in the early years of the nineteenth century. See St. Martin Parish Estate 406. For more on Jesse McCall on Avery Island, see Gertrude C. Taylor, "The Saga of Petite Anse Island," *Attakapas Gazette*, XIX (1984),

92. This is the approximate site of present-day 513 - 525 East Main Street.

93. IPCB 1, p. 363.

The land south of East Main, between Bank and Prairie avenues, was duly surveyed and subdivided. The property north of Main Street, however, was not divided into lots but was sold in two large segments. The first of these parcels contained the home and ancillary buildings of Miller's plantation. Thus, on February 16, 1871, Smith sold to the Catholic Archdiocese of New Orleans a parcel of land four-hundred-feet wide along East Main, beginning at the Henshaw line (that is, the west side of Bank Avenue, if that street continued to the bayou) and running to the south property line of present-day 525 East Main, with a depth to the bayou.[94] The church bought the house and property for use as a boys' school.[95]

Twenty-five years later, the archdiocese sold most of the old Miller homesite, then known as the "Old College Place," to George W. Fitzhugh.[96] The Fitzhughs apparently lived in Miller's house until their daughter Kate and her husband, Joseph Russell, demolished the old building and built a new residence in 1905. The Russells, and then their daughter and her husband, Dr. Frank Courts, resided there until the house was destroyed by fire in 1933.[97]

John Miller was a man of popularity and pleasing address and for a time represented the southern ward of St. Martin Parish. He was a bachelor and was fond of horses and horseracing. He owned a racetrack on Jefferson Island where gentlemen of this section raced their horses for many years.

Miller was also connected with the story of Sally Muller, a German immigrant girl who was sold into service for a year as a redemptioner to pay her passage over the sea and then through someone's criminal act, was sold as an African slave. Miller became the purchaser, probably in all good faith, and the girl was brought to New Iberia and remained in slavery at the Miller home

---

94. *Ibid.*, 2, p. 572.

95. For more on this school, see the essay entitled "The Story of Education in New Iberia."

96. IPCB 30, p. 223. Before the sale to Fitzhugh, the church had sold to Lucius LaSalle one sixth of the 400-foot front (approximately 70 feet) adjoining the Henshaw line. This later became the homesite of the Albert Estorge family. The sale to LaSalle is mentioned in *ibid.*

The present-day east boundary line of the Civic Center corresponds to the east boundary line of the property purchased by LaSalle.

97. *New Iberia Enterprise*, March 11, 1933.

Facts and Traditions

The Fitzhugh - Russell Home

for long years until, over thirty years of age, she was discovered by her people. Suit for her freedom was brought and was argued in the state supreme court, the case being reported in 11 Robinson, page 339, and her right to liberty was decreed. After the publication of this story by George Cable, some of the former Miller slaves stated that they distinctly remembered the girl.[98]

To return to the land sold to Brainerd Smith for subdivision purposes, the area on the south side of Main Street, between Bank and Prairie avenues, was

---

98. The case, as reported in 11 Robinson 339, presents the following facts: John Fitz Miller stated that in August, 1822, a certain Anthony Williams, then of Mobile, left him with a certain mulatto girl, then named Bridget, and that she was then about 12 years old. Miller advanced Williams $100 against the girl, the amount to be repaid when the girl was sold. When Williams did not claim the slave, Miller sold her to his mother, Mrs. Canby. She, in turn, raised the girl as a domestic and retained her until 1834 when the slave, together with her children, were sold back to Miller. Then, in 1838, Miller sold the woman to Louis Belmonti of New Orleans. Perhaps it was then that her people found her, for it was then that she brought suit against Belmonti for her freedom.

The woman claimed that she was Sally Miller, daughter of Daniel Miller, and that she had emigrated with her parents from Germany in 1817 or 1818. She stated that her mother died during the Atlantic crossing and that her father died shortly thereafter. See Merritt M. Robinson, *Reports of Cases Argued and Determined in the Supreme Court of Louisiana* (New Orleans, 1846), XI, 339.

subdivided into eight lots, the sale of which had begun when Smith lost the property to the Citizens' Bank. On January 25, 1876, the district court ordered Smith's land seized and sold at auction.[99] The property was once again acquired by the Citizens' Bank. It was the bank, then, using the plat of Smith's proposed addition to New Iberia, which began to sell lots in the area.[100] The purchasers of the eight lots facing Main Street were (from Bank to Prairie) C. C. Weeks, George Colgin, Mrs. Susan Devers, Mrs. L. Fontelieu, D. U. Broussard (2 lots, shortly afterward purchased by William Southwell), and William Schwing (2 lots).[101]

The Frantz Home, 1985
The William Schwing Home, 1876

99. IPCB 5, p. 377.
Excluded from the seizure and sale were the two parcels of land on the north side of Main Street between Bank and Prairie avenues.

100. Bank Avenue was named for the Citizens' Bank, not, as it is sometimes said, for General Nathaniel Banks.

101. The sales are found in IPCB 5, p. 521 (Weeks); IPCB 2, p. 322 (Colgin); IPCB

The Jones Home, 1985
The William Southwell Home, 1881

The only area of the block between Bank and Prairie avenues remaining to be discussed is the second parcel of land on the north side of Main Street, the 225-foot lot between the Fitzhugh property and Prairie Avenue. It will be recalled that John F. Miller acquired a parcel of land seven arpents wide from Martha Crauford Nicholls, widow of Nathan Morse. Mrs. Morse, however, excepted from the sale the two houses on the property, the one in which she resided and the one for her sister-in-law and her husband, Jonas Marsh. It was not until 1839 that the Marshes sold these homes to Miller.[102]

As has been recounted, Miller held the property until his death when it was inherited by his niece, Cordelia Lewis, who, in turn, lost it to the Citizens' Bank, which, in turn, sold it to Brainerd T. Smith. Smith divided the area north of Main Street into two parcels, one of which he sold to the Catholic church. The second parcel of land, the 225-foot width between the church property and Prairie Avenue, with a depth to the bayou, was not sold and therefore returned to the Citizens' Bank when it seized Smith's property in 1876.

Then, on May 8, 1877, Mrs. John R. Davis (Margaret Winters) bought from the Citizens' Bank eleven lots of ground, containing eighteen arpents, bounded north by the bayou, south by the public road (Main Street), west by the property of Holy Cross College, and south by the property of Cordelia Lewis (or the present-day east boundary line of 623 East Main Street).[103]

On July 18, 1878, Mrs. Davis sold to Frederick Gates a lot of ground fronting 211 feet on Bayou Teche with a depth of 210 feet from the bayou, bounded north by the bayou, east by Prairie Avenue, and south by the vendor.[104] The following year, Adam Winters sold to Gates a parcel of land

---

5, p. 358 (Devers); IPCB 7, p. 527 (Fontelieu); IPCB 7, p. 527 (Broussard-Southwell); and IPCB 5, p. 583 (Schwing).

102. It is quite possible that Miller's home was the former residence of Jonas Marsh. This would have been the same house which later served as Holy Cross College (the boys' school) and the residence of George Fitzhugh and his family. The editor has not been able, however, to document this fact.

103. IPCB 6, p. 41.

104. *Ibid.,* 436

Facts and Traditions 63

sixty-five feet wide, fronting on the bayou, by a depth of 210 feet and located just east of Prairie Avenue.[105]

On December 18, 1881, the Citizens' Bank repossessed Mrs. Davis' unsold property, and, on May 23, 1882, sold to John Emmer a lot of ground measuring 225 feet facing Main Street by a depth of 338 feet, bounded west by the property of George Fitzhugh, east by Prairie Avenue, and north by Frederick Gates.[106] Several years later, in November, 1885, Emmer sold this parcel of land to Gates.[107] Shortly thereafter, Judge Gates built his home on this prop-

The Gates Home
in the record snowfall of February 14, 1899

105. *Ibid.*, 7, p. 426.

106. *Ibid.*, 10, p. 22

107. Iberia Parish Mortgage Book R, p. 109.

erty. The judge died on September 4, 1897, and on December 31, 1901, his widow sold the property to Mrs. Annie Lee Gebert.[108] It is from this family that the beautiful oak on the property derives its name. In 1978 the Gebert heirs sold the property to Mr. and Mrs. Lonnie Bewely.

The Gebert Oak, 1985
at 150 years old

108. IPCB 33, p. 228.

The portion of the Davis property east of Prairie Avenue between the Teche and Main Street was also acquired by John Emmer.[109] It was then an empty space, but was quickly developed.

The John Emmer Home
about 1937

Section 40 of Township 12 South, Range 6 East, is bounded by the west line of Bank Avenue and west by the west boundary line of the Civic Center, an area of about two arpents in width by a depth of forty arpents (that is, to Admiral Doyle Drive). This area constituted the Henshaw Addition to New Iberia when it was subdivided in 1869. The land was originally a portion of a

---

109. Emmer acquired the property from the Citizens' Bank on May 23, 1882. IPCB 10, p. 22. He built his home at 623 East Main Street shortly thereafter. East of the home, Mr. Emmer established a brick kiln which he operated from 1884 to 1899. *New Iberia Enterprise*, April 8, 1899.

grant to Joseph Carlin, who also owned large tracts of land near Franklin.[110]

As recounted above, Carlin sold a portion of this tract, six arpents wide, to François Prévost.[111] In 1802, Prévost sold the six arpents to John Kershaw.[112] It was Kershaw who divided the tract into two parts, selling what became Section 40 to François Mongault, and the remainder to Edward Church Nicholls.[113] On May 30, 1828, Section 40, together with other land, was sold to John C. Marsh.[114] Then, in 1851, at a private sale, Marsh sold Section 40 plus about 210 acres on the opposite bank of the Teche to his son George and his sons-in-law, Daniel Dudley Avery and Ashbel Henshaw.[115] That same day, June 26, 1851, Marsh and Avery sold their interests in the New Iberia lands to Henshaw.[116]

The property remained with the Henshaw family until well after 1900; however, John M. Henshaw, Ashbel's son, continued to sell lots in the Henshaw Addition. After his death, his sons, continuing these sales, disposed of the home place, between the bayou and the street. It was sold to the Catholic church for the purpose of establishing a boys' school, later known as St. Peter's College.[117] That school was closed in 1957, and the site of the campus, plus the adjoining Estorge property, was purchased for the proposed Civic Center.

Next above the Henshaw Addition (that is, toward the west) was the tract which about 1858 and subsequently was divided into, and was sold as, the Weeks

---

110. For a biographical sketch of Joseph Carlin (c. 1730-1809), see Conrad, "Wilderness Paradise," pp. 53-54

111. See footnote 8 of this essay. The sale occurred on February 15, 1791.

112. SMOA, Bk. 21, no. 110.

113. SMOA, Bk. 22, no. 120. For the sale to Nicholls, see SMOA, Bk. 24, no. 5.

114. See footnote 25 of the essay entitled "The Obituary of William Weeks."

115. This private sale was recorded the next year in East Baton Rouge Parish, but did not enter the record books of St. Martin Parish until 1867. See SMCB 32, p. 96.

116. *Ibid.*, 29, p. 49.

117. John Henshaw's sons, Charles, Nevil, and Harold, sold the homesite to the Catholic church on October 17, 1913. IPCB 76, p. 215. St. Peter's College did not begin operation, however, until 1918.

Addition.[118] This land formed a part of the Prévost grant. On September 20, 1825, David Weeks bought from the estate of Henry Pintard a tract of land measuring about 915 feet along the bayou, by a depth of forty arpents. The only house on the property, the one into which Weeks and his family moved, was located on the site of 424 East Main Street. About 1831, David Weeks began building the home now known as Shadows-on-the-Teche.[119]

It is due to the memory of Congressman John Moore to say that in 1841 he married David Weeks' widow, Mary Clara Conrad, and lived in New Iberia until his death in 1867. Largely through his efforts a two-story frame building was erected on the estate property. It was known as the Odd Fellows' Hall, and served them as a lodge room for several years. After the Civil War, it was used for a public school and later, about 1878 to 1881, for the school taught by Mr. Wellington Blend. About 1898 the building was demolished when the property was sold for the site of the old post office building.[120]

It remains now only to discuss the various ownerships of the land between present-day Weeks Street and Iberia Street. This might best be accomplished by the series of maps that follow.

---

118. The Weeks Addition incorporated the area between Weeks Street and the Civic Center's western boundary (that is, the line immediately behind the shrine of the Immaculate Conception). Center Street derives its name from the fact that it runs down the center of this tract of land. Charles, Harriet, and William streets are named for the children of David Weeks. There was also an Alfred Street, named for another son, but that street has since become an extension of Hacker Street.

119. The owners of the property which was ultimately purchased by David Weeks in 1825 are traced in the essay entitled "The Obituary of William Weeks."

120. This is the building at 300 East Main Street.

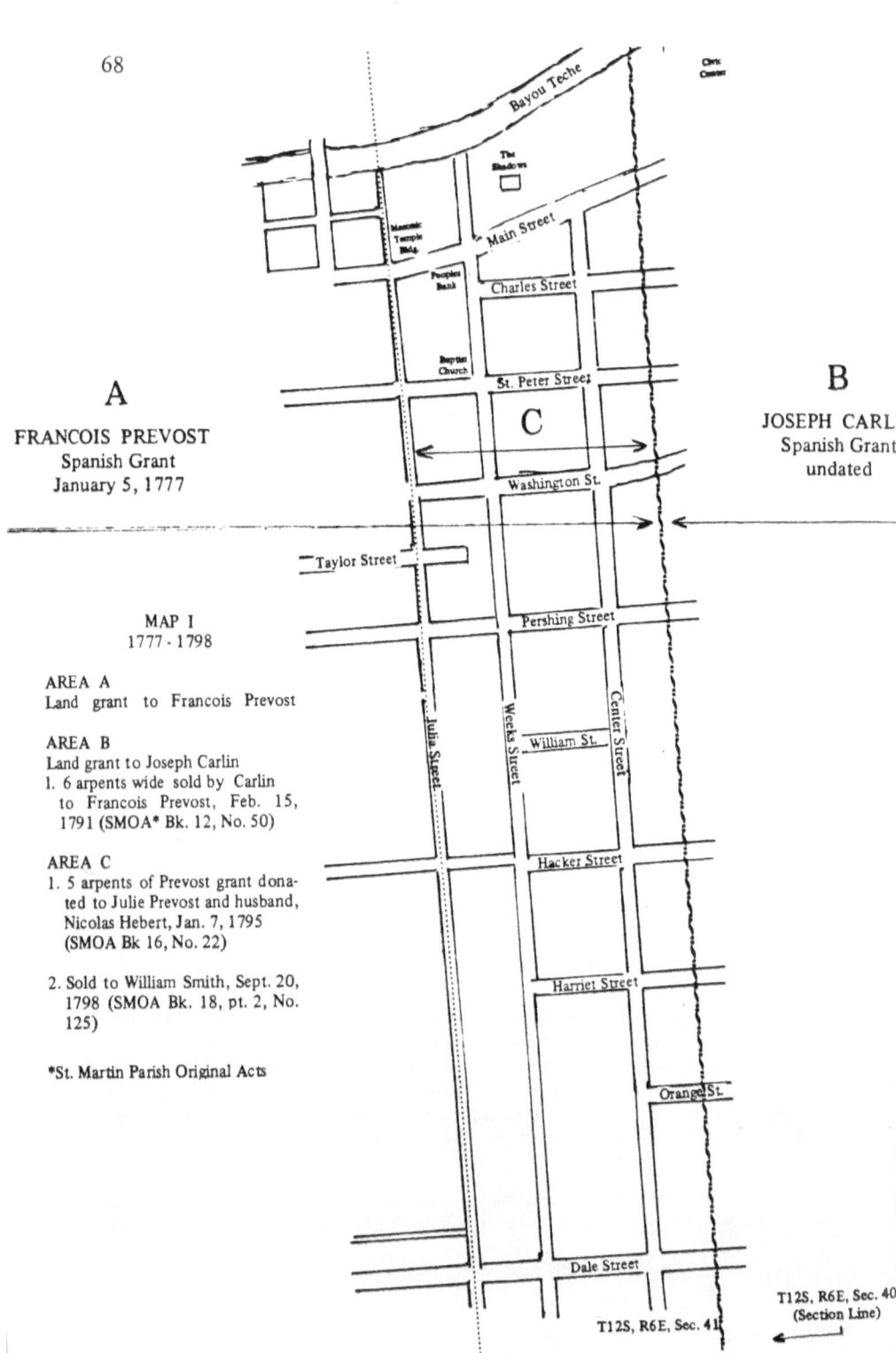

MAP I
1777 - 1798

AREA A
Land grant to Francois Prevost

AREA B
Land grant to Joseph Carlin
1. 6 arpents wide sold by Carlin to Francois Prevost, Feb. 15, 1791 (SMOA* Bk. 12, No. 50)

AREA C
1. 5 arpents of Prevost grant donated to Julie Prevost and husband, Nicolas Hebert, Jan. 7, 1795 (SMOA Bk 16, No. 22)

2. Sold to William Smith, Sept. 20, 1798 (SMOA Bk. 18, pt. 2, No. 125)

*St. Martin Parish Original Acts

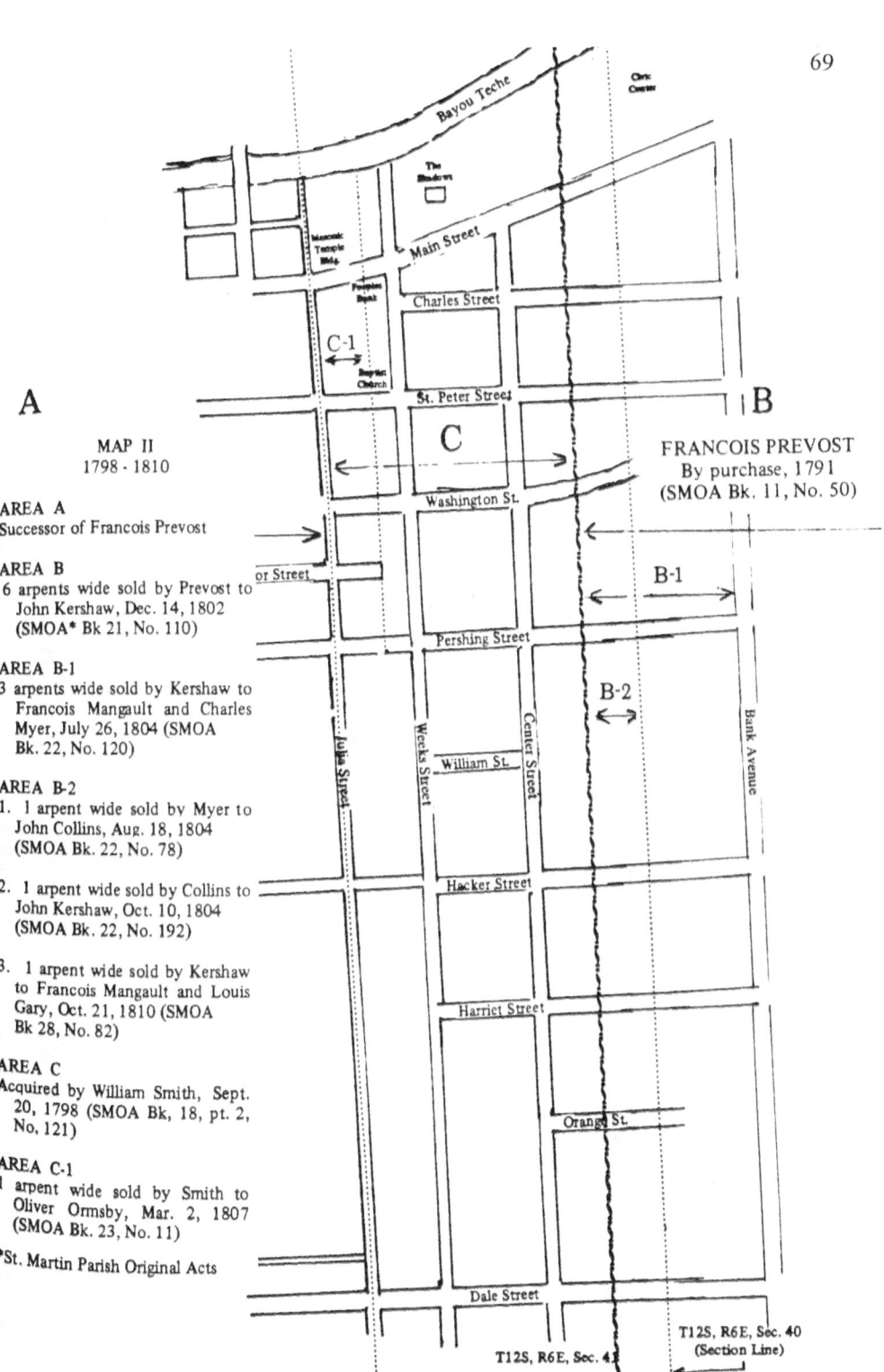

MAP II
1798 - 1810

AREA A
Successor of Francois Prevost

AREA B
6 arpents wide sold by Prevost to John Kershaw, Dec. 14, 1802 (SMOA* Bk 21, No. 110)

AREA B-1
3 arpents wide sold by Kershaw to Francois Mangault and Charles Myer, July 26, 1804 (SMOA Bk. 22, No. 120)

AREA B-2
1. 1 arpent wide sold by Myer to John Collins, Aug. 18, 1804 (SMOA Bk. 22, No. 78)

2. 1 arpent wide sold by Collins to John Kershaw, Oct. 10, 1804 (SMOA Bk. 22, No. 192)

3. 1 arpent wide sold by Kershaw to Francois Mangault and Louis Gary, Oct. 21, 1810 (SMOA Bk 28, No. 82)

AREA C
Acquired by William Smith, Sept. 20, 1798 (SMOA Bk, 18, pt. 2, No. 121)

AREA C-1
1 arpent wide sold by Smith to Oliver Ormsby, Mar. 2, 1807 (SMOA Bk. 23, No. 11)

*St. Martin Parish Original Acts

MAP III
1807 - 1829

AREA C-1
1. 1 arpent wide sold by Oliver Ormsby to Margaret Reynolds, Mar. 3, 1807 (SMOA Bk 23, No. 22)
2. 1 arpent wide sold by Reynolds to Manna Arial, Nov. 24, 1819 (SMCB* 1-B, p. 642)
3. 1 arpent wide sold by Arial to Jean Labarth, Feb. 24, 1821 (SMCB 1-B 1/2, p. 206)
4. 1 arpent wide seized and sold by sheriff to John Brownson, Feb. 7, 1824 (SMCB 3, p. 64)
5. 1 arpent wide sold by Brownson to Manna Arial, Mar. 15, 1827 (SMCB 3, p. 65)
6. 1 arpent wide sold by Arial to Joseph Aborn, Mar. 15, 1827 (SMCB 3, p. 62)

AREA C-2
1. Purchased by Wm. Smith from Nicolas Hebert, Sept. 20, 1798 (SMOA Bk. 18, pt 2, No. 121)
2. One-half arpent sold by Widow Smith to Nicholas Edgar, Oct. 15, 1813 (SMOA Bk 28, No. 128
3. One-half arpent wide sold by Edgar to William Vernought, Dec. 1, 1817 (SMCB 1-B, p. 256)
4. One-half arpent wide sold by Vernought to John R. Howe, Mar. 3, 1826 (SMCB 1-B 1/2 p. 12)
5. One-half arpent wide sold by Estate of Howe to Frederick Henry Duperier, May 13, 1821 (St. Martin Parish Estate No. 397
6. One-half arpent wide sold by Duperier to William Conbrough, May 22, 1826 (SMCB 2, p. 229)
7. One-half arpent wide sold by Conbrough to Joseph Aborn, May 15, 1829 (SMCB 5, p. 112)

*St. Martin Parish Conveyance Book

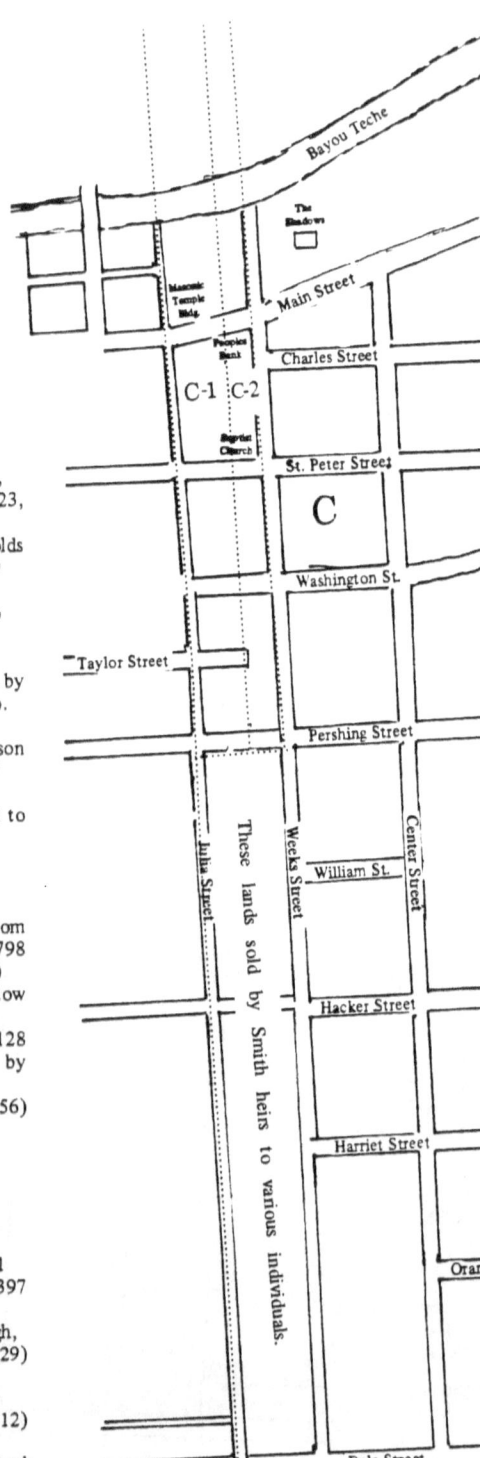

MAP IV
1807 – 1828

AREA C
Three and one-half arpents acquired by Henry Penne through the following purchases:
  a. 2 arpents seized by sheriff and sold to Penne, Nov. 4, 1814 (St. Martin Sheriff's Book A, p. 14)
  b. 1 arpent seized by sheriff and sold to Wm. L. Brent, Nov. 3, 1814 (St. Martin Sheriff's Book A, p. 12)
  Same arpent sold by Brent to Penne, May 15, 1815 (SMCB* 1-A, p. 23)
  c. One-half arpent sold by John M. Smith to Penne, Oct. 12, 1814 (SMOA Bk. 28, No. 190)

AREA B-2
1 arpent wide sold by Mongault and Gary to Henry Penne, 1811 (SMOA 1059:1151, document missing)

AREAS C and B-2
Four and one-half arpents sold by Penne to Henry Pintard, Aug. 30, 1821 (SMCB 1-B 1/2, p. 339)

Four and one-half arpents sold by estate of Pintard to David Weeks, Sept. 20, 1825 (SMCB 2, p. 64)

AREA B-1
2 arpents wide sold by Mongault to Elizabeth Norwood, July 9, 1813 (SMOA Bk. 28, No. 82)

2 arpents wide sold by Norwood to John C. Marsh, May 30, 1828 (SMCB 29, p. 49)

*St. Martin Parish Conveyance Book

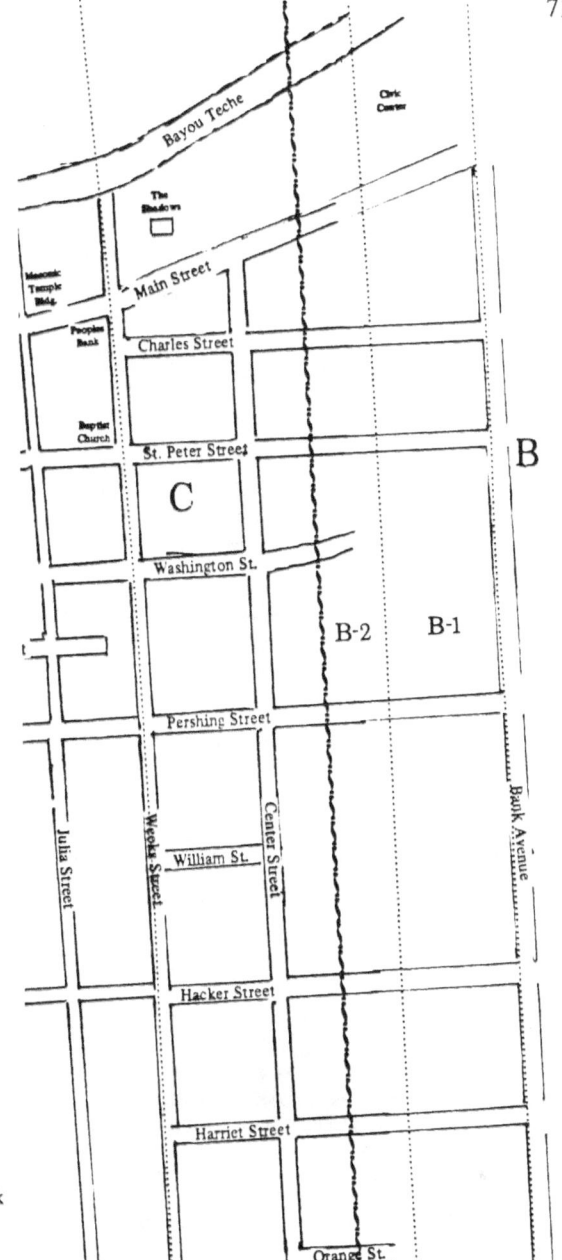

MAP V

1. Part of a land grant to Francois Prevost, January 5, 1777
2. 5 arpents wide by 40 arpents deep sold by F. Prevost to Josef Artacho, April 25, 1780. SMOA* Bk. 2, No. 6
3. 5 arpents wide sold by Artacho to Joseph Prevost, Mar. 24, 1789, SMOA, Bk. 7, No. 89.
4. 5 arpents wide sold by J. Prevost to Nicolas Hebert, Jan. 10, 1794, SMOA, Bk. 16, No. 72.
5. 5 arpents wide sold by N. Hebert to Alexandre Hebert, Oct. 30, 1794, SMOA, Bk. 16, No. 72.
6. Of the 5 arpents, A. Hebert sold 2 1/2 arpents wide by 40 arpents deep to John Kershaw (see Fig. 5) and 2 1/2 arpents deep to Thomas Collins, Feb. 16, 1801, SMOA, Bk. 20, No. 24.
7. 2 1/2 arpents wide leased by Collins to James Murphy, Jan. 3, 1804, SMOA, Bk. 22, No. 9. Murphy subsequently came to own this tract of land but the conveyance from Collins to Murphy cannot be located in St. Martin Parish records.
8. 2 1/2 arpents wide sold by Widow Murphy to Henry Pintard and Charles Olivier Devezin, February, 1816, SMCB** 1A, p. 137
9. C. Olivier Devezin sold his one-half interest in this property to Pintard, Feb. 19, 1817, SMCB 1B, p. 77.
10. 2 1/2 arpents wide belonging to Pintard inherited by his wife upon his death in Oct. 1821. Widow Pintard then married Bernard Lafosse. Mrs. Lafosse died in January, 1825.
11. 2 1/2 arpents wide in the estate of Mrs. Bernard Lafosse (Esther Teare) sold by her husband to Frederick H. Duperier, Oct. 25, 1825, SMCB 2, p. 103.
12. Partially subdivided in 1839 and became part of New Iberia.

*St. Martin Parish Original Acts
**St. Martin Parish Conveyance Book

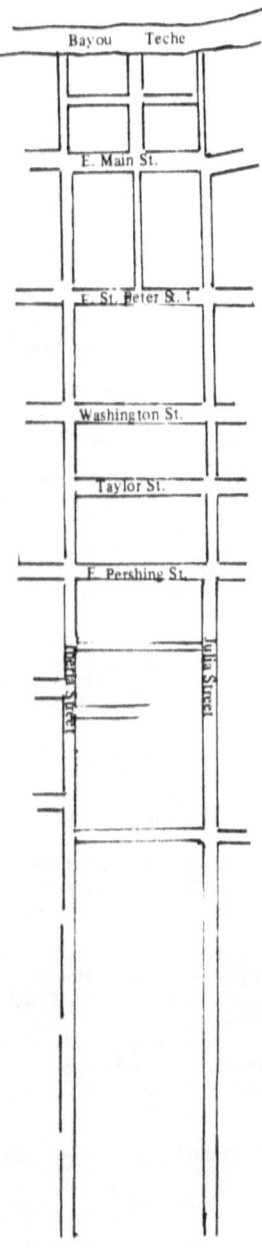

III

A Narrative of Events Connected with the Early Settlement of New Iberia

by
Dr. Alfred Duperier

edited and annotated by
Glenn R. Conrad

New Iberia has had a history of her own closely connected with the whole Attakapas country. Unlike Rome or the other great cities of antiquity, she has no monuments to mark the epoch of her origin[2] and different periods of development, or a contemporaneous history, to which we can refer. The offspring of a generation that followed in the footsteps of the original Spanish, French, and Acadian pioneers, I am familiar with all that transpired in the early 1830s, and such other incidents in the earlier history of New Iberia as were transmitted to me by my immediate predecessors. New Iberia can boast a history and is destined to have a future much more rapid in development and prosperity. Her first period, or that of her early settlement, if we are to judge by remaining landmarks, dates back to the commencement of the nineteenth century or may

---

1. This historical sketch of New Iberia appeared in the *New Iberia Enterprise* on March 25 and April 1, 1899.

2. In September, 1976, Bouligny Plaza in downtown New Iberia was officially dedicated and a bust of Bouligny was erected to the memory of the founder and the first settlers of the town. For a discussion of the founding of the town and its early years, see the essay entitled "New Iberia: The Spanish Years."

MAP VI
LANDOWNERS AT NEW IBERIA
May 15, 1829

A Dr. Raphael Smith, Sr.   E David Weeks
B John Stine   F John C. Marsh
C Frederick H. Duperier   G Widow Nathan Morse
D Joseph Aborn   H Daniel Coxe

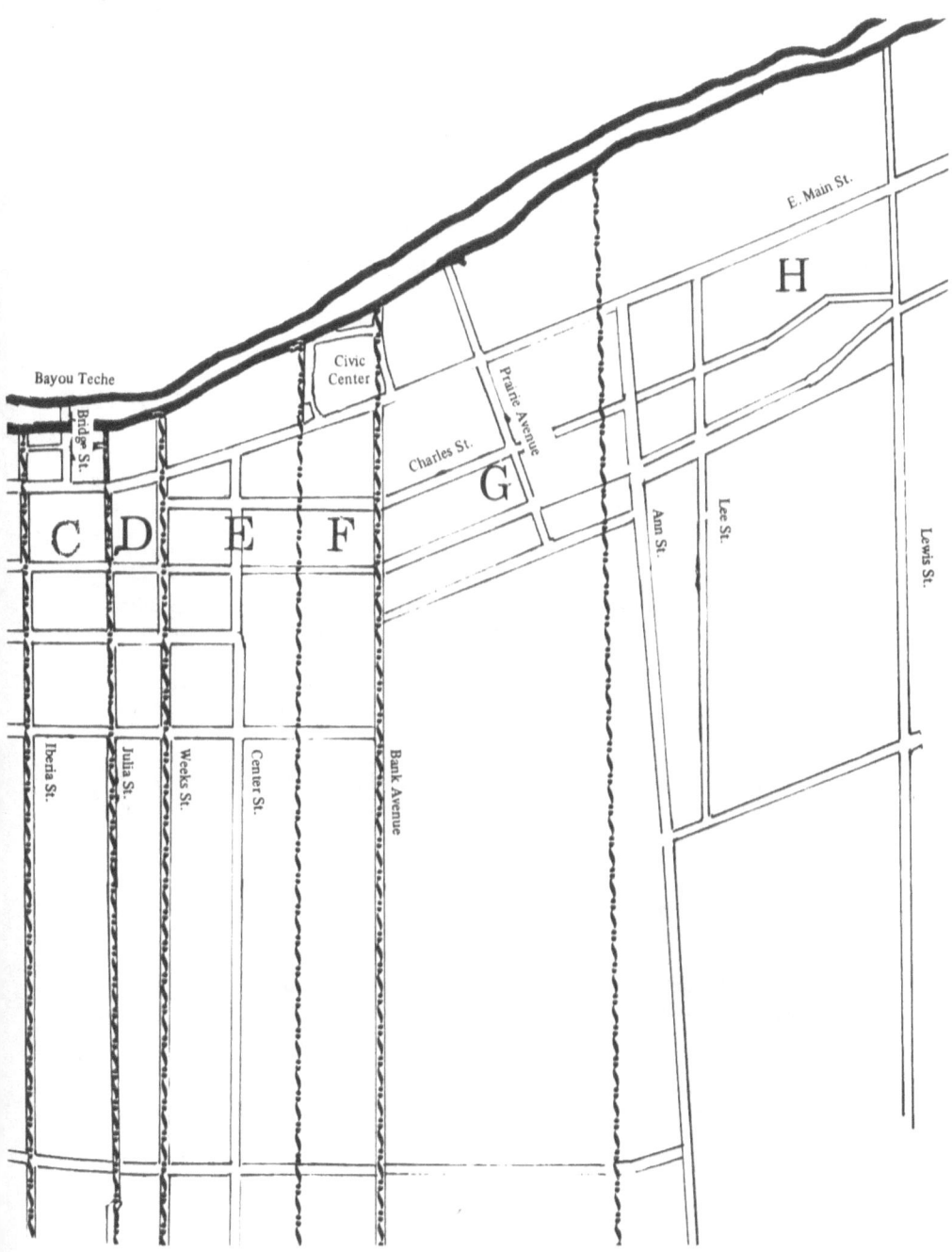

extend a few years into the previous century.[3] I knew in the 1840s a couple, man and wife, original Spanish colonists who attained four score and more.[4] The only remaining structure that has resisted the test of time is the residence of Max Mattes. This house was familiar to me in my boyhood days when occupied by Louis Segura, the original owner. Segura was a descendant of one of the first Spanish colonists and his home dates back to the commencement of the nineteenth century.[5] This is the only remaining landmark of the first epoch of New Iberia as a trading post to the date of its incorporation as a village about

---

3. It is a fact, of course, that the town was founded by Francisco Bouligny in April, 1779.

4. Possibly one of the last survivors of the Spanish emigration of 1778 was Antonio Romero. The 1850 U. S. census of St. Martin Parish (p. 182) records that he was then 75 and was living at Petite Anse.

5. This structure, located on West Main Street, just west of Swain Street, may have been considerably older than Dr. Duperier suggests. When it was being demolished in March, 1927, the *New Iberia Enterprise* (March 5) reported that

> . . . The building was erected in the year 1775, or one hundred and fifty years ago, by the Spanish government for the Governor [commandant] of the Attakapas country. . . . [Subsequently,] this building was occupied as a home by Mr. Pat Heirs, a civil engineer. . . .
>
> Later, it was occupied by the late William Kramer who for a number of years operated a bakery and confectionery where the Gulf Station now stands. Subsequently, the late Charles Flockerzie acquired the property, later transferring it to the late Max Mattes who . . . [operated] the bakery and confectionery. . . .
>
> After the death of Mr. Mattes, Mr. John R. Taylor acquired the property when the bakery and confectionery made way for the Gulf Tire Station, which now occupies the corner. With the steady advance of the automobile and the great demand for storage room for parking and storing of cars, the old home is being demolished to make way for an up-to-date storage plant. . . .

The newspaper was incorrect concerning the building date of the house and probably incorrect about its original occupant. The house was apparently built in the early 1780s as a residence for the long-time Spanish commandant of New Iberia, Jean-Baptiste St-Marc Darby.

Further evidence that there was a house on the lot at the time it was purchased by Louis Segura is found in the fact that he purchased two adjoining lots from the estate of John Stine, Sr., both of comparable size. For Lot 8 he paid $705, but he paid only $420 for Lot 9. He purchased the lots in July, 1829. See St. Martin Parish Estate 623.

1835.[6] Simultaneously with the period of its incorporation, the first Roman Catholic church was erected by contributions from the wealthy members of its congregation.[7] It was under the control of a board of regents[8] and the Rev. de St. Aubin was the first pastor. The original church was demolished in 1888 and replaced by the present structure; a monument to the frugality, generosity, and good taste of the Rev. Jacquet who did not long survive the completion of the temple erected by him to the glory of his Maker.[9] With the erection of the first

---

6. New Iberia was incorporated by Act 16 of the legislature on March 13, 1839. The original boundaries of the town were "That tract or portion of land lying and fronting on both sides of said bayou, and which is included on the West side of said bayou, between the lower line of Doct. L. J. Smith [the lower line of Dr. Smith's property was approximately 100 feet west of present-day Swain Street] . . . and the lower line of the plantation of John F. Miller [this would have put the southeastern boundary in the vicinity of present-day Ann Street; the boundary was subsequently revised to place it at the "upper line" of Miller's plantation, or in the vicinity of Bank Avenue]." The town was officially named "Iberia," but this name was later changed to "New Iberia" by Act 160, April 24, 1847.

For the official acts dealing with these developments, see *Acts Passed at the First Session of the 14th Legislature of the State of Louisiana* . . . (New Orleans, 1839), pp. 34-42.

7. The property for the Catholic church of New Iberia was donated by Frederick Henry Duperier and his wife, Hortense Berard, on January 30, 1837. The donation comprised a parcel of land measuring one arpent wide on Petite Anse Road (Iberia Street) by two-and-one-half arpents deep (there was no St. Peter Street at the time). This parcel of land was located within the town limits when the town was incorporated in 1839. For the donation of this land, see St. Martin Parish Conveyance Book 13, p. 363.

8. The board of regents, or commissioners, at the time of the donation were Maximilien Decuir, Francois St-Marc Darby, Zenon Decuir, F. H. Duperier, and L. J. Smith. *Ibid.*

9. The original St. Peter's Church, a brick structure, was completed in 1838. It was built under contract with John Johnson. The bricks used in its construction were made on the present-day site of Mt. Carmel Convent. The pastors to serve in this church were Father St-Aubin (1838-39), Genetenlane (1839-40), Prioux (1840-49), Therion and Mitelbron (1849-51), Beln (1851-52), Theve (1852-54), Outenderck (1854-66), Marion (1866-67), Hoste (1867-68), Chasse (1868-73), Le Cozie (1873-75), and Jacquet (1875-88).

The second St. Peter's Church was begun in 1888 by Father Claude Jacquet. The old church was demolished during the last ten days of April and the excavation for the foundations began on May 8. The first bricks were laid on May 14 and the cornerstone was set on May 27. The architect was James G. Freret of New Orleans. Contract for brick work was awarded to William Southwell at $5.50 per thousand. Carpentry work was done by George Francis and Bertrand Langla. The bricks came from John Emmer's brickyard and cost $7.00 per thousand. Seventy-five thousand bricks from the first church were incorporated into the second edifice. The church measured 126 x 55 feet and stood on the site of the

The Mattes house during demolition, March, 1927
(Said to have been the home of the Spanish Commandant Jean-Baptiste Darby)

Catholic church and the town's incorporation, we can date the second epoch in the development of New Iberia.[10] Around this first permanent improvement

---

first church. Pastors to serve in the second St. Peter's were Fathers Jacquet (1888-90), Jouan (1890-1909), Langlois (1909-47), and Bacque (1947-54).

The third St. Peter's Church (the present church) was completed in 1953. The architect was Owen J. Southwell. The church was built just east of the 1888 church, on the site of the old rectory, which was, at the time it was demolished, the Knights of Columbus hall. The pastors who have served in this church are Fathers Bacque (1953-54), Boudreaux (1954-71), Benedict (1971-73), Disch (1973 to present).

10. This is a fair statement. When James Leander Cathcart visited New Iberia in February, 1819, he stayed at Pintard's Tavern, which would be presently located between Bridge and Iberia streets. Cathcart recorded in his journal that there were no more than six houses in New Iberia. See Walter Prichard, Fred B. Kniffen, and Clair A. Brown,

Narrative of Events 79

The Santiago Lamperez House, c. 1843
One of the oldest extant houses in New Iberia

there very soon radiated others, showing that a new impetus had been given to the village, with its steeple, that supplanted the old Spanish and French trading post.[11] A small Methodist church was at that time erected on the corner of

---

eds., "Southern Louisiana and Southern Alabama in 1819: The Journal of James Leander Cathcart," *Louisiana Historical Quarterly*, XXVIII (1945), 821-22.

11. Dr. Duperier is being more poetic than factual here. The original church was surmounted by only a cupola topped with a cross. The tall steeple of this church was a later

The second St. Peter's Church as it appeared about 1903

The third St. Peter's Church as it appeared in January 1986

The third Methodist Church as it appeared about 1903

The Methodist Church on fire, January 1907

The present-day Methodist Church

The Episcopal Church of the Epiphany about 1903

The Episcopal Church of the Epiphany, January 1986

Washington and French streets on a lot donated by John Stine, the generous donor of the land upon which the Catholic graveyard is located.[12] The leading members of the Methodist congregation in those early days were the Stines, Riggs, Johnsons, and others. The Richardsons followed, giving weight and support to the small congregation. The small church was the scene of interesting debates, inaugurated by the Attakapas Debating Society, to which Charles Gayarré, the historian of Louisiana, once took part. The society lasted several years, with a good membership.

---

addition and was the work of Father Joseph Outenderck and a black man named Azor. The steeple was built during the Civil War. See W. R. Burke, "St. Peter's," *Weekly Iberian*, December 21, 1895.

12. Dr. Duperier is completely in error regarding the donor of the land for the Methodist church and the facts surrounding the creation of the Catholic cemetery.

The lot on the corner of French and Washington streets was donated to the Methodist congregation by Thomas Johnson, Josiah French's son-in-law, as a result of his wish "that the said church may have, own and possess in property a place of worship in the town of New Iberia. . . ." The trustees of the church, who received the donation, were William Kilgore, John G. Richardson, Edward W. Richardson, John C. Gordy, Henry C. Wilson, Thomas J. Jones, and Joseph Knight. The trustees were represented by their attorney, John R. Reynolds. Witnesses were John DeValcourt and Robert H. Marsh. On this lot a frame building was erected, and it fulfilled the needs of the small congregation until 1858. For the record of the donation, see St. Martin Parish Conveyance Book, 20, p. 310.

The Methodist church of New Iberia was organized by the Reverend B. M. Drake in April, 1829. On July 3, 1859, the congregation purchased from John Moore a lot on the northwest corner of Iberia and Washington streets, and in 1859 a new house of worship was built under the pastorate of the Reverend Thomas B. White. Then, on March 17, 1868, Ebenezer Mount, possessing power of attorney, sold to Jasper Gall and David Riggs the old Methodist church lot on the corner of Washington and French streets. The Iberia and Washington streets location of the church proved untenable with the laying of the Southern Pacific railroad on Washington Street in 1879. A decade passed, however, before the Reverend F. S. Parker was sent to New Iberia by Bishop Duncan with instructions to relocate the church. Before that could be done, however, the church and parsonage burned on May 24, 1890. On August 8, 1890, the Board of Trustees purchased from J. P. Russell a lot on the corner of West St. Peter and Jefferson streets, and the cornerstone for the new church (the present church) was laid on March 30, 1892. For a detailed account of the Methodist church in New Iberia, see Sam White, comp., "Methodism in New Iberia," a copy of which is on deposit in Iberia Parish Library. Also see the *Weekly Iberian*, December 28, 1895. The sale to Jasper Gall and David Riggs is recorded in St. Martin Parish Conveyance Book 32, p. 383.

The property where the Catholic cemetery is now located was sold to St. Peter's Parish by Josiah French on March 24, 1838, for $250. Receiving it for the parish was Francois St-Marc Darby. For this transaction, see St. Martin Parish Conveyance Book, 14, p. 168.

Msgr. J. M. Langlois
(1868 - 1947)
Pastor of St. Peter's Parish
1909 - 1947

The substantial brick mansion erected by David Weeks,[13] and that erected by Dr. L. J. Smith, now the "Alma House,"[14] followed closely the completion of the Catholic church.[15] New buildings brought from the East by sailing vessels, were erected as if by magic, and a new class of men became their inmates.[16] New merchants, representing Northern capital, entered the field of competition.

13. For the story of David Weeks' acquisition of the land upon which stands the Shadows-on-the-Teche, and the building of that house, see footnote 15 of the essay entitled "The Obituary of William Weeks."

14. The Alma House was built as the residence of Dr. Leonard J. Smith. For more on the history of this building, see footnotes 20, 21, 22 of the essay entitled "Some Facts and Traditions About New Iberia."

15. Dr. Duperier's memory did not serve him well in this instance. Both houses were completed before the Catholic church was even started. The Shadows and the Alma House were completed about 1834.

16. "Prefabricated" homes were common in the nineteenth century. James Michener mentions the fact in his book *Hawaii.* Apparently, many of the purchasers of town lots (see footnote 23 below) improved the property with prefabricated homes.

Narrative of Events 89

It was at this time that Shute and Taylor, Edgar, Camors,[17] Faisans and Bourda,[18] opened businesses in New Iberia. The first two firms were American and the last two were French. Shute and Taylor succeeded to my father's business; John DeValcourt succeeded to this firm after the retirement of Shute and the subsequent death of Taylor.[19] His descendants, as well as those of John Taylor, Sr., are among the most worthy of our citizens. Josiah French, from New York, was among the first who settled here, conducting a large tannery on the bayou front, now owned by McMahon and Fisher. Two generations of his progeny

17. Dominique Henri Camors was a native of Nay, Basse Pyrenees, France. He married Marie Marguerite Irma Beauvais, the daughter of Jean-Baptiste Beauvais and Suzanne Ozenne, in St. Martinville, on December 21, 1837. The Camors had only one child, a son, Jean-Marie Camors who was born August 29, 1838. In January, 1839, the Camors took up residence in New Iberia after buying a house and lot on Main Street (located just east of present-day Church Alley) from the estate of John Taylor. Camors was apparently in partnership in the mercantile business with Ulger Decuir. Later in 1839, on September 10, Camors purchased the lot directly behind his earlier purchase from the estate of Frederick Duperier; thus, he owned a strip of land from Main Street to St. Peter Street.

On September 25, 1839, Mrs. Camors died, perhaps a victim of the yellow-fever epidemic then raging. Camors remained in New Iberia but did not remarry. In the early 1850s he became the partner of Jean-Jacques Mistrot in the general merchandise business. Shortly thereafter, he returned to France on a visit and apparently decided then to close out his American holdings and return to his homeland. Back in New Iberia in September, 1854, Camors sold a part of his property (that facing Main Street) to Jean-Jacques Mistrot. The back portion of his property he sold to Gaspard Ratier.

The final mention of Camors in local records occurs in 1859 when, from France, he records that he has settled with his son the child's inheritance from his mother. The son was then living with his father in France. For documentation concerning the Camors, see Hebert, *Southwest Louisiana Records,* III, 32, 125; St. Martin Parish Estates 877 and 898; St. Martin Parish Conveyance Book 20½, p. 490; Book 22, p. 127; Book 27, p. 494.

18. Little is known about Silvain Faisans and Jean Bourda. The fact that they were in partnership is reflected in St. Martin Parish Conveyance Book 11, p. 518.

19. Shute of this firm was Theodore Shute. Little is known about him. The Taylor mentioned here was John Taylor, Sr. He was the son of Joseph Taylor and Ann Graff. On October 24, 1837, John married Martha Morse Marsh, daughter of Jonas Marsh and Elizabeth Morse. Taylor died unexpectedly in December, 1838, leaving a son, John, Jr. For records of these events, see Mary Elizabeth Sanders, *Records of Attakapas District, Louisiana, III, St. Martin Parish, 1808-1860,* p. 75, and St. Martin Parish Estate 877.

John Taylor, Jr., married Kate Richardson, daughter of Daniel Richardson of Jeanerette. They had six children. Taylor died September 21, 1888. See his obituary in the *Daily Picayune,* September 23, 1888, p. 2.

now replace him.[20] Many accessions to the town and many improvements sprang into existence during this period. The first public sale of vacant town lots extending ten arpents in depth, with a frontage of three arpents on Main Street between Iberia and Corinne streets, realized over $30,000. This was in 1839.[21]

John Richardson Taylor, the eldest son of John J. Taylor and Kate Richardson, was born April 4, 1875. He married Lonie Lietmeyer of New Iberia in 1918. The couple had no children. For years Taylor was associated with James A. Lee in the drugstore business before entering the business in his own right. Taylor's Drug Store was originally in the building on the southwestern corner of French and Main streets (then known as the Decuir Building, later as the Speciality Store, and today as Main Mall). In 1906 Mr. Taylor built a new building for his business on the southeastern corner of Main and French streets. Taylor's Drug Store, constructed of a white, glazed brick, remained for many years a well-known landmark. Following Mr. Taylor's death Felix Mestayer, Sr., succeeded to the business. After the drugstore business moved to new quarters on West St. Peter Street in September, 1967, the building remained vacant for several years. In 1978, it was renovated and occupied by Radio Station KDEA. Taylor Street is named for this family. For John R. Taylor's obituary, see *New Iberia Enterprise*, May 12, 1928.

20. Josiah French married John and Elizabeth Stine's daughter, Mary, on April 1, 1810. They were married before Judge Seth Lewis. Although there is no succession for French, it would appear that he died in 1865 or 1866. French Street is named for his family.

21. This statement requires elaboration. The property mentioned here was not between Iberia and Corinne streets but between Julia and Iberia streets. Moreover, the sale of town lots in September, 1839, was not the first for New Iberia. When John Stine died in 1829, his property between Iberia and French streets was divided into town lots and sold by his heirs. Buyers of the lots at that time were Stine's widow (Elizabeth Clark), Josiah French, John Stine, Jr., Louis Segura, Nelson Johnson, Thomas Johnson, John C. Marsh, Parker Rupel, and William Stine (whose lot was on the east bank of the bayou adjoining that of Frederick Duperier). For these sales, see St. Martin Parish Estate 623.

When Mrs. Stine died in 1832, her property between Iberia and French streets was further divided into town lots and sold to Theodore Shute, John Stine, Jr., Thomas Johnson, Cornelius Guyon, Josiah French, and Ely Riggs. *Ibid.*, 687.

Moreover, St. Martin Parish conveyance records indicate that Frederick Henry Duperier was selling lots on Main Street long before 1839. On October 27, 1831, he sold Lot 3 of a subdivided area, surveyed by Auguste Gerard on July 7, 1831, to Theodore Shute. See St. Martin Parish Conveyance Book 7, p. 170.

The sale which took place on September 10, 1839, may have been planned by Frederick Duperier before his death on March 15, 1839. In 1837 he commissioned William B. Jackson, a surveyor from Opelousas, to lay out some of his property between Julia and Iberia streets in town lots. That same year he donated the land for the Catholic church. Next, Duperier was the prime mover for the incorporation of the town, which was ap-

Five Generations of Iberians

Standing from left: Mrs. Louis Indest, Sr. (the former Marie-Mathilde Duperier); holding child: Mrs. William Lourd, Sr. (the former Felicite Indest); child: Fay Lourd (later (1) Mrs. Elvin Sarradet and (2) Mrs. Roger D. Smith). Seated from left is Mrs. Frederic Henri Duperier (the former Marie-Mathilde Berard); and Mrs. Jean-Baptiste Berard (the former Marie-Aurelie Huval).

When it is considered that this boom in the value of real estate occurred at the time of one of the greatest financial disasters witnessed in Louisiana, it was truly wonderful. The tampering with the tariff legislation in 1837, having reduced the price of sugar far below the cost of production, entailed complete ruin upon the leading industry of Louisiana. Sugar property, including lands and slaves, was being sold daily under expropriation. It was this condition of things that called into existence the Citizens Bank, and the Consolidated Association Bank.[22] To those who were willing to avail themselves of the relief tendered

---

proved by the legislature two days before his death. Thus, it would appear that Duperier had long been planning to subdivide his property--at least that lying on the west bank of the Teche. Indeed, the idea to do so may have come through action of his wife's family. After the death of their father and mother, Jean Berard and Anne Broussard, the Berard heirs subdivided much of the Berard property adjoining St. Martinville into town lots. The sale of these lots occurred in the early 1820s (see St. Martin Estate 404). Nevertheless, the sale of the town lots which occurred in September, 1839, was also in the form of a succession sale by Duperier's heirs, namely, Hortense Berard, his widow; Alfred and Frederick, his sons; and Marie, his daughter (Note: Marie, Henry and Hortense streets and Duperier Avenue, on the east side of Bayou Teche, are named for this family and certain of its members.

Buyers of the New Iberia town lots were Dominique Henri Camors, Joseph Lion, Francois St-Marc Darby, Gaspard Ratier, Casimir Olivier, Evan Pindasois (?), Jean Berard (Jr.), August Cesar, Achille Berard, Nicolas Loisel, A. B. Dauterive, Dubreuil Olivier, Leon Frilot, Hyacinthe Olivier, Zenon Olivier, Victor Labauve, Joseph Labauve, and Cornelius Voorhies. Jean-Baptiste Hacker and Nicolas Loisel bought lots with houses upon them. Antoine Segura bought a strip of land two arpents wide and 10 arpents deep located about 10 arpents from the west bank of the Teche. John Riggs bought several hundred fence posts. The lot bought by Cornelius Voorhies was at the corner of Julia and Main streets, where the New Iberia National Bank now stands. The sale of this property brought $19,117.55, not in excess of $30,000 as stated by Dr. Duperier. That figure, in fact $33,312, was the total value of the estate. For more detail regarding this matter, see St. Martin Parish Estate 881.

22. The Citizens Bank of Louisiana was incorporated on April 1, 1833, fully four years before the Panic of 1837. It was one of several "planters' banks" in the state. Planters bought stock in the bank which was secured by mortgages on their property. Thus, a planter holding stock in the bank was always assured of credit to improve his property, plant his crops, etc. The system worked well so long as harvests were good. A planter could easily survive one poor, or even disastrous, harvest, such as the sugar planters experienced in 1856, because his loans could be paid off the following year after a normal or better-than-average harvest. What planters did not take into consideration was the possibility of a series of poor harvests, such as occurred between 1865 and 1869. As a result of poor returns from a given year's crop, the planter borrowed on the success of the next

Narrative of Events 93

by these monied institutions, representing foreign capital, a temporary relief was afforded. None, however, accepted the inevitable ruin which resulted from the fetters which merciless capitalists had riveted around them.

As before stated, the first important sale of real estate, consisting of town lots made at New Iberia on the 10th day of September, 1839, realized over $30,000 to the astonishment of everyone.[23] The frugality with which the

---

year's crop. When that failed, he would borrow again, speculating on the profits to be generated by the next year's crop. After a series of three or four crop failures, the bank would lend no more and the planter was bankrupt. The bank would then seize and sell the planter's plantation at public sale. Because many plantations were seized in the immediate post-Civil War era, many people have mistakenly believed that this action was taken as a result of the carpetbagger government. In many instances, however, the real reason was a long series of disastrous harvests resulting in foreclosure. For the act incorporating the Citizens Bank, see *Acts Passed at the First Session of the Eleventh Legislature of the State of Louisiana* . . . (New Orleans, 1833), pp. 172-94.

23. The area subdivided and sold on this day, that is to say between Julia and Iberia streets, had had a long history before Frederick Henry Duperier's heirs sold it (see Map V, p. 72).

The area was part of the Spanish land grant to Francois Prevost dated January 5, 1777. From that grant, Prevost sold to Josef Artacho, on April 25, 1780, 5 arpents wide by 40 arpents deep. Artacho, on March 24, 1789, sold these five arpents to Joseph Prevost (Francois' brother). Prevost then sold the tract of land on January 10, 1794, to his brother-in-law, Nicolas Hebert. On October 30 of that same year Hebert sold the tract to Alexandre Hebert. Then, on February 16, 1801, Hebert divided the tract in half, selling the western half to John Kershaw and the eastern half to Thomas Collins. Collins leased his portion of the tract (corresponding to the area between present-day Julia and Iberia streets) to James Murphy on January 3, 1804. Murphy, probably through private sale not recorded in St. Martin Parish, acquired the property. After his death in August 1815 (see St. Martin Parish Estate 209) Murphy's widow, Sarah, sold the land to Henry Pintard and Charles Olivier Devezin, together with the tavern and general merchandise business established by her husband. On February 19, 1817, Olivier Devezin sold his share of the property and business to Henry Pintard.

Henry Pintard was a merchant. He was a native of St. Roman de Sevenne in the French province of Languedoc. On January 4, 1821, at the age of 70 he married Esther Teare, a native of Liverpool England. Pintard died ten months later, in October, 1821. (For the marriage contract of Pintard and Teare, see St. Martin Conveyance Book 1B½, p. 179. Pintard's death is recorded in St. Martin of Tours Catholic Church, vol. 4, no. 1484.)

Esther Teare was born in 1784, the daughter of Daniel Teare of Liverpool. Family tradition holds that she was in Santo Domingo at the time of Toussaint L'Ouverture's revolution and fled the island with her nephew, Frederick Henry Duperier, after the execu-

people of the country lived in those days--the result of nomadic pursuits, copied from their ancestors--rendered their wants limited. Their herds of cattle, grazing upon the public domain, all free from taxation, relieved them of almost every burden. They indulged in no extravagance. The men rode on horseback; their wives and daughters used the *caleche,* a homemade gig suspended by means of rawhide straps from arms projecting from the shafts; the wheels were often without tires, the axles were of wood and the cushions consisted of feather pillows. Among the more prosperous, these vehicles were painted. The harness was either all of rawhide or leather tanned at home. The principal luxury of the people, to which they still adhere, was coffee. Their clothing consisted of homespun goods, known as "Attakapas cottonade." They indulged in the purchase of only a few articles, principally calicoes, domestic cotton goods, and shoes brought from the East or imported from England and France. Shoes were a luxury, men and women often went barefooted; the men wore moccasins made of rawhide or buckskin. Girls going to church, or to a ball, would often carry

---

tion of his parents by revolutionaries. She supposedly joined other French exiles making their way to Philadelphia. The records of St. Martin's Church, however, indicate that Duperier was born in Philadelphia on September 11, 1802 (St. Martin of Tours Catholic Church, vol 7, no. 186).

Esther Teare was first married to Joseph Hart. There is no record of Hart in St. Martin Parish, and the only mention of his name occurs in the Pintard-Teare marriage contract. Upon Pintard's death, his wife inherited most of his property.

On January 11, 1823, Teare married Bernard Lafosse, Jr., a merchant from Port-au-Prince, Haiti (this supporting the family tradition that Teare had come to the United States from Haiti). Together they ran the tavern and general merchandise business in New Iberia until Teare's death in January, 1825, at the age of 41. They had no children. (See St. Martin Parish Marriage Book A, no. 66, for the marriage contract of Lafosse and Teare and St. Martin Parish Estate 526 for Teare's death.)

On October 25, 1825, while in the process of settling his wife's estate, Lafosse sold the two-and-one-half arpents of land on both sides of Bayou Teche, with a depth of 40 arpents on the west side and to the "second" bayou on the east side, bounded above by the property of John Stine and below by that of Joseph Aborn, to Frederick Henry Duperier for $3,200. The tract mentioned on the west side of Bayou Teche would presently correspond to that portion of New Iberia lying between Julia and Iberia streets and the bayou and Admiral Doyle Drive.

The general merchandise store which was opened by the Murphys on this property passed to Pintard, Teare, Lafosse, and Duperier. After Duperier's death, the store was sold to Theodore Shute who, later, went into business with John Taylor. After the death of Shute and Taylor, the store was bought by the DeValcourt family.

Documentation for the conveyances mentioned in this footnote can be found accompanying Map V, p. 72.

their shoes in hand, to be worn only when they reached their destination. At home these shoes were faithfully hung from the ceiling.

The principal industry of the country was grazing large herds of cattle that ranged from the Cypremort to the Mermentau and Calcasieu. The entire Opelousas country, including Lafayette and St. Landry parishes, was used for grazing purposes. The Pellerins, the Wickofs, the Dupres, and Moutons branded thousands of calves annually. The cattle trade of the early days supplied the Mississippi River plantations with beef. The use of Western pork and cured meats was unknown at this period. Francois Duplessis, a refugee from Santo Domingo, a civil engineer by education who subsequently owned a sugar plantation immediately fronting Morbihan plantation in consideration of some engineering work executed by him at the mouth of Bayou Plaquemine, secured an exclusive privilege for transporting cattle and livestock from Bayou Portage, in the rear of Loreauville, to Plaquemine. This proved a valuable franchise over a short route and has often suggested itself to me as a proper line for the building of a railroad from the east bank of the Teche to the Mississippi. Immense herds of cattle were constantly driven to the point of embarkation on the Duplessis steamers, which after a few hours were landed on Bayou Plaquemine to be driven thence up and down the Mississippi coast. Many of our old inhabitants were engaged in this cattle traffic. Antoine and Michel Romero and Athanase Hebert were among my earliest recollection; The latter, "Tanasse," as he was universally known, was a descendant of the earliest Acadian emigrants who had settled Fausse Pointe. A large progeny, reputed for their frugality and honesty, still inhabit that section of Fausse Pointe.

"Tanasse," on account of his witticism, became a favorite among the aristocratic planters who lived along the Mississippi coast. Upon reaching a large plantation, he would drive his herd into the pasture with the assurance of a hearty welcome. On one occasion, arriving at the plantation of Mr. Fortier, he walked into the dining room, unaware that it was the anniversary of the host. He entered the crowded dining room with his homespun suit and moccasins. Seating himself quietly in a faroff corner until the libations of champagne, which were many, opened the eyes of the host to his uninvited guest. "What news do you bring from the 'land of cattle,' friend Tanasse:" "Nothing," was the reply, until resuming after a lengthy pause, he said: "Ah! I forgot, Mr. Fortier, a very extraordinary event happened just before my departure." "What can it be?" was the simultaneous interrogatory of several guests. "Well," said Tanasse, "just before my leaving home, a cow gave birth to five calves." "Please tell me, friend Tanasse," interrupted Mr. Fortier, "how does the fifth calf participate in the festive board?" "He does as I have so far done," rejoined Tanasse, "he awaits his turn in the corner." It is useless to say that this witty and appropriate repartee was the signal for increased conviviality. Tanasse was pressed to the table at the proper moment, for he was fond of champagne which he imbibed to the amusement and delight of all the guests. He forgot for the remainder of the day about his herd. Next day he was compensated by a large deal with his host who continued to be his best friend and patron. It is not strange that under the circumstances a great deal of money accumulated in the hands of such frugal people. To exemplify the existing condition, I will relate an incident that came under my personal observation.

A very responsible friend, engaged in business in New Orleans, wishing to bridge a temporary bank crisis, came to the country to effect a short loan. At his request I accompanied him to a farmer's house, the owner of which I knew to have money. The demand being apparently extravagant to the farmer, he appealed to his wife, who was knitting at the time. Her reply was, "We can only lend him all we have." At this conclusion, the wife and husband retired to an adjacent room where, in a short while, they returned with $30,000 in bank bills and gold. This amount of money was handed to my friend, with the promise of returning it in sixty days. This was evidently the accumulation of years of frugal economy from the sale of cattle, from a large herd that could be seen grazing from the house. Life and property at that time were perfectly secure in the rural districts of Attakapas.

It is not strange, therefore, that under the existing condition of things the sale of the property referred to was not affected by the financial crisis that had preceded some two years. The crisis of 1837 only affected those who had embarked in the sugar industry. The varied products of those early days made most farmers independent.

The sale referred to was effected on the 10th day of September, and on the 19th was followed by an outbreak of yellow fever. On the 14th, the body of Dr. Raphael Smith,[24] the cousin of Dr. L. J. Smith, already referred to as the builder of the present Alma House, having died of yellow fever at Plaquemine, was transported to New Iberia for interment. The funeral service took place at the Catholic church. A few days after the service, the pallbearers, and others,

---

24. The Dr. Raphael Smith referred to here was one of four children, namely, Raphael, Mary Elizabeth, Charles, and Francis, born to Dr. Raphael Smith, Sr., and his wife, Sarah Hardy. Raphael Smith, Jr., was educated at Georgetown University in the District of Columbia. He died September 10, 1839, at the age of 23 (St. Peter's Catholic Church, vol.

Narrative of Events 97

who had attended the funeral were taken sick with yellow fever. The epidemic developed rapidly. The leading physician of the place, Dr. Neal,[25] was one of the earliest victims; Mr. Burke, the father of Wm. Burke, and the ancestor of two worthy generations now living in New Iberia, was another of the numerous victims. Dr. S. F. R. Abbey, a brother-in-law of DeValcourt, was incapacitated, for service at the onset. In the absence of medical assistance and the epidemic raging, he placed himself under the immediate charge of an old Santo Domingo servant who had always lived in my family. "Aunt" Félicité, as she was universally known, became the physician and nurse, for all the cases that followed in rapid succession. Her experience, as a nurse, made her successful in her practice. She was kindly assisted by Mrs. Maximilien Decuir, Mrs. David Hayes, Mrs. Baron Bayard, and Mrs. Don Louis Broussard, all residents of the country who constituted themselves a corps of good samaritans.[26] The sense of charity and humanity that prevailed in those days contrasted greatly with the cruel and selfish treatment that we have witnessed in late epidemics of a much milder character. This change is largely due to the senseless panic engendered by shot-

---

1, p. 2). These children were the cousins of Dr. Leonard J. Smith, mentioned above. For more on the Smith family, see footnote 38 of the essay entitled "The Obituary of William Weeks."

25. Dr. Duperier speaks of yellow fever as though it were a contagious disease. He wrote the *Narrative* before it was discovered that *Aedes aegypti* mosquito transmitted the disease from one individual to another.

Dr. Benoni Neale of St. Mary's County, Maryland, died at the Widow Duperier's boarding house on September 29, 1839, at the age of 39. It is possible that Dr. Neale and Dr. Raphael Smith, Sr., were relatives. They were both from Maryland, and Dr. Smith's mother's maiden name was Neal (see St. Martin Parish Estate 892). Dr. Neale had practiced medicine in New Iberia from the mid-1820s until his death.

26. Mrs. Maximilien Decuir was the former Susanne Broussard. She married Decuir on November 11, 1811. They had ten children. One of them, Eugene, died on October 2, 1839, at age 20, probably of yellow fever.

Mrs. David Hayes was the former Josephine Lambert. She married David Hayes on January 28, 1834.

Mrs. Baron Bayard was the daughter of Francois Cezar Boutte and Marie-Therese Degruy. She first married Achille Berard, and it was their daughter, Hortense, who married Frederick Henry Duperier. After Berard's death, she married Benoit Baron Bayard, a native of France, on December 17, 1819.

Mrs. Don Louis Broussard was the former Felonise Broussard. She married on August 6, 1810.

gun quarantines organized since. The epidemic of 1839 was disastrous in its mortality list as well as in the prosperity of the entire state of Louisiana. It was several years before New Iberia recovered from its effects; fortunately, the sale of real estate before referred to had taken place before the outbreak of the disease.[27]

The generosity displayed by our national legislature in appropriating $50,000 for the erection, within the corporate limits, of the public buildng to be used as a post office, suggests a retrospective as well as a forward view of New Iberia.[28] Strangers, so we are informed, and members of the late Congress failed or feigned not to be able to locate the place on the map. With the sole object of enlightening those who should, like myself, feel a deep interest in their native or adopted home, I have attempted to write my recollections of what has transpired within my personal observations; and also much of the events which were transmitted to me by a preceding generation.

From the date of its incorporation until some time in the 1840s, New Iberia, despite natural advantages, remained stagnant of existing rivalries and because of her entire dependence upon St. Martinville, the county seat of St. Martin Parish, of which New Iberia was a part.

St. Martinville, at the time referred to [the antebellum period], was the most attractive town in the whole of the Attakapas and Opelousas country. Settled principally by a class of intelligent French emigrants, such as the De Blancs, DeClouets, Delahoussayes, Pellerins, Darbys, Dauterives, Gonsoulins, and others, she gave tone to society. Her merchants, Rousseau and Tertron, S. B. Bellocq, Bonaton and Vivien, Durand, and others, were thrifty and intelligent. They were assisted by a large capital in trade supported in her early days by two banks, the Union and the Louisiana State Bank, both liberal in their discounts towards the farming as well as the mercantile interests. Rous-

---

27. The impact of the epidemic on New Iberia may be exaggerated by Dr. Duperier. Volume one of the register of deaths at St. Peter's Church reveals that only eleven people were buried from the church between the day Dr. Smith was buried (September 10) and the end of October. They were Raphael Smith, Jr., Salvador Migues, Sr., Joachim Etie, Irma Camors, Benoni Neale, Eugene Decuir, Widow Etie, William Booth, Jerome Monjean, Louis Eloi de Blanc, and Marie Boutte. The cause of death is not given in the records; thus, some of the above persons may have died from causes other than yellow fever.

28. In February, 1899, Congress appropriated $50,000 for the construction of the post office building at the corner of Weeks and Main streets. This building, completed in 1903, is a fine example of latter-day Williamsburg architecture. For the story of the building of this post office, see the essay entitled "New Iberia Gets a Post Office."

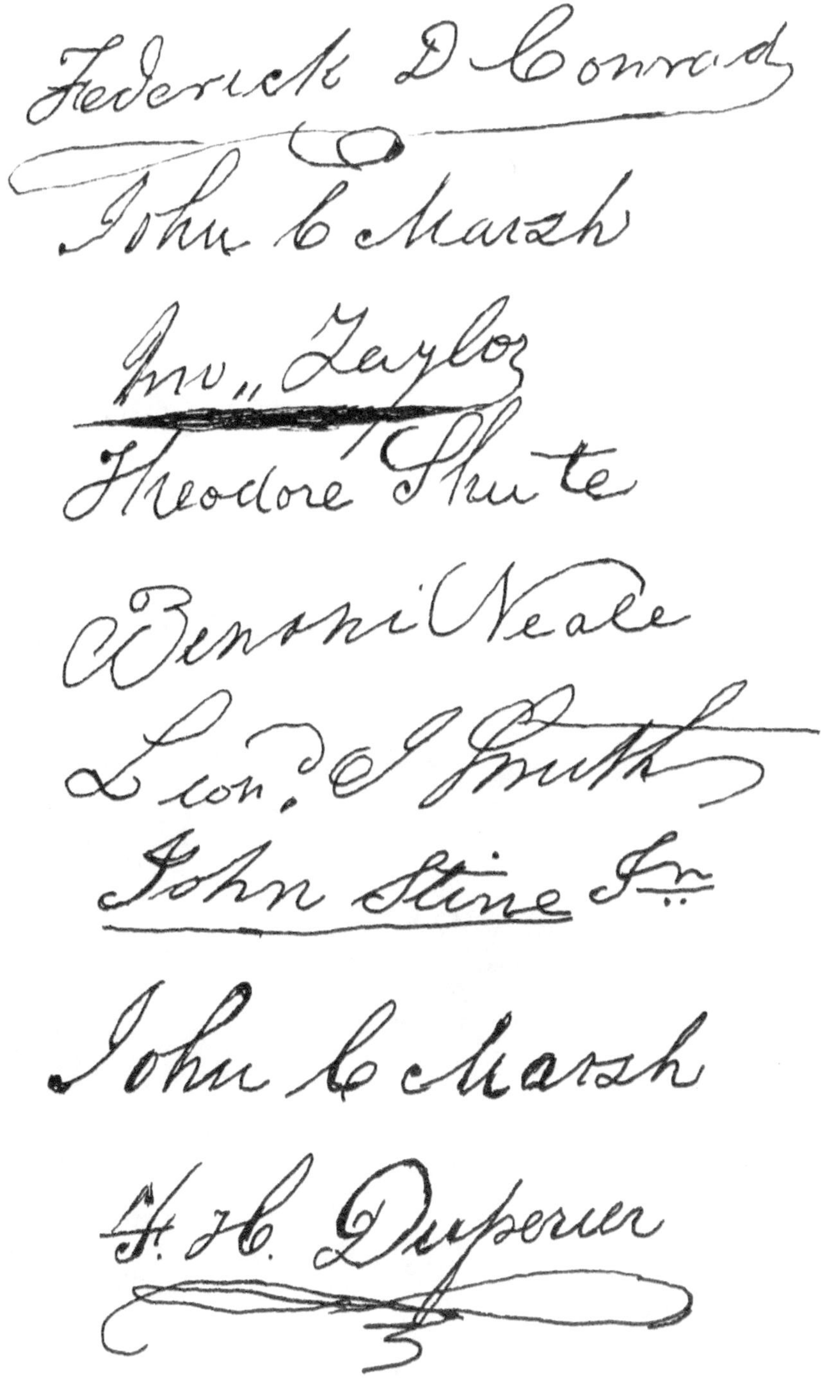

Narrative of Events

Federick D Conrad

John C Marsh

Jno. Taylor

Theodore Shute

Benoni Neale

Leond. J Smith

John Stine Jr

John C Marsh

A. H. Duperier

Facsimile signatures of some nineteenth-century New Iberians

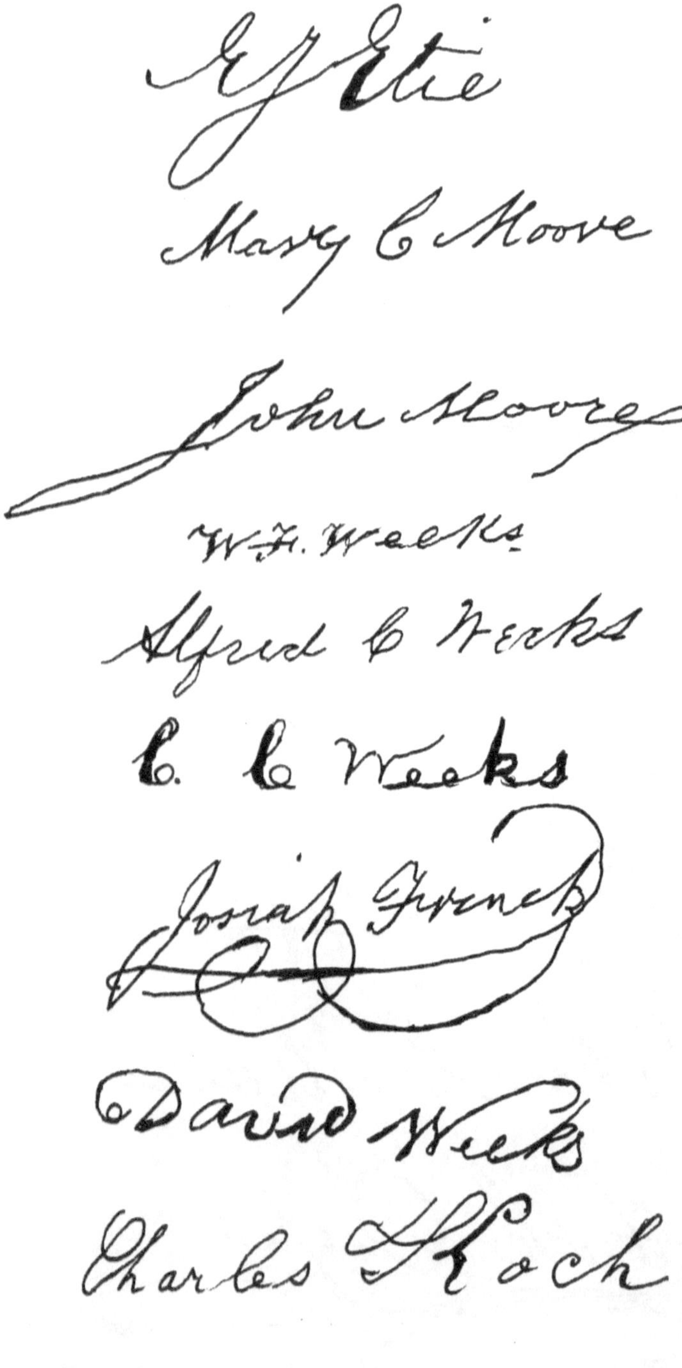

E J Etie

Mary C Moore

John Moore

W. F. Weeks

Alfred C Weeks

C. C Weeks

Josiah French

David Weeks

Charles Koch

Facsimile signatures of some nineteenth-century New Iberians

seau and Tertron furnished full loads from their immense warehouses to steamers plying between the Teche and New Orleans via Plaquemine. This company was of such a size that it could dictate the terms for transportation to and from New Orleans. The class of steamers that navigated the Teche in those early days were luxurious in their treatment of passengers. Freight and passage, the result often of contracts, were moderate considering the length of the journey. The regular passenger fare for a three-day trip to New Orleans was from seven to eight dollars. Annually, with the end of winter, there was a general exodus of farmers and merchants to New Orleans. The first of March, being the accepted period for settling all business transactions, merchants and planters would return from the commercial metropolis with their yearly supplies. In connection with St. Martinville, I should not omit to state that besides her businessmen, she could also boast of a class of men of rare attainments. Judge Paul Briant, a refugee from Santo Domingo, and for years parish judge, was an able and model jurist. Judge Ransom Eastin was the prototype of General Jackson in physique and character. Judge Dumartrait was a financier of rare ability conducting successfully the Union Bank until it closed its doors. The legal fraternity was represented by men of distinction at the bar such as Judge Simon, Jr., Judge Cornelius Voorhies, Isaac Morse, William Brent, and John Brownson. The medical profession was led by men licensed from the French schools. It was after the annual pilgrimage to New Orleans that the gala days were transferred from the latter place to St. Martinville. The removal of the opera troupes for the summer made St. Martinville the center of gaiety, pleasure, and amusements. Visitors from all sections of Attakapas and Opelousas would flock to the "Petit Paris" to enjoy the society of her intelligent population.

The failure of the expedition under General Leclerc, Napoleon's brother-in-law, to quell the revolution in Santo Domingo, due to mortality among the troops, including the commander of the expedition who succumbed early to yellow fever, led to a general exodus of the French population to avoid the cruelties perpetrated by Toussaint l'Ouverture and his followers. Many of these immigrants, including my own ancestry, were transported to Wilmington, to Philadelphia, whence they removed to Louisiana. Derbes and Bruno, two respected citizens of St. Martinville, were among the early refugees.[29] Many others, such as Pierre Lassalle, St. Julien, and Lefebre who settled in Cote

---

29. Derbes and Bruno may have come to Louisiana from Santo Domingo, but in the 1850 U. S. census, Derbes indicated that he was a native of France, and Bruno gave his native place as Italy.

Gelée, may have been among these refugees who came to different parts of Louisiana. The final capture of Toussaint l'Ouverture by Rochambeau, and his transportation to France, did not subdue the revolution in Santo Domingo, nor did it accomplish much toward the civilization of the barbarians of that island. At this hour, it looks very much as if history is about to repeat itself. The inauguration of a political war, on humanitarian grounds, may cost valuable lives and billions of treasure, to raise someone to the presidency.[30]

My first trip to New Orleans on a Teche steamer was in 1830, on my way to college.[31] The steamer was *Plough Boy*, built by her commander, Captain Patterson, the first settler of Pattersonville, on the Lower Atchafalaya. The ascent of the rapid current of Bayou Plaquemine was too much for the single engine steamers of those days and could only be effected by the *cordelle*. Imagine how ludicrous such a method would be at this age of progress in machinery and steam navigation. To see ten yoke of oxen, harnessed to a hawser made fast to a steamer, and the engine puffing away with all its might, in order to ascend the rapid stream, appears today incredible. The narration, true as it is in the experience of men of my age, sounds like a "fish story" to those of the present generation.

It is not strange that in those fairy days of the country metropolis of St. Martin Parish, New Iberia, with its many natural advantages, could not rival the "Petit Paris." The name of New Iberia, to those not familiar with its history, would seem to imply that it always was the county seat of Iberia Parish. Until 1868, when the parish of Iberia was created, New Iberia was located within St. Martin Parish, whose southern limits extended to the line of the Satterfield property.[32] Marsh Island [Avery Island] and Grand Cote [Weeks Island] formed a part of St. Mary Parish.

The early Spanish colonists, attracted by the beauties of the Teche, gave to their trading post the name of "Nueva Iberia," in commemoration of the land of

---

30. Dr. Duperier is, of course, referring to the Spanish-American War which broke out with the declaration of war by Congress on April 21, 1898.

31. Something is wrong with this statement, probably the date may be a printer's error. Dr. Duperier was born April 28, 1826, and could hardly have been going off to college at the age of four.

32. The boundary between St. Martin and St. Mary parishes crossed East Main Street at a point approximately 150 feet east of present-day Evangeline Street.

flowers as purported the Iberia of their native land. Letters held by me with the postmark "Nueva Iberia," coming from Baltimore as early as 1824, show that this Spanish appellation clung to the place for a period.

The healthfulness of this particular location, the fertility of its soil, the immense mineral salt deposit, the immunity from overflows,[33] and the accessibility for commercial intercourse with the mother country through the Mississippi River and the several inlets leading into the Gulf of Mexico, show how wise the early Spanish, French, and Acadians were in their selection. As the New Iberia of today progresses, we become more and more impressed with the wisdom and thrift of the original colonists. The labor performed by the early emigrants, before steam navigation, shows how much they appreciated commercial intercourse. Although more of a nomadic race--devoting much of their time to grazing--the works of internal improvement performed by them, with the crude appliances of those days, are worthy of imitation by our present agricultural and mercantile population. The digging of the Attakapas Canal, to link the valley of the Teche with the Lafourche and Mississippi through to New Orleans, shows how much they appreciated the importance of commercial intercourse. Other works do, too, such as the canal leading from Petite Anse prairie into the waters of Vermilion Bay. Grand Cote canal leading from Isle Piquant prairie into Grand Cote Bay, Lake Tasse Canal leading from the lake of that name to the Teche on the property owned by the French commandant [Louis-Charles] De Blanc; to supply water in default of steam. The two first canals were utilized for commercial purposes by the original colonists; also by Randolph, Mongault, and Gerbeau, agents of Lafitte in their smuggling operations; as well as in the slave traffic. Mongault's residence at New Iberia became the property of John C. Marsh, who removed early from New Jersey to this place.[34] The Averys and McIlhenneys are among his worthy descendants, holding still his early possessions, including the Avery Salt Mines. Much of the Marsh property was also acquired from Joseph Gerbeau, whom I personally knew, and who lived on a portion of Barnett's place in St. Mary.

If I have referred to undertakings which to the casual observer of today seem insignificant, it is to show that a spirit of enterprise prevailed among

---

33. The immunity ended with the flood of 1927. For an account of that flood, see the essay entitled "The Teche Country in the Flood of 1927."

34. For background on John C. Marsh, see footnote 25 of the essay entitled "The Obituary of William Weeks."

the early pioneers of southwestern Louisiana, a spirit well worthy of imitation by the present generation.

Up to the time of the incorporation of New Iberia, it had remained comparatively stagnant; notwithstanding the valuable additions of a class of intelligent and worthy emigrants who had settled in her adjacent territory. John Fitz Miller was among the first; a Virginian, from Norfolk,[35] he removed from New Orleans, purchasing the property of Nathan Morse, the father of Isaac E. Morse, for a long time our representative in Congress.[36] With this property, Miller subsequently acquired some Daniel Clark lands that became involved in the long-pending litigation with Mrs. Myra Clark Gaines.[37] All of this property was transformed into a sugar plantation now absorbed by what is known as the East End extension of New Iberia.[38] Miller was, for a long time, a controlling spirit in the turf association, being among the first to import racing stock from England. He imported "Sorrow" and "George Martin" as may be ascertained from the turf register. He organized the Attakapas Turf Association and opened on his land a mile-long track which for many years was liberally patronized by Colonel Minor, Duplantier, Kenner, Lecompte, Parrot, Harding, and others. These annual races were a great attraction to New Iberia and contributed much to bring it into notice. Miller became the owner of what is now Jefferson Island, which he used as a stock ranch and sugar plantation. Dying a bachelor, his estate went to a niece, Mrs. John Lloyd Lewis.

Among the other immigrants who imparted tone and vigor to the immediate neighborhood of New Iberia were John D. Wilkins, Dr. James S. Peebles, and Henry Peebles. John D. Wilkins was the first of this group. He came from

35. Miller may have lived in Norfolk, Virginia, but he was a native of Philadelphia. For some background on Miller, see footnote 28 of the essay entitled "The Obituary of William Weeks" and the section on Miller in the essay entitled "Some Facts and Traditions about New Iberia."

36. For a background sketch of Isaac Morse, see footnote 27 of the essay entitled "The Obituary of William Weeks."

37. The Daniel Clark-Myra Clark Gaines story has not yet been fully told. To date, however, the best account is that of Nolan Bailey Harmon, *The Famous Case of Myra Clark Gaines* (Baton Rouge, 1946). For more information on the Miller lands bought from Clark, see the essay entitled "Some Facts and Traditions about New Iberia."

38. John Fitz Miller's plantation was located between Bank Avenue and Evangeline Street. The foundations of Miller's sugar mill can still be seen along the banks of the bayou just west of the point where Prairie Avenue would meet Bayou Teche.

Virginia possessed of considerable means and a liberal education received at the University of Virginia; he was far above the average. He purchased for himself a large domain which was utilized as a sugar plantation and stock farm. His intelligence and education made him a favorite among the elite of the French population. He soon became the controlling spirit of the banks of St. Martinville. He was the first to introduce the "short hours" into the country. Virginia-style, he raised and cured all his meat. He was a great reader and the friend of the young man who would display industry and ambition. He was liberal in his contributions to all undertakings. He contributed to the first phanlanstery erected by the disciples of Charles Fourier, $5,000. He was a man of deep thought and a natural philosopher. He once announced himself as a candidate for governor on what he called a triangular platform. His address to the people was full of reform suggestions. He pledged the salary of the office, if elected, to charitable objects. During the yellow fever of 1839, he was a public benefactor to all who had shared in the distress. He was a man *sui generis* full of charitable impulses. Upon arriving to settle permanently upon his lands, he had brought a letter of introduction from Henry Clay to Colonel Eugene P. Olivier. Landing at the latter's plantation, he was received with the princely hospitality characteristic of the French gentlemen of those days. The boat that brought him had also landed a cargo of fine stock of all descriptions that were at once driven to Mr. Wilkins' newly acquired possessions, three miles in the rear of the Olivier place. Mr. Wilkins died at his Louisiana home, regretted by all classes of people living in the Attakapas country. He left considerable means to his heirs, who have long since followed him to his last resting place.[39]

---

39. For two accounts of the life and career of John D. Wilkins, see Glenn R. Conrad, "Virginians in the Teche Country," *Attakapas Gazette* XVII (1982), 5-18, 52-67, 100-19; Carl J. Guarneri, "Two Utopian Socialist Plans for Emancipation in Antebellum Louisiana," *Louisiana History*, XXIV (1983), 5-24.

John D. Wilkins was the uncle of Henry D. Peebles. Together, they purchased approximately 8,000 acres of public land southeast of New Iberia in the area known as Isle aux Cannes (presently the area between the Commercial Canal and the community of Lydia). When Wilkins died in 1852, his heirs sold his portion of this property to Francois Optat Darby. Darby sold it to Dr. Leonard J. Smith in 1856, and Smith sold it to Desire Hebert in 1869. See Iberia Parish Probate Book 3, p. 411.

Henry D. Peebles and his family retained his portion of the plantation, which is popularly known as "Peebles Plantation," well into the twentieth century. For the story of the Peebles family in the New Iberia area, see Gertrude C. Taylor, "Virginians in the Teche Country," *Attakapas Gazette*, XVII (1982), 152-65; XVIII (1983), 2-14.

One of the many causes of the stagnation of New Iberia was her having to pay tribute to the county seat without receiving a *quid pro quo* of the contributions for the maintenance of public roads and ferry privileges. The grievances became so overt that as early as 1837 a public meeting, numerously attended, was convened and was presided over by Neuville Declouet, a descendant of one of the French commandants. The abortive efforts of those early days to create the parish of Iberia culminated in 1868 in severing from St. Martin and St. Mary parishes a territory of sufficient extent to form one of the richest parishes of Louisiana, with New Iberia as its county seat. The result was finally attained through the united efforts of the best citizens of New Iberia and its immediate vicinity, under the administration of Governor Warmoth.[40] It was the result of methods for the first time made public. Enjoying the intimate friendship of John Ray, an old-time Whig, once a candidate for lieutenant governor on the same ticket with our much to be regretted citizen, Alexandre DeClouet,[41] I confided to him the bill that had been carefully drawn setting forth the boundaries of the contemplated parish of Iberia, with a carefully prepared census of the population within its prescribed limits. The preliminary work absorbed a small sum for the labor performed at home. Joachim Etie,[42] a young man highly respected, attended to all the details at home, transmitting to me in New Or-

---

40. For an account of the creation of Iberia Parish, see the essay entitled "New Iberia Becomes the Parish Seat."

41. John Ray was not the running mate of Alexandre Declouet on the Whig ticket in 1849. Duncan Kenner ran that year for lieutenant governor. Ray ran for lieutenant governor on a ticket headed by Louis Bordelon in 1852. See William H. Adams, *The Whig Party of Louisiana* (Lafayette, 1973), pp. 185, 242; Albert Leonce Dupont, "The Career of Paul Octave Hebert, Governor of Louisiana, 1853-1856," *Louisiana Historical Quarterly*, XXXI (1948), 501.

42. Emanuel Joachim Etie, Jr., was the son of the senior Etie and Claire Migues. He was born on February 18, 1829. On February 22, 1851, he married Elvina Segura, the daughter of Antoine Segura and Marguerite Marcellite Viator. They had several children. Etie and others were responsible for drafting the bill for the creation of Iberia Parish which was presented to the legislature. After the creation of the parish in 1868, Etie was named parish judge. He died on September 27, 1870, at the age of forty-one. *Southwest Louisiana Records*, II, 311; V, 196, 505; IX, 136

Judge Etie's grandsons, Aristide and Alfred were well-known contractors at the turn of the nineteenth century. They were the sons of Dubuc Etie and Leontine Broussard (Iberia Parish Probate Book 2, p. 281). A good example of their craftmanship can be seen in the brick work for the building on the northwest corner of Weeks and Main streets.

Narrative of Events 107

leans all the papers when completed. The bill, when presented by Senator Ray[43] went through the senate and lower house without any great solicitation. After its enrollment, I was summoned to the governor's office. With his usual promptness, laying his hand on the enrolled bill that lay on his desk, he said: "Doctor, must I sign this bill?" Affecting ignorance and replying slowly, he said: "You have fathered this bill, and if you want it signed, so-so, otherwise it will be consigned to the waste basket." Without further hesitation, I requested that he should sign the bill, which he did in my presence, adding: "I have signed the bill on one condition, to wit: that you shall formulate the slate for all appointments deemed acceptable by your people. Upon tomorrow, bring me a list of all the appointments, and I will issue their commissions."[44] I could not overcome my joy at the opportunity of crowding out the hungry scalawags who were building hopes upon the Negro influence, which they felt sure would influence the governor in his appointments. I had had previous assurances from the governor that he had determined to cut loose from his surroundings, if the best element of Louisiana would join him in this movement. I had no reason to doubt his sincerity and had abundant proof of his devotion to the best interests of the state, as represented by the white element of the Republican party, and the entire conservative body of white voters. The names as handed in to him by me were those of Patrick Burke, William Robertson, George Stubinger, Joachim Etie, and Judge Daniel Avery as president of the police jury. These were promptly commissioned. The administration of the parish of Iberia under a set of officers unsurpassed, if ever equaled since, gave a deserved impetus to the new parish. Judge Robert Perry[45] and Judge

---

43. Senator John Ray, in the 1868 legislature, was a Republican representing Ouachita and Caldwell parishes. He was a most prolific sponsor of legislation and was quite active on the floor of the senate. For a discussion of this man's background and career, see Frederick W. Williamson, *Northeast Louisiana: A Narrative History of the Ouachita River Valley and the Concordia Country* (Monroe, 1939).

44. Governor Warmoth signed the bill creating Iberia Parish on October 30, 1868. For the provisions of the bill, see *Acts Passed by the General Assembly of the State of Louisiana, 1868* (New Orleans, 1868), pp. 272-74

45. Robert S. Perry was born in Lafayette Parish on December 5, 1834. As a youngster he went to Kentucky where he attended Kentucky Military Institute. He studied law at the University of Louisville and afterward entered a law office in Anderson, Texas. Shortly thereafter, he moved to Vermilion Parish and established his law practice there.
During the Civil War, Perry served in Company C of the 8th Louisiana Regiment and fought in Virginia until captured at Rappahannock in November, 1863.

Joseph A. Breaux
Chief Justice
Louisiana Supreme Court
1904 - 1914

Joseph A. Breaux,[46] both men of influence in their respective communities, were the first to avail themselves of the new field of operations. Both have

---

After the war he resumed his law practice in St. Martinville and there married Bertha Gary in July, 1870. The following year he moved to New Iberia. Before his wife's death in 1878, the couple had three children, Bertha (born 1872; later Mrs. Walter Burke), Lilia (born 1874), and Joseph Robert (born 1876). In 1883 Perry married Camille Vedrines, but his second wife died that same year.

In 1874 Perry was elected to the state legislature and served one term. In 1888 he was elected circuit judge and served in that capacity until approximately 1896.

Judge Perry died February 24, 1900. For a review of his life and career, see the *New Iberia Enterprise*, March 3, 1900.

46. Joseph A. Breaux was born at Bayou Goula, La., on February 18, 1838, the son of John B. Breaux and Margaret Walsh. He attended the University of Louisiana and received his law degree from Georgetown College, Georgetown, Kentucky. In 1859 Breaux was admitted to the Louisiana bar and began the practice of law in New Iberia. Two years later he married Eugenia Mille, the daughter of Thomas Mille of Iberville Parish, and sister of Emma Mille, wife of Dr. Alfred Duperier of New Iberia.

His law practice interrupted by the Civil War, Breaux served the Confederacy throughout the conflict. After the war he returned to New Iberia where he engaged in the practice of law from 1868 to 1888. In 1887, he was elected president of the New Iberia National

met with merited success. Many more followed adding daily to the wealth and intelligence of Iberia Parish. Possessed of a soil unsurpassed in extent and fertility for the production of cane, corn, and other products, with its numerous central sugar factories, with its southern territory underlaid with an inexhaustible deposit of mineral salt, the future of Iberia Parish and of its metropolis is beyond all conjecture.

The discovery of the hidden treasure was the result of pressing wants, engendered by the Civil War. As early as 1848, a French geologist and scientific explorer named Thomassy, arrived at New Iberia with a letter of introduction to my ever-lamented friend and classmate, Eugene P. Olivier. Together we visited Marsh [Avery] and Grand Cote [Weeks] islands. On Marsh Island there remained traces of salt springs, with crude appliances that had been resorted to for the evaporation of salt between 1812 and 1815.[47] The result of Mr. Thomassy's cursory exploration was the publication of a brochure in which he predicted the existence of rock salt on Marsh Island and much of our southern territory.[48] A complimentary copy of his work was mailed to my friend and to me from Paris. It was reserved to the period of the War Between the States to verify the predictions made by Thomassy. In digging out some of the old salt springs, the solid rock was struck. Since then, Marsh Island or Avery mine has been operated by companies with large capital. The recent discovery of an

---

Bank, a position he held until 1924. Breaux also had many business interests and was long associated with the P. L. Renoudet Lumber Co. of New Iberia. In addition, he served as superintendent of education in Iberia Parish with such success that in 1888 he was elected state superintendent of education. The latter position he held until April 24, 1890, when he was appointed associate justice of the state supreme court. In 1904 Judge Breaux became chief justice and served in that capacity until his retirement from the bench in 1914.

After retirement, Judge Breaux resided in New Orleans, where he died July 24, 1926. His wife preceded him in death by four years. The couple had no children. For more on Joseph A. Breaux, see the *Louisiana Sugar Bowl*, December 2, 23, 1875; the *New Iberia Enterprise*, February 10, 1912; the *Weekly Iberian*, March 16, 1912; Henry E. Chambers, *A History of Louisiana*, 3 vols. (Chicago, 1925), III, 201; and the New Orleans *Times-Picayune*, July 24, 1926.

47. This was the salt works belonging to Jesse McCall. See footnote 54 of the essay entitled "Some Facts and Traditions About New Iberia."

48. (Marie-Joseph) Raymond Thomassy, *Geologie pratique de la Louisiane* (Paris, 1860).

equally extensive bed of rock salt underlying Grand Cote, soon to be operated by a company possessed of large capital, will make the parish of Iberia the basis of supply for the entire South.[49] This extensive deposit of mineral salt, limited apparently to the parish of Iberia, is truly wonderful.

The original map of New Iberia, by Dowd, comprised the territory between what is now Weeks and French streets, fronting Bayou Teche, running ten arpents in depth, with Iberia Street as the only inlet and outlet of Petite Anse into New Iberia. Corresponding to Corinne Street[50] from Main Street, a narrow passage led to the ferry landing on the Teche. Thence through a small woods the public road leading to Fausse Pointe was reached. Loreauville, Jeanerette, Burke, and Cade at the time were *non est*. The territory known as Fausse Pointe was settled by the most worthy class of immigrants from Acadia, the Decuirs, Broussards, Breauxs, Dugas, and others. The descendants of the persecuted race bear the impress of their noble ancestry.[51]

Within the limits of Dowd's map, comprising the village of New Iberia, there were at my earliest recollection, twenty-five residences, four stores, one blacksmith shop, one bakery, one tannery and two saloons. The capital in trade in those early days was very large, equal probably to a million dollars. Local merchants like Shute and Taylor, afterwards Taylor and DeValcourt, did a large wholesale and retail advancing business. They held large cash deposits for such men as J. D. Wilkins, and the many stock raisers who enjoyed their confidence. Selling on a credit of twelve months, replenishing their stock twice a year from Boston, New York, Philadelphia, and other Atlantic ports, through sailing vessels returning with cargoes of country produce in exchange, they were compelled to carry heavy stocks of goods. Western produce, such as flour, whiskey, soap, candles, etc., were floated down the Mississippi and Atchafalaya on flatboats. The use of cured meats, such as pork, bacon and ham, were in those days almost unknown.

New Iberia, being the real terminus of deep-water navigation on the Teche, began to assert its commercial importance in the 1840s. The interruption of navigation through Plaquemine during the low stage of water in the Mississippi

---

49. The reference here is to General F. F. Myles, founder of the Myles Salt Company of Weeks Island.

50. Present-day Serret Alley was once known as Corinne Street.

51. The Decuir family does not have its origins in Acadia. The family came to the

Narrative of Events

created a demand for a class of gulf steamers of large carrying capacity. These steamers, not being able to ply above New Iberia, landed their large cargoes, destined for all points south and west on the Vermilion and Calcasieu, at New Iberia. It was then that she became the radiating point for the trade of a large territory, extending some sixty miles in all directions. About the same period, and continuing until the completion of the New Orleans, Opelousas and Great Western Railroad from Morgan City to its western terminus, New Iberia became the distributing point for mail and passenger traffic overland to Texas. New Iberia also controlled a large cattle trade from Texas and adjacent territory. It was at this juncture that she assumed commercial supremacy over St. Martinville and Franklin.

In 1867, a second visitation of yellow fever came to mar her prospects. Every inland town in Louisiana fell prey to this epidemic. It prevailed with great virulence in the neighboring towns of St. Martinville, Lafayette, and Abbeville. New Iberia was fortunate in escaping the scourge that affected most other towns in 1852, 1854, 1878, 1897, and 1898.[52] Owing to these exemptions, she has been less impeded in her prosperity....

Having looked backward as well as forward, at everything connected with the welfare of New Iberia, within my sphere of observation, as connected with the past as well as the future of New Iberia, I will close my lengthy and somewhat uninteresting narration of events connected with my native town and parish.[53]

Fausse Pointe area from Pointe Coupee Parish. Before that the family had come to Pointe Coupee from France.

52. For details of the 1867 yellow-fever epidemic in New Iberia, see the essay entitled "New Iberia and Yellow Fever: Epidemic and Quarantine."

53. Dr. Duperier prepared this historical sketch about the same time that another important event in the history of New Iberia was developing, the organization of the Jewish congregation. The Congregation's efforts to secure a temple were successful just about the time that Dr. Duperier died in April 1904.

During the late nineteenth century the Jewish community of New Iberia contemplated the formation of a congregation and the erection of a place of worship. Toward the end of the century, Joseph H. Wise led a movement looking toward the formation of a congregation. Although Wise died before seeing the fruits of his labor, success was nevertheless forthcoming and climaxed with the organization of the Congregation Gates of Prayer on April 26, 1897. Shortly thereafter a plot of ground on the corner of Charles and Weeks streets was purchased by the Congregation.

In early 1903 the membership called for plans to be submitted for the construction of a temple, and work began on the building in September of that year. On February 26, 1904, the tenth day of Adar, 5664, the cornerstone of the edifice was laid, although work on the interior still had to be completed.

At the time of the temple's erection, the officers of the Congregation were Leon Dreyfus, president, Leopold Kling, vice-president, Max Levy, secretary, and Lazarre Kling, treasurer. The building commitee was composed of Leon Dreyfus, Morris Scharff, and Lazarre Kling. Members of the Congregation at the time were Leon Dreyfus, M. Weil, Jules Dreyfus, Joseph Weil, Henry Myer, E. Taul, Henry Levy, A. Rosenzweig, Lazarre Kling, E. Wallfish, Leopold Kling, D. Wallfish, Fernand Kling, Lichtenstein, Chas. Gugenheim, Chas. Kahn, Joseph Scharff, Sam Weil, Morris Scharff, Moses Immergluck, Jake Weil, Jake Immergluck, Schoeneman, Max Levy, Eli Wise, Dave David, L. Sokolosky, Louis Ochs, Sol Wise, L. Wormser, M. Wise, Meyer Wormser, L. Weil, A. Silverman, M. Maritzky, and N. Silverman.

The dedication of the completed temple occurred on September 2, 1904, with Dr. J. Miller of Omaha, Nebraska, officiating. The program included an organ prelude by Mrs. Joseph Weil, hymns by the choir, a prayer by the Rev. C. C. Kramer of the Church of the Epiphany, a violin ceremony by Mrs. Leon Dreyfus, the address by Dr. Miller, remarks by Porteus R. Burke, and a vocal solo by Anna Grant Miller.

Through the years of the twentieth century, the temple has continued to stand on its original site; however, assembly rooms and reception rooms have been constructed nearby for the use of the Congregation.

The above information has been gleaned from the *Jewish Ledger* of New Orleans and the *Weekly Iberian* for March 5 and August 27, 1904. The annotator is especially indebted to Mrs. Percy Creim who provided information from the Congregation's archives.

Temple Gates of Prayer as it appeared in February 1986

IV

*The Obituary of William F. Weeks**

by
Dr. Alfred Duperier

edited and annotated by
Glenn R. Conrad

Died, at the Weeks home, at New Iberia, on Thursday, the 24th day of January, 1895, at 10 o'clock a.m., William F. Weeks, age 71 years. *Requiescat in pace.* Whilst this simple epitaph, fulfilling all the aims of a life well spent in the service of the Lord should satisfy the vanity of any mortal, and prove a sufficient solace to the relatives and friends of the departed, it becomes, in this instance, the duty of a life-long friend to perpetuate, in type, the deeds of one who has been so intimately connected with the origin and development of the country. In this way, his numerous good traits may serve as an example to the rising generation.

Shortly after the admission of Louisiana as one of the states of the American Union, the immigration from the original states was directed to it. Already the home of the Spanish and French colonists under the two regimes that had preceded the treaty of cession to the United States, St. Martin Parish, the home

---

*Editor's note: The following obituary probably appeared in the *New Iberia Enterprise* on January 16, 1895. That edition of the paper, however, has been lost. The obituary printed here is a typewritten copy of the original found in Southwestern Archives, University of Southwestern Louisiana.

of the "commandant" and the elite of the French immigration, attracted thereto the early American settlers.[1]

"Nova Iberia," as indicated in letter in the possession of the writer stamped from Baltimore, Maryland, as late as 1824, seems to have been the name adhered to for New Iberia by the Spanish colonists who had settled at this point.[2]

St. Martinville, the home of "Commandant" De Blanc, the Declouets, Dubuclets, Delahoussayes, Fuseliers, Oliviers, Devezins, Delhommes, Dumartraits, Briants and others, continued for a long time, the most attractive point for the French colonists, whether coming from the mother country or from its West Indian possessions. Outside of New Orleans, St. Martinville was the most attractive city of *Nouvelle France,* on account of the intelligence and wealth of its citizens. Its proverbial gaiety and unbounded hospitality had entitled it to the well-merited surname of *Petit Paris.* It was not surprising, under these circumstances, that the elite among the early Anglo-Saxon immigration found their way to St. Martin Parish, then including within its boundaries the present parish of Iberia.[3] The Palfreys, Bakers, Conrads, Morses, Towles, Eastins, Brownsons, Hickeys, Brents, Porters, Weekses, Wilkinses, and others were among the first to fraternize with the customs and manners of the Latin race who had preceded them under an earlier regime.[4] The conviviality and unbounded hospitality of the French chevaliers soon captivated the esteem and friendship of the American friends.

1. The Attakapas District, at least those segments of Bayou Teche from St. Martinville to Berwick Bay, and Bayou Vermilion from Lafayette to Abbeville, was settled by Acadians and Creoles in the mid-1760s. In 1779 Francisco Bouligny settled a group of Spaniards at New Iberia (see the essay entitled "New Iberia: The Spanish Years"); however, except for their surnames, these Spanish settlers soon lost their cultural identity in the midst of the prevailing Gallic environment.

2. For a brief discussion of the name changes of New Iberia, see the essay entitled "New Iberia Gets a Post Office." New Iberia was also frequently called "New Town" in antebellum days. Note that "Nova" is the Latin word for "new." "Nueva" is the Spanish term; however, the editor has also seen envelopes postmarked "Nova Iberia."

3. Iberia Parish, of course, was formed in 1868 from parts of St. Martin and St. Mary parishes. The line dividing St. Mary and St. Martin parishes before that date was about 125 feet below Evangeline Street on the east side of New Iberia.

4. John Stine, of Pennsylvania, was probably one of the first Americans to settle in what is now New Iberia. He was not, however, the first Anglo-American to settle along Bayou Teche. In 1781 a group of Anglo-Saxon settlers were recorded as being at "New

The Shadows sometime before 1894

The Shadows about the turn of the nineteenth century

The Obituary of William F. Weeks

The Shadows about 1930

The Shadows from the east garden, November 1985

William F. Weeks was the son of David Weeks and Mary Conrad, who were among the early settlers of St. Martin Parish.[5] Deceased was born at "Parc Perdu," the first home of his father.[6] There was, at that time, and for a long

---

Iberia," a designation that probably included much of the lower Teche Valley. They were Thomas Berwick, Ephraim Hormel, Thomas Beard, William Bundick, Joseph Carr, John Brandon, John Hair, William McCullogh, Ebenazer Crene (Craine ?) Cameron, Patrick McCarthy, John Abshire, Abraham Stuart, and William Dickson. For more on these Anglo-Saxon settlers, see Glenn R. Conrad, "Friend or Foe? Religious Exiles at the Opelousas Post in the American Revolution," *Attakapas Gazette*, XII (1977), 137-40.

By the turn of the nineteenth century, a group of Anglo-American merchants had established themselves at New Iberia. They were John Kershaw, the Collins brothers, and James Murphy. For more on these individuals, see the essay entitled "Some Facts and Traditions about New Iberia."

5. David Weeks was born in Baltimore in 1786. He was the son of William Weeks, born in Bristol, England, in 1743. Upon coming to America, William married (1778) Rachel Hopkins of New Jersey, the widow of Steven Swayze. Together with Mrs. Weeks' two children by her first marriage, Steven and Rachel Swayze, the Weeks family moved to Natchez and then to' West Feliciana Parish. William subsequently acquired property in Rapides, St. Mary, and St. Martin parishes (see the *American State Papers: Land Grants and Claims [1789-1837]*). William Weeks died on his plantation in West Feliciana Parish on October 22, 1819. See West Feliciana Parish Succession No. 451, Box 113.

David Weeks married Mary Clara Conrad on December 31, 1818, in St. Mary Parish. They were married by John Towles, a justice of the peace and a doctor, who, two months earlier, had married Mary's sister, Ann Alexander Conrad. (Towles was born in Spotsylvania County, Virginia, on May 8, 1779, and died in St. Mary Parish, October 26, 1832.)

Most of this information on Weeks and Towles is taken from Mary Elizabeth Sanders, comp., *Selected Annotated Abstracts of Marriage Book 1, St. Mary Parish, Louisiana, 1811-1829* (privately printed, 1973), pp. 24, 26-27. Much of the Conrad and Weeks genealogy used in these annotations has been graciously supplied by Mrs. Henry Dauterive, Sr., of New Iberia, the great-granddaughter of David Weeks. For a brief genealogical chart of the Weeks family and its Swayze branch, see Avery O. Craven, *Rachel of Old Louisiana* (Baton Rouge, 1975), p. 113.

6. David Weeks acquired "Parc Perdu" from Pierre Petit of Bordeaux, France, by act of sale recorded in St. Martin Parish on April 24, 1819. Petit had acquired these lands from the Boutte and Prevost families. Although he had married in St. Mary Parish a short time before, the act of sale states that Weeks was then a resident of Bayou Sara in West Feliciana Parish (but see footnote 14 below). The plantation, located on Bayou Parcperdue, was probably in the westernmost part of Iberia Parish in the area of the present-day community of Parcperdue. Weeks sold the plantation to James Mather of East Baton Rouge Parish on October 5, 1825, for $12,000. Mather subsequently sold the property to Frederick Daniel Conrad, David Weeks' brother-in-law. Conrad made the final payment on the plantation on May 31, 1832. For the acts of sale, St. Martin Parish Conveyance Book 1, p. 247; Book 2, p. 79; and Book 6, p. 227.

period subsequent, considerable traffice between the Atlantic ports of the East and the Valley of the Teche. Among the articles brought over for sale and barter were potatoes, onions, lime, codfish, soap, candles, and the noted "Connecticut Yankee" clocks. These wares were exchanged for hides, horns, bones, tallow, molasses, etc. Large invoices of cotton and woolen goods, shoe leather and numerous other wares, the product of Yankee thrift and energy, were brought to the commercial firms of Edgar and Shute & Taylor--afterwards Taylor and DeValcourt--both firms then doing an extensive business at New Iberia.[7]

On his mother's side, William F. Weeks descended from Mary Conrad,[8] a sister of Alfred, Frederick, and Charles M. Conrad; the first was, for a long time, cashier of the Gas Light Bank of Franklin, La. The two last were distinguished members of the New Orleans bar.[9] Charles M. Conrad married the niece of

---

7. For additional information on early business establishments of New Iberia, see the essay entitled "A Narrative of Events Connected with the Early Settlement of New Iberia."

8. Mary Clara Conrad was the daughter of Frederick Conrad and Frances Thruston. Frederick, the son of Frederick Conrad (born June 28, 1723) and Mary Clara Leigh (originally Ley, born September 14, 1736) was born in Fredericksburg, Virginia, in 1758. Frances Thruston, the daughter of the Reverend Charles Mynn Thruston and Elizabeth Rutherford, was also born in Fredericksburg on February 3, 1774. (It is interesting to note that Frederick Conrad and Mary Clara Leigh were married by the Reverend Thruston, the future father-in-law of their son.)

Frederick and Frances Thruston were married at Fredericksburg on April 25, 1793, and then moved to Winchester, Virginia, where Mary Clara was born in 1797. She was one of several children: Frederick Daniel, Frances, Alfred, Charles, Sydney Ann, Elizabeth Frances, Frank, and Henry.

Frederick and Frances Conrad moved from Winchester to Louisiana in 1808 and established a plantation on Bayou Teche between New Iberia and Jeanerette (on the west bank of the Teche, just upstream from the Experimental Farm Road). They were joined in their trip to Louisiana by her parents. Frances died in St. Mary Parish on October 24, 1813. Frederick died in 1822 in St. Martin Parish.

Mary Clara Conrad married David Weeks in December 1818. They had six children: Frances Sydney, Harriet Clara, William Frederick, Alfred Thruston, Charles Conrad, and David, Jr. After Weeks' death, Mary Clara married (1841) John Moore of St. Mary Parish. She died at The Shadows on December 29, 1863.

9. Frederick Conrad read law in the New Orleans office of Abner L. Duncan. Duncan, a Pennsylvanian who arrived in Louisiana shortly after the Purchase and who served as aidede camp to Andrew Jackson in 1815, was able, through investments, to accumulate a large fortune. Some of that wealth was invested in plantations along the Mississippi. Thus, when his daughter Fanny married Frederick Conrad, Duncan gave the young couple a plantation on what subsequently became known as Conrad Point, located below Baton Rouge, and

Mary Clara Conrad
First Mistress of The Shadows

George Washington.[10] Her remains rest, side by side, at Mount Vernon, with those of the "Father of his Country." Upon the election of General [Zachary] Taylor to the presidency of the United States, Charles M. Conrad was made secretary of state. He filled this position with credit to himself and the nation,

---

built a magnificent home for them which was paradoxically called "The Cottage." Thereafter, Frederick Conrad practiced law in Baton Rouge. For a brief and undocumented account of the Duncans and the Conrads, see Herman Seebold, *Old Louisiana Plantation Homes and Family Trees,* 2 vols. (privately printed, 1941), I, 157-62.

Charles Magill Conrad was also a lawyer and was deeply involved in antebellum Louisiana politics. When Alexandre Mouton resigned from the U. S. Senate to run for governor of Louisiana, Conrad replaced him in the upper house of Congress. For Conrad's role as a Whig politician, see William H. Adams, *The Whig Party of Louisiana* (Lafayette, La., 1973).

10. She was Mary Eliza Angela Lewis, the grandniece of George Washington.

until the end of the Fillmore administration.[11] Among the aunts of deceased, on his mother's side, were Mesdames Harding, Palfrey, and Towles; the latter being the mother of our worthy citizen Philip Towles.[12]

Many years after the death of deceased's father, his widow was wedded to the Honorable John Moore, a man of sterling merit, who rose from the position of parish judge of St. Mary Parish to that of state senator, and finally to that of representative in the federal Congress.[13]

From "Parc Perdu," deceased's father having purchased the large sugar estate of "Grand Cote," removed to New Iberia.[14] Upon a lot now the resi-

11. Charles Conrad was not a cabinet officer in the Taylor administration, a fact that came as a great disappointment to many Louisiana Whigs. They had firmly believed that President Taylor, a resident of Louisiana at the time of election, would routinely name a Louisianian, probably Conrad, Duncan Kenner, or Judah Benjamin, to a cabinet post. The president surprised many people when he did not name a single Louisianian to his official family. Conrad did subsequently serve as secretary of war in the Fillmore administration, the last Louisianian to hold cabinet rank until Moon Landrieu, former New Orleans mayor, was named to President Jimmy Carter's cabinet. For the reaction of Louisiana Whigs to Taylor's election and Conrad's appointment, see Adams, *The Whig Party*, pp. 182, 202-03.

12. Mrs. Harding was Frances Elizabeth Conrad who married Winthrop Sargent Harding, son of Lyman Harding, May 12, 1828; Mrs. Palfrey was Sidney Ann Conrad who married William Taylor Palfrey; Mrs. Towles was Ann Alexander Conrad, second wife of John Thomas Towles (see footnote 5 above). For the record of these marriages, see Mary Elizabeth Sanders, comp., *Annotated Abstracts of the Successions of St. Mary Parish, Louisiana* (privately printed, 1972), p. 28.

13. For more on John Moore, see footnote 88 of the essay entitled "Some Facts and Traditions about New Iberia."

14. The author of the obituary has glossed over a large and important segment of the Weeks saga in this rather bland sentence.

The Weeks family, particularly William, David's father, became interested in Grand Cote Island (now Weeks Island) at an early date. On August 16, 1809, William purchased from Evan Williams of Smith County, Tennessee, 480 arpents of land on the island for $300. But William was not the first of his family to buy land on the island, for the Williams-Weeks instrument records that the property was bounded on one side by that belonging to Rachel Bell. Rachel Bell, wife of Richard Bell, was William Weeks' stepdaughter. For the record of this transaction, see St. Mary Parish Mortgage Book BA (copy), p. 222, recorded December 28, 1815.

Then, on May 14, 1814, William Weeks purchased from Louis-Charles de Blanc, the "commandant," 2,080 arpents of land. David Weeks negotiated the sale for his father, paying De Blanc $2,000 for the land. This act of sale is found in St. Mary Parish Mortgage Book BA (copy), p. 190. On July 2, 1814, William Weeks transferred title to the 2,080

dence property of H. Gouguenheim, adjacent to Charles Sonneman, and fronting Main Street, stood, for many years, the early home of the Weeks family in New Iberia.[15] Whilst the old home has long since disappeared, there stands, and will

---

arpents to his son David. This transfer is found in St. Mary Parish Mortgage Book BA (copy), p. 222, recorded December 28, 1815.

Next, on July 23, 1818, Jesse McCall, a resident of St. Martin Parish, sold to David Weeks (referred to as a resident of St. Mary Parish) 480 arpents of land on Grand Cote Island for $1,400. This would appear to be the same tract of land which William Weeks bought in 1809 from Evan Williams and apparently sold to Jesse McCall, for both tracts recorded the same arpentage and both were bounded by the same neighbors. For the Weeks-McCall transaction, see St. Mary Parish Mortgage Book BA, no. 608.

Finally, on February 5, 1832, Rachel O'Conor (Rachel Swayze Bell married Hercules O'Conor following the death of Richard Bell) sold to her half-brother, David Weeks, 400 arpents of land on Grand Cote for $2,000. It is stated in this instrument that the land was acquired by Rachel Bell and her former husband. For the record of this transaction, see St. Mary Conveyance Book F, folio 275, recorded July 11, 1844.

Thus, between 1814 and 1832, David Weeks acquired nearly 3,000 arpents of land on Grand Cote Island, but was not, as a result, sole owner of the island. In addition, David Weeks inherited approximately 1,755 arpents in West Feliciana at the time of his father's death. See West Feliciana Parish Succession no 451, Box 113.

15. Contrary to the author's statement about David Weeks selling "Parc Perdu," acquiring "Grand Cote," and removing to New Iberia, this was not the case (see footnotes 6 and 14 above).

About the time of the sale of "Parc Perdu," David became interested in properties in and quite near New Iberia. At a sheriff's sale on September 20, 1825 (just before the sale of "Parc Perdu" and perhaps anticipating that sale), he purchased the land which is probably most associated with his name. This was recorded as being four-and-one-half arpents wide on the right bank of Bayou Teche by forty arpents deep located in "Nova Iberia." This would be the site of "The Shadows." The land was acquired from the estate of Henry Pintard for $1,567.

Henry Pintard was a native of St. Roman in Sevenne, France, the son of Jacques Pintard. He arrived in New Iberia in 1811, and in 1821 married Hester (or Esther) Teare of Liverpool, England, daughter of Daniel Teare (see footnote 23 of the essay entitled "A Narrative of Events Connected with the Early Settlement of New Iberia"). Earlier, however, Pintard began to acquire property in the area of the present-day Shadows. On August 30, 1821, Pintard purchased four-and-one-half arpents from Henry Penne. The Penne property had a house and barn upon it and sold for $3,000. This was to be Pintard's last major transaction, for he died in October, 1821. For the civil records of Pintard's activity, see St. Martin Parish Conveyance Book, 1A, p. 137; Book 1B, pp. 77, 130, 351; Book 1B½, pp. 179, 339; and Book 1C, p. 178.

Henry Penne acquired the four-and-one-half arpents width by forty arpents depth piecemeal. In 1811 he purchased one arpent width by forty arpents depth (the property with the house and barn on it) from Francois Mongault and Louis Gary (see Map IV, Area B;2, p. 71).

continue to stand, until felled to the ground by the vandalism of civilization, a cluster of trees, nature's ornaments, around which there still dwell pleasant recollections of the boyhood days of one surviving septuagenarian.[16] Perched under their dense foliage and fanned by the balmy gulf breeze, during the long summer solstice, the mockingbirds warble sweet anthems of praise to the memory of the departed ones who were so considerate to provide for them this pleasant retreat.

In 1834, David Weeks conceived the plan of building the present antique and attractive brick residence, now the home of a fourth generation.[17] It was reserved to the projector of this elegant home to be disappointed in the realization of his plans, for *l'homme propose et Dieu dispose* was verified in this in-

---

On October 31, 1814, at a sheriff's sale called to satisfy a suit brought by Jesse McCall against the heirs of William Smith, Penne purchased a tract of land two arpents wide by forty arpents deep for $315. Then, on May 15, 1815, William L. Brent sold to Henry Penne an adjoining tract of land one arpent wide by forty arpents deep for $400. This piece of land was bought by Brent at a sheriff's sale called on November 3, 1814, to satisfy a debt owed by the succession of William Smith to John Wells. Finally, on June 8, 1817, John M. Smith, William Smith's son, sold one-and-one-half arpents wide by thirty arpents deep to Ely Riggs. This land was subsequently acquired by Penne to round out the four-and-one-half arpents in width sold to Henry Pintard. For these transactions, see St. Martin Parish Original Acts 1059, 1151; St. Martin Parish Sheriff Book A, pp. 12, 14; Conveyance Book 1 B, p. 168.

William Smith, a silversmith and watchmaker, acquired the above-mentioned four-and one-half arpents width together with additional arpentage from Nicolas Hebert in 1798. Papers in Hebert's possession and remitted to Smith indicate that the land in question (The Shadows property) was granted to Francois Prevost (Collet) on January 5, 1775 (see Map I, Area C, p. 68). Smith died in 1811. His wife was Prudence Bonner and their children were John Moses, Adolphus Frederick, William Henry, Augusta Matilda and Elizabeth. For the transactions involving Smith, see St. Martin Parish Acts of Notaries, Book 1, no. 77, dated July 27, 1805; and St. Martin Parish Estate no. 27, dated March, 1811.

Finally, Weeks bought a small piece of land, 87 feet wide by six arpents deep, above and adjoining the property purchased from Pintard's heirs, from the succession sale of Joseph Aborn. This purchase was made on June 12, 1830, and would round out the properties referred to by the author as being "at New Iberia." For the Aborn-Weeks transaction, see St. Martin Parish Conveyance Book 6, pp. 243-45.

16. This would be the present-day site of the home at 424 East Main Street.

17. Work on The Shadows actually began in 1831.

Judge John Moore

stance. Having gone to Connecticut on a visit to relatives and friends, he met with an untimely death away from home.[18]

The present Weeks mansion, the home of Dr. Leonard J. Smith [the Alma House], and the Roman Catholic church were built about simultaneously, and were, up to 1836, the only brick structures in New Iberia.

It was at the Weeks home, at New Iberia, that William F. Weeks, Alfred Weeks, Frances Weeks, Harriet Weeks, and the writer received their first educational training under Hiram Stetson, a graduate of Yale University. Stetson had been engaged by David Weeks as a private teacher. Following the untimely death of the latter, the widow determined to send her two sons to the University of Virginia. The preceptor Stetson, having been appointed by Governor

---

18. "David Weeks died in New Haven, Conn., at the home of Capt. A. Heaton on 25 Aug. 1834." Sanders, *Selected Annotated Abstracts,* pp. 26-27. David Weeks' last will and testament can be found in the succession records of St. Mary Parish.

[Andre] Roman as professor of English literature at Jefferson College, it was allotted to the writer to share the fortunes of this preceptor.

The critical condition of the sugar industry which developed early in the 1840s caused the return of the two brothers, Alfred and William, to their native land.

When barely 21 years of age, William F. Weeks was wedded to Mary Palfrey, the daughter of Judge Palfrey, at one time parish judge of St. Martin Parish, and a brother of Senator Palfrey of Massachusetts.[19] The father of Judge Palfrey and Gorham Palfrey of Massachusetts died possessed of a sugar estate near St. Martinville. Mr. Gorham Palfrey caused the removal of the slave property which had fallen to his inheritance, to Massachusetts where he could, under the laws of that commonwealth, enfranchise the unfortunate victims of the most cruel and barbarous institution, the result of a traffic now repugnant to the entire civilized world.[20] When such acts are the result of fanatical interference, as in the case of John Brown, they are to be condemned. Many of the descendants of the slaves emancipated by Gorham Palfrey are still living in the city of Boston, blessing the memory of their liberator.

Possessed of a thorough moral training and a well-cultivated mind, William F. Weeks was enabled, while quite young, to grapple with the management of

19. The Judge Palfrey referred to was William T. Palfrey. He had two brothers, John Gorham Palfrey who was not a senator but rather a representative from Massachusetts from 1847 to 1849. The other brother was Henry T. Palfrey who resided in New Orleans. They were the sons of John Palfrey, owner of the large St. Martin Parish plantation known as "Isle Labbe." John Gorham Palfrey's biographical sketch can be found in the *Biographical Directory of the American Congress*, p. 1647.

20. The author's account of what happened in this case is fairly accurate. John Palfrey, master of Isle Labbe Plantation, died on October 19, 1843. Upon being notified of his father's death and of his slave inheritance, John Gorham Palfrey, a Unitarian minister, directed that his share of the slave property be hired out until such time as he gave further instructions. The proceeds of their labor was also to be held for further instructions.

The partition of John Palfrey's estate was made on March 1, 1844, and Gorham Palfrey received twenty slaves as his share. Apparently he had sixteen of the slaves transported to Boston either before or after manumission. Four slaves were old and sickly; therefore, Palfrey petitioned the St. Martin Parish Police Jury to allow him to free these four and permit them to spend their remaining days in Louisiana. He wrote that he wished to free them "not only on account of loyal and faithful service by them rendered to their late master John Palfrey, but also because it would be cruel and unjust to take the said slaves at their advanced age to the cold and foreign climate where the said owner resides." For the documents connected with this episode, see St. Martin Parish Estate 995 and Conveyance Book 15, p. 26.

the Grand Cote sugar estate--a task that had baffled the most expert managers of such property. With undaunted energy, industry, and perseverance, thoroughly enslaving himself and his family from the pleasures of life, he was enabled to master, one by one, the numerous difficulties that surrounded this gigantic undertaking. In a few years, he was not only enabled to pay all indebtedness, but also to purchase the several interests of his co-heirs, thereby enabling each one to make separate investments. Alfred C. Weeks, the second brother, died at the commencement of the war [Civil War] on his sugar plantation near Jeanerette.[21] After his death, the widow and children removed to Washington D. C., where they now reside. Frances Weeks, the eldest sister, married David Magill, a Virginian and lawyer of distinction at the St. Martinville bar. The latter died, leaving a widow and child who met with a sad and untimely death at the time of the Last Island storm.[22] Mrs. Weightman and Charles Weeks are the only surviving sister and brother of the deceased. Mrs. Weightman and her two sons and one daughter are now in Chicago. Charles Weeks, now one of the oldest among the native residents, is a member of the New Iberia bar. The elegant Swiss cottage, immediately fronting the old Weeks home, is the residence of the Charles Weeks family.[23]

21. Alfred T. Weeks died in December, 1864. See St. Martin Parish Estate 1811.

22. Frances Weeks was married to Augustin S. Magill, and the couple had three children, David, Augustin, and Ida.

David Magill was born March 18, 1842. His father died in September, 1851. In May, 1855, his mother married a second time, to Buford A. Prewitt of Terrebonne Parish. Mrs. Prewitt and her two younger children, Augustin and Ida Magill, were on Last Island at the time of the disastrous hurricane. All three perished in the storm.

David Magill, however, had not accompanied his mother and therefore survived the disaster. His stepfather, Prewitt, died in 1858; thus, David came under the care and protection of his grandmother Mary Clara Moore.

When the Civil War began, David joined the Confederate army. He was wounded in May, 1863, at the siege of Vicksburg and died a few days later.

The above information can be found in St. Martin Parish Estates 1614 and 1811, and *Southwest Louisiana Records*, VI, 490.

23. Charles Conrad Weeks married Margaret Glassell. They had six children. He died on November 18, 1900.

Dr. Duperier's reference to "the old Weeks home" is to the house that stood on the present-day site of 424 East Main Street, not to The Shadows.

The Obituary of William F. Weeks

The Charles C. Weeks home, built in 1894, as it appeared about 1903 (above).
The house as it appeared in February 1986

The Henshaw Home, built 1885
Later residence of Christian Brothers of St. Peter's College

Below the cluster of trees which still marks the spot whereon stood the old Weeks residence, and immediately fronting the elegant Henshaw home, stood the Edgar store. Henshaw's residence was then, as it is now, at the extreme lower corporate limits of New Iberia.[24] Upon the site of elegant mansion stood the "Mignons," the original owner was said to be associated with Lafitte in his smuggling operations around Vermilion Bay.[25] Engaged in the heinous slave traffic,

24. Ashbel B. Henshaw was a resident of New Orleans when he married Margaret Marsh, the daughter of John C. Marsh of New Iberia, in the summer of 1846. On June 26, 1851, Henshaw, Dudley Avery, husband of Sarah Marsh, and George Marsh formed a planting partnership and purchased from John Marsh a tract of land two arpents wide by forty arpents deep, bounded above by the property of Mrs. John Moore (Mary Clara Conrad Weeks) and below by that of John F. Miller. This land was called the "New Town Property." The same day Henshaw acquired sole ownership of this tract and also one opposite it on the east side of Bayou Teche. It was on this land (the site of the present-day Iberia Parish Library) that John Henshaw (Ashbel's only child) built his Victorian-style home in 1885. For the above transaction, see St. Martin Parish Conveyance Book 29, p. 49.

25. John C. Marsh, husband of (1) Eliza Ann Baldwin and (2) Euphemie Craig, and the father of George, Sarah, Margaret, Eliza Ann, and Helen, was a native of Rahway, New

their memories are associated with all that is barbarous in the annals of civilzation.

In those early days, the aristocratic East End of New Iberia consisted of the old college building,[26] which had been the Morse home,[27] and was subsequent-

---

Jersey. He apparently came to Louisiana with his brother Jonas and was in business in the Attakapas area with his brother-in-law, Samuel Stone. Marsh acquired the New Iberia property from Elizabeth Norwood, a free woman of color, by act of sale dated May 30, 1828. Norwood had acquired the property from Francois Mongault by act of sale dated July 9, 1813. Whether or not Mongault was associated with Lafitte remains a matter of speculation. For information on the Marsh family and the above transactions, see Sanders, *Annotated Abstracts of the Successions,* pp. 90-91; St. Martin Parish Conveyance Book 29, p. 49.

26. The home site of John F. Miller (see footnote 28 below) was mortgaged after the Civil War to the Citizens Bank of Louisiana (as was all the property between Bank and Prairie avenues). Bank Avenue gets its name from the Citizens Bank, not, as some people have suggested, from General Nathaniel P. Banks. The bank then sold the site to the archdiocese of New Orleans to establish a boys' school. This school, first called Holy Cross College and then renamed St. Peter's Academy, operated for a few years in the 1870s and 1880s before closing.

27. Nathan Morse, the son of Dr. Isaac Morse of Elizabethtown, New Jersey, settled in New Iberia about 1805 or 1806 and launched his law practice from an office in James Murphy's inn (see footnote 23 of the essay entitled "A Narrative of Events Connected with the Early Settlement of New Iberia"). In 1808, Nathan married Martha Craufurd Nicholls, the daughter of Judge Edward Church Nicholls, the grandfather of the future governor Francis T. Nicholls. Nathan's sister, meanwhile, married Jonas T. Marsh, the brother of John C. Marsh.

Isaac Edward Morse, the only child of Nathan and Martha Morse, was born in New Iberia in 1809. Educated in the North, he graduated from Harvard in 1829, four years before Nathan drowned in the Mississippi River in the wake of a steamboat accident.

After graduating from law school, Isaac travelled abroad for two years, and in 1831 established his residence in New Iberia (the Morse home was located on the bayou side of East Main Street about midway between Bank and Prairie avenues). Morse practiced law in New Iberia and St. Martinville until he entered politics in 1842. He was elected to the Louisiana senate and then served in Congress from December 2, 1844, to March 3, 1851. An ardent Democrat and political rival of John Moore, the two men were nevertheless good friends. From 1853 to 1855, Morse was attorney general of Louisiana. On December 2, 1856, President Pierce appointed him special representative to New Grenada (Colombia). He died in New Orleans in 1866 and was interred in that city.

Morse married Margaretta Wederstrandt in 1835. She was the daughter of Philomen Charles Wederstrandt, of Maryland, who had arrived in Louisiana in 1806 to assist in apprehending Aaron Burr. The Morses had three sons, Charles Nathan, Edward Malcolm, and Alexander Porter.

ly the home and sugar plantation of John F. Miller, extending to the upper limits of the Satterfield home.[28] A large sugar mill and distillery, with numerous Negro cabins fronting the Teche, comprised, with one exception, all the

---

For additional information on Isaac Morse and the Morse family, see Dr. Edward C. Morse, "The Morse Family in Louisiana," *Louisiana Historical Quarterly*, VII (1924), 441-46; Sanders, *Selected Annotated Abstracts of Marriage Book 1*, p. 113; *Biographical Directory of the American Congress*, p. 1594; Lyle Saxon, *Old Louisiana* (New York, 1929), pp. 102-20.

Closely associated with the Morse family and the subsequent land acquisitions of John F. Miller was the Nicholls family. Edward Church Nicholls was the son of John Nicholls and Cecilia Church of Cornwall, England. From an old Catholic family, Edward was educated at the Jesuit college of St. Omer in France until it was closed in 1762. When Edward refused to continue his studies for the priesthood, his family disinherited him.

He made his way to America and settled in Upper Marlboro, Prince George's County, Maryland. He studied law and was admitted to the bar. About the same time he married Wilamina Hamilton, daughter of Robert Hamilton and Martha (Patsy) Craufurd. His marriage to a Protestant further alienated his family, but they did leave him an inheritance. Leaving his family in America, he sailed for England, conducted his business, and returned to America just after the Louisiana Purchase.

He was appointed judge of the County of Attakapas on May 5, 1805, and the family moved to New Iberia. Judge Nicholls, however, soon became quite controversial and the source of considerable popular discontent. On December 11, 1805, James Brown, the U. S. district attorney, wrote to Albert Gallatin that Governor Claiborne had "gone on an excursion to the County of Attakapas, where the extortion, resistance to law, and oppressive acts of the County Judge Nicholls *are said* to have rendered the presence of the Executive [Claiborne] necessary in order to tranquilize the public mind. The conduct of Mr. Nicholls has excited much clamor. . . ." In his correspondence, however, Governor Claiborne makes no mention of this problem. Nevertheless, when the parish system was introduced in 1807, Nicholls was succeeded by Judge James White, father of Governor E. D. White and grandfather of the chief justice of the Supreme Court.

Edward Church Nicholls and Wilamina Hamilton bought the property between present-day Ann Street and Bank Avenue (see page 53), with a depth of forty arpents. Their heirs subsequently sold the property to John F. Miller. The Nicholls had several children, Robert Hamilton, Thomas C (the father of Governor Nicholls), David Craufurd, and Martha Craufurd (who married Nathan Morse). For additional details on Edward Church Nicholls and his family, see "The Nicholls Family In Louisiana," *Louisiana Historical Quarterly*, VI (1923), 5-18; Clarence Edward Carter, comp. and ed., *The Territorial Papers of the United States*, IX, *The Territory of Orleans, 1803-1812* (Washington, D. C. 1940), 286, 547, 598.

28. John Fitz Miller, the son of John Fitz Miller and Sarah Wessel (whose second husband was Joseph Canby), was a native of Philadelphia. He settled in New Iberia with his mother and sister, Mary Ann Jane (who later married Nathan William Wheeler of Cincinnati), in the 1830s or early 1840s.

In September, 1835, Miller purchased the Morse property which was described as

improvements on this extensive front. The house now occupied by R. F. Hogsett [640 E. Main Street] was, in those early days, the home of Simon Walsh, brother-in-law of Judge D. D. Avery. Above the present Henshaw property, on both sides of Main Street and extending to Weeks Street, stood the old and present Weeks home, with barns, stables, etc., and an open field back forty arpents [present-day Admiral Doyle Drive]. From Weeks Street to Corinne [present-day Serret Alley], on both sides of Main Street, there stood one bakery, two saloons, and on the bayou front, where now stands Serret's hotel,[29]

---

being seven arpents wide by forty arpents deep, bounded above by the property of John C. Marsh and below by that of Daniel Coxe of Philadelphia.

Daniel Coxe was one of the principal heirs of the enigmatic Daniel Clark of New Orleans. During the Territorial period, Clark acquired large tracts of land around the state. One of his holdings was acquired from the heirs of Jean-Baptiste Macarty in 1810. The land measured twenty arpents wide by forty arpents deep and was located in the area approximately between Ann and Evangeline streets. Upon Clark's death in 1813, the New Iberia property passed to his partner Daniel Coxe. On April 23, 1839, Coxe sold the property to Miller.

This is the tract which became involved in the famous case of Myra Clark Gaines, a civil action brought by Mrs. Gaines in 1866 to prove that she, not Coxe and others, was the legitimate heir of Daniel Clark. In the end, Mrs. Gaines produced evidence which convinced the courts of the merits of her claim, and she obtained judgments recognizing her rights.

In the meantime, John Miller died and his estate passed to his niece, Mrs. Cordelia Lewis (the daughter of Nathan and Mary Ann Jane Wheeler). In 1869, Mrs. Lewis compromised with Mrs. Gaines and thereby received clear title to the tract from just above Ann Street to just below Evangeline Street. For additional information on the Miller lands, and the Gaines-Lewis matter, see the essay entitled "Some Facts and Traditions About New Iberia."

For the real estate transactions mentioned above, see St. Martin Parish Conveyance Book 9, p. 360; Conveyance Book 11, p. 344.

The Satterfield home is now known as Mintmere Plantation house and is the property of Dr. Roy Boucvalt. The original subdivision of the Francois Cezar Boutte grant ran from a line about 125 feet east of Evangeline Street to Bayard Street. It was purchased by E. B. Smedes from S. C. and M M. Hartman in 1860. The house was built between 1857 and 1859. After Smedes' death, his widow, Sarah Cade, sold the place to the Satterfield family. The property was the first in St. Mary Parish before Iberia Parish was created in 1868. The house was subsequently owned by the McMahon, Caulking, Collie, and Trappey families. Dr. Boucvalt, the present owner, has undertaken extensive restoration work, and the house is now a tourist attraction.

29. Serret's Hotel was located on Serret Alley (formerly known as Corinne Street) near the bayou.

The Hogsett Home, built c. 1895

Mintmere Plantation House, built c. 1859

was the residence of [Joseph] Aborn, the U. S. Customhouse officer.[30] The property between Weeks and Julia, running forty arpents back, was known as the Boutte property.[31] From Julia to Iberia streets, fronting Main Street and running back forty arpents, was the Duperier property. On this stood the old homesite, the Taylor and DeValcourt store,[32] the stables, barns, etc. On the south side of Main Street, where now stand the Daigre and Gouguenheim stores, stood a one-story brick building known as the Washington Ballroom. Above Iberia Street, and extending to Swain Street, running back forty arpents was the Stine property. On this property at the north and south corner of Iberia and Main streets, stood two Yankee residences that had been brought "knocked down" by sailing vessels.[33] Upon the site of the courthouse stood the Stine residence.[34] On the rear of McMahon's store,[35] on the bayou front, stood the "old tan yard," and Squire French's home.[36] The Boyer residence was that of Thomas Johnson, engaged in making rum puncheons for the distillery of Miller and Marsh. The residence of Max Mattes, the oldest structure in New Iberia, was built by Louis Segura, oldest brother of Raphael Segura, whose father and mother were among the original colonists.[37] The Alma House, built in 1835 by Dr. L. J. Smith, was the last house on Main Street within the corporate limits. All above the Alma House and extending to the St. Marc Darby estate

30. This was Joseph Aborn who was postmaster at New Iberia for a time.

31. See Map 2, p. 69.

32. For the interesting history of this store, see footnote 23 of the essay entitled "A Narrative of Events Connected with the Early Settlement of New Iberia."

33. This was probably the home of Cornelius Guyon, located on the northwest corner of Main and Iberia streets. "Prefabricated homes" in the nineteenth century must have been rather common. James Michener mentions them in his novel *Hawaii* (New York, 1959).

34. See footnote 4 of this essay.

35. Until recently the Davis Furniture store.

36. See footnote 4 of this essay.

37. For more information on this house, see footnote 5 of the essay entitled "A Narrative of Events Connected with the Early Settlement of New Iberia."

was the Raphael Smith sugar plantation.[38] The entire south side of Main Street, extending from the upper to the lower corporate limits, and forty arpents in depth, with the exception of the Catholic church and graveyard, established in 1835, was an open prairie, where grouse, ducks, and snipes were found in abundance.

At the end of the 1840s, William F. Weeks, having met with success in his agricultural pursuits and being freed from the arduous task of closely supervising his sugar estate, made New Iberia his home. Vast changes had taken place. After the yellow-fever epidemic of 1839, it had gradually become the head of navigation and the commercial emporium of the Attakapas country. Up to the time of the breaking out of the Civil War, the home of William F. Weeks was noted for its genuine hospitality to visitors from all sections. The ending of the war, with the complete annihilation of slave property, entailed upon him, as it did upon every slaveholder, heavy financial losses. He was among the few who

---

38. Dr. Raphael Smith, Sr., the son of Leonard Smith and Elizabeth Neal, was a native of Maryland. He moved to New Iberia about 1821 from St. Landry Parish and bought the large plantation formerly belonging to Louis-Charles de Blanc. Three Smith brothers are known to have settled in the Opelousas area in the 1790s. They were Charles, Benjamin, and Raphael. Another brother, Joseph, and a sister, Jane, remained in Maryland.

It was the Smith and Brent families of Maryland who aided the exiled Acadians during their sojourn in that colony. Members of both families eventually made their way to Louisiana to live among the Acadians. For the story of the Smith and Brent assistance to the Acadians, see Felix Voorhies, *Acadian Reminescences* (1907; reprint ed., Lafayette, La., 1977).

Raphael Smith, Sr., married Sarah Hardy of Opelousas, and they had four children, Mary Elizabeth, Charles, Raphael, Jr., and Francis. Mrs. Smith preceded her husband in death. Dr. Smith died in October 1829. His will provided that his children should be educated in the East. Mary Elizabeth was sent to St. Joseph's House in Emitsburg, Maryland, where Dr. Smith's sister, Jane, was a religious; Charles went to the seminary at Emitsburg; Raphael and Francis attended Georgetown College (now University) in the District of Columbia.

Dr. Smith appointed his nephew, Dr. Leonard Smith of New Iberia, to be executor of his will. Thus, on January 11, 12, and 13, 1830, the estate of Dr. Raphael Smith was auctioned. The plantation, comprising 2,400 arpents was sold to David Weeks for $13,500. Weeks also brought eight slaves for approximately $4,500.

On April 27, 1833, David Weeks sold the plantation and slaves which he had acquired three years earlier to Dr. Leonard Smith for $18,000. Apparently, Dr. Smith began construction of his home (later called the Alma House) immediately, for records indicate that it was completed by August, 1834. Leonard Smith was married to Ladoiska Darby, the daughter of Francois St-Marc Darby. See St. Martin Parish Estate 632; Conveyance Book 6, pp. 39-41, and Conveyance Book 8, p. 122.

Dr. Raphael Smith, Jr., returned to Louisiana after finishing at Georgetown and was a victim of the 1839 yellow-fever epidemic. See footnote 24 of the essay entitled "A Narrative of Events Connected with the Early Settlement of New Iberia."

retained possession of their landed estates. With undaunted energy, he contracted new liabilities, that he might, with new methods, adopt himself to the new order of things. In the numerous changes necessary for success, whether in the manufacturing process, or in the advanced methods of agriculture, he was always in the front ranks of progress. All that he realized from his vast sugar estate was paid out freely to the laborer, the mechanic, and for such improvements as his judgment dictated, for the success of the industry in which he was engaged.[39] It was only a few years back, that realizing his failing energies, and his inability to cope with the inimical legislation that threatened the sugar industry, he concluded to sell Grand Cote. Since the sale of the latter, he had been almost unremittingly at his New Iberia home. The death of the companion of his life, a few years later,[40] in the identical room in which he himself surrendered his soul to his Maker, was the first death warning since that of his mother in 1863.[41] The Weeks home, now occupied by a fourth generation, has been noted for its hospitality. To friends and strangers, its broad avenues, its shaded grounds, its wide galleries, its spacious dining room, its numerous bedrooms, were always ready to extend a hearty welcome to all.

William F. Weeks was by nature a true and sincere friend. Scrupulously honest, he was self-sacrificing in his business relations. Having but few individual wants, he lived for the enjoyment of his family. Devoted to agricultural pursuits, he was also a great horse fancier. His greatest enjoyment, away from the cares of his plantation, was to visit occasionally the Blue Grass region of Kentucky, where, with the Alexanders, the Swigerts, the Martins, and others, he could talk "pedigrees." His fondness for the turf and fine stock came to him from inheritance. His father, David Weeks, John F. Miller, Parrot, Kenner, Minor, Duncan, Duplantier, Harding and Penniston were among the organizers of the Attakapas Jockey Club Association, which proved a source of great satisfaction for New Iberia during several years. It was through this organization that "George Martin" and "Sorrow," two English thoroughbreds, were imported to the country as early as 1835.

---

39. In addition, he served on the Board of Trustees of New Iberia from June 19, 1871, to August 24, 1872.

40. Mrs. Weeks died in 1889.

41. His mother died on December 29, 1863, see footnote 8.

Having during a septuagenarian life enjoyed the closest intimacy with the deceased, always sympathizing--if not always agreeing upon matters of minor important--no one more thoroughly appreciates the loss that has been sustained by the death of William F. Weeks to his family, his friends, and the community at large, than this friend of his youth, his manhood, and his old age.

The Last Days of the Darby House
Built c. 1816; destroyed by fire, February 6, 1979

V

*The Reflections of John M. Weeks**

edited and annotated

by

Glenn R. Conrad

I have been asked to write an article containing my recollections of some of the principal incidents and happenings during the years of my life in New Iberia. The chief difficulty in preparing such an article seems to be to select that which is best suited from a flood of memories which date back to my early childhood. Dates and names are sometimes confused or dim, but events are clearly defined in my mind.

My father, Charles Conrad Weeks, was born in New Iberia in his father's home which was then located on the site of the present home of Dr. and Mrs. Henry Dauterive.[1] He met my mother, Margaret Somerville Glassell, in her native state of Virginia. They were married in 1857, and he brought his bride to his new sugar plantation which he had purchased from Mr. Etie.[1] Below and

---

*John Moore Weeks, son of Charles C. Weeks and brother of Edward T. Weeks, Sr., and William G. Weeks, was born October 12, 1858. He spent most of the latter half of the nineteenth century in Louisiana. In 1901 he moved to Florida where he spent the remainder of his life. Mr. Weeks died May 16, 1948. His recollections have been edited for the present work.

1. Charles Weeks' plantation, "Sunnyside," was not purchased from "Mr. Etie." Mr. Weeks purchased the plantation, on the east side of Bayou Teche just upstream from Bayside plantation, from Paul Goodloe in January 1859. Goodloe, however, had only recently acquired the property from Mrs. Mary E. Leake and Mrs. Ann C. Rucker in May 1858. The

adjoining his plantation was that of Mr. Vaughan. Next was Bayside, the property of F. D. Richardson; below that was the plantation of David Ker; next was that of my uncle, Alfred Weeks. Other plantations along the Teche at that time were the Provost's, the Grevemberg's, Druilhet's, John Richardson's, Dr. Duncan's, Devezin's, Jules and Eugene Olivier's, "Yankee" Thompson's, Bussey's, Reggio's, Nelson's, Smedes', Bayard's, Lloyd Lewis', Henshaw's, and Berard's.

Probably everyone advanced in years can look back to some incident as being the first thing which they can remember. My first memory--or recollection--is that of a cane cart backed up to the gallery of our plantation home. It was being loaded with furniture and household goods, for we, like other neighboring planters, were about to become refugees. The cause of our flight was the retreating Confederate army in the face of a Union army's advance up the Teche.[2] A skirmish between the two armies took place at Ricohoc Plantation; another at Franklin; another at Nelson's Canal, just below New Iberia; and another just above the town, on the Lourd [Hopkins] plantation. The breastworks thrown up by the Confederates at the latter location were for years after the war plainly visible. Boys would dig into those breastworks looking for "Yankee" bullets.

When we left the plantation, my mother, sisters, Eudora and Harriet, the baby, and I travelled in mother's carriage. Father rode his horse in order to keep together the procession of carts being driven by his slaves. Father's slave driver

---

ladies, sisters-in-law, had purchased the land from Judge Moses Liddell, Francis Richardson's father-in-law, in March 1846. Judge Liddell had acquired the plantation in June 1843 at a sheriff's sale brought to satisfy a debt owed to Henry Dwight by John G. Richardson. Richardson had acquired the property from James L. Johnson in March, 1829. Johnson had acquired the property from Elizabeth Davis, widow of Ramus Davis, in June 1828. Davis had purchased the land from the heirs of Alexandre LePelletier de la Houssaye who had exchanged a tract of land on Bayou Vermilion for this tract on Bayou Teche. The original grantee of the Teche tract that ultimately came to be owned by Charles Weeks was Jean-Baptiste Labauve. For the foregoing conveyances, see St. Mary Conveyance Book M, 9822; Book M, 9610; Book 12, 5936; Book 11, 8463; Book B4, 702, and *Martin's Reports of Cases . . . in the Supreme Court of the State of Louisiana*, vol. 12, old series, 223-37; vol. 1, new series, 696-718; vol. 6, new series, 140-143.

2. It had been widely reported throughout the Teche country that the advancing Union forces were watonly pillaging plantations and homes in their path. For many individuals, this was sufficient reason to flee with their most precious belongings. Union pillaging in the Teche country is discussed by Morris Raphael in *The Battle in the Bayou Country* (Detroit, 1975), pp. 129-31, 136-37.

was a Negro named Denis Joe, and he drove Mother's carriage. Our destination was the home of Mother's cousin, John Glassell, in De Soto Parish, near a little town called Mansfield.

After reaching Cousin John's home, Father used his slaves, carts, and mules to haul provisions, etc., for the Confederate army. Thus, both he and Cousin John were absent from home when the Battle of Mansfield was fought. The Union army was severely defeated in that engagement and retreated in disorder. Although too young to realize or to appreciate what was being done, I distinctly remember seeing Cousin Mary Glassell, Mother, and other ladies picking lint while the battle was being fought--lint to be used in dressing the wounds of unfortunate soldiers. The day after the battle we drove into Mansfield with the lint, and I vividly recall the gruesome sight of many dead soldiers. The dead had been placed side by side, heads to the walls and feet to the street, on galleries of homes which had been commandeered and converted into impromptu hospitals.

After the war we returned to New Iberia, then a part of St. Martin Parish. The last night before reaching home we made camp atop the "hill" near Spanish Lake, at the point where the road turns--or did turn--to go to the Wyche Plantation. Early next morning we heard the bell in the tall steeple of the Catholic church calling the faithful to prayer.[3]

In 1867 a violent epidemic of yellow fever swept over South Louisiana. Hundreds of persons in the village of New Town, as New Iberia was sometimes called, died from the disease.[4] Hoping to escape infection, Uncle William Weeks, Aunt Mary, and Cousins Lily and Harriet moved from town to our plantation. A few days later the fever developed in Cousin Lily, and Father and my sister Harriet also contracted the disease. Fortunately, under the skillful treatment of Doctor Duncan, they all recovered. Around the close of 1868 my father sold his plantation to Carlos Grevemberg and in early 1869 we moved to New Iberia, into a house which stood at the corner of Washington and Center streets.

---

3. Mr. Weeks probably mentions the bell and the "tall steeple" because the steeple was constructed during his absence in North Louisiana. For a discussion of the building of this steeple, see W. R. Burke's history of St. Peter's Church, *Weekly Iberia*, December 21, 1895.

4. For an account of the 1867 epidemic, see the essay entitled "New Iberia and Yellow Fever: Epidemic and Quarantine."

New Iberia, La. From Bridge St. East
June 29th 1933

New Iberia, La. From Bridge East
June 3rd 1863

Reflections of John M. Weeks

New Iberia, La., from Bridge East, January 19, 1986

South side of Main St. from Bridge looking west, November, 1985

As I was of school age, I attended the school for boys run by R. S. Isabel, located on Washington Street between Iberia and French streets. Isabel was an excellent teacher and his pupils were well grounded in the "three R's." Among my early schoolmates were Benny Lourd, Robert Smedes, L. Paul Bryant, C. T. Cade, Overton and William Cade, Avery French, George and John Robertson, Jackson Colgin, Joseph Reynolds, William A. Marsh, E. F. Millard, Henry Fuller, J. W. Wyche, W. E. Walker, H. P. Hilliard, and many others. Between the last three boys and myself was formed a life-long friendship.

There were no public schools in the town at that time. About 1871 or 1872 a public school was being taught by a Mr. Freeman. It was located on Main Street on a lot south of the Stubinger home, and opposite the present *Weekly Iberian* building.[5] Later, the public school was kept in a one-room building on the Fontelieu property on Iberia Street, just back of what is now the Hugonin Building.[6] It was taught by Miss Mollie Hartman, who later became Mrs. Knight. The entire public school system of New Iberia, at that time, consisted of one school in one room and with one teacher. Later, the school grew in size and L. O. Hacker was the teacher for several years. About 1880 the school board of the parish consisted of W. R. Burke, secretary, Joseph A. Breaux, James A. Lee, and others. They organized public schools in the different wards as well as in the towns and built the first high school in New Iberia. It was located on Julia Street. A Mr. Harnish from Pennsylvania was the principal and a Mr. Swearingen was his assistant. The school system developed more and more up to the present time.[7] It is due to the memory of William R. Burke to add that he labored long and faithfully in this work of laying the foundation of the Iberia Parish public school system.

Among the private schools which were established in the 1870s was Mount Carmel Convent on the east side of the Teche. This school has been

---

5. The reference here is to the approximate site of 233 West Main Street. The *Weekly Iberian* was across the street in the building at 232 West Main Street, long the location of the Steinberg Fur Co.

6. The "Hugonin Building" is the structure located at 101 West Main Street. An earlier generation referred to it as the "Gouguenheim Building." A later generation of New Iberians called it the "Morgan and Lindsay Building." A future generation may refer to it as the "Hallmark Building." The school was about mid-block, behind this building. The building was built by Charles Gouguenheim in 1898 and played an important role in the downtown fire of October 1899.

7. For a more detailed discussion of the development of the New Iberia school system, see "The Story of Education in New Iberia, 1848-1983."

splendidly supported and thousands of its graduates are among the housewives, mothers, and business women of New Iberia. Also established about the same time was the Howe Institute on Washington Street, between Iberia and Providence streets. It was a blessing for the colored population of town and country.

In the 1870s New Iberia was a small, very compact town in a thinly populated countryside. Any part of the town was in easy walking distance from any other part. In winter the prairie--which began immediately where the town ended--was a veritable sportman's paradise. On the numerous ponds which watered cattle, and on the more numerous bayous in the marshes and swamps were black ducks, mallards, teal, and wood ducks. Out on Vermilion Bay were the canvasbacks which are considered to be the best flavored of the duck family. A few geese were seen at times. Jacksnipe were thick. A friend of mine once shot seven snipe in seven shots without changing his position. Deer and bear abounded in the marshes, and the baying of hounds trailing deer was sweet music to the hunter. From the country, men would ride into town having long strings of ducks tied to their saddles. These were then sold to eager housekeepers for twenty or twenty-five cents for mallards and ten cents for teals. Poultry and eggs were very cheap. An almost grown turkey could be purchased for fifty cents, hens for twenty-five cents, and a dozen eggs for six to eight cents. In summer dewberries and blackberries were abundant. These sold for twenty-five cents a water bucket. Many housekeepers made their own preserves, jams, and delicious blackberry cordials. Native cherries were also used to make cherry bounce.

In the autumn of 1873, Father placed me in school in Virginia, and I remained there until the summer of 1876. When I returned, Mr. Bagarry had established an ice factory, and thus for the first time ice was brought within the reach of everyone. Prior to that time the only supply of ice for the town was a small amount which Pierre Artigue brought in once a week from New Orleans.

I returned home just in time for the Fourth of July Celebration of 1876. It was the first time since the Civil War that New Iberia had celebrated the Fourth.[8] On that occasion a small detachment of federal troops, stationed at St. Martinville, were invited to participate, and they did. They marched in

---

8. For an account of the Centennial celebration in New Iberia on July 4, 1876, see the essay entitled "The Centennial Celebration at New Iberia, 1876."

the procession down Main Street, across the bridge, and into the Duperier woods, that is, the wooded property which was then back of what is now Dauterive Hospital.[9] This land, at the time, belonged to Mrs. Hortense Duperier and her daughter, Mrs. Athanase Hebert. The soldiers fired a salute with a small cannon. In the procession was a troop of boys dressed in white. Also the fire companies participated as well as other organizations, including Aurora Lodge of Free and Accepted Masons. Joseph H. Wise was at that time Master of the lodge.

In 1876 I was employed by the firm of A. Lehman and Company as a clerk in their three-storied store at the corner of Main Street and Church Alley. Adrien Vuillemot was the managing partner. The store adjoining was that of Hayem Gouguenheim. He employed his two nephews, Charles and Aaron, as clerks. After some years, Aaron left for Central America, but Charles remained in New Iberia. He was very thrifty so that at the time of his death he had accumulated a large fortune. In 1878 I resigned my position at Lehman's and went north again. With the exception of a short vacation spent in New Iberia about 1880, I did not return until February, 1884.

The 1870s were the Reconstruction days throughout Louisiana.[10] Blood was shed and men were killed that Reconstruction might be accomplished. Louisiana for years after the Civil War was under the control of carpetbagger governors. They were all Republicans as to politics. One faction of the party was called "Black" Republicans, because they used the newly enfranchised Negroes for their own ends. The other faction was called the "Lily Whites" and refused to use the Negro vote. The outstanding Lily White in New Iberia then was Captain John T. White, the genial father of Dr. Junius White, a prominent dentist and civic worker.[11]

---

9. Dauterive Hospital, the old Duperier home, was located at the intersection of Duperier Avenue and Marie Street (facing Marie Street) until 1973. The property was subsequently acquired by the Order of the Carmelites. The hospital moved to new facilities on North Lewis Avenue.

10. Most historians agree that Reconstruction in Louisiana ended shortly after the presidential election of 1876.

11. John T. White, a native of Troy, N. Y., was born January 4, 1842. During the Civil War, White served with the Union army in Louisiana and afterward settled in the Loreauville area as a sugar farmer. A short time thereafter he moved his farming operation to Bayside Plantation and remained there until 1894. Abandoning his agricultural interests, he moved to New Iberia where he entered the insurance

After the exciting campaign of 1876, Francis T. Nicholls became the first Democratic governor of Louisiana since the Civil War. Thus, the Reconstruction regime was turned out of office in Baton Rouge, but Iberia Parish did not succeed in turning out the local Republican administration until 1884. During these years Theodore Fontelieu was parish judge and Theogene Viator was sheriff. In 1884, Samuel McEnery was the Democratic candidate for governor, and in Iberia Parish, Fred Gates, a former resident of St. Mary Parish, ran as the Democrat candidate for judge against Fontelieu. By this time the Democrats had the powerful assistance of the Democratic state administration, and thus made a determined effort to gain control of Iberia Parish. They were further assisted in achieving that goal by P. A. Veazey, a one-time Republican, who now joined forces with the Democrats and ran as their candidate for sheriff. The resulting campaign was exceptionally bitter and concluded with the so-called Battle of Loreauville.[12]

---

business. He was the husband of Sarah Hull of Pittsfield, Illinois, and the father of Junius and Lizzie White. Captain White died on August 4, 1917. *New Iberia Enterprise*, August 11, 1917.

12. The animosity existing between Republicans and Democrats in Iberia Parish reached fever pitch in the April, 1884, election of local officials and in subsequent events during the summer and early fall of that year. Thus, it was clear to any observer that neither the April election nor the litigation which followed it had settled the issue of the political future of Iberia Parish.

During September and October, 1884, shots had been fired at Sheriff Veazey, Judge Gates, and others. Fortunately, all had escaped injury, but the incidents only increased tensions between the political factions.

Then, on November 1, 1884, three days before the congressional and presidential elections, a Republican rally was held in Loreauville on behalf of the Republican candidate for Congress from the Third District. About three hundred blacks and a number of whites attended the meeting. Among the whites were two prominent Loreauville Democrats, Joseph Guilbeau and Captain R. Bell.

According to one account, the speechmakers were confronted by a group of Loreauville citizens who asked that what they considered to be verbal abuse of the Democratic candidate, Edward J. Gay of Iberville Parish, to be toned down. During this face-to-face encounter, a shot rang out and apparently passed through the hat being worn by Guilbeau. He, in turn, immediately drew his pistol and fired. What followed was described as "a general resort to firearms."

The crowd panicked and many individuals were trampled while trying to flee the area. When the shooting ended, Guilbeau, Bell, and an undisclosed number of blacks (estimates range between six and twelve) were dead. An unknown number of the rally participants were wounded by gunfire or by the melee which accompanied it.

About the same time the Democrats had organized as part of the state militia a military company known as the Iberia Guards. A short time thereafter, a cavalry company was also formed with C. T. Cade as its captain. The first officers of the Iberia Guards were D. D. Avery, captain; A. G. Barnard, first lieutenant; E. A. Pharr, second lieutenant; A. C. Burkhart, first sergeant; Timothy Moity, second sergeant. The Guards were an artillery company having a six-pound brass cannon. For a short time after its organization, the armory was in the second story of the second building below Iberia Street on the east side of Main Street--that is, above the J. C. M. Robertson grocery store.

The present courthouse of Iberia Parish[13] was built in 1884 by the police jury which was at the time headed by Dominique Ulger Broussard, father of Silvio Broussard, the postmaster. D. U. Broussard was an able, honest, and popular man. Once the courthouse was completed, the armory of the Iberia Guards was transferred to the third story of that building.

In the campaign of 1888, Francis T. Nicholls was again the Democratic nominee for governor and James E. Mouton was the Democratic candidate for judge of this district. Former Judge Theodore Fontelieu was the Republican candidate. The whole Sixth Ward [New Iberia and its immediate environs] then voted at the courthouse. On the day of the election the Iberia Guards had been "mobilized" to prevent fraud and violence. The balloting proceeded in an orderly manner all day. After the sun had set and the ballots were counted, Mouton was overwhelmingly elected and the Demoractic candidate for sheriff, Alfred Barnard, was equally successful.

In 1886 the New Iberia Literary Club was organized. Sidney J. Heard and his brother Joseph were among the principal movers in the matter of organization. They were Western Union telegraphers and were quite popular among the townspeople. The club charter was signed by L. T. Dulany, L. A. Burgess, E. F. Millard, Douglas Duperier, George E. Sonneman, T. Lee Hebert, R. F. Broussard, and others. Some of the members of the organization were Charles

---

The "Battle of Loreauville" thus ended shortly before dark on November 1, 1884. Three days later the Democratic candidate for Congress easily won election. Local Republican leaders who had attended the rally were arrested and held for a time in guarded cells. Judging from the temperament of the times, their arrest was probably more a safety precaution than a punitive measure. For accounts of the event, see the New Orleans *Daily Picayune,* November 2, 3, 4, 1884; and the New Orleans *Times-Democrat,* November 2, 3, 4, 1884.

13. Mr. Weeks is, of course, referring to the old courthouse on Main Street.

Burgess, F. J. Mestayer, Walter J. Burke, W. G. Weeks, E. T. Weeks, and this writer.

It was a splendid organization, and undoubtedly had a beneficial effect on the young men. Rumor had it, for example, that W. J. Burke intended to study medicine before he became a member of the club and thereafter decided to become a lawyer. Who can tell what help Bob Broussard derived from this early experience?

In 1885 J. B. Lawton established the *New Iberia Enterprise,* a staunch Democratic paper, which Lawton fearlessly edited in the interests of the party and of good government. The *Enterprise* had much to do with securing for the parish and the state the good government which later did prevail. When Lawton left New Iberia in 1902 for a new home in Orlando, Florida, he sold the paper to M. W. Fisher, one of his employees. Fisher successfully edited the journal until his death.[14]

In July, 1894, the *Weekly Iberian* was established by E. F. Millard in connection with his printing business. Later, the writer was associated with Millard until going to Florida about the beginning of 1901. Both newspapers, the *Enterprise* and the *Iberian* contributed much to the advancement and prosperity of the town and country.[15]

Among those prominent in the Democratic party following the struggle of 1884 was Robert F. Broussard. "Cousan Bob," as he was called, was admitted

---

14. In 1884, J. B. Lawton, a young typesetter for J. Y. Gilmore's *Louisiana Sugar Bowl,* a New Iberia weekly newspaper published through the 1870s and into the 1880s, quit his job to start a paper of his own which would proclaim the principles of the Democratic party. Lawton was obviously motivated by the upcoming parish election (see footnote 12) which pitted the incumbent Republicans against the Redeeming Democrats.

Thus, on May 1, 1884, Lawton moved into a one-room printing shop on Bridge Street. His paper was immediately successful as a weekly. On March 1, 1902, he sold the paper to one of his employees, Melvin W. Fisher, who then served as editor for many years until his death in 1933. The paper continued as a weekly until July 6, 1947. Clarence Daigle was editor when the paper suspended publication.

15. The editors of the *Weekly Iberian* were E. F. Millard, John M. Weeks, W. Ledger Grant, A. J. Reynolds, Lawrence L. Luehm, Ralph W. Frame, J. J. McMahon, C. J. Edwards, B. F. Reno, C. D. Harper, Max Thomas, and Matt Vernon.

On August 1, 1946, the newspaper became a daily. The paper was for many years located on the southeast corner of Bridge and Burke streets. In May 1963, it moved to the southwest corner of East Main Street and South Lewis Avenue. The plant was extensively enlarged and remodeled during the summer of 1978.

E. F. Millard

John M. Weeks

J. B. Lawton

Millard's Printing House

The *Daily Iberian* offices and plant

to the Iberia bar and shortly thereafter became district attorney. He was then elected representative from Louisiana's Third Congressional District, and after serving several years in the lower house, he was elected to the U. S. Senate. During his entire life, he retained a devotion to principle and to the people of Louisiana. He was staunch opponent of the Louisiana State Lottery, and in Congress he fought many a bitter and unpopular fight on behalf of a tariff for sugar to aid the farmers of South Louisiana.

The years between 1879 and 1890 witnessed a great deal of activity for New Iberia. In 1879 Morgan's Louisiana and Texas Railroad was built through the town and connected it with Houston and New Orleans. Shortly thereafter, the Gebert Shingle Mill and the Joseph Russell shingle factory opened. Breaux, Renoudet and Broughton built, and for years operated, a sawmill just above the present Celotex factory [The Chas. Boldt Paper Mill on East Main Street]. For many years George W. Dallas was associated with them.[16] Three sash, door, and

---

16. George Dallas, a native of Plaquemine, La., was born in 1860. When about the age of 17 he came to New Iberia and found employment in a sawmill. In his early twenties

The George Dallas home shortly after construction in 1903

blind factories were established--those of O. J. Trainor, Callahan and Lewis and C. W. George. Two iron foundries were operating: Lutzenberger's and Stott's. Other industries then being operated in the town were the Erath Ice and Bottling Works, the Bagarry Ice Factory, Broussard and Decuir sawmill, Gall and Pharr sawmill, Gates Cotton Seed Oil Mill, the cotton gins of James A. Lee and Robert Brown.

About that time there appeared a change in the process of sugar making. Central factories were established instead of the small plantation sugar houses,

---

he supervised the construction of a large sawmill at Franklin. Thereafter, he became manager of the Planters' Lumber Co. in Jeanerette and the manager of the "Big Jim" sawmill in New Iberia. In addition to lumbering, Dallas had interests in Dallas and Bertram Hardware, LeBlanc and Broussard Ford agency, Iberia Jewelry Co., and the State National Bank. He was married to Bertha Bernard, a native of Vermilion Parish. In 1903, Mr. Dallas built the home at 812 East Main Street for his residence. Members of his family still reside in it. Mr. Dallas died on February 15, 1922.

and the smaller growers now sold their cane to these central factories. With the central factories came an improved method of hauling cane to the mill. Instead of the slow method of hauling with mules and carts through a sometimes endless sea of mud, the narrow-gauge railroad was introduced. The rails would extend for miles, and this system greatly aided the growing sugar industry.[17] Among the central factories of the New Iberia area were Oasis, near Cade; Segura, just north of town; Pharr [also known as Orange Grove], at Olivier; Patout [Enterprise], at Patoutville; the Gonsoulin factory at Loreauville; Monnot's; Provost's; Sanders'; Bussey's; and Delgado, at Jeanerette; and the Keystone mill near St. Martinville. In recent years, since the advent of the automobile, large trucks and trailers are used to haul cane to the mills.[18]

In 1887 the New Iberia National Bank was organized with Judge Joseph A. Breaux as president; Felix Patout, vice president; P. L. Renoudet, cashier. Prior to its organization, the only attempt at banking in the parish was something of the kind done in connection with various businesses, as for example, those of Breaux and Renoudet, James A. Lee, and Zenon Decuir. In 1889 the People's National Bank was formed by W. E. Satterfield. He was joined by John and James Gebert, the Kling brothers, the Laughlin brothers, and others. The People's Bank began business in the building opposite the courthouse.[19]

In 1897 J. Paul Suberbielle and others organized the State Bank of New Iberia which was reorganized into the State National Bank. It is located about mid-block between Julia Street and Church Alley. Finally, the First National Bank of Jeanerette was organized by Hypolite Patout, Beaulieu and Bourgeois, George Labau, Dr. Paul Cyr, and others. In 1930 banks in the United States began closing their doors, and in 1931 there was an even greater number of

---

17. One of the last, if not the last, sugar mill in the area to have the narrow-gauge railroad to haul cane was the St. John mill near St. Martinville. Cane was hauled to the mill in this fashion until the late 1950s.

18. The annotator remembers hearing stories from those who saw the narrow-gauge plantation railroads at their height that it was nearly possible, during cane season, to ride these trains across the plantations from New Iberia to Franklin.

19. This is the building on the site of 119 West Main Street. In 1963 the main offices of the bank moved to the northwest corner of Weeks and Main streets. In 1979 the main offices of the bank moved to a new building on the northeast corner of the intersection of South Lewis Avenue and Admiral Doyle Drive. For more information on this bank and other banks of New Iberia, see the essay entitled "An Historical Sketch of New Iberia's Banks."

failures. Yet, these four banks functioned as though no depression existed. It is much to the credit of the parish and its four banks [at that time] that in March, 1933, after President Roosevelt ordered the closing of all banks in the nation, out of the nine banks in the state of Louisiana which were first allowed to reopen, four of these were located in Iberia Parish.

In 1887 the New Iberia Building Association was organized. Judge Fred Gates was its first president; Mr. M. H. Lewis was its first secretary. Among other prominent in the formation of this institution were William Robertson, J. W. Callahan, and E. F. Millard. Millard was for many years the president, and W. G. Weeks was secretary for over fifty years.

These reminiscences would not be complete without mention of the three immense salt mines within the border of the parish. The Avery Salt Mine is the oldest. In later years the salt mines on Jefferson and Weeks islands were developed, and train loads of salt were removed from these mines each day.

A word must also be said for the good cooks of Iberia. Nowhere is there so rich a variety of food as in South Louisiana, and especially in the New Iberia area. There is always something new to delight the palate.

First St. Peter's Church with its unusually tall steeple

VI

Reminiscences of the '60s and '70s

by
Louis Paul Bryant

edited and annotated
by
Glenn R. Conrad

I was born in the town of St. Martinville, but was brought to New Iberia by my parents at the age of three, and it was in New Iberia and environs that I grew to manhood.

My mother, Hermance de Laureal, was a native of Guadeloupe, a French possession. Her parents died when she was quite young, and she was sent to Paris by her brothers. She was placed in the Convent Ste-Clothilde where she remained until she finished her education at the age of eighteen. Her brother, Dr. David de Laureal, a graduate of the College Louis Le Grand, in Paris, had, previous to the completion of my mother's education, emigrated to the United States and had located in New Orleans for a while and from there had gone to St. Martinville, which was generally known as *le petit Paris*, because of its exceptional culture and gayety. After my mother's graduation, she came to live with Dr. de Laureal in St. Martinville.

My father was a Virginian, a native of what is now the state of West Virginia; and through Mr. [Francois] St. Marc Darby, who, together with his family, was a frequent visitor at White Sulphur Springs, he was induced to come to Louisiana. My father was a Methodist by birth, rearing, and tradition, but when he came to Louisiana, through his contacts and through the persuasion of the

Darby family, he joined the Catholic church. Mr. St. Marc Darby became his godfather and Mrs. Dubuclet, his godmother. From the time that my father came to Louisiana until after the close of the Civil War, he was identified, in one way or another, with the Darby family. My father and mother were married in 1856.[1] At that time my father had a very meager knowledge of French and my mother a meager knowledge of English; hence, this courtship must have been beset with linguistic difficulties.

A short time after reaching St. Martinville, my mother engaged in teaching French in a private school then existing in that town, under the principalship of Mrs. St. Laurent. In or about the year 1861, my mother, together with Mrs. Leonce de la Croix and Mrs. Emile Soulier, established a school in New Iberia in a dwelling which stood at the corner of Main and Swain streets and which, in recent years, was demolished. Incidentally, this dwelling was said to have been one of the oldest in New Iberia.[2] This school was succeeded by another school for young ladies which occupied the dwelling still existing and presently known as the Howe Institute on Railroad Avenue [Washington St.]. The teachers at this school were Mrs. Dr. de Rene and her daughter Alphonsine, who had come to New Iberia from one of the northern states, Mrs. Emile Soulier, Miss Henrietta Andrus, subsequently Mrs. John N. Pharr, and my mother. A German, known as Professor Muller, who lived to a ripe old age and who died in New Iberia in the early eighties, was the professor of music. English French, Latin, and music were taught. This school was very successful until 1867, when a yellow-fever epidemic swept over this section and Mrs. de Rene and her daughter left for California. About this time, Miss Henrietta Andrus became Mrs. John N. Pharr, and thus the school passed out of existence.[3] Sometime thereafter Mrs. de la Croix left for Costa Rica where she continued to reside until her death. My mother continued, however, to conduct a school of

---

1. Louis Paul Bryant's father was Martin Bryant, the son of William Bryant and Minerva Eicher. Martin Bryant married Hermance Coudroy de Laureal, the daughter of Marie-Rene-Jules Coudroy de Laureal and Angele Augustine Deymar, on April 8, 1856, in St. Peter's Church, New Iberia (see St. Peter's Marriage Records, vol. 1, p. 189). This family should not be confused with the family of Judge Paul Briant of St. Martinville.
Louis Paul Bryant died in 1935 and is buried in Rosehill Cemetery.

2. This house is discussed is the essay entitled "A Narrative of Events Connected with the Early Settlement of New Iberia." See footnote 5 of that essay.

3. Henrietta Clara Andrus, the daughter of Louis Andrus of Opelousas, was born November 6, 1836. She was the wife of John Newton Pharr. She died January 17, 1903.

her own in New Iberia until 1890, when she went to New Orleans to reside. She died in 1893; and I pause to pay tribute to her sacred memory.

There are still a number of prominent citizens of New Iberia, men and women, who at different times, were her pupils and who have repeatedly given expression to their admiration of her.

I also recall another school for girls that existed in New Iberia in the late sixties [1860s] and that there was one conducted by Mrs. Sarah Cade Smedes. I do not recall her assistant or assistants, but I remember her as a woman of fine personality, education, and culture. She was a half-sister of Captain C. T. Cade, who came to the front in political affairs in Iberia Parish in about 1884 and who exercised for a long time a dominating political influence in Iberia Parish and South Louisiana.[4]

The schools for boys that were conducted in New Iberia during my boyhood and early manhood were the following: one under Professor R. S. Isabel, which was located on Railroad Avenue [Washington St.], opposite the DeValcourt homestead.[5] This school was largely patronized, for Professor Isabel was regarded as a very erudite teacher. There was another under the principalship of Professor P. O. Lydon, and this was located in the building known as the Odd Fellows' Home, situated where the post office now stands.[6] For a time Judge Thomas Balch, the father of Mrs. L. O. Hacker, conducted a successful school

---

4. Charles Taylor Cade, the son of Robert Cade (a native of South Carolina), was born in Lafayette Parish on September 24, 1849. At the age of 14, he served as a Confederate scout during the Civil War. After the war, he attended Spring Hill College and the University of the South. In 1878, he married Elizabeth Ker, the daughter of David Ker and Sarah Brownson. Cade's interests were quite varied. He superintended the building of Sterling sugar house in Franklin. A resident of Iberia Parish for many years, he served on the parish police jury and was elected sheriff for two terms. Upon retiring from politics, he moved to High Island, Texas, where he raised cattle and where he built the Seaview Hotel. He died March 6, 1912, in Mineral Wells, Texas. His wife died on Christmas Day, 1920. The couple was survived by two daughters and a son.

5. The Devalcourt residence was the large home now situated about mid-block between Iberia and French streets on the south side of St. Peter St. The house was later acquired by Dr. J. W. K. Shaw. When Mr. Devalcourt died in 1863, the description of his residence property in the succession inventory states that it fronted on Main St., indicating that St. Peter Street had not yet been put through from Iberia to French sts. See St. Martin Estate 1781.

Indeed, St. Peter St. between Iberia and French was opened in June, 1870. See Iberia Conveyance Book 2, pp. 220, 222, 224.

6. Reference is, of course, to the old post office at 300 East Main Street.

in a building where the Elks Theater Building now stands.[7] In the middle part of the seventies [1870s], as I recall, Mr. Theodore Minvielle with an assistant, whose name I do not recall, conducted a school in a building which stood where the present Catholic presbytery was recently constructed.[8]

In the late seventies, a college under the auspices of the Catholic church was established, which had a successful career for a number of years. This college was located on what is now the property of Mrs. Joseph P. Russell on East Main Street.[9]

The Mt. Carmel Convent was established in the latter part of 1872 and has since that time been an outstanding educational institution in New Iberia.

When I left New Iberia for Texas in 1881, the public schools were just being established along permanent lines, and many of the most prominent citizens of the parish were identifying themselves with them and were giving them cooperation and assistance. In a few years the public schools largely supplanted the private schools.[10]

My first vivid recollections are connected with the occupation of New Iberia and its environs by the Federal army. A detachment of this army was camped near the Darby Plantation, where my mother and I were living; my father was, at that time, in the service of the Confederacy in North Louisiana.

I recall that the Union soldiers treated us with kindness and consideration and there is one incident that I vividly recall. A Union soldier had appropriated a leather saddle that belonged to me. Upon his captain learning of it, he sent for him and ordered him to return my saddle. I do not recall any acts of depredation committed by the Union army on the Darby Plantation. After the close of the war, my parents moved into New Iberia, where my adolescence was uneventful and my experiences were only those usual to a poor, growing

---

7. The Elks Theater was located on the northwest corner of Main and Fisher streets. It was constructed in 1907 and was demolished in 1940.

8. Early in 1874 it was announced that Minvielle would open a school in Jeanerette in the home of Paul Druilhet (*Louisiana Sugar Bowl*, February 5, 1874).
This is the rectory located on the southeast corner of Iberia and St. Peter streets.

9. For additional information on the home site, see footnote 102 of the essay entitled "Some Facts and Traditions about New Iberia." For mention of Holy Cross school, see the essay entitled "The Story of Education in New Iberia."

10. For a complete discussion of education in New Iberia, see *ibid.*

boy in a small, poor, and remote community, greatly impoverished as a result of the war.

I was always socially inclined and when about seventeen, I began taking a lively interest in all social activities in the community and continued so identified from that time until my departure in 1881. Among my contemporaries and friends in the city of New Iberia were

Rufus Colgin	Henry Palfrey	Octave Renoudet
Jackson Colgin	John Weeks	Embry Tolson
Robert Smedes	Emelius F. Millard	Ernest Darby
Adolph Mestayer	Michel Hebert	James Vidrine
William Marsh	Henry L. Fuller	Dayton DeValcourt
Robert Olivier	Peebles Hilliard	James W. Wyche
Louis Indest	Joinville Hebert	Joe Reynolds
William Walker	Beverly Campbell	

David Ker and his family, including his sons, Brownson and Willie, came to reside in New Iberia about 1879, as I recall, and became identified with the social life of the community. There were others who were also identified with the social life of New Iberia, but those whom I have mentioned are the ones with whom I had the closest contacts and who generally constituted a group to be found connected with social events.

There was a great deal of visiting at the homes, where dancing and singing were engaged in, but chaperonage, by parents or elder relatives of the young ladies, was always the order of the day. All-day picnics and fishing parties were very popular and were generally arranged for weeks in advance. The only dance hall in New Iberia was one operated by Mrs. Octave Boutte, generally known as Mrs. "Gugueche" Boutte. Her place was located at the corner of Julia and Hacker streets.

Occasionally this dance hall would be rented for private affairs, but on every Saturday and Sunday night, Mrs. Gugueche conducted public dances. The music for these dances was furnished by a trio consisting of Joe LeBlanc, a fiddler, and another fiddler, whose name I do not recall, and an accordionist, whose name I do not recall. These musicians were afforded a bandstand in a corner of the ballroom and this bandstand was nothing more than a large four-posted bed with the mattresses removed and a platform substituted. This bed with its canopy furnished quite an imposing bandstand. Refreshments were generally sold and consisted principally of gumbo, coffee, and anisette. On these occasions, I remember, for Mrs. Gugueche's amusement, the dancers would join in singing a doggerel, a snatch of which is as follows:

> Mo' cher cousin; mo' cher cousine;
> No' l'aime la cuisine
> Mo' manger bien; mo' boi du vin;
> Ca pas couter moin a rien

Mrs. Gugueche was a kindly, cheerful, and deserving old soul and was universally esteemed.

It was also the custom for the young people to attend vesper services at the Catholic church on Sunday afternoon, and thereafter the boys and girls would pair off and walk down East Main Street, which was then known as Lovers' Lane. These walks would extend no further than to a bridge which spanned a large canal at a point where Ann Street now intersects East Main. This bridge was called "Lovers' Bridge." These walks did not extend any further because it was unwritten law that the young ladies had to be back at their homes by sundown. I will not undertake to name all of the songs, nor do I recall all of the popular songs of the era to which I am referring, but there comes back to my memory a few outstanding ones which I find myself, every now and then, humming. There were the following: "Il va partir et il n'a jamais connu une larme" (This was Joinville Hebert's favorite and he sang it with great feeling and pathos); songs from the French operas and some of Thomas Moore's and Robert Burns' poems rendered to music; "Juanita"; "The Mocking Bird"; "In the Gloaming"; "Old Black Joe"; "Shoo Fly Don't Bother Me"; and "My Love is Like a Little Bird."

The girls of that era pass in mental review before me and in memory's eye; they are beautiful, winsome, and charming as of yore. I will not undertake to mention names, as my memory may play me a trick and I may omit the names of some of those fair contemporaries of mine, which might render me chargeable of invidious distinctions.

Horse racing was very popular; and Iberia Parish boasted of possessing fine imported racers from Kentucky. I remember a famous race between a horse belonging to Mr. William F. Weeks and another belonging to Devezin Romero (or Dorcellie Romero). This race attracted a great deal of interest and was attended by a very large crowd. Colonel Brown, who was the owner at the time of Keystone Plantation, was present in company with Miss Lily Weeks, who became Mrs. Gilbert L. Hall, the mother of our young friend Weeks Hall. As the race started, whether due to the tension produced by it, or other causes, Colonel Brown, while seated next to Miss Weeks, suddenly collapsed and died. This caused considerable gloom over the community as this erstwhile enemy had become socially popular in New Iberia. Colonel Brown was a Northern man and had been an officer in the Union Army.[11]

From the late sixties [1860s] until the advent of the railroad, in 1879, marked an era of luxurious steamboats plying the Teche.[12] I recall the *Minnie Avery* as one of these luxurious boats. It was owned by the firm of Price, Hine, and Tupper, who maintained a commission house in New Orleans, and who had the mail contract from Morgan City to New Iberia by boat and thence by stagecoach from New Iberia as far west as San Antonio, Texas. The Price of this firm was the father of Andrew Price, who represented the Third District in Congress for a great number of years and whose domicile at the time was in St. Mary. Mr. Hine of this firm was T. D. Hine of Franklin, the grandfather of my highly esteemed friend, Mrs. Porteus R. Burke, and the Mr. Tupper of the firm resided in New Orleans and was a relative of the Weeks family. Mr. H. B. Smith, the father of my good friend, Henry L. Smith, was their resident agent in New Iberia. In the course of time, the mail contract was given to Captain John N. Pharr, who from thence operated several boats, plying between Morgan City and New Iberia.[13]

11. Bryant's memory partially failed him in this instance. The race, which occurred on September 28, 1878, was between a horse owned by Dudley Avery and one owned by Devezin Romero. Romero's horse won the race.

During the race, Colonel William H. Brown of Keystone Plantation (near the present-day lock of that name on Bayou Teche) collapsed of an apparent stroke. He was in the company of William Weeks and his two daughters. Removed to the Weeks home, Brown, later the same day, suffered a second attack which resulted in his death. Drs. Colgin and Duperier were in attendance.

Colonel Brown was a native of York, Pennsylvania, who had served in the Federal army during the Civil War. After the war, he bought a plantation between New Iberia and St. Martinville and named it "Keystone" in honor of Pennsylvania, the "Keystone State."

At the time of his residence near New Iberia, Colonel Brown was a widower. He was also childless. Last rites for him were conducted in the Church of the Epiphany (*Louisiana Sugar Bowl*, October 3, 1878).

12. For a more detailed discussion of the steamboat era and New Iberia, see the essay entitled "New Iberia's Steamboat Days."

13. This statement may be somewhat misleading. During the 1860s and into the 1870s, the mail did go by stagecoach from New Iberia to Texas. In the mid-70s, however, the mail

There were also packets, or round boats, plying between New Orleans and New Iberia that were veritable floating palaces and the last word in luxury for the times. One of these boats, known as the *Ingomar,* I recall particularly as it was one of the largest and the most luxuriously fitted boats that ever navigated the Teche. It contained even spacious quarters for dancing. I always connect the *Ingomar* with its captain, P. E. Burke, a brother of James L. Burke and William R. Burke. Captain Burke was a veritable Chesterfield, handsome, always immaculately dressed and exceedingly popular with the fair sex. He was over six feet in height, slender, and erect; and, as I recall him, he had a most attractive personality. The trip on the *Ingomar* from New Iberia to Morgan City was regarded in the nature of a social event. With the advent of the railroad in 1879, Captain Burke became identified with it as a general agent, and so remained up to the time of his death in the early eighties.[14]

In the early seventies and throughout the seventies, at intervals, travelling theatrical companies, circuses, and showboats would visit New Iberia; and, of course, these visits were regarded as events in the community. Under the influence of these visits, a dramatic society was organized in New Iberia known as the Jefferson Dramatic Club (so named because the great actor and noble character Joseph Jefferson had in 1870 become identified with Iberia by purchasing Orange Island, now Jefferson Island, and his name and fame added to the enthusiasm of our local talent), and on frequent occasions plays were produced under the auspices of this club. The local actors were generally L. O. Hacker and his brothers, Numa and Charles, Jackson Colgin, Rufus Colgin, Joinville Hebert, and few others whom I do not distinctly recall. The ladies of the casts were, occasionally, Misses Alice and Kate Smith, Miss Sarah Balch (Mrs. L. O. Hacker), Miss Mattie DeValcourt, Miss Johnny Mitcheltree, Miss Sarah DeValcourt, and others whom I do not recall.[15]

The active members of the medical profession in New Iberia in the late sixties and in the seventies were, as I recall, Dr. Robert Hilliard, who died in

---

route was changed and the Texas mail went by boat from Morgan City to Galveston. For editorial comment about the mail service, see the *Louisiana Sugar Bowl,* October 31-December 26, 1878.

14. Burke also served as clerk of court of Iberia Parish from 1868 to 1872.

15. For a more detailed discussion of theatrics and other entertainment in New Iberia, see the essay entitled "Sports, Entertainment and Recreation in New Iberia."

the yellow-fever epidemic of 1867; Dr. William Walker [Dr. Hilliard's brother-in-law], Dr. Henry Stubinger; Dr. Vermentoir; Dr. Abadie; Dr. Alfred Duperier; Dr. Frederick Duperier (who abandoned the active practice of medicine because of planting interests in the seventies); Dr. Gustave Blanchet; Dr. George Colgin; and Dr. Gaston Mestayer.

In the late sixties and the early seventies, the leading mercantile firms of New Iberia were Vidrine and Hebert and Mistrot and Decuir, Mistrot and Decuir (Ulger Decuir) in the late sixties went out of business, and thereafter the firm of Soulier and Decuir (Zenon Decuir) became established and prominent.[16] The firm of DeValcourt and Taylor was also a leading mercantile firm in the early and middle sixties. After Mr. DeValcourt's death in 1863, John J. Taylor of the firm, who was much beloved in the community, continued in business for some years and then in the seventies became a member of the firm of Lehman, Hayem, and Taylor, which for a number of years did a very large mercantile business at the corner of East Main and Church Alley. There were other mercantile firms in New Iberia, but I am making reference to the largest ones existing in the sixties and seventies. I do not remember Mr. [John] DeValcourt, of the firm of DeValcourt and Taylor, very well, as I was quite young when he died, but I remember, as I grew up, that his memory was very much revered in New Iberia.[17]

When the parish of Iberia was created in 1868, the upstairs in one of the buildings in the Duperier Block [between Bridge and Iberia streets] was for a time used as the courthouse; thereafter, the upstairs of a two-story building, situated next to where the Masonic building now stands, was converted into a courthouse. The courthouse there remained until 1884 when the present one [the old courthouse] was constructed. During all of the seventies, there was a great deal of political activity in New Iberia. The Republicans were well entrenched in power with a considerable white and with an overwhelming Negro vote in the parish, but the Democratic party, though a minority, possessed aggressive and determined leadership. At times, very tense situations would arise

---

16. Mistrot and Decuir did not go out of business in the sixties. It was the downtown fire of June 1870 that destroyed their building (corner of Julia and Main streets) and its contents.

17. John Devalcourt died January 2, 1863, leaving his widow Sarah Marsh and several children, Alexander, John Taylor, Elizabeth, Charles Dayton, Mary Margaret, Martha Hamilton, and Sarah Abby. See St. Martin Estate 1781.

The Mistrot House, circa 1859

and strong enmities resulted.[18] In the late sixties and throughout the seventies, the two outstanding and uncompromising Democratic leaders in New Iberia were D. U. Broussard, affectionately known as "Gachon" and James L. Burke. In addition to their political activities, they were always identified with everything connected with the life of New Iberia and were affectionately regarded as friends, counselors, and guides by most of the population. These two were close friends and inseparable in their personal relations and, as the fates would have it, they both died in a comparatively few months of each other in the early eighties.

There were, of course, a number of other men prominently identified with the life and activities of the community, and I will undertake to mention some of the outstanding ones, as I recall them. William Robertson, a highly polished gentleman, much beloved and a sage in the community, a West Point graduate, and an ex-army officer, who located in New Iberia in the forties [1840s];[19] William F. Weeks, prominent as a sugar planter, who maintained his residence in New Iberia; A. B. Henshaw, an Englishman by birth, who had married a Miss

---

18. For a detailed discussion of the beginnings of Iberia Parish, see the essay entitled "New Iberia Becomes the Parish Seat."

19. William Robertson married Eliza Ann Marsh, the daughter of John C. Marsh.

Marsh of New Iberia, and who was mayor of New Iberia before the Civil War and again in the sixties and early seventies; Jasper Gall, noted for his public spirit and general kindness; Judge Theodore Fontelieu, who was the leader of the Republican forces in the parish of Iberia, despised by the Democrats, but he was personally popular; Emanuel J. Etie, who was the first parish judge of Iberia; Thomas J. Allison, who succeeded Etie as parish judge; Zenon Decuir, P. A. Veazey, John J. Taylor, William R. Burke, John Lamperez, William Lourd, and John Emmer; these were always interested in all public matters: James A. Lee, who located in New Iberia long before the Civil War, always identified himself with the progress of the town; J. Y. Gilmore, who owned and edited a splendid paper known as the *Louisiana Sugar Bowl* throughout the seventies; Dr. Alfred Duperier and Dr. Frederick Duperier. The creation of the parish was said to have been largely due to Dr. Alfred Duperier, who was a close friend of Governor Warmoth, during whose administration the act creating Iberia Parish was passed by the legislature. Dr. Alfred Duperier was a forceful man, very progressive and up to the time of his death enjoyed the reputation of eminence in the medical profession. His brother, Dr. Frederick Duperier, was also a forceful, well-educated man, who exercised a considerable influence in public affairs. There were a number of other citizens who lived in the environs of New Iberia and were, more or less, identified with its activities and with its life and I will mention a few of them. Colonel E. P. Olivier, who resided on his plantation now known as Orange Grove, and who was a man of strong personality and of great personal charms; Adolph Segura, who resided on Spanish Lake, a man of ripe education and of solid judgment whose opinion and advice were generally sought (he was proficient in Spanish and while attending a college in Kentucky was made the Spanish teacher on the faculty); Major James Fletcher Wyche, the father of my good friend James W. Wyche, who located on the Belmont Plantation in the late fifties, and who always took a live and positive interest in public affairs and who was a fervent Democrat. The names that I have mentioned are not to be regarded as constituting exclusively all of the prominent men of the era to which I am referring, but are those that I recall most vividly. It is probable that I have omitted some names deserving of mention for having given of themselves and of their personalities to the making of New Iberia and Iberia Parish.

In the late seventies, Judge Fred Gates and his nephew, Alfred Barnard, moved from Franklin to New Iberia and established a cotton oil mill.[20] In

---

20. Gates' oil mill was located just off Prairie Avenue, near the bayou. The mill was

eighty-four Judge Gates became district judge, succeeding Judge Theodore Fontelieu. Judge Gates was thus the first Democratic judge after the Civil War in the district then consisting of Iberia and St. Martin parishes.

As I have heretofore stated, I left New Iberia in 1881, and at that time younger men in New Iberia and its environs were forging into the front in leadership. Among these were Captain C. T. Cade, Alfred Barnard, E. A. Pharr, George M. Robertson, Alphonse Landry, Albert Landry, Charles E. Smedes, Albert Decuir, Octave Romero and J. B. Lawton (I cannot undertake to mention others who became active and prominent after my departure).

After the creation of Iberia Parish and throughout most of the seventies, the lawyers constituting the local bar were R. S. Perry, Joseph A. Breaux, P. L. Renoudet (a young man at the time, who in after years became an outstanding financial and industrial figure in New Iberia),[21] Octave Delahoussaye, Robert Belden, Julius Robertson, William Schwing, and W. B. Merchant. Robert Belden was the first Republican district attorney and he was succeeded by W. B. Merchant, also a Republican, as district attorney. Merchant remained in that office until the election fo 1884. In course of time, Joseph A. Breaux became state superintendent of education and later became a justice of the [state] supreme court, eventually serving as chief justice of that body. R. S. Perry became a justice of the court of appeals. The orator of the group was Octave Delahoussaye, who was, both an English and a French scholar, and who was unusually gifted as a public speaker.

The first sheriff of Iberia Parish was George Stubinger, son of Dr. Henry Stubinger. A short time after he had been in office, he was killed by a man

---

completed in late 1878. It housed a cotton gin and press and corn mill. Initially, the mill was designed to make fertilizer; however, in time it produced cooking oil and soap.

21. P. Laurent Renoudet was born near Loreauville on March 12, 1848. He was the son of Antoine Renoudet and Virginie Dutel. In 1871 Renoudet and Joseph A. Breaux formed a law partnership. They further cooperated in the establishment of New Iberia National Bank in 1887. Renoudet remained an officer of the bank until his death. With Breaux and Victor Aucoin, Renoudet established the Iberia Cypress Co. He was also responsible for founding the wholesale grocery company that became known as Renoudet and Dietlein.

Renoudet married twice. His first marriage was to Cecile Duperier, daughter of Dr. Alfred Duperier. They were the parents of Alfred; Anthony; Joseph; Marie, who married Fritz Dietlein; and Mathilde, who married L. A. Walet. A son, Laurent, preceded his father in death. Mr. Renoudet married a second time to Lucille Folse of Napoleonville. He died August 18, 1917. *New Iberia Enterprise*, August 25, 1917.

whom he was endeavoring to arrest. An enraged citizenry dealt summarily with this murderer, and he was hanged, a short time after perpetrating the deed, from the limb of an oak tree on the bayou at a point back of the present courthouse [the old courthouse on Main St.]. Sheriff Stubinger was, at the time of his death, a young man, but exceedingly popular. Some few years thereafter, Dr. Stubinger died and the remaining members of his family returned to Baltimore from whence Dr. Stubinger and his family had originally come.[22]

The principal hotels in New Iberia during the seventies were Serret's Hotel, which was situated on the bank of Bayou Teche at the foot of what is now known as Serret Alley (this was the largest hotel); the Two Lions Hotel, which was situated on Main Street at a point about where the State National Bank is now located (this hotel was rather an attractive two-story structure of the Spanish type of architecture with a patio in the center); and the Pointis Hotel, situated on Lower Main Street at a point about opposite the building presently occupied by the Ford agency (this hotel consisted of two, two-story frame buildings erected close to each other and connected by galleries). All three hotels mentioned were regarded as having splendid cuisine. At an earlier time, there was also the Decourt Hotel which stood about where the Estorge Drug Store now stands and which was noted for its cuisine and for the affability of it owners, Joe Decourt.[23]

New Iberia during the period of which I am writing possessed quite a few industries, but depended largely on agriculture and cattle for its support. It was,

---

22. George Stubinger was not the first sheriff of Iberia Parish. That honor went to James Griswell who was sheriff for about six months in 1868-1869. The man accused of murdering Sheriff Stubinger was lynched from the bayou bridge. For an account of the Stubinger murder and its aftermath, see Glenn R. Conrad, "The Murder of Sheriff Stubinger," *Attakapas Gazette*, XIV (1979), 43.

Dr. Henry Stubinger was a native of Canada. He resided in New Iberia from the 1840s until he moved to Maryland in 1875. He died there the following year.

23. The Estorge Drug Store was located at 128 East Main, or about midway between Julia Street and Church Alley. During the remodeling and expansion of the main offices of the State National Bank in 1975, the building formerly housing Estorge's was incorporated into the bank.

Other hotels in New Iberia over the years were the Bazus Hotel on East Main between Weeks and Julia streets (the building still stands at 210 East Main and is quite possibly the oldest extant structure in the commercial district of Main Street), the Eureka Hotel (on the southeast corner of Fisher and Main streets, it burned in 1931), the Teche Hotel which has been located at 824 West Main for many years; the Evangeline Hotel on Iberia Street, about mid-block between St. Peter and Washington streets; Paul's Hotel (now the

Hotel Frederic, 1915 (above) and 1923 (below)

Hotel Frederic in April 1972 (above); during demolition, June, 1975

The former annex of Hotel Frederic was converted into the Francois Office Building in 1976

Royal Hotel and Motel at 213 West Main St.)
    By far the largest of New Iberia's hotels was the Hotel Frederic, located at 207 West Main. The Frederic was built by Felix Patout in 1913. The architect was W. F. Nolan of New Orleans and the contractor was Eugene Guillot of New Iberia. The largest hotel in the area when it opened on November 13, 1913, the Frederic soon became a headquarters for salesmen and various commodity buyers.
    In 1913 the hotel boasted two rooms with private bath, but business was such that soon forty rooms had complete bath facilities. Prices, then as now, reflected type of accommodation. A room without bath was $1.50 per night. A room with bath was $3.00.
    Anticipating that the hotel would be a headquarters for salesmen, there was a large showroom for their displays. In addition to this convenience the hotel was steam heated and included an elevator. Incorporated into the main building was a large dining room and a handsome bar.

in the steamboat era, quite an important distributing point for freight for the neighboring parishes; and it was not an unusual sight to see many carts and wagons drawn by oxen conveying freight from the steamboat warehouses to remote points. This fact added somewhat to the commerce of the town.

The chief industries consisted of two sawmills, one first owned and operated by Jasper Gall and then by Gall and Pharr (E. A. Pharr) and the other owned and operated by D. U. Broussard and then by the firm of Broussard and Decuir (Albert Decuir). In the early seventies, F. S. Lutzenberger, the grandfather of my esteemed young friend, Emile Simon, moved to New Iberia and established a foundry and machine shop, which is now quite an extensive plant, known as the New Iberia Foundry and Machine Shop.[24] Mr. Lutzenberger became very popular in the community and always enjoyed the confidence and respect of the people. There were also a few cotton gins and a few brickyards. In the very late seventies, Judge F. L. Gates, as I have stated, established a cotton oil mill.

I recall with a sense of amusement an experience which occurred to me wherein I displayed a ludicrous lack of judgment through an overwrought sense of duty. It was when Kellogg, the then Republican governor of Louisiana, had ordered a military detachment to St. Martinville to overawe Colonel Alcibiades de Blanc and his followers who were endeavoring to redeem St. Martin Parish.

After World War II, the hotel was expanded (the expansion wing being the basic structure for the present Francois Building), the architect then was Owen Southwell. When the hotel closed in 1972, it had 128 air-conditioned rooms.

Among those inseparably associated with memories of the Frederic Hotel are Frederic Patout and his wife Yvonne, later Mrs. Owen Southwell: clerks, such as Clarence Louviere, Dudley LeMaire, John Upton, and Louis Dugas; switchboard operators and clerks Betty Labauve and Louise Blanchet; accountant Marcus de Blanc; chef Jack Gurin; dining room managers Fred Mestayer and Blanche Hulin; bar managers Mayo Bessan and Dominic Bonin; housekeepers Lena Lemaire and Mrs. E. David; bell captain Jack Color; and bellmen Louis Henry, Robert Landry, and Morris Chapman.

In 1976 this landmark passed from the New Iberia scene, but it and the people associated with it will long be remembered by New Iberians and others.

Among motor hotels, the Teche Motel at 1830 East Main Street is by far the dean of New Iberia motels. Other existing motels are the Beau Sejour Motel on West Main; Sugarland Motor Lodge at 1211 West Main; Dixie Motel at 1506 Center St.; Acadiana Motor Lodge and Holiday Inn, both located on U. S. 90, just outside the city limits. The Best Western, on Center St., is also just outside the city limits. Motels of the past were Deare's, on the street of that name; Kiper's, just outside the west city limits of New Iberia on the old U. S. 90, now La. 182; and Colonial Courts, in the 1700 block of East Main Street.

24. The brick building that still stands on Jane Street near its intersection with Corinne St. was part of the Foundry complex.

military detachment landed in New Iberia from a steamboat and then marched on to St. Martinville. For some reason, which I cannot recall, armed guards were hastily summoned by Mayor James L. Burke and placed at different strategic points in New Iberia. I was assigned as a guard at the courthouse with instructions from Mayor Burke not to allow anyone to enter the building. I was armed with a double-barrelled shotgun. After being on duty a little while, Allen Hayes, who was then sheriff and whose office was in the courthouse, undertook to enter the building. I halted him and told him that he could not enter. He thereupon reminded me that he was sheriff and that he had a right to enter the building. Notwithstanding, I warned him that my instructions were not to allow anyone to enter. Hayes paused for a minute, then turned and left. I subsequently learned that he had gone to Mayor Burke and protested against my conduct. Mayor Burke laughed heartily over this little incident and it became a joke. At the same time, however, I was complimented for my determination to carry out orders as were given to me. I might add that I had such respect and affection for James Burke that his word to me was law.

In connection with the military detachment going to St. Martinville, as above mentioned, I recall that Colonel Alcibiades de Blanc and General Declouet were arrested and brought to New Orleans to be tried, either by the federal court, or by a military court, because of their determined stand against carpetbagger domination of St. Martin Parish. When they reached New Orleans, they were welcomed by thousands of citizens at the river landing, and a procession was formed to accompany them. In the enthusiasm of the moment, an effort was made to unhitch the horses from the carriage in which the distinguished prisoners had been seated and to drag the carriage by willing hands in the midst of the procession. Whereupon Colonel de Blanc leaped from the carriage and exclaimed: "Non, citoyens, remettez les chevaux; votre fardeau et notre fardeau sont déjà assez lourds et pénibles." ("No, citizens, put back the horses; your burden and our burden are heavy and lamentable enough.")

They were ultimately released and on their return they landed from a boat in New Iberia and were escorted by a large number of citizens to St. Martinville, where a public celebration was held in the nature of a grand barbecue, with speech making and general felicitations.[25]

---

25. For an account of these events, see Suzy Shea, "A Man for the People: Alcibiades DeBlanc and the St. Martinville Insurrection of 1873," *Attakapas Gazette*, XIV (1979), 3-10.

Another amusing experience that I recall was one which occurred to me on an Easter Sunday in the early seventies. Easter was a gala day in New Iberia; it was a day which, aside from its religious significance was the occasion of general gayety. On that day it was the custom to allow the black women, members of the Roman Catholic church, to sell, during the entire day, exclusively to the white people of the congregation, gumbo, cakes, pralines, and coffee at tables or booths immediately in front of St. Peter's Church. I do not recall whether this was for the benefit of the Church or for the private benefit of the sellers. Easter was also the day on which the pews of the Catholic church were auctioned off for the next ensuing year and these auctions drew large numbers of bidders, as the congregation was a very large one. On that certain Easter Sunday, I was asked by an old lady friend to attend the auction of the church pews and to bid as much as $30.00 for a pew in a certain section of the church. This I did, causing others to pay more for their pews than they had expected to pay, and thereby causing irritation. My bidding continued until an irate group came to me and told me that I was in collusion with the priest to raise the amount of the bids for the pews and that they would abstain from bidding. I assured them that it was not the case; thereupon, I made a bid of $30.00 on the next offering which proved to be the only bid. I had, then, to go hurriedly to my principal to get the money to demonstrate my good faith. Nevertheless, I can recall vividly the indignation that prevailed.

In 1879, I began the study of law in the office of William F. Schwing, but I did not pursue my law studies without many interruptions. In 1881, an opportunity presented itself for me to go to Texas to teach in a school in Laredo on the Mexican border. I continued my legal studies and was admitted as a member

Felix Patout
Businessman - Banker

of the Texas bar in 1883. I remained in Texas until 1895, when I returned to Louisiana and was elected to the legislature of Louisiana from New Orleans in 1896.

The Felix Patout home shortly after the turn of the century.

VII

*New Iberia and Yellow Fever: Epidemic and Quarantine**

by
Glenn R. Conrad

The summer of 1867 was not unusually disagreeable. Temperatures and rainfall were typical for that season along the Gulf Coast. Nevertheless, for New Iberians, the summer of '67 would be, to parody Shakespeare, the summer of their discontent.

The Civil War had ended in April, 1865, but there was no quick return to normalcy. To begin, it had taken three, four months or more for the tired, sick men in gray to trudge back to their homes in the Teche country. Then, after recuperating, they had houses to repair, barns to rebuild, acres of weeds to till where sugarcane, corn, and cotton had grown abundantly only a few summers before. Thus, even though dazed by recent events, bewildered by seemingly insurmountable problems, and anxious about the future, these veterans of

---

*Information for this essay was gleaned from several sources: New Orleans *Daily Picayune;* the Baton Rouge *Triweekly Advocate;* the *New Orleans Republican;* and the Opelousas *Courier.* Unfortunately for posterity, there is no extant newspaper from New Iberia for the year 1867.

The account of the quarantine of New Iberia in 1878 was gathered from the *Louisiana Sugar Bowl.* The major source of information on the 1906 case of yellow fever in New Iberia is the *Weekly Iberian.*

the Valley Campaign, Shiloh, Bisland, Port Hudson, and Mansfield, took up their task of creating a new life in that summer after Appomattox.

Upon reaching home, few veterans had time to plant a crop which could be harvested before first frost. Even if there had been time for the grain to ripen, where would the seed have come from? Most veterans therefore resorted to growing a few vegetables, scaring up a few chickens, a coon, or rabbit while waiting for spring to come.

The spring of 1866 was about normal for Louisiana until late April and early May when drought virtually destroyed the corn crop. Shortly thereafter, cotton fell prey to worm infestation and the crop proved to be a complete failure. Sugarcane, stunted by drought and choked with weeds, froze in the fields in the fall of '66, waiting for harvesters who never came. Poverty gripped the Teche country that winter and people went hungry. Commerce stalled as there was nothing to barter or buy. Only tremendous courage kept hope alive for spring and another start.

Planting went well in the spring of '67. Conditions were more settled, the desperate reality of survival was recognized by all. By late March the corn, pea, rice, and sugarcane crops were looking good. Disaster, however, was imminent.

On March 27, the west-bank levee of the Mississippi in Pointe Coupee Parish broke, producing a half-mile crevasse through which the flood of muddy waters poured into the area between the Teche and the Lafourche. Thousands of people, fleeing the approaching waters, took refuge on the west bank of the Teche. The steamboat *Teche* made trip after trip into the flood areas east of the bayou and brought out families, furniture, animals, and whatever. Flood victims crowded into New Iberia, and the townspeople did all in their power to assist them. Finally, in late April, the flood crested with less than twenty-four inches to go before spilling over the west bank of the Teche. Then, during June, following the receding waters, the refugees returned home, if a home existed. New Iberians gave thanks for their deliverance and looked forward to a more routine way of life.

With the arrival of July came the distressing news that the cotton worm had wiped out the crop in St. Landry Parish. Lafayette Parish cotton was heavily infested, and St. Martin's production was threatened. Sugar and cotton farmers along the lower Teche shook their heads despairingly and hoped they would be spared. No one along the Teche during those muggy July days could know that before long they would face a peril far greater than that found on any recent battlefield, a calamity of greater magnitude than any flood or agricultural failure. About to descend upon the Teche country, particularly New Iberia, was the scourge of yellow fever.

It is generally agreed among historians that yellow fever was introduced into Louisiana in the 1790s, probably arriving in New Orleans on board ship from a Gulf or Caribbean port. For the first forty years or so following its introduction into the state, yellow fever remained a distinctly New Orleans problem. But when the steamboats began to ply the bayous, they carried among their freight the pesky, but seemingly harmless insect, the *Aedes aegypti* mosquito. Here, completely ignored by science until the beginning of the twentieth century, was the carrier of misery and death which made battlefield casualties pale by comparison.

In May, 1819, Francois Duplessis' steamboat *Louisianais* inaugurated a new era in transportation and communication when it steamed up the Teche and docked at New Iberia. Unknown to the excited townspeople who viewed the hissing machine was the fact that steamboats would, in the future, carry the yellow-fever mosquito into their midst.

In September, 1839, New Iberians experienced their first bout with yellow fever. The epidemic spread rapidly up and down the Teche. Joachim Etie and Dr. Raphael Smith, Jr., were early victims and were followed to the grave by a score of Iberians. A black woman named Felicite, a native of Santo Domingo, apparently immune to the disease, worked day and night nursing the sick, comforting the dying, and arranging for the burial of the dead.

As New Iberia moved into the 1840s, many people forgot the yellow sword of pestilence. Even the terrible epidemic of 1853 in New Orleans did not bother the Teche country, and, almost miraculously, yellow fever virtually disappeared during the Civil War years.

An ominous event occurred, however, in mid-July, 1867, when a traveller arrived in New Iberia complaining of fever and vomiting. The next day he left for Abbeville, but word soon spread that he had died within twenty-four hours-- of yellow fever.

On July 17, a New Iberia doctor was called to a home on Main Street where he diagnosed the patient's illness as black vomit (an euphemism for the dreaded words "yellow fever"). The patient died the next day, and the doctor declared that if another such case was reported, he would label the illness yellow fever. The next case developed quickly. By the first of August fifty cases were reported, more than the local physicans--Drs. Thomas Mattingly, Frederick Duperier, Alfred Duperier, and Robert Hilliard--could handle. Drs. Dungan and Maguire from Franklin hurried to New Iberia to be of assistance.

Meanwhile, several men organized a citizens' committee to deal with the growing epidemic. An empty house on East Main Street was rented to serve as a hospital. Mayor Ashbel Henshaw appealed to doctors and nurses from New Orleans to help with the sick in New Iberia.

The response was immediate. Dr. J. Dickson Bruns and Samuel Logan of the New Orleans Medical College, together with nearly a dozen nurses and two Sisters of Charity, boarded a steamboat for the Attakapas. In addition, incomparable service was to be rendered by the Howard Association of New Orleans and its president Dr. E. F. Schmidt. The Howard Association, a benevolent society founded in 1837, assisted the sick and destitute in epidemic seasons. In addition to making home visits, the members provided medical care, nursing and medicine, alms for the poor, and established temporary yellow-fever hospitals.

Under the auspices of Dr. Schmidt, who could be seen at all hours of the night and day at the side of the sick and dying and at the graves of the dead, the Howard Association of New Iberia was founded. Its officers were James A. Lee, president; David Riggs, vice president; Jules Blanchet, secretary; and the Reverend A. E. Goodwyn, treasurer.

By early August the number of fever victims increased sharply, and the town of 1,500 people became virtually cut off from the outside world by strict quarantine. There were eighty cases by August 8; thirteen people were dead, including Mrs. R. S. Isabel, wife of the local schoolteacher, Francois Fourcade, and A. B. Dauterive.

The illness spread rapidly and took its toll. On August 13, Dr. Mattingly, Fred Mestayer, and Tertule Broussard succumbed. The town's two bakers fell ill and no bread was baked. On August 14, Dr. Schmidt telegraphed Howard headquarters in New Orleans: "Great distress and poverty here. Ask members to raise money and remit as soon as possible." A few days later Mayor Henshaw appealed for two hundred loaves of bread per day and two casks of ice per week.

Shortly thereafter the telegraph signal from New Iberia fell silent. Barnes, the telegrapher, remained at his key until the end, but he too fell victim of the fever. The number of persons with the disease passed 160 on August 21, between six and ten people dying each day. So bad had the epidemic become that steamboat captains were ordered not to enter town, but to dock about a mile downstream at the Smedes' Mintmere Plantation. At that point Dr. F. E. Piquette had set up what amounted to a medical station. In a plea for help, Dr. Piquette wrote: "These people are in a miserably destitute condition."

The appeals for assistance were answered from far and wide. In addition to doctors, nurses, medicines, and money furnished by the Howard Association, the

Shakespeare Club of New Orleans staged a benefit performance of "The Wife, or a tale of Mantua" at the New Opera House. The play was presented on August 28 to an overflow crowd, and the proceeds were sent to New Iberia. The citizens of Opelousas, under the leadership of Dr. James Ray (James Lee's brother-in-law), subscribed $250.00 for the New Iberia yellow-fever victims. The people of Franklin bought two hundred loaves of bread per day for a week and sent them to New Iberia by steamboat. H. M. Isaacson of New Orleans dispatched two casks of ice a week for several weeks. The Morgan Railroad to Morgan City and the Attakapas Mail Transportation Company, which operated the boats on the Teche, offered free transportation to doctors, nurses, and aid bound for New Iberia. Mr. T. Tupper, president of the Attakapas Company, subscribed hundreds of dollars of aid from friends and business associates. A more genuine concern for fellow human beings would have been hard to find.

But heroism and charity did not cure yellow fever. Not knowing the cause of the virus, there was very little doctors could do to cure it. Even the doctors became victims of the scourge. On August 21, Mayor Henshaw reported that all doctors, except Hill and Walker, were ill and that one nurse, Mrs. Tully of New Orleans, had died.

By late August, James Lee wrote to Tupper that there were seven hundred cases of fever in New Iberia and that one hundred people had died. He also noted that the outbreak of the fever in New Orleans, Franklin, St. Martinville, and other towns, had caused doctors and nurses from those places to leave New Iberia and return home.

New Iberians and their doctors were thus left to their own devices as the epidemic climaxed in early September. On September 4, Lee telegraphed an appeal for any help available, but there was little, for every town had its own problems. Silently, then, Lee recorded that William Robertson's son had died; that Mrs. Henshaw, the mayor's wife, had taken ill; that the highly esteemed Harvey Hopkins was dead; that the brave Dr. Hilliard had become ill and then died on September 10. No more fitting tribute to this physician can be found than the words inscribed on his tombstone: "He lived without fear and without reproach and fell at his post in the full tide of his usefulness."

All in all, nearly two-thirds of New Iberia's population had suffered in varying degrees from the disease. The list of dead included someone from nearly every household in the town. Some of the families in mourning were French, Fourcade, Etie, Lamperez, Pellerin, Dauterive, Mestayer, Olivier, Bienvenu, Delahoussaye, Lassus, Provost, Hopkins, Bergerie, Derouen, and Decuir.

As the silence of death, mourning, and exhaustion descended upon New Iberia in late September, 1867, the *Opelousas Courier* ran a small three-line announcement: "The yellow fever has almost entirely disappeared from New Iberia. Deaths are now very uncommon." Although no accurate figure has been compiled, it is safe to say that at least one hundred persons had died at New Iberia between August 1 and October 1, 1867.

The town's medical profession had acquitted itself well in the face of the mysterious killer. Truly, it could be said of New Iberia's doctors in 1867 what had been said of their predecessors: they "labored and died in the heroic exercise of professional duty and Christian charity in time of pestilence."

The old Dauterive Hospital (1919-1973)

The new Dauterive Hospital as seen in January 1986

Iberia General Hospital as it appeared in 1979

Iberia General Hospital with new wing as it appeared in January 1986

Yellow Fever

The yellow-fever epidemic in New Iberia in the late summer and fall of 1867 had been a costly affair in terms of lives and money. Scores of New Iberians had perished as the disease spread through the Attakapas country. Many more had spent weeks on the sickbed, often hovering near death.

Thus, when it became apparent that the incidence of yellow fever would be of epidemic proportions in 1878, New Iberians lost no time in taking the commonly accepted methods of prevention. Chief among these were the burning of sulphur, "disinfecting," and quarantining.

Although medical science was still uncertain of how the disease was transmitted from individual to individual (and the germ theory was still widely accepted), doctors and others recognized the benefits of certain preventive measures, especially quarantining.

The decision to quarantine, however, was always a difficult one to make, especially for urban centers which relied on the flow of commerce and the free movement of people into and out of the community. Because of these and other reasons, there was, therefore, a tendency for town and city authorities, merchants, and the local press to play down or completely deny that yellow fever had made its appearance in their communities. Thus, it was usually only after the disease was obviously entrenched and several deaths had occurred that the city fathers and others would reluctantly concede that their town had been invaded. By that time, however, it was too late for preventive measures, and the saffron scourge cut a wide swath across the community until such time as the days turned cool and the first frosts appeared. Normally, the yellow-fever season extended from July into October or November. No one, as yet, had realized the connection between the frequent summer showers along the Gulf Coast, the warm days and nights, the appearance of clouds of mosquitoes, and the arrival of yellow fever. For that matter, no one seemed to connect the disappearance of mosquitoes after the first cool days of fall and subsequent frosts with the end of an epidemic. These discoveries would be made only toward the turn of the century.

But why should these connections be made? It was a well-known fact that yellow fever did not visit the Gulf Coast every year, thereby enforcing the belief that yellow fever was a communicable disease, probably brought into the United States by travellers from Central and South America.

In brief, then, such was the popularly accepted view of yellow fever when the tyrant struck in the summer of 1878. True to form, the New Iberia newspaper, the *Louisiana Sugar Bowl*, commented on August 15 that in New Orleans there were 466 cases of some disease and that within the last week 126 people had died of the affliction. The comment continued: "We honestly believe the majority of cases in New Orleans are not yellow fever, but a malarial fever, caused by the filthy conditions of their streets."

A week later, however, the New Iberia paper confirmed that yellow fever had, indeed, appeared in New Orleans; there were 975 cases of which 266 had been fatal. The paper also noted that the fever had appeared in Vicksburg and Memphis. On August 29, the paper reported that fever cases were found in Plaquemine and along the Mississippi River.

With Plaquemine being the gateway for all steamboat traffic (the only means of mass transportation) to the Attakapas country, the people of New Iberia, harboring memories of the 1867 epidemic and alarmed by the current rapid spread of the disease, decided to hold a mass meeting to decide whether to take preventive measures.

On August 31, a group of New Iberians, including J. H. Wise, J. Y. Gilmore, Louis Miguez, Norwood Stansbury, Michel Heymann, Theodore Fontelieu, and others, met to discuss possible implementation of safety measures in the face of the imminent danger. Meanwhile, a mass meeting was called for the following evening at the courthouse.

With a large crowd in attendance, the meeting commenced at 6:00 p.m. J. H. Wise called the citizens to order and then asked Mr. Stansbury to read a resolution prepared by his committee. The resolution read:

> Resolved: That the President of the Board of Health and the Mayor of New Iberia [James L. Burke] be requested to notify the owners and commanders of the steamboats now plying between this place and other points below and above, that no passengers will be allowed to debark here from and after Sept. 5th, 1878, until this quarantine is raised. . . .

Then, in what was obviously a concession to the merchants of New Iberia, it was further resolved that

> under existing circumstances, it is not expedient to so completely isolate ourselves, by the violent stoppage of the boat, the needed supplies and the mails, as to place us beyond the reach of aid, should the enemy [yellow fever] effect an entrance. . . .

A minority report, presented by John Emmer and L. A. Dupuy, favored the quarantine of all freight. After a short debate, John Robertson moved the adoption of the majority report.

It was further agreed that a municipal committee, composed of Stansbury, C. O. Delahoussaye, and J. Y. Gilmore, would meet with the police jury to urge upon that body adoption of a parishwide quarantine. As these events unfolded, numerous young men volunteered to serve in the quarantine guard. They were

Chas. Gouguenheim	John M. Senac	Wm. Gankendorff
Felix Lacaze	L. G. Roth	Samuel Goldbey
H. Fauvel	C. B. Vest	Chas. Fontelieu
Frederick Decourt	J. E. Tolson	Alex Dinjery
E. Guerin	Alex Fauvel	Joe Camors
Jules Andre	L. S. Miguez	J. C. Montagne
A. D. Blanc	Joe Martinez	J. M. Frasher
A. J. Colgin	P. Meehan	C. P. Hacker
Chas. Sangez	A. Cestia	J. A. Miguez
Henry Gankendorff	A. Guerin	F. E. Montagne
P. F. Castille	P. Decourt	Chas. Bar
A. Fontelieu	F. J. Hebert	George Doerle
N. P. Hacker	Adolphe Orillion	

At a subsequent meeting, the volunteers elected J. M. Frasher to be their captain and pledged themselves to serve day and night in the enforcement of the quarantine.

On September 2, 1878, William R. Burke, president of the police jury, presided over an extraordinary session of the body. Jurors present were J. A. Provost, E. P. Olivier, J. A. Fagot, L. P. Serret, and Hilaire Decuir. Unable to attend were H. Steckler, Sr., Honore Miguez, Joseph Bourriaque, and Etienne Frilot.

The president stated that he had called the meeting for the purpose of obtaining from the police jury the cooperation necessary to establish a rigid quarantine throughout Iberia Parish. The jurors agreed that no person coming from a district infected with yellow fever would be allowed into the parish. Anyone breaking this ordinance would be fined not less than $25 nor more than $50.

By September 3, 1878, then, the necessary steps had been taken to establish the quarantine and the municipal quarantine station was erected on the bayou just east of town, between the Smedes and Clerc estates (the area of present-day Evangeline Street).

Probably with vivid memories of outside help to New Iberians during the yellow-fever epidemic of 1867, townspeople called a mass meeting for September 3, for the purpose of establishing a committee to collect funds and solicit contributions to assist yellow-fever victims in other localities.

At the subsequent meeting, held in the B'nai B'rith Hall, the group organized as the Iberia Relief Committee. Patrick Burke was chosen president; Michel Heymann, vice president; Dr. J. G. Mestayer, treasurer; and J. Y. Gilmore, secretary. The committee to collect funds and solicit contributions was composed of L. B. Duffard, Joseph H. Wise, J. G. Mestayer, Jules Blanchet, Jacques Fourcade, Oscar Dupre, J. N. Landry, D. U. Broussard, Jules Dubus, A. Grouset, Mrs. L. Fontelieu, Mrs. Sarah DeValcourt, Mrs. J. N. Landry, Mrs. Ellen Fuller, Mrs. D. Levy, F. J. Hebert, Michel Heymann, J. Y. Gilmore, F. Gonsoulin, and William Robertson.

As the drive to collect funds and contributions for yellow-fever victims accelerated, the *Sugar Bowl* took special note of the Jewish community's contribution to this endeavor. The newspaper commented: "No group of our citizens have contributed so large as our Jewish townsmen to relieve yellow fever sufferers in other cities. . . . If citizens everywhere would do as well, there would be much less suffering among the destitute."

Apparently the Relief Committee members were hard at work, for at a meeting of the committee on September 11, the treasurer reported receiving a total of $415 in cash and a considerable amount of livestock. It was decided to forward $400 in cash to the Howard Association of New Orleans and the livestock to the Peabody Subsistence Association of the same city. D. U. Broussard offered to take all corn donated and grind it into meal at no charge, and it was reported that the Morgan line of steamboats would transport the livestock to New Orleans at no charge.

Soliciting donations for the yellow-fever victims was only one way of supporting the work of the Relief Committee. There were other ways to raise money for the sick. The Creole and Quickstep baseball clubs of New Iberia announced that they would hold a benefit game "back of the Catholic cemetery" and all proceeds would go to the Howard Association.

The game was played on September 20, and the Creoles won 21 to 17. Playing for the Creoles were Alphe Fontelieu, Charles Sangez, J. A. Miguez, Charles Fontelieu, Alex Cestia, S. Miguez, J. M. Senac, M. Fourmigrie, A. Miguez, and F. Mestayer. Members of the Quickstep team were A. Escudier, C. Montagne, Arthur Escudier, Henry Gankendorff, Alphonse Severin, A. Orillion, M. Keller, and H. Gascon. The game netted $50 which was handed over to the Relief Committee.

About the same time, the Ladies Relief Committee met at Temperance Hall and decided to give a public picnic at the Weeks Grove (opposite the present-day "Shadows"). Taking part in the preparations were Mesdames Leon Couget, L. Fontelieu, J. N. Landry, D. Levy, S. DeValcourt, M. R. Millard, J. H. Wise, M. Heymann, Alexis Lague, Antoine Comeaux, L. Bazus, Fourcade, J. G. Mestayer, R. Oubre, T. Fontelieu, Dauterive, Jules Dubus, Frederick Mestayer, Charles Clerc, Octavia Blanchet, Henriette Ermann, Louisa Chaignon, and Misses Ezelda Darby, Clemence Landry, Leontine Fontelieu, and Regina Duperier. The event went off well with the Iberia Brass Band joining in. The picnic netted $300.

In mid-September, J. Henry proposed to give two magic lantern exhibitions, the first for the benefit of charity and the second for his benefit. The first showing was well attended, but Mr. Henry realized little at the second showing.

While the Relief Committee and its allied groups engaged in these activities, the fever spread westward from the Mississippi during September. On September 18, B. F. Winchester, president of the Morgan City Relief Committee appealed to the New Iberia group for cash and produce. He reported that the fever had recently broken out in Morgan City and that there were then 75 cases and 13 deaths. Three days later he reported 115 cases and 21 deaths. In light of Winchester's appeal, the Iberia group decided to send all available produce and approximately $60 in cash to the Morgan City committee.

The popular fear engendered by the epidemic and the extent of the quarantines is clearly reflected in the following item reported in the *Sugar Bowl:*

> Mr. and Mrs. John B. Marsh arrived in town from New York yesterday [September 18]. They came a most circuitous route--via Cincinnati, St. Louis, Sedalia (390 miles west of St. Louis), down through Texas to Orange, thence overland here. They met innumerable obstacles, as Texas had quarantined against everybody who did not have good papers, and Lake Charles is quarantined against Texas. They could get no one to bring them this side of the Mermentau, for fear of being quarantined, so they telegraphed Mr. Overton Cade, who met them. They had to leave their baggage in Houston. This was certainly traveling under difficulties. They were from the 4th to the 18th between New York and here. [Editor's note: normally the trip took no more than five days by train between New Orleans and New York.]

The popular fear may have been well warranted, for, by the end of September, the fever had spread northward into the Mississippi Valley, and along the East and Gulf coasts.

Locally, the report came that the fever was spreading up Bayou Teche from Morgan City. By early October it had invaded Patterson and was moving onto plantations between there and Franklin. By early October, Morgan City reported over 200 cases and 50 deaths, Thibodaux cited 149 cases and 14 deaths, Baton Rouge listed 1,000 cases and about 100 deaths.

As the disease spread, the Iberia Relief Committee redoubled its efforts. By September 30, Dr. Mestayer reported that a total of $1,000 had been collected during the month and that this, plus the contributions of produce, had been divided and donated to the Howard Association, the Peabody Association, Touro Infirmary, and the Morgan City Relief Committee.

Then, in early October came still another plea for help. President Burke read a letter from New Orleans begging the Relief Committee for assistance for the New Orleans orphanages which were becoming overcrowded as a result of the epidemic. After discussing what could be done, the Committee agreed to D. U. Broussard's motion to send cash donations to the Jewish Widows' and Orphans Home, the Mt. Carmel Orphanage, the Little Sisters of the Poor, the St. Vincent de Paul Society, the St. Mary Boys' Asylum, and the Catholic Relief Association.

By mid-October the spread of the fever throughout the Teche area seemed to halt. Nevertheless, the *Sugar Bowl* reported on October 10 that Morgan City had 350 cases and 160 deaths, and that in Thibodaux the disease was not abating. The climax had been reached, however. In the last fortnight of October, the number of cases around the state dropped dramatically. By the first of November, the officers of the Iberia Relief Committee decided that they would be able shortly to terminate the group's activities.

On November 9, the Committee held its final meeting. It was reported that the Committee had raised a total of $1,569.25; that it had received as contributions 24 calves, 37 sheep, 7 hogs, 729 chickens, 80 dozen eggs, 26 bbls. of cornmeal, 3 bbls. of potatoes and 13 bbls. of corn. As important as this aspect of its work had been, the president joyfully announced that the quarantine of New Iberia had achieved its end, not a single case of yellow fever had been reported in the town. Mr. Blanchet moved that a day of thanksgiving for the town's deliverance be set aside. The Committee decided that no better day could be found than the approaching Thanksgiving Day.

New Iberia had a great deal to be thankful for in the fall of 1878. Statistics from neighboring communities proved that the 1878 yellow-fever epidemic had left nearly 4,000 dead in New Orleans, over 100 in Morgan City, 47 in Patterson, 88 in Thibodaux, and nearly 200 in Baton Rouge.

Yellow Fever

Although New Iberia's escape from the epidemic of 1878 is noteworthy, there is a postscript in connection with the town and yellow fever. The last reported and authenticated case of yellow fever in the continental United States occurred in New Iberia in 1906. The victim, a young teenager, was treated by Dr. I. T. Rand and by Drs. P. E. Achinard and Charles Chassaignac, yellow-fever experts from New Orleans. The victim recovered.

St. Peter's Cemetery

VIII

New Iberia Becomes the Parish Seat

by

Glenn R. Conrad and Carl A. Brasseaux

The roots of the popular movement which produced Iberia Parish in 1868 can be traced to 1837 when Neuville DeClouet organized a New Iberia group advocating secession from St. Martin Parish. Throughout the late 1830s and the 1840s, public meetings were periodically held to air the separatists' grievances, foremost among which was the alleged misuse of public funds by the police jury.

Between 1847 and 1850, the separatists' ranks were swollen by hundreds of residents of the contiguous portions of St. Martin and St. Mary parishes who were unhappy with the necessity of traveling great distances to conduct their legal affairs at either St. Martinville or Franklin. These rural enlistees were welcome additions to New Iberia's separatist forces.

In a meeting called by separatists at New Iberia in January 1850, committees of vigilance and correspondence were formed for the dual purpose of intimidating politicians and silencing opposition. In addition, the secessionists appointed a group to lobby their interests in the state legislature.

By late March 1850, the political power of the DeClouet faction was manifested in Resolution No. 297 which directed the state engineer, A. D. Wooldridge, to compile statistics concerning the area encompassed by the prospective parish. (The projected boundaries lay four miles south of St. Martinville and ten

*Data for this essay was gathered from various state and local newspapers of the era.

This building on Main Street was the Iberia Parish Courthouse between March 1875 and July 1876.

miles northwest of Franklin.) This report, as well as lists of voters in the proposed parish, compiled by the assessors of the mother parishes, were to be presented at the next session of the state legislature. According to the state constitution, however, the minimum area necessary for the creation of a new parish was 1,875 square miles. Excepting Marsh Island, which apparently no one wanted, the areas of St. Martin and St. Mary parishes proposed for the new parish contained only 1,720 square miles. Rejoicing that the separatists' plans had gone awry, the editor of the Franklin *Planters' Banner,* strongly opposed to the proposed new parish, fired a tongue-in-cheek volley at his opponents.

> The only way in which a new parish can be formed without infringing largely on the old ones, is to transfer New Iberia, town lots and all, to Marsh Island, and by taking in Vermilion and Cote Blanche Bays on the one side, and a liberal slice of the Gulf of Mexico on the other, a very large parish might be formed without infringing upon any-

An 1886 woodcut of the first Iberia Parish Courthouse

thing except the Gulf of Mexico, and there is no doubt that town lots would then be in good demand. The editor is referring to his previous allegations that the advocates of secession were motivated solely by a desire to enhance the value of their New Iberia property holdings. Under such circumstances, New Iberia might become a second Venice. Instead of being an obscure town on the Teche, of a modest and retiring appearance, it would become the 'pride of the ocean,' as valuable as a gold mine, and as conspicuous as a light house.

Although the flames of separatism were extinguished by these reverses, the embers of discontent remained very much alive. In 1868 the election of numerous legislators sympathetic to the divisionists' cause gave rise to a new wave of covert activity on the part of the St. Martin and St. Mary secessionists. After compiling census figures from the "sugar bowl" parishes, several New Iberia residents, under the leadership of Joachim Etie, drafted carefully worded legislation for the creation of Iberia Parish. (Ironically, the bill's authors followed the editor's mordant advice and incorporated Marsh Island and a generous portion of Vermilion and West Cote Blanche bays into the prospective political unit.) The legislature reacted favorably and Governor Warmoth signed the measure creating Iberia Parish in October 1868.

The governor was directed by the terms of the act to appoint, with the advice and consent of the state senate, numerous parochial officials, including the judge, sheriff, and recorder. Nevertheless, Governor Warmoth unofficially delegated this authority to Dr. Alfred Duperier who "could not overcome his joy at the opportunity of crowding out the hungry scaliawags [sic] who were building hopes upon the Negro influence, which they felt sure would influence the governor in his appointments."

Upon receiving his commission, the parish judge was required to convoke a meeting of the local justices of the peace for the purpose of dividing the infant parish into four wards. Having completed this task, the regional magistrate was to authorize a special police-jury election supervised on the precinct level by the justices of the peace. The newly elected members of the parish legislature and the parish judge were to assemble at New Iberia, designated by the act as the seat of justice, "for the purpose of causing to be erected the necessary public buildings."

Acting in accordance with the dictates of the state legislature, Police Jury President Daniel D. Avery leased the upper story of a brick and frame structure on Main Street from Louis Miguez for $800 annually. Under the terms of the

The 1884 courthouse before being remodeled in 1922

agreement the parish assembly was authorized to use the cistern at the rear of the buildings and to remove all partitions on the second floor. After the destruction of this temporary courthouse by a fire which destroyed the north side of Main Street in June 1870, the police jury met in emergency session on August 2, 1870, to secure new quarters for the parish government. Apparently unable to find suitable accommodations, the jurors adopted a resolution advocating construction of temporary quarters; however, during October the jurors reversed this decision and accepted P. A. Veazey's offer to rent the second story of a building then under construction on Main Street near Serret Alley. The Veazey Building, however, was completely unfit for use as a court building. The roof leaked to the extent that the bench, spectators, and parochial records were frequently soaked during court sessions. The proprietor's failure to repair the rapidly deteriorating structure prompted the police jury to search

The Parish Seat

The 1884 courthouse after remodeling in 1922

for a new home. On March 15, 1875, the parish assembly, acting upon the grand jury's recommendations, appointed P. E. Burke, J. A. Lee, and D. U. Broussard to make arrangements for the construction of a new courthouse and jail. Meanwhile, the seat of justice was transferred to temporary quarters in the Duperier Block.

On July 3, 1875, Jasper Gall purchased the Veazey Building and opened ultimately successful negotiations with the parish solons to persuade them to return to their former quarters. Gall's promise to repair and remodel his recent acquisition and the paucity of building bonds in the parochial treasury prompted the police jury to rescind its decision to build. The parish government therefore occupied its former quarters in mid-July 1876.

Iberia Parish Court Building upon completion, 1940

Despite the upgrading of its facilities, the police jury continued to be unhappy with its new home. Apparently dissatisfaction stemmed from the Gall Building's unsavory atmosphere (the ground floor housed a saloon) and the excessive cost of guarding prisoners in the rented, minimum security facility. The parish assembly therefore adopted a resolution on December 15, 1877, urging the state legislature to authorize the police jury to borrow $15,000 for construction of a permanent courthouse and jail. Although the state general assembly failed to enact this legislation, the jurors entered into negotiations for acquisition of a courthouse site. On December 2, 1882, Police Jury President D. U. Broussard announced that the parish legislature had purchased a lot from the firm of Taylor and DeValcourt for $4,000. Under the terms of the purchase agreement, the vendors received $1,000 as a down payment and six annual installments of $500 with eight percent per annum interest.

In 1883 the parish assembly authorized construction of a three-story courthouse to be built at a cost of $24,447. Fred Gates, C. T. Cade, J. A. Lee, and William R. Burke were subsequently appointed building commissioners. Shortly after its completion in the spring of 1884, the new courthouse became the scene of a pitched battle between Republicans and Democrats.

The Albrizo fresco

The courthouse controversy was precipitated by Alfred G. Barnard's (the Iberia Parish returns officer) decision to create a new electoral precinct on the eve of the April 22, 1884, parochial election. The 958 ballots cast at this, the Bayou Pigeon box, subsequently became the Democratic ticket's margin of victory. Once the votes were tallied, Theodore Fontelieu, an incumbent Republican candidate for district judge and the local head of the party, placed armed guards at the entrance to the courthouse to ensure that the Democratic candidates, Frederick L. Gates, P. A. Veazey, and Adolph Wakefield, would not take office while he appealed the outcome of the election to the state courts. On May 28, the Republican jurist obtained an injunction from

An Art Deco rendering of Justice

Judge DeBaillon prohibiting Gates, Veazey, and Wakefield from assuming their respective duties as district judge, sheriff, and clerk of court; however, on June 16 DeBaillon reversed his decision and dissolved the injunctions on the grounds that he lacked jurisdiction in the case. Iberia Parish was consequently left without a slate of public officials.

Understandably, tensions ran high in New Iberia, especially as a result of the Republican administration's failure to check a wave of burglaries, shootings, and attempted assassination of some prominent Democrats. In an effort to restore order to New Iberia Sheriff-elect Veazey, accompanied by twenty men, occupied the courthouse at 2 a.m. on July 12. During the following morning

The Parish Seat

Iberia Parish Court Building with 1976 additions to wings

the Fontelieu faction prepared to storm the courthouse; however, a confrontation was averted through the efforts of Captain Dudley Avery, the commander of the local militia unit, the Iberia Guards. At a meeting of the area's political leaders, arranged by Avery, Fontelieu agreed to allow Veazey to post bond, which was necessary for him to assume office. This was done in exchange for Judge Gates' assurances that the armed Democrats would abandon the court building. Informed of the terms of the agreements, Veazey ordered his followers to disperse; the number of courthouse guards was subsequently increased.

Fontelieu refused to relinquish his office despite Gates' gubernatorial appointment as his replacement in late July. Nevertheless, the Democrat actively discharged the duties incumbent upon his position as district judge. On August 5, he approved P. A. Veazey's bonds and submitted them to Clerk of Court P. H. Segura for his inspection. Shortly thereafter the new sheriff demanded the keys to the courthouse from his predecessor, but the outgoing Republican refused to comply with this request. Moreover, Segura refused to accept Veazey's bond, thus preventing him from officially taking office. When Judge Gates summoned the Republican clerk of court to appear before the bench to explain his actions, it was learned that the clerk of court was out of town. The judge then ordered Veazey's bond to be filed.

Fontelieu supplemented the actions of his political friends by reinforcing

The courthouse addition of 1985-86

the courthouse guard. Determined to resist to the bitter end, Viator, the former sheriff, refused to surrender the courthouse to Colonel Faries, Governor McEnery's adjutant-general, on August 11. Two days later, the governor mobilized a unit of the Louisiana Field Artillery to enforce Faries' orders. These Crescent City militiamen arrived in New Iberia during the night of August 14. During the next morning they took positions around the courthouse while Sheriff Veazey and six deputies entered the building and found that the parish archives had disappeared during the preceding night.

During the tense days which followed the incarceration of the former parochial officials, New Iberia was plagued by a rash of destructive fires. Veazey was therefore forced to devote much of his energies and attention to the maintenance of order in the town, while at the same time continuing to search for the missing documents. On August 18, the sheriff "searched the coffee house on the ground floor of the old courthouse building, and found secreted in the ten-pin alley, back of the saloon, a large portion of the archives of the clerk of court's office. Additional records belonging to the sheriff's department were found in a private residence during the night of August 25.

Defiant to the end, former Sheriff Viator, refused to relinquish the courthouse keys, thus forcing the police jury to spend approximately $250 to change the locks. Although the Republicans were allowed this face-saving gesture, Vea-

The Parish Seat

zey's incumbency signaled the end of the "GOP's political ascendency in Iberia Parish."

The region's rapid growth following the turn of the century caused a proportional increase in the volume of business conducted by the parish government. In 1921, prompted by the necessity of enlarging the courthouse, the police jury commissioned an unnamed architect to submit a plan to raise the roof (literally) and remodel the third floor "as to afford room for the Assessor's office, Police Jury room and Grand Jury, when it was in session." (The sheriff's and clerk's offices were to be located on the ground floor, while the second story was to contain the courtrooms.) In addition, a "nice" elevator and staircase were to be installed at the rear of the structure. Finally, a Greek Revival facade was to be erected. The parish legislature allocated $35,000 for this project in early November 1921. On March 11, 1922, the police jury awarded a building contract toalling $37,500 to Caldwell Brothers of Abbeville. Work on the project began approximately two weeks later.

Although contemporary news reports claimed that the renovations would extend the life of the building for another thirty years, such was not to be the case, at least insofar as a courthouse was concerned. In early 1938 the police jury, under the presidency of Rufus McIlhenny, began laying the ground work for construction of a new parish building. Apparently the primary motive was to create jobs for local people. On February 10 the parish legislature adopted Ovey Romero's resolution advocating that Overstreet and Town be appointed architects for the parish's capital improvements project, that they be paid six percent commission, and that the district attorney be ordered to draft an appropriate contract. In mid-April, after weighing the advantages and disadvantages of building an annex on the undersized public square or constructing a new courthouse on another site, the police jury decided on the latter course of action. In late May the police jury approved Paul Hebert's motion that the project be financed through the sale of bonds totalling $300,000 and that they apply for a WPA grant (45 percent of the projected construction costs). The federal agency approved the request in early August 1938, and approximately one week later John Schwing, acting on behalf of the police jury, purchased the Howe Institute property as the new public square.

The present Iberia Parish Courthouse, designed by A. Hays Town and constructed by the firm of Gravier and Harper in 1939, is a fine example of federally funded Art Deco style building of the Great Depression period. It was constructed under the Public Works Administration of the Federal Works Agency.

At that time the federal government required that a certain percentage of the total cost of a federally funded structure be set aside for art work, such as murals, mosaics, relief, and sculpture in-the-round. The architect for the Iberia project exploited this requirement and produced a building which is outstanding for its marriage of architecture, painting, and sculpture. The remarkable fresco in the original court room was the work of Conrad Albrizio, a member of the LSU art faculty. He also executed frescoes in the State Capitol.

The Iberia Parish Court Building (as it is officially dubbed) was occupied in 1940. The official dedication of the building took place on Armistice Day, 1941. Since then, there have been two additions to the building. In 1976 the wings were extended, and in 1985-86, a massive addition was built to the rear facade of the original building.

The memorial to D. U. Broussard, "father" of Iberia Parish's first courthouse stands in front of the present courthouse.

IX

The Centennial Celebration at New Iberia, 1876

by
Glenn R. Conrad

With cannon booming and bells ringing, New Iberians ushered in the celebration of America's centennial of independence, July 4, 1876.*

The New Iberia celebration is remarkable for many reasons, but two are truly outstanding. First, with the exception of events in New Orleans, the local festivities were the largest and best organized in the state. Secondly, the local celebration should be considered phenomenal when one realizes that less than a dozen years before Iberians were fighting to separate themselves from the Union.

But the factor which most definitely sparked the local event was a desire to put aside, hopefully forever, the fractricidal hatred that was rampant in the land. Indeed, the theme of the celebration became "to destroy all national prejudice, to set aside race, and the issues of the day . . . in order to cement hitherto repellent factions into one common and fraternal bond." That this goal was seriously pursued is amply borne out in the accounts of New Iberia's celebration of July 4, 1876.

Long before the eventful day a group of Iberians set about the task of planning and organizing the festivities. D. U. Broussard was named chairman of preparations and was designated grand marshal. Assisting him were innumerable

---

*Information for this essay was derived from the *Louisiana Sugar Bowl*, June 29, July 6, 19, 1876.

people who were designing and building floats, sewing costumes, making decorations, or planning some other aspect of the celebration. The black community, under the leadership of their Centennial Committee, began constructing floats, enlisting paraders, and securing planners and workers.

Charles Clerc acted as chairman of the barbeque committee. His group solicited meat and other food to be served during the course of the celebration. Several saloonkeepers donated casks of beer, and at the last minute many ladies made gallons of lemonade.

Maurice Heymann served as chairman of the finance committee. Captain J. N. Pharr, owner of a Teche steamboat line, agreed to reduce roundtrip fares by seventy-five percent on all boats going to New Iberia on July 4. Moreover, he announced that a special excursion boat, the *Rene Macready* would leave Morgan City on the night of July 3, making frequent stops along the bayou to take aboard all those wishing to attend the New Iberia event.

Then, the planning was finished, the preparations completed, the day had arrived. As the sun slowly rose over the hushed, dew-soaked countryside, Iberians were suddenly awakened to the booming of cannon, a thirteen-gun salute. Bells, from church spires to plantation quarters, peeled their joyous message and urged citizens to converge on the town. Anxious children raced out of their homes, each carying a small American flag, and almost all exasperatingly urging their parents to hurry along.

By seven o'clock, as the human tide steadily swelled, a long blast of its whistle announced the arrival of the *Rene Macready*, its decks jammed with celebrants from the lower Teche. Meanwhile, wagons crowded with laughing, waving country folk poured into town from Coteau, Cade, Petite Anse, and Patoutville.

By 8:30 everyone taking part in the first event of the day, the religious observance, gathered at the Weeks Grove in front of "The Shadows." At the sound of a drum roll, this procession, headed by the national colors, a military honor guard and a brass band playing "Hail, Columbia," moved up Main Street to Iberia, out Iberia to St. Peter's Church, where thousands heard, or thought they heard, Father Jacquet say Mass.

In another part of town the steamboat *Mary Lewis* arrived to the sounds of whistle blasts and cannon reports. Hundreds of people aboard the boat waved flags and handkerchiefs to those greeting them at the wharf.

At 10:30 the grand parade was launched into the streets. Beginning at the Weeks Grove, the procession was led by the grand marshal, followed by the national colors and guard of honor. Then came the band playing patriotic music, followed by a company of soldiers in full dress.

Next to move out onto the parade route was the Centennial Float, drawn by four bay horses. Lavishly decorated in a red, white, and blue motif, the float carried thirteen young ladies representing the Thirteen Colonies. They were presided over by the Goddess of Liberty, as portrayed by Ilma Clerc. The float was flanked by thirty-eight young men, each representing a state of the Union.

The next float, a representation of the ship *Old Ironsides*, was designed by Captain Thomas Morse. It, too, carried fourteen young ladies, thirteen representing the colonies, and the fourteenth portraying Freedom.

Then came a brass band and two fire companies from New Iberia. These were followed by the fire departments of Morgan City, Franklin, St. Martinville, and Breaux Bridge, each preceded by the visiting town's band. Next came a veritable horde of chattering, laughing school children, waving flags and an occasional hand to beaming parents on the sidelines. Finally, there proceeded up Main Street a host of decorated carriages and buggies, followed by an equal number of equestrians.

But if the casual bystander thought the parading had ended, his thoughts were soon corrected, for now the black parade began. This segment of the overall event was extremely well organized and reflected the day-and-night planning which had preceded it. Stretching out for over a mile, the black parade included lively bands, smart-looking fire companies, innumerable children, decorated vehicles, and horsemen.

The parade flowed up Main to Corinne, out Corinne to St. Peter, down St. Peter to Iberia, Iberia to Main, Main to Bridge Street and then across the bayou to the Duperier Grove, near the convent. At the Grove, the grounds were thronged long before the procession arrived. Then, at high noon, a two hundred voice choir opened the program with the national anthem.

As the throng settled down, Robert Perry rendered a dramatic reading of the Declaration of Independence. Donelson Caffery next addressed the crowd on the meaning of patriotism. Following a few selections by the choir, Colonel Alcidiades de Blanc of St. Martinville, speaking in French, traced the history of America from Columbus to the Centennial. Finally, Frank McGloin, a New Orleans attorney, gave the concluding address before a sea of rapidly moving palmetto fans. Throughout the afternoon, "short recesses were had, facilitating vigorous and repeated charges upon the viands furnished by the Barbeque Committee."

At sunset the crowd stood on the bayou banks and cheered as a thirteen-gun salute honored the patriots of a century before. For many this marked the end of a full day of activity, and they began to make their way home. The final event of the day, however, was yet to take place.

The grand ball, sponsored by Fire Company No. 2, was staged in the Weeks Grove. Beneath decorated lanterns and torches, friends, neighbors, and acquaintances of the day chatted, danced and sipped lemonade.

All to soon the *Rene Macready* and *Mary Lewis* summoned passengers, and shortly thereafter the two boats, illuminated from stem to stern like two fairy-tale palaces, glided away from the wharf.

The celebration concluded as the last dancers, discovering that July 5 had come around, hurried home, their heads like those of countless others, filled with memories and dreams of this most remarkable day, memories so vivid that they survived in New Iberia for nearly a century.*

THE BICENTENNIAL CELEBRATION OF THE FOUNDING OF NEW IBERIA, APRIL 1979: A PHOTO ESSAY

In the spring of 1979 New Iberians celebrated the bicentennial of the founding of their town. The festivities, over a period of three days, April 8 - 10, included a childrens' parade, arts and crafts shows, Spanish music and dancing, gospel singing, and religious services. Local officials hosted the event. The guest of honor for the occasion was the Marques de Casa Mena, consul-general of Spain in New Orleans. The photo essay that follows depicts scenes from the three days of celebration.

---

*There was no public celebration in New Iberia on July 4, 1976, the bicentennial of American independence. Even a fireworks display, scheduled at the Acadiana Regional Airport, was cancelled because of a late afternoon rain.

The Bicentennial Celebration

Mayor Allen Daigre and friends officially open the Bicentennial Celebration April 8, 1979

The Marques de Casa Mena, consul-general of Spain in New Orleans, opens the Arts and Crafts Exhibit during New Iberia's Bicentennial Celebration. The ladies assisting him, from left, Rita Viator, Virginia Moore, Sylvia Conrad, the Marquesa, and Helen Marin.

An Arts and Crafts Exhibit on the lawn of The Shadows and neighboring Weeks Street during the New Iberia Bicentennial Celebration

The Bicentennial Celebration

Spanish dances and music were part of the Bicentennial Celebration

A childrens' parade commemorated the ethnic groups which have settled in New Iberia

The Little Zorah Church Choir sang for the Bicentennial Celebration

X

The Iron Horse Comes to New Iberia*

by
Glenn R. Conrad

At the beginning of 1879, the Teche country was astir with news and rumors of progress in railroad building in that area of the state. Morgan's Texas and Louisiana Railroad had finally begun the project of extending the railroad westward from the Atchafalaya to the Sabine River. This stretch of track, cutting across South Louisiana's numerous swamps and bayous, had been planned for construction in the years just before the Civil War. In June 1851, Alexandre Mouton of Vermilionville (Lafayette), along with several other enterprising Louisianians, founded the New Orleans, Algiers, Attakapas and Opelousas Railroad. Alfred Mouton, Alexandre's son and the future hero of the Battle of Mansfield, served this company for a time as a civil engineer, surveying the roadbed of the railroad. But when the Civil War came the line had only been completed between Algiers and Brashear City (Morgan City). The war and its aftermath, plus the fact that the Teche country had seemingly adequate service from steamboat lines, contributed to the fifteen-year delay in completing the railroad through the state.

*Information for this essay was drawn from the New Iberia *Louisiana Sugar Bowl* and the New Orleans *Daily Picayune* for 1879 and 1880.

By the late 1870s, however, transportation needs had become critical as local businesses boomed and more and more people moved westward for settlement. These factors, among others, prompted the Morgan line to complete the train link between Morgan City and Orange, Texas. Work on the line progressed westward from Berwick and eastward from Orange, with plans for construction to meet in Lafayette about January 1, 1880. For the people of the Teche country, however, it was the line coming up from Berwick that held their interest.

In late January, 1879, three gangs of railroad workers, or "gandy dancers" as they were called, were engaged in building a bridge near Pattersonville, elevating roadbed on Fairfax Plantation, and filling in the Lacey swamp a few miles below Centerville. When equipment was available, work progressed at the rate of a quarter mile per day, but there were the usual, and sometimes unusual, delays. Weather was always an unpredictable factor, not only locally but also when, for example, the steamboat bringing rails from Pittsburgh became trapped in ice on the Ohio River.

Despite these problems, known to every section boss, the ribbons of steel continued to stretch across South Louisiana. In late March the railroad reached Bayou Sale. Continuing at that rate of construction, predicted Superintendent George Pandelly, the railroad would be in New Iberia by September 1.

The novelty of the whole enterprise thrilled some Iberians, but worried others. Some merchants were particularly disturbed by the prospect of local customers taking the eight-hour trip to New Orleans, the great commercial center of the South, instead of spending their shopping dollars at home. To allay such fears, J. Y. Gilmore, editor of the *Louisiana Sugar Bowl*, wrote that, because of the railroad, "New Iberia is destined to become a great business center, having transportation lines in at least six different directions, adding greatly to the trade of her sawmill owners, oil factory, foundrymen, manufacturers of all classes, and merchants and businessmen generally. More than that, New Iberia will be, at no remote date, a noted place of resort...."

About May 1, the people of Franklin watched the first locomotive chug through their town with a work crew. By mid-June about one hundred laborers had brought the railroad to Jeanerette and a week later had pushed onto the Bussey place between Jeanerette and New Iberia. Then occurred the event anticipated by many people who probably waited for it with an excitement as great as that of a later generation waiting to see the first man to land on the moon. On June 24, 1879, Judge Alcibiades de Blanc of St. Martinville left New Orleans at 8 a.m. and arrived on the train at Dr. Bussey's place before 3 p.m. and was home for 5 p.m. Total travel time was nine hours. Gilmore reported, "This is the first arrival on the railroad. We are rejoiced to note a beginning."

The Iron Horse

In July, with its almost endless rain, the railroad arrived at the Rosedale place, but, because of the weather, it was a month later before it reached the Nelson Canal crossing. Then, on August 28, as many New Iberians looked on, the rails were laid through town and the 125th mile post was planted. To mark the occasion a group of citizens led by Captain S. Boudreaux assembled at the corner of Washington and Corinne streets to salute the first train to enter New Iberia. As the work train approached, pulling one passenger car, the receptionists fired the town's cannon eight times (perhaps one shot for every month of construction work from Berwick), and the engineer returned the salute with eight short blasts from the locomotive's whistle. This exchange was followed by a considerable amount of cheering on all sides, and, when the frolic ended, many townspeople, joined by some railroad employees, repaired to a local saloon in a demonstration of comradery.

In early September the line between New Iberia and Berwick was tested for safety and, after a locomotive raced over the rails at the amazing speed of thirty miles per hour, it was adjuged safe for trains to run between the two points--at a much slower and saner speed, to be sure. But the railroad did not begin operations as planned. In late August and early September a yellow-fever epidemic struck the Morgan City-Berwick area causing the two towns to be quarantined. This, plus a particularly bad hurricane in early September, forced a delay in railroad activity until November when a combination freight-passenger train began moving between New Orleans and New Iberia. Meanwhile, the road was completed to Lafayette in January, 1880. Work on the New Iberia depot began in February, and by the end of April, the finishing touches were put on the building.

Once the construction work was completed, everybody was anxious to get the railroad company to organize excursions. One such event, planned for April, 1880, was cancelled when the company announced it could not supply the necessary equipment.

Then, in mid-June came the announcement that the first excursion from New Orleans over the Morgan railroad to New Iberia would occur on July 4, and would be under the auspices of the Benevolent Association of the Army of Northern Virginia. The round-trip fare would be $2.00. Because the Association anticipated about 1,000 persons joing the excursion, they arranged with several New Iberia societies to prepare food and entertainment for the travellers. A Committee of Arrangement was formed with Jules Dubus, of the New Iberia Mutual Aid and Benevolent Association, serving as chairman. Numa P. Hacker, representing the Musical and Dramatic Association, served as treasurer, and A. J. Colgin, of America Fire Company No. 2, assumed the post of secretary. Others on the committee were Oscar Dupre, Charles Escudier, and A. Dore.

The Southern Pacific depot about 1915

The depot about 1940

The Southern Pacific depot, April 1972

The abandoned Amtrak depot, January 1986

Over 100 years after being laid in 1879 to connect the railroad with steamboat traffic on Bayou Teche, this spur on Railroad Avenue is still evident.

The committee took up its task. Dozens of ladies and numerous little girls were organized to make sandwiches, while innumerable young boys squeezed crates of lemons for a veritable flood of lemonade. Bands, marching groups, decorated carriages and carts, and sheet-covered mules were rounded up for the event. Men of the town built tables and benches at Davis' oak grove on the east side of town. There, the visitors would be fed and entertained.

Meanwhile, in New Orleans the proposed excursion was proving to be quite popular. By Saturday, July 3, the Association had sold all of its 1,200 tickets, but apparently hundreds of people were still seeking to join in the adventure. That afternoon the Association's officers arranged with the railroad for a second train. All seats on it were quickly sold. Still people came, and all night Saturday many stood in line at the railroad ticket office hoping to buy someone's ticket who could not make the trip, or hoping to get someone to sell their ticket for an inflated price.

At dawn Sunday morning, July 4, two-and-one-half hours before departure, hundreds of people were waiting to be ferried across the river to the railroad terminal in Algiers. Some held tickets, many did not. At 7 a.m. literally thousands, perhaps as many as 3,000 people were politely (and not so politely) elbowing their way in the general direction of the gateway to the ferry. Railroad and Association officials, determined to control the flow of people onto the ferry, placed a committee of men at the gate to exclude all but ticket holders. When boarding time arrived, however, the gate together with the committee and almost every other stationary object in the immediate vicinity were swept aside by a human tidal wave seeking to board the boat.

As the crowd pushed onto the ferry, the captain began to fear the weight of the onslaught might capsize the boat. He therefore ordered it to be moved away from the wharf, even though many people were still trying to board. Fortunately, other ferries were nearby and soon took on the remaining crowd. Once the ferries landed at Algiers, 3,000 chattering, sandwich-eating, cigar-smoking, fun-loving excursionists raced ashore, bound for the Morgan railroad terminal. In what must have appeared to waiting trainmen as a local rendition of the Exodus, the crowd engulfed the waiting trains. As soon as the startled railroad personnel regained their composure, they worked hard to bring some order out of the developing chaos. Finally, the two waiting trains, loaded to capacity (and then some), pulled out of the station, bound for the Teche country. Hundreds of people, however, were left standing in the station, but they would not be disappointed. Railroad officials had the three-coach mail train brought up and, when it was filled, it too pulled out in the direction of New Iberia. But people still stood in the station. Thus, a fourth train was put together and, a little after 9 a.m., everyone was on his way to the picnic in the country.

It would be a fun trip. In addition to the excessively crowded conditions, sticky July heat, liberal quantities of cinders from the locomotive, a horde of mosquitoes, and the din of a thousand happy voices, the drinking water on each of the trains gave out in and around Des Allemands. Furthermore, one eyewitness later remarked that, in addition to these problems, "ladies were not provided with proper accommodations." It was, therefore, a thankful, but none the less high-spirited, group that arrived at Morgan City to be ferried across the Atchafalaya to Berwick.

The Atchafalaya railroad ferry at the time was a small boat, capable of doing its job under normal circumstances, but these were not normal circumstances. So much time was required to ferry the first three trains across the river that by the time the fourth train arrived it was realized that it could not possibly reach New Iberia until sometime that night, probably long after the festivities had ended. This last train therefore terminated at Morgan City, turned around, and returned its passengers to the Crescent City before nightfall.

After crossing Berwick Bay the intrepid excursionists pushed on into the Teche country. New Iberia was only two hours from Berwick. In New Iberia, hundreds of people from the town and surrounding countryside had poured onto the streets, first of all to see the arrival of the passenger trains, and then to view the members of the Benevolent Association of the Army of Northern Virginia in their bright uniforms. One eyewitness has left this description of the scene: "From early dawn, all the avenues and roads were crowded, vehicles of every kind came loaded with people from all the surrounding towns. . . . Before 12 o'clock, standing room could scarcely be found on the sidewalks in some parts of the principal streets, and the roadway was blocked with a countless array of carriages and horsemen."

New Iberians, waiting on the railroad and peering off in the direction of Olivier, had been told the trains would arrive about 1 o'clock. After that hour passed, every unusual sound produced a false alarm that the trains were approaching. Finally, about 4 o'clock, a young boy sitting on the track with his head buried in his arms folded on his knees, and with disappointment creeping over his body, suddenly jumped up, and pointing in the direction of an approaching cloud of smoke, screamed "The Train! The Train!" Enthusiasm surged through the crowd.

The trains slowly pulled up to the oak grove, stopped and discharged most of the travel-weary but joyous passengers. The members of the Association stayed on board and went to the depot where they, together with local veterans' groups and bands, formed a parade and headed out East Main Street to the picnic grounds.

Received by a cheering crowd, the paraders and their admirers then settled down to hear appropriate speeches from Judge De Blanc, himself a Confederate veteran, from Congressman J. H. Acklen, and from other notables. Sitting in the audience and attracting no small amount of attention from all who recognized him was former Governor Francis T. Nicholls.

At 6:30 the trains (only two now, the mail train having gone on to Lafayette) approached the picnic area and sounding their whistles announced departure time. The first train, filled to capacity, left at 7 o'clock. The second train pulled out at 8 o'clock. Some visitors concluded the return trip was not worth the effort and made arrangements to stay overnight in New Iberia. Most New Iberians, hoarse from cheering and exhausted by the activities of the day, went home to bed. Everyone was well aware that the iron horse had come to town.

XI

The New Iberia Conflagration of 1899*

by
Glenn R. Conrad

The angelus was ringing at St. Peter's Church as Pierre LeBron, standing in the doorway of his grocery on the corner of Julia and St. Peter streets, checked his watch. It argued that the sexton was three minutes early. Although darkness was enveloping the community, LeBron could still see many pedestrians on St. Peter Street in the direction of Iberia and on Julia Street toward Main. Most of these people were going home after an unusually warm October 10. The temperature had pushed into the middle eighties. LeBron surveyed the crystal-clear sky, looking not for stars, but for rain clouds. New Iberia's last rain had been in

---

*AUTHOR'S NOTE: Although the activities of the persons named are fictitious (except Mayor Broussard's appeal telegrams), the facts of this story are documented in the New Orleans *Daily Picayune*, October 11, 12, 1899; the *New Iberia Enterprise*, August 26, October 7, 14, 1899; the *Weekly Iberian*, October 14, 1899.

The 1899 conflagration was not the first disastrous fire in the commercial district of New Iberia. On June 28, 1870, fire broke out at Jeanty's (Gentil's?) grocery store on the north side of Main Street. The fire destroyed all buildings between Bridge and Weeks streets and Main Street and the bayou. Across Main, the fire burned from Church Alley to near Weeks Street. Among those businesses destroyed were Hebert & Co., general merchants; Wm. Burke & Co., grocer; J. L. Burke Livery Stable; Jacques Fourcade, general merchant; Ferrall and Serret, commission merchants; Eugene Dariet, coffeehouse; L. Bazus, coffeehouse; the courthouse; Boutte and Gonsoulin Livery Stable; Weeks' buildings; Mistrot and Decuir, general merchants; Mestayer's drug store; Lion Hotel; A. Renaud, watchmaker; Soulier and Decuir, general merchants; Lehman & Hayem, general merchants; E. Montagne, general merchant and furniture dealer; the U. S. Mail Co. (stage coach company). No lives were lost in the 1870 fire which broke out about 11 p. m. Damage was estimated at $250,000. For a brief account of the 1870 fire, see the New Orleans *Daily Picayune*, June 30, 1870, and the *Lafayette Advertiser*, July 2, 1870.

The second, third, and fourth buildings from left, known as the Duperier Block, were built shortly after the fire of June 1870. The first building from left was built by Octave Renoudet in 1898; its facade has been remodeled. These buildings are in the 100 block of East Main Street.

late August, and by now the drought had reached critical proportions as cisterns with drinking water ran dry. The dry spell nurtured other inconveniences as well. Clouds of dust billowed up each time a team tramped past the LeBron store, and all day a steady east wind ushered the finely powered earth into the building and onto the wares. Flies, which had been a constant annoyance during the first month of the drought, were seemingly reduced in number because of the new municipal garbage service. This daily service, provided by a mule and cart, was one more achievement of Mayor John Broussard's administration.

Indeed, only minutes before, LeBron had stopped the mayor, on his way home, to assure his honor that he would certainly be happy when the municpal waterworks went into operation. The bond issue to finance the water and electric works had been hotly debated back in the summer, and J. B. Lawton, editor and publisher of the *New Iberia Enterprise* and proponent of the bond issue, had informed his readers on the eve of the election that "New Iberia is the only town of 5,000 population, or over, in the state, without a waterworks system." He called upon townspeople to vote to "install that healthgiving, labor-saving and property-protecting triumph of the mechanics art, the gravity system of waterworks." On election day his efforts and those of other New Iberia civic leaders had helped to produce a majority vote favoring waterworks.

Leaving LeBron, Mayor Broussard strolled toward home, a block away on St. Peter Street. Crossing Weeks Street, he stopped to chat with Fernand Dauterive, whose store-residence, a two-story brick structure on the corner of Weeks and St. Peter, was nearing completion. Earlier that day, the builders, Alfred and Aristide Etie, had assured Mr. Dauterive that his family would be enjoying their new quarters by Christmas. Mayor Broussard was pleased to have the Dauterives as his next-door neighbors.

On Main Street many businesses were closing as the angelus sounded. E. J. Carstens locked the front door of his store in the Segura Building on the corner of Main and Julia streets and hurried off toward Center Street where his new home was nearing completion. A few days before, the local newspaper had described Carsten's house as "beautiful in design, modern in arrangement and equipment, . . . it will be a source of joy to the family."

Carstens had just ended a "Close Our Sale of Summer Shoes" before displaying his Christmas stock. The advertisement pages of the local paper gave evidence of the little city's prosperity at the turn of the century. In his grocery on Julia Street, directly behind the New Iberia National Bank, Victor Aubry took the opportunity of a business lag around supper time to browse the pages of the hometown newspaper. He saw his advertisement and smiled approvingly. He noted that his neighbor across the street, Charles Horner, the blacksmith and wheelwright, advertised "Pipe Fitting Done Under Full Guarantee." Another neighbor, J. Jacquemoud, advertised that he was a "Manufacturer of Carriages, Buggies, Wagons, and Vehicles of All Kinds." Dr. T. J. Woolf's advertisement reminded Aubry that he should go by the Attakapas Sanatorium and get the doctor to remove a wart from his left thumb. Aubry wondered if Dr. Woolf would use his new-fangled electrical treatment, for the doctor's advertisement read: "Treatment of Disease by Electricity--A Specialty." Aubry's thoughts tumbled along one after the other as he scanned the paper. He spotted a headline that proclaimed it to be six weeks since the last rain. This, in turn, brought to mind the August bond issue and Aubry was thinking of the convenience of "city water" and the luxury of electricity when his reverie was interrupted by a customer.

Albert Estorge had just closed his wholesale and retail drug company on Main Street and was going home when he remembered that he was expected to pick up a few items at the grocery store. Aubry remarked that Estorge was late getting away from the store this evening; the druggist agreed, adding that he had waited for his cleaning boy to finish his work. Tucking the groceries into the crook of his arm, Albert Estorge headed toward home as the angelus rang.

On Main Street, in the busy commercial block between Julia and Iberia streets, merchants were suspending operations for the day. P. A. Ross was closing his dry goods store next door to Estorge's drug emporium. The Two Lions Hotel in the middle of the block had a fair number of guests for a Tuesday night, mostly salesmen scouting the Christmas trade. Sol Adler's and Nathan Dreyfus' grocery stores were still open as the glow of kerosene lights attested. J. W. Eckert stood in the doorway of his jewelry store telling young Dr. George Sabatier about the latest shipment of merchandise received. C. P. Moss nodded to James Lee, the druggist, as he rounded the corner on Iberia for home a half-block away.

The angelus was ringing as a young Adler skipped across the front porch of the family home on Iberia Street and headed toward George Doerle's bakery on the corner. A block down St. Peter from the bakery, Oklar Hebert stepped into Pierre LeBron's grocery just in time to hear the storekeeper mutter that the sexton's watch was three minutes fast.

For the next few minutes activity in the heart of New Iberia was normal. Nothing heralded the impending disaster. A few minutes past six, G. W. Peters walked to the back of his office in the old post office building on Julia Street and locked the rear entrance. In the half-light of twilight he saw the mass of wooden cottages clustered along Church Alley as well as the sheds and other outbuildings that crowded into the center of the block. Each cottage displayed from its doorway and windows a dim kerosene light; each little chimney above the wooden shingled roof smoked from the preparation of the evening meal. The potential fire hazard here had frequently entered Peters' thoughts. Tonight was no exception. As he turned from the door he heard a muffled sound, like the thud of a heavy object hitting the ground, or perhaps a small explosion. His glance shot toward the back entrances of the cottages, but nothing appeared to be amiss. Returning to the front of the building, Peters stepped out onto Julia Street, and barely had time to lock the front door when he heard the fearful cry--"Fire!"

At 6:15 p.m., the large bell in the tower of the city hall on Main Street announced the emergency and warned of disaster. From all sides people gathered to watch and to fight the fire that originated from an exploding lantern in a warehouse behind the Estorge drug store. Surrounded by wooden buildings on Church Alley, St. Peter Street, and John Broussard's livery stable on Julia Street, the fire was free to move in almost any direction. Feeding on the chemicals and other inflammables at its origin, secure for the moment from the water of Iberia Fire Company Number 1, the blaze was free to become a roaring inferno before it burst through the roof of the Estorge building.

The Conflagration

The Municipal Fire Bell
that tolled the emergency
of October 10, 1899

The ringing bell brought Mayor Broussard running from his house. Reaching Main Street, the mayor immediately realized that the local fire company was inadequate to control the blaze. He therefore went directly to the Western Union office in the Gouguenheim Building on the corner of Iberia and Main streets and dashed off telegrams appealing for help from Jeanerette, Lafayette, St. Martinville, and Franklin. Within minutes he had the replies. Jeanerette and St. Martinville would dispatch their engines and fire companies. Lafayette had no engine; Franklin's engine was in need of repair. Knowing that valuable time would be lost if the engines were brought over the poor roads from Jeanerette and St. Martinville, Broussard next phoned the Southern Pacific depot and, learning from a company official that one of the locomotives in the yard still had steam up, asked that it be sent with a flat car to Jeanerette to pick up the fire engine and company. A second locomotive, he was informed, would be sent to St. Martinville as soon as its crew could raise steam. Minutes later, the locomotive and flat car raced out of New Iberia in the direction of Jeanerette. At the same moment, the Southern Pacific telegraph operator tapped out orders for all trains on the main line to halt at Jeanerette and Cade, thereby keeping the tracks open for the emergency trains.

As Mayor Broussard left the Western Union office, he could see the flames spreading rapidly. From its starting point in the rear of Estorge's, the fire had moved swiftly through the timber-dry buildings in the heart of the block and

The devastated area of downtown New Iberia included the entire block bounded by Main, Iberia, St. Peter, and Julia streets. The above picture was taken from St. Peter St. looking northwestward toward the intersection of Main and Iberia streets.

had attacked the rich fuel supply of Mayor Broussard's livery stable. At the same time the inferno began to move up Main Street toward Iberia as the gentle east wind fanned it to great frenzy.

By 7 o'clock the fire had consumed the buildings on the corner of Main and Julia, including the New Iberia National Bank, and was marching relentlessly up Main toward Iberia. Meanwhile, most of the block of Julia between Main and St. Peter had become engulfed in flames with the fire threatening to leap the narrow street and move into the block toward the east. New Iberia's only fire engine and its company concentrated on the Main Street buildings, but with little effect.

By 7:30 p.m., the fire was moving ever nearer Iberia Street. It had consumed P. A. Ross' store, Jules Landry's saloon, the Two Lions Hotel, LaSalle's

The Conflagration

The burned area of downtown New Iberia looking westward from Julia St. to Iberia Street.

saloon (at the corner of Church Alley and Main) and was moving rapidly toward the Moss Hotel. So intense was the heat on the opposite side of Main Street that the plate glass shattered in the windows of the new Kling Building on the corner of Bridge Street. People moved back as the heat of the fire burned their exposed faces.

As the fire approached each building, its owner, his employees, and friends were seen rushing in and out of the wtore in an effort to save merchandise. Suffocating smoke was everywhere. The fire roared toward Lee's drug store on the corner of Main and Iberia.

The firefighters came to the realization that there was no chance of saving any building between Julia and Iberia streets. The first possible line of defense was Iberia Street itself. The street, however, was narrow; the steady breeze from the east made it questionable whether the width of the street was sufficient to prevent the flames from leaping across. On the west side of Iberia Street

The south (left) side of Main Street as rebuilt after the fire of 1899.

The south (right) side of Main Street about 75 years after the fire of 1899.

The Conflagration

three structures proved dangerous to the safety of the entire block. These were the Gouguenheim Building on the corner of Main and Iberia, a residence owned by Charles Fontelieu in mid-block, and the residence of Judge Joseph Breaux on the corner of Iberia and St. Peter. If the fire successfully crossed to one of these buildings, the probability was that the entire block would be doomed. Nevertheless, there was cause for hope: the Gouguenheim Building was constructed of brick and had a metal roof; Judge Breaux's house was protected on the front by shade trees. Only the Fontelieu house was dangerously exposed, but the house was surrounded by empty lots, a natural firebreak. Thus, with a strategy adopted of making a stand on Iberia Street, the local fire department began wetting down the Gouguenheim Building galleries.

As these plans materialized, the fire spread quickly to Lee's drug store and turned southward, engulfing the residences of Max Levy and C. P. Moss. Within moments Sol Adler's house and the next one burst into flames. Only one structure now stood between the inferno and St. Peter Street--George Doerle's bakery. Once again the question arose: could the fire be contained--this time at St. Peter Street? Opposite Doerle's bakery was the colored convent, a frame building which, if ignited, would threaten St. Peter's Church, the rectory, and still another block of wooden structures. Anticipating this danger to the block south of the disaster area, one bucket brigade began wetting down the convent while a second group concentrated on Judge Breaux's home.

George Doerle's bakery had but minutes before burst into flame when, above the noise and tumult of the scene, a train whistle blared forth. The locomotive and car had returned from Jeanerette with that community's fire company and pumper. Sliding to a halt, the locomotive stopped at the corner of Iberia and Washington streets. Without lost effort, the Jeanerette firemen unloaded their engine and sped to the corner of Iberia and St. Peter. Their arrival was decisive. Despite the heroic efforts of the bucket brigade, the front wall and roof of the convent had, on several occasions, ignited from the heat of the fire across the street. With the Jeanerette pumper on the scene, water was applied directly to the source of the fire--the burning Doerle building--thus reducing the probability of flames crossing either Iberia or St. Peter streets.

About the time that the Jeanerette fire department arrived in New Iberia, so did the St. Martinville contingent. Tiring of waiting for the train to arrive to take them to New Iberia, the St. Martinville firemen hitched six mules to their pumper and, beating the animals, covered the ten miles between the two towns in seemingly record time. Without a moment's hesitation, they took up a position next to the New Iberia firefighters, and together the teams worked to halt the fire at Iberia Street.

The fire now appeared to be contained by the width of Main Street and the strategically located fire companies. One area, however, remained unprotected--

the east side of Julia Street. The firefighters had hoped that the prevailing east wind would prevent the flames from crossing the narrow street, and so it had, until the fire burned to the corner of Julia and St. Peter streets. During a momentary lull in the breeze, the heat of the fire caused Charles Flockerzie's livery stable on the east side of Julia Street to burst into flames. From that point the fire travelled down St. Peter toward Weeks Street, consuming the houses owned by Laurent Bazus, Mrs. Emile Theriot, and Mrs. P. L. Renoudet. At the same time the fire moved along the east side of Julia destroying the wheelwright and blacksmith shops and threatening the Segura Building on the corner. Only the heroic efforts of a bucket brigade saved that building.

By 10 o'clock the crisis had passed. Nevertheless, a few anxious moments were had when the Fontelieu house on the west side of Iberia Street burst into flames. The empty lots surrounding it did, however, insulate the fire from the remainder of the block.

By midnight the fire had burned its course. The block bordered by Julia, Main, Iberia and St. Peter streets was totally destroyed. The east side of Julia

At the time of the downtown fire, this building housed James A. Lee's apothecary. The masonry walls withstood the fire and the present building incorporates those walls. Lee's name is still discernable on the masonry block atop the structure.

The Conflagration

Buildings erected on Julia Street after the fire of 1899. Facade of building at right of later construction. Above photo taken March, 1972; below, the buildings as they appeared in January 1986.

and the north side of St. Peter between Julia and Weeks were also burned out. As New Iberians took stock, they discovered the following victims of the holacaust. On the south side of Main Street the fire burned the New Iberia National Bank, Estorge drug store, P. A. Ross's general store, Jules Landry's saloon, the Two Lions Hotel, LaSalle's saloon, Sol Adler's grocery, C. P. Moss' restaurant and hotel, Decourt's barber shop, Smith, De Blanc, and Suberbielle's dry goods store, Nathan Dreyfus' grocery, J. W. Eckart's jewelry store, Harry and Muller's clothing and dry goods store, the State Bank of New Iberia, J. J. Craig's insurance company, the Postal Telegraph Co., Pfister Brothers jewelry store, James Lee's drug store, the law offices of Foster and Broussard, the lodge rooms of the Catholic Knights of America, Justice Breaux's office, and the offices of Drs. J. W. K. Shaw, C. Pierson, and George Sabatier.

On Iberia Street the fire burned the residences of Max Levy, C. P. Moss, Sol Adler, and the unoccupied house belonging to Charles Fontelieu.

On St. Peter Street the fire consumed George Doerle's bakery and residence, the boarding house belonging to Oklar Hebert, Mrs. Decuir's cottage occupied by the Frank Blanc family, the Pierre LeBron residence and store, the harness shop and residence of Charles Flockerzie, a cottage owned by Laurent Bazus, Mrs. Emile Theriot's home and the house owned by Mrs. P. L. Renoudet.

On Julia Street the victims included Vincent Piraro's fruit stand, G. W. Peters' office in the old post office building, the residence of Homer Daigre, John Broussard's livery stables, carriage barns, etc., Joe Hughes' horseshoeing shop, J. Jacquemoud's wheelwriting and blacksmithing shops, Benthall and Horner's blacksmithing shop, A. A. Flory's harness and saddlery shop, and Victor Aubry's grocery.

No surviving records reveal the names of those who suffered property damage on Church Alley. Miraculously, only one fatality resulted from the conflagration. The victim's remains were found in the ashes of what had been the Harry and Muller store on Main Street.

An exhausted citizenry trudged home after midnight. Friends and relatives of the fire victims offered shelter until new accommodations could be found. Everyone awaited daylight to determine the extent of the damage, and to begin the job of rebuilding.

As the last doors closed and the last lamps went out that long October night in 1899, New Iberians still awake heard a most unfamiliar sound--it was raining.

XII

New Iberia Gets a Post Office

by
Glenn R. Conrad

In the twilight years of the nineteenth century, one of the most needed improvements for the thriving little town of New Iberia was permanent premises for the United States Post Office. Since the first post office was established on March 2, 1814, local postal facilities had always been housed in leased or rented space.[1] As a result, the postmaster and his clerk were usually sandwiched into the corner or unused side room of someone's store. Invariably, these wooden buildings were miserably cold in winter and suffocatingly hot in summer. Moreover, the tenancy of the post office in any one of these habitats was often abruptly ended by fire. As late as October, 1898, the post office had moved

---

1. Post Office records disclose that "a post office was established in Louisiana shortly prior to April 1, 1809, listed as Attakapas, or St. Martinville, or New Iberia." Nathan Morse was the first postmaster (for more on Morse, see footnote 27 of the essay entitled "The Obituary of William Weeks.") Then, in 1814, this post office was simply designated "St. Martinville," and on March 2 of that year another post office was established in the same parish and given the name "New Iberia." James Murphy was the first postmaster (for more on Murphy, see footnote 23 of the essay entitled "A Narrative of Events Connected with the Early Settlement of New Iberia."). The foregoing information is contained in a letter to Edward T. Weeks, Sr., from K. P. Aldrich, November 2, 1934. Aldrich was, at the time, with the Post Office Department in Washington, D. C. A copy of the letter is in the possession of Mrs. Henry Dauterive, Sr.

A listing of the postmasters of New Iberia appears at the end of this essay.

from Julia Street to the *Enterprise* building in the first block of West Main. Whether or not the postmaster had a premonition of things to come is unknown, but the former Julia Street home of the post office burned a year later in the great fire of 1899.

For years the plight of the post office was a frequent topic of conversation among the town's businessmen. They often expressed wonder over the fact that although the town was growing rapidly, the federal government did not act to construct a permanent post office. True, the 1890 census had listed only 3,400 residents of the community, but in the seven or eight years after the enumeration it was apparent that the population had nearly tripled. Large sawmills employing many men had located their factories and workmen's quarters just outside the city limits. The construction of a major sugar mill on the outskirts of town had attracted additional families from nearby rural areas. Further evidence of New Iberia's need for a permanent postal facility was the fact that the town was the head of navigation for steamboat traffic on the Teche. This meant that the local post office was the collection and distribution center for a large volume of freight and mail for the surrounding region. In addition, not only did the Southern Pacific's main line run through the town, but also in recent weeks there had been reliable reports that New Iberia would soon become the terminus of another major railroad. All of these factors therefore served to constantly prod local leaders to urge, through the Third District congressman, that the government build a post office in New Iberia. But Representative Andrew Price lived in Thibodaux and really was not too concerned about the state of postal facilities in New Iberia.

Prospects for the post office project took a dramatic turn for the better when, in November, 1896, a local man and long-time advocate of a new postal facility, Robert F. Broussard, was elected to Congress from the Third District. Upon entering the House of Representatives on March 4, 1897, the freshman legislator was assigned to the Post Office Committee. New Iberia's town fathers were delighted.

Over the next few months the congressman began investigating the possibility of securing a government appropriation for the erection of a post office in his hometown. Almost at once he encountered a host of formidable problems, most of which were completely unknown to his constituents. First, of course, were the problems of politics, party, and regionalism. Broussard was a freshman Democrat from the South sitting in a chamber dominated by Eastern Republicans. Moreover, thirty years or so after the Civil War, there was still no rush on the part of Northern legislators to spend federal money in the South, especially in a little-known place like . . . "What's the name of that place? . . . Oh yes, New Iberia." Then there were problems of a more practical nature. For example, postal authorities in Washington informed Congressman Broussard that

The Post Office

U. S. Representative, later
U. S. Senator
Robert F. Broussard
(about 1900)

his proposal would receive little attention because of New Iberia's small population as reflected in the 1890 census. Only towns of approximately 10,000 population would be seriously considered for permanent postal facilities. Furthermore, it was a Post Office Department regulation that there be no free mail delivery in towns of less than 10,000 people.

Undaunted, the congressman pursued his goal, seeking ways around the uncompromising obstacles. In Washington, Mr. Broussard contacted his friends in Congress, presented his arguments in favor of the project, and asked for their support of a bill he would soon introduce seeking an appropriation for New Iberia's federal building. Then, at home, he urged Mayor John Fisher and the city council to extend the limits of the town to include the hundreds of people living nearby. Following such action a new census would be taken and the figures used to support Broussard's argument that the town was large enough to warrant expanded postal facilities.

The wheels of progress, however, were not well greased. Throughout 1897 and most of 1898 little was done locally to get the project moving; hence, Congressman Broussard was unable to introduce his appropriation bill for a public building.[2] Nevertheless, by late 1898, two events coincided to rejuvenate

---

2. *New Iberia Enterprise* (November 12, 1898) reported that Congressman Broussard had not introduced the bill during his first term of office because of "the restricted limits of the corporation, causing a poor showing in population."

the project. The city fathers succeeded in incorporating the large population formerly living outside the resctricted city limits, and Congressman Broussard was elected to a second term of office in November.

Owing to the outbreak of the Spanish-American War in April, 1898, Congress was sitting in special session, obviating the need for Broussard to await the convening of the new Congress to introduce his measure. Accordingly, on December 20, 1898, House Resolution 11314 was introduced "to provide for a public building at New Iberia, La." The bill stated, in part, that the cost of buying the site and erecting the building should not exceed $50,000. Moreover, "the site purchased shall leave the building unexposed to danger from fire by an open space of at least 40 feet, including streets and alleys." Following normal legislative procedure, the bill was then referred to the Committee on Public Buildings and Grounds.[3]

Arriving home for Christmas, Congressman Broussard was happy to learn that the city's limits had been extended and that a census of the enlarged town would shortly be taken. In early February, 1899, W. B. Davis took the initiative with regard to the census and, securing an appropriation of $50.00 from the city, set a force of young men to work enumerating the population. The final count stood at 7,856 people in New Iberia.[4]

Meanwhile, in Washington, Mr. Broussard continued soliciting support for his bill. On February 6, the Committee on Public Builidngs and Grounds reported the bill and referred it to the Committee of the Whole House on the State of the Union.[5] The measure passed the House Committee of the Whole without opposition and, of sixty similar measures to be brought before the House for a vote, was placed in eighth position. Mr. Broussard was encouraged by the bill's prospects for passage, and reported this to the editor of the local newspaper who, in turn, informed his readers.[6] Then, disaster struck. Writing to his

---

3. U. S. *Congressional Record*, 55th Cong., 3rd Sess. 1898, XXXII, Part 1, 356. Hereafter cited as *Congressional Record*.

4. Even after the city limits were extended, the total population amounted to only 7,856. See *New Iberia Enterprise*, February 4, 1899.

Probably with his fingers crossed, Mr. Broussard, when asked by another member of the House of Representatives about the population figure for New Iberia, responded, "about 10,000," the exact number needed for further consideration of his bill. For some of the congressional debate on building a post office in New Iberia, see *ibid.*, Part 2, 1571, and Part 3, 2586.

5. *Ibid.*, Part 2, 1519.

6. *New Iberia Enterprise*, February 25, 1899.

The Post Office

Foundation for the old post office, Weeks and Main streets, is laid December 1902

Construction on the old post office as of January 1, 1903
Buildings in the background are Benthall's and Horner's Blacksmith Shop (far left), a cottage residence; the spire of St. Peter's Church above the cottage; the Bazus Hotel (long, two-story building), and the former home of Judge E. J. Etie (in front of Bazus Hotel).

Construction work as of February 1, 1903

Construction work as of June 1, 1903

The Post Office

The front facade of the completed post office, October, 1903. The Koch home is at left

The rear facade of the completed post office. The Pascal Building is at left.

friend, E. F. Millard, Broussard explained what had happened. "When the bills were considered in the house, a filibustering party consumed the entire time allotted us by the committee on rules, so that we failed to put any of the bills through. This is a dreadful setback. . . . [but] we have not given up hopes."[7] Nevertheless, hope was waning, for the special session ended on March 4, and in late February it seemed almost impossible to get the measure reconsidered in the final days of the Fifty-fifth Congress.

Through adroit legislative maneuvers, however, Broussard and his congressional allies succeeded in having the bill reconsidered. On February 28 the Speaker of the House called up House Bill 11314 to provide for a public building in New Iberia.[8] Instantly reacting, Congressman Sereno E. Payne of New York, chairman of the Committee on Ways and Means and leader of those opposing the measure, leaped to his feet and inaugurated a series of parliamentary maneuvers designed to consume once more the time allotted for the bill's consideration. The Speaker *pro tempore* would not, however, tolerate such delaying tactics and thus forced Mr. Payne into a defense of his opposition. Payne stated:

> I object to the consideration of this bill. . . . Here is a small village, a place, even according to the report of the committee, without material importance, where no courts are held; a small post office, where receipts are insignificant, a place practically unknown, except as we see the name on the maps and in the geographies of that region. There is no need of this building there. It is a large expenditure of public money, without, in my judgment, any justification. There is no court of the United States and no custom house there, and only a few few inhabitants, and the post office receipts are so insignificant that the advocates of the bill do not even put them in the report. . . . Here is a bill making an appropriation of $50,000, when every man knows that the Government never rented a post office building there in the past that cost $5,000 for construction...[9]

As Mr. Payne concluded his remarks, Congressman Albert Berry of Kentucky, a relative of Ledger Grant of New Iberia and a close friend of Bob Broussard, rose and noted

---

7. *Ibid.*

8. *Congressional Record*, XXXII, Part 3, 2586.

9. *Ibid.*

that it seems a little strange . . . that when three separate bills were proposed, considered, and passed for New York we heard not a single word or objection from Mr. Payne. Now, however, there is great objection because of the introduction of the pending bill. Of course, I know New York is the center of population--a metropolitan center . . . and there can be no possible objection to the erection of public buildings . . . in the metropolis of the country.[10]

At this juncture Congress Jerry Simpson of Kansas injected a thought: "Let me suggest to the gentleman from Kentucky that the gentleman from New York was acting upon his 'convictions' in regard to New York."[11] This comment evoked hearty laughter from House members and was followed by several cries of "Vote," "Vote." Clearly, congressional opposition to New Iberia's public building was crumbling. The division confirmed this fact as the House voted 92 to 20 in favor of Broussard's bill.[12] The Senate considered and passed the bill the same day, and, on March 2, President William McKinley signed HR 11314, providing for a public building at New Iberia, Louisiana,[13] The presidential pen used to sign the appropriation was handed to Congressman Broussard who, in turn, forwarded it to James A. Lee, the New Iberia druggist, a prime mover among those seeking a new post office for New Iberia.

Reacting to the good news, a group of New Iberians planned a reception for Congressman Broussard in recognition of his achievement. The gala was held at City Hall on March 8. Upon their arrival for the occasion, Mr. and Mrs. Broussard were given an enthusiastic ovation, and were escorted to the platform by the Reverend C. C. Kramer and Captain A. N. Muller. On behalf of Mayor Fisher, W. R. Burke acted as master of ceremonies. Welcoming speeches were made by Dr. Alfred Duperier and Captain Muller. Congressman Broussard was introduced "amid deafening applause" and then recounted the battle waged to secure the $50,000 appropriation. He concluded by informing his audience that in a few weeks the government would invite proposals for the building site. To mark the occasion, Victor Aubry presented Mr. Broussard with a gold-headed cane.[14]

10. *Ibid.*

11. *Ibid.*

12. *Ibid.*

13. *Ibid.*, Part 3, 2932.

14. *New Iberia Enterprise*, March 11, 1899. It can be noted here that the brief his-

The government's call for site proposals for the post office appeared in the newspaper on April 1, 1899. James K. Taylor, supervising architect of the Treasury Department, stated that the government was seeking preferably a corner lot at least 130 feet wide by 120 feet deep, but in the event a corner lot was unavailable, then an interior lot at least 170 feet by 120 feet would be considered. He reminded New Iberians that "the United States has not got money to burn, and it does not expect to pay three or four times the value for property which it intends to purchase." An editorial suggested that the Jackson and Taylor property on Main Street, stretching from Fisher Street to McMahon's furniture store (shortly thereafter the site of the Elks Theater) or a distance of 144 feet, would be a desirable location. Also mentioned as a possibility was the residence site of Judge R. S. Perry on the corner of Jefferson and Main streets.[15] A week later five sites were known to be available: the Jackson and Taylor properties; Judge Perry's residence property; the Gilmore and Winters property, opposite the Methodist church; the Opera House lot; and the Pointis and Delcambre properties on the corner of Main and Weeks streets.[16]

A month afterward, in early May, 1899, Inspector W. D. Windom arrived to investigate the merits of the various sites offered for the post office. His instructions concerning the selection of a site were specific. The overriding factor was proximity to the center of business rather than proximity to the center of population. In drawing up his report, Windom stated that the main business district was on Main Street between Weeks and Jefferson--its center being at Iberia Street. In addition to steady growth along Main Street, Windom noted that the town was also spreading out along Duperier Avenue, or the Fausse Pointe Road, and on Center Street. The business district, he speculated, would not continue to grow along Main Street, but would invade St. Peter Street and cross streets linking Main with St. Peter. It was his conclusion, however, that sometime in the future Center Street would probably be the town's main avenue of commerce. Windom then reported that the Southern Pacific Railroad was planning a new passenger station for New Iberia. The railroad had picked a site just off Center Street for the depot, but had put off construction of the new facility un-

---

tory of New Iberia prepared by Dr. Alfred Duperier, and which subsequently appeared in two installments in the *Enterprise* entitled "A Narrative of Events Connected with the Early Settlement of New Iberia," was originally written for presentation at this function. A lack of time, however, precluded its presentation, and the piece later appeared in the newspaper.

15. *New Iberia Enterprise,* April 1, 1899.

16. *Ibid.,* April 8, 1899. The Opera House lot was approximately where the Frederic Hotel later stood.

til the post office site was selected because, by law, if the depot was within a quarter mile of the post office, the railroad company was required to make free delivery of mail to the post office. Hence, the site of the railroad station would be determined only after the post office site was selected. The depot would then be built just outside the quarter-mile limit.[17]

The Treasury Department had received a total of twenty-six site proposals from New Iberia's landowners. Of these, six proposed sites were south of the Southern Pacific railroad. Windom believed that it would "be unwise to place the building in a location that compelled the majority of the population to cross these dangerous tracks when visiting the post office." Hence, no further consideration was given to the proposals of A. C. Boas, L. A. Pellerin, U. S. Haase, A. F. Daunoy, and two sites proposed by Peters and DeGeneres.[18]

Next, the two proposals of Mrs. N. P. Millard for the corner of Main and Railroad Avenue and St. Peter and Railroad Avenue were rejected because "Railroad Avenue is not a public street but the property of the railroad company through which its tracks run to a wharf on the bayou."[19]

The proposal of George Simon offering a lot at the corner of Main and Hopkins was excluded because of its "remoteness from the center of business population." Meanwhile, John T. White withdrew his proposal of a site at the corner of Washington and French streets.[20]

Three proposals were dismissed from further consideration because of insufficiency of land dimensions or because the price was greater than the appropriation would allow. This included a site of three varying widths on Main Street between French and Jefferson offered by Todd and Davis and two proposals by Levy and Davis, realtors, for the two corners of Weeks and Main, south of Main because the owners resubmitted proposals for the same sites for a lesser price.[21]

Windom found that three sites proposed were across the bayou from the business district in the vicinity of Duperier Avenue and Bridge Street. One of these lots was being offered by Mrs. F. H. Duperier and two by Millard and Weeks. While one of the Millard and Weeks lots presented "advantages superior to any other from an artistic point of view," Windom found, however, that "it was dis-

17. *Ibid.*, June 17, 1899.

18. *Ibid.*

19. *Ibid.*

20. *Ibid.*

21. *Ibid.*

The Vaccaro-Jennaro Store (cor. Jefferson and St. Peter) about 1898.

tant from the business quarter and in the opposite direction from the probable growth thereof." A serious objection, of course, was that the property was on the opposite side of the bayou from the business district.[22]

The result of this culling process was that four sites were finally considered by the government for the new post office. These were the John T. White property on the corner of Jefferson and St. Peter, diagonal from the Methodist church (then the location of the Vaccaro and Jennaro Store); an interior lot offered by A. C. Gayle on the northwest side of French Street; the southeast corner of Jefferson and Main, offered by Levy and Davis; and finally, the corner of Weeks and Main extending back to Charles Street, also offered by Levy and Davis, realtors.[23]

Windom recommended that last site because that lot "has the advantage over the three others of being bounded on three sides by streets and from this fact it results that a great portion of this lot is available for building purposes after deducting 40 feet of fire limit." Furthermore, the Main-Weeks location was favored because it was larger than the other three; aesthetically more desirable

22. *Ibid.*

23. *Ibid.*

owing to the slight angle in Main Street which allowed the building to present a pleasing appearance; and finally, it was near Center Street which "gives promise of rapid increase in population and importance." Windom therefore recommended the purchase of this lot for a price of $8,000.[24]

Once the decision was made--once the excitement ended of speculating which site would be chosen--there was naturally a sense of disappointment for various reasons among some New Iberians. The editor of the *Enterprise*, J. B. Lawton, commented editorially on the "disappointed portion of our population at the location selected" and, he said, he was to be counted "as one of the disappointed ones." He emphasized, none the less, that the many rumors in circulation concerning the selection of the site were definitely untrue. In particular, the story that a deal had been proposed to Mr. Windom to the effect that if the Main-Weeks site was selected, the remaining property in the block bounded by Main, Weeks, Center, and Charles streets would be bought by several civic-minded individuals and donated to the city as a public park. The post office, according to the story, would then have been placed squarely in the center of the block, facing "The Shadows." The editor labeled the story "greatly elaborated" and published a letter from Mayor John Broussard in which his honor stated that it had been casually suggested in a private discussion by New Iberia businessmen that if the Main-Weeks property was selected, it would be nice "if" the additional land could be acquired for a public park. To his knowledge the mayor continued, Mr. Windom was entirely unaware of the suggestion. But rumors are thick-skinned and possess incredible longevity; thus, the story caused many New Iberians to harbor had feelings toward the entire post office project.

Then, too, many Iberians had thought that the site selection was the last bit of business before the erection of the post office. Actually the site selection was only the beginning of the entire project. Thus, when nothing happened on the local scene for the next twenty-five months, a sense of keen disappointment crept across most townsmen. In Washington, however, the wheels of the government bureaucracy turned slowly. On June 25, 1901, in reply to an inquiry by Congressman Broussard, J. K. Taylor stated that working drawings of the building were being prepared.[25] Then, seven months later, in January, 1902, Taylor announced the completion of the specifications and the advertisement for construction bids for the post office building.[26]

24. *Ibid.*

25. *Ibid.*, June 29, 1901.

26. *Ibid.*, February 3, 1902.

E. W. Phillips and J. W. Taylor (no relation to the supervising architect), local architect and building contractor, submitted a bid as did the Congressional Construction Co. of Chicago. Phillips' and Taylor's bids were the lowest at $45,245, and everyone delighted at the prospect of a local firm, hiring local people, doing the construction work. Even these hopes and expectations were dashed, however, when, a week later, it was learned that all bids had been rejected by the government because they were in excess of available funds.[27] In mid-April, therefore, the government advertised anew for construction bids. The local builders again submitted a proposal, but when the bids were opened it was determined that Brandt and Co. of Atlanta were low bidders and were therefore awarded the contract. Deep disappointment again engulfed the community over the prospect of the construction money going elsewhere. As a result, the community developed a tacit "hands-off" policy toward their new post office.[28]

In early October, 1902, Colonel O. J. Muchmore, superintendent of public buildings, and his wife arrived in New Iberia and, after settling into his temporary home on the corner of Center and Main streets, the colonel prepared to oversee the construction work. By late October the Georgia contractor moved into town with a sizable work force, hired some local laborers, and began work in earnest.[29]

Just before Christmas the foundations of the building had been laid and the placing of the stone facings and walls had begun. Many citizens felt that by-gones should be by-gones, that any heretofore hard feelings should be forgotten and plans developed to recognize the new addition to New Iberia. In that season of goodwill, Editor Lawton wrote: "We hear of no effort on the part of our citizens to celebrate the event of laying the cornerstone with appropriate ceremonies. . . . A movement should be made toward some public recognition of a great work." He suggested that the civic organizations and fraternal lodges should take the lead in planning an appropriate event. He concluded: "No other public building in this city has been allowed to go up with-

---

27. *Ibid.*, March 29, 1902

28. *Ibid.*, April 12, 1902.

29. *Ibid.*, October 18, 1902. Colonel Muchmore took up his quarters in the Clerc home.

The Post Office 243

out an appropriate and reasonable ceremony."[30] To this appeal there was but little response. One civic group appointed a committee to make arrangements for laying the cornerstone, but its efforts came to nothing as the committee members disagreed among themselves as to what action should be taken. Attempting to mollify public sentiment, Colonel Muchmore provided a cornerstone; but not even this action would induce the community to stage an appropriate ceremony.[31]

Throughout spring and summer of 1903 the construction work continued apace. In early June the cupola was completed marking the end of exterior work on the Williamsburg-style building. By mid-August the interior work was nearly finished. Once again, many individuals believed that there would be a formal dedication of the gleaming new building dominating Main Street. One letter to the editor commented that

> our beautiful Post Office is nearing completion. . . . Surely there should be a mass meeting called by our progressive City Council to accept the gift from Uncle Sam with appropriate expressions of thanks, the band could give some rousing national airs. Our local fraternities could turn out and have a number of very short speeches. Congressman Broussard should be publicly thanked for his part of the good work. No, let us drop our intense provincialism as the time grows. Let our various factions quit the old game of always 'playing for keeps' and grow large enough to consider the public good once in a while.[32]

This plea, however, fell on seemingly deaf ears. Few New Iberians would so quickly shed their pique. As a consequence, as the day approached for the new facility to open its doors to public business, most of that public staunchly ignored any suggestions for a dedication ceremony. Hence, on October 10, 1903, the pastmaster, Captain T. R. Morse, and his assistant, Mr. Sam Weil, opened the front doors of the building and postal business began at the loca-

---

30. *Ibid.*, December 27, 1902.

31. *Ibid.*, January 3, 1902. The civic group was the Progressive League.

32. *Ibid.*, August 22, 1903.

tion where it would remain until July, 1965.[33] In that month and year postal operations in New Iberia moved to the Civic Center complex. It was announced in the fall of 1985 that a new main post office would be built on East Dale, just west of South Lewis Avenue.

33. *Ibid.*, October 10, 1903.

The Main Post Office, 1965 -

POSTMASTERS OF NEW IBERIA

	Date of Appointment		
James Murphy	March 2, 1814	Samuel Wakefield	July 27, 1871
Joseph Aborn	November 30, 1819	Charles Decuir	March 12, 1873
Josiah French	January 6, 1825	Carmelite C. Guilfoux	October 7, 1885
Clarkson Edgar	February 20, 1830	Robert Brantley	December 21, 1889
Achille Berard	November 14, 1834	Casimir Burkhart	February 14, 1894
John Taylor	March 22, 1837	Alexander Cestia	July 19, 1897
Abner D. Minor	January 15, 1839	Thomas R. Morse	January 28, 1902
John DeValcourt	March 5, 1839	Alphonse Davis (acting)	February 11, 1914
Josiah French	December 22, 1845	Silvio Broussard	February 20, 1914
John DeValcourt	July 6, 1846	Buvens P. Lemoine (acting)	November, 1941
Luther M. Sugg	July 25, 1856	Van J. Harry	November 1942
Robert I. Epperson	December 24, 1857	Junius H. White	March, 1966
Abner D. Minor	January 17, 1860	Carl G. Landry, Sr.	February, 1973
William G. Daunt	August 31, 1865	Earl Lacombe (acting)	June, 1979
Pierre L. Renoudet	March 21, 1867	Louis D. Noel	November, 1979
I. R. Esnard	June 15, 1869	Don Higginbotham (acting)	January, 1985
William A. Riggs	August 13, 1869	Dale E. Dooley (acting)	June, 1985
		Billy Ray Brewer	June, 1985

XIII

The Electric Railway

by
Glenn R. Conrad

The electric interburban railway played a major, but short-lived, role in the development of intercity passenger traffic around the turn of the nineteenth century. Basically, the interurban was a transitional step from almost sole reliance upon the steam railroad to an almost equally complete dependence upon the automobile. Indeed, the two modes of transportation, interurban car and automobile, were developed in roughly the same period, and had the auto manufacturers perfected their product sooner, the interurban would have died in infancy. Because of this lack of auto development and the poor condition of America's roads nearly a century ago, interurban electric rail transportation sprang up, blossomed, and quickly faded away.

Although some interurban lines were built in the 1890s, and a few were opened as late as the 1920s, most were built in two great bursts of activity, the first between 1901 and 1904 and the second between 1905 and 1908. The first spree ended with the financial panic of 1903, the second with the panic of 1907. There was a limited revival of construction in the years between 1908 and 1912, and it was during this era and shortly thereafter that Louisiana's only two interurban lines were constructed. They would operate between New Iberia and Jeanerette and from New Orleans to Kenner.

The Electric Railway

By 1918 the automobile was beginning to assert itself as the popular mode of transportation; thus, beginning that year and continuing for the next ten years, interurban rail traffic declined rapidly. The problems of the interurban lines were further compounded by the Great Depression when hundreds of companies suffered financial failure. By 1937 the industry had been virtually annihilated. By 1960 only skeletal remains--abandoned cars, stations and lines--could be found in junk yards, museums, or rotting and rusting beside the gleaming interstate highway system.[1]

Nevertheless, it was a romantic era, not only for the short-lived interurban lines but also for the automobiles, airplanes, the crack passenger trains, the trans-Atlantic liners, and a host of other technological developments. Alive to the excitement of the times, the people of New Iberia and the Teche country joined the national parade to progress. They would build an interurban line to connect the towns of the Teche Valley. Enthusiasm ran high for the project which was given many names ranging from "The Electric Railway" to "The Streetcar" to "The Trolley."

Iberians' interest in rapid transportation began early in the era of interurbans. In 1889 a group of New Iberians planned to build a streetcar line along Main Street. Mr. Daguesseau Etie presented the plan to the city fathers and sought permission to build the line, but the mayor and board of trustees could see no merit in the proposal, and this attempt died aborning.[2]

Ten years later, in 1899, a plan was put forth by a group of area businessmen to build an interurban line from Lafayette to Berwick, thus connecting the several towns and numerous plantations between the terminals. Lack of capital, however, prevented this plan from maturing.

But the national interurban fever, like autumn pollen, was in the air. Interurban lines were meeting with tremendous success in the East and Midwest. It was, therefore, only a matter of time before another individual, recognizing the potential of heavy population concentration in the narrow corridor of the Teche Valley, proposed the building of an interurban line.

In October, 1900, F. F. Myles, who had but recently organized and chartered the Myles Salt Co., Ltd., to exploit the vast salt deposit beneath Weeks Island, proposed to the Iberia Parish Police Jury the construction of an interurban line from New Iberia to Berwick and asked for a franchise to build the line down the main public road of the parish (presently State Highway 182). A similar proposition was put to the St. Mary Parish Police Jury shortly thereafter.

---

[1]. George W. Hilton and John F. Due, *The Electric Interurban Railways in America* (Stanford, 1960), VII, 3.

[2]. Louis C. Hennick and E. Harper Charlton, *Louisiana: Its Street and Urban Railways* (Shreveport, 1962), p. 130.

On November 2, 1900, the Iberia Parish Police Jury, in regular session, granted to Myles and his associates a franchise to build, own, and operate an electric railway through the parish of Iberia from New Iberia to Jeanerette. The franchise was for ninety-nine years. At the same time the police jury authorized Myles to construct a loop for his line from Main Street down Ann Street to the Southern Pacific Railroad, along the railroad to Lewis Avenue, and out Lewis to the main line on Main Street.[3] In mid-January, 1901, the St. Mary Parish Police Jury granted Myles a similar franchise to run an interurban line through that parish from Jeanerette to Berwick.[4] It appeared, therefore, that work on the line would begin at any moment.

It was, however, to be a false start. In mid-March, Myles was in Franklin to locate track and select property for his powerhouses and stations. At the time he told a reporter that the building of the interurban would increase property values by fifty percent.[5] All of the excitement of getting the project underway was soon cooled, however, when, in late April, 1901, a suit was filed in 19th Judicial District Court challenging the right of the Iberia Parish Police Jury to award a franchise to a person to use the public road for a railroad line.[6]

W. R. Farmer, a planter residing about three miles south of New Iberia, filed suit through his attorney, A. J. Cammack, contending that the police jury of the parish had no authority to grant to any person or corporation the right to conduct a railway over the public roads that had been dedicated to public use for the accommodation of persons on foot or in vehicles. In response to the plaintiff's petition, Myles asserted that he did not seek to use the public highways in any manner different from that contemplated by the law--that he only sought to apply to their use new and improved methods of locomotion and conveyance.[7]

As the case opened and arguments were presented, Solange Sorrel, a neighbor of the plaintiff, testified that the erection of a trolley line would have "a demoralizing effect" on laborers in the sugarcane fields along the way. He stated that "the rule is almost invariable, they will stop working as soon as a train is in sight and gaze idly upon it until it has passed away. They will lose

---

3. *New Iberia Enterprise*, November 10, 1900.

4. *Ibid.*, January 19, 1901.

5. *Ibid.*, March 16, 1901.

6. Louisiana. Parish of Iberia, Original Suits No. 3605, *W. R. Farmer v. F. F. Myles*, April-May, 1901.

7. *Ibid.*

the time necessary for the train to pass by and that will amount to a couple of minutes each time."[8]

The district court ruled in favor of Myles, and the decision was appealed to the state supreme court. Chief Justice Francis T. Nicholls rendered the court's opinion in overturning the district court's ruling. He stated, "Police Juries have no legal authority to grant a right to construct . . . railways over and through the public roads in the parishes. . . . F. F. Myles . . . is hereby enjoined from constructing or operating said line of railway under said ordinance or resolution."[9]

This legal action, however, would only delay the project, not end it. As early as November 23, 1901, the *Enterprise* editor suggested that the court's ruling was only a temporary setback until the state legislature could amend existing laws.[10]

In the May, 1902, session of the legislature, a bill was introduced by the chairman of the Committee on Parochial Affairs to authorize police juries to sell and grant franchises on the public roads and highways of the parishes for "railways utilizing electric or other motive power than steam." The bill passed both houses and was signed into law in July, 1902.[11]

The action of the legislature did more than prompt interurban activity along. In July, John McIlhenny petitioned the City of New Iberia for a franchise to operate a streetcar line in the town. Mr. McIlhenny proposed a line that would have run along Main Street from the east city limits to Ann Street, out Ann to St. Peter, along St. Peter to Chestnut, out Chestnut to Washington and along Washington to the west city limits. An intersecting line was proposed for Bank Avenue from St. Peter to Alfred (Hacker) Street, along Alfred to Weeks, doglegging on Weeks to Hacker and doglegging again on Iberia to Robertson to Hopkins and then to Washington where it would link with the other line.[12]

At the same time, General Myles proposed a streetcar system for the town that would have basically operated along Main and Pershing and connecting streets.[13] Early in September the corporation granted a twenty-five-year

---

8. *W. R. Farmer v. F. F. Myles*, 19th Judicial District Court, Parish of Iberia, State of Louisiana. The suit was filed April 22, 1901.

9. *W. R. Farmer v. F. F. Myles*, 106 Thorpe, 333-345 (1901-1902).

10. *New Iberia Enterprise*, November 23, 1901.

11. *Official Journal of the Proceedings of the House of Representatives of the State of Louisiana*, Regular Session, 1902 (Baton Rouge, 1902), p. 111.

12. *New Iberia Enterprise*, July 23, 1902.

13. *Ibid.*

New Iberia

Main St. looking east from French St. about 1905 (above) about 1910 (below)

The Electric Railway 251

Main St. looking east from French St., April 1972 (above)
and November 1985 (below)

franchise to both men.[14]

In early October, the police jury took advantage of the new state law to draw up an ordinance fixing the terms, conditions, and specifications of a franchise to construct an electric railway on the public roads of the parish and specifically the road paralleling Bayou Teche between New Iberia and Jeanerette.[15] On December 27, 1902, Police Jury President James F. Brittain sold the franchise to the only bidder, General F. F. Myles. The general agreed that work on the interurban line would begin within one year.[16]

By May, 1903, however, no work had started on the line; the obstacle, it was believed, was difficulty in getting a franchise from the St. Mary Parish Police Jury to run the line through that parish to Berwick.[17] Nevertheless, toward the end of summer, those favoring the construction of the interurban line were encouraged when General Myles advertised for bids for erection of poles to carry the streetcar's electric cable. A few days later there was a brief ceremony inaugurating the building of the interurban line. Mayor Jules E. Dupuy turned the first shovel of dirt.[18]

But the happy expectations of summer 1903 turned to gloom as later that year a financial panic gripped the country. In the light of that, all work on the interurban line was halted indefinitely. On March 3, 1904, the Iberia Parish Police Jury received a request from Myles for an extension of the time to get the project started. After due deliberation the police jury granted an extension of the time, provided that Myles would build and operate a line at least one-half mile long during the next ten months and would complete the line through the parish during the next twenty-four months.[19]

During July, 1904, the editor of the *Enterprise* had a long interview with General Myles during which the general painted a beautiful picture of the progress and prosperity that would come to the Teche region as soon as the New Iberia and Berwick interurban was constructed. He commented, "We expect to have everything in shape to begin work on the road in early fall." In addition, Myles stated that his company would build and operate streetcar

14. *Ibid.*, September 6, 1902.

15. *Ibid.*, October 4, 1902.

16. *Ibid.*, December 27, 1902.

17. *Ibid.*, May 9, 1903.

18. *Ibid.*, August 22, 29, 1903.

19. *Ibid.*, March 12, 1904.

The Electric Railway

The Dietlein Home, c. 1905
Presently The Evangeline Funeral Home

The Porter Home
Built by Ed Estorge, c. 1905

lines in New Iberia and Franklin and would develop the Charenton beach.[20]

By Christmas Eve, 1904, not a single section of track had been laid, and the editor's comments conerning the Myles project had turned caustic: "General Myles has had his privilege extended and every chance given him to commence this work, but up to this writing nothing has been done but the erecting of a few posts which have served as obstacles to our sidewalks and to advertise the inability or indifference of the recipient of the franchise. The people feel that they should have better treatment than this . . . now after nearly two years the patience of the public is about exhausted and it is tired of those 'talks' the General gives us every once in a while."[21]

The editor's words were but an apparent reflection of popular opinion, for on January 5, 1905, by a vote of ten to one, the police jury refused to extend Myles' franchise.[22] Thus, this project to build an interurban between New Iberia and Berwick had failed to materialize, mainly because of the financial crisis of late 1903. Although this first attempt to construct a street railway failed, the idea of linking the towns along the Teche in such a fashion remained very much alive. So, also, did the idea of building a streetcar system for New Iberia.

The next burst of activity to construct a streetcar system for New Iberia came in late 1905 and occupied the public's attention for two full years. Like the initial attempt, it would end in failure. It all began when F. A. Augur petitioned the corporation for a franchise to build a streetcar system for New Iberia.[23] A month later, on January 10, 1906, the town council awarded him the franchise. By the terms of the agreement, Augur was to have a minimum of $5,000 worth of material on the ground within five months of starting his operation.[24]

Work on the streetcar line was determined to have begun on February 10, but did not proceed apace. Therefore, by early June, 1906, the popular consensus was that the necessary money for the project could not be raised and

---

20. *Ibid.*, July 9, 1904.

21. *Ibid.*, December 24, 1904.

22. *Ibid.*, January 7, 1905.

23. *Ibid.*, December 16, 1905.

24. *Ibid.*, January 13, 1906.

that the franchise would be allowed to lapse.[25] As expected, Augur did not deposit the $5,000 on June 10, and the franchise lapsed.

Barely a month later, the city council granted a franchise to W. P. Conery to build and operate a municipal streetcar system and interurban line to Franklin and St. Martinville. With the franchise in hand, Conery left for New York to raise the necessary capital.[26] By September 22, the local newspaper reported that Conery expected to start work on the streetcar line within sixty days.[27] But a month later the paper was beginning to hedge its bets.[28]

Nevertheless, by late November, Conery made the last installment on the deposit of $5,000 guaranteeing the completion of the line within fifteen months. At the time he announced that the project would begin in January, 1907, with the building of the interurban line to Jeanerette.[29] Then, a month later, he transferred his franchise to the Bayou Teche Railway Company.[30]

By April, 1907, the company had succeeded in getting the necessary right of way with few exceptions. To convince the recalcitrant property owners to deal with the company, a committee composed of H. R. Fine, the company representative, Captain John T. White, Henry Pharr, and Emile Gajan called upon each of these individuals.[31]

The next issue to be settled was the site of the powerhouse for the trolley line. The franchise had stated that it would be built within the city limits or within one mile of the city limits. The mayor and city council wanted the powerhouse within the corporation, the company wanted it located on the Nelson Canal, which was then more than a mile outside the east city limits, but was willing to accept the Bayard property (on East Main near Bayard St.) as a compromise site for the powerhouse. A problem arose, however, when Porteus Burke told the city fathers that he had serious objections to the company establishing a powerhouse on the Bayard place. In the end, the mayor

---

25. *Ibid.*, June 9, 1906.

26. *Ibid.*, July 21, 1906.

27. *Ibid.*

27. *Ibid.*, September 22, 1906.

28. *Ibid.*, October 20, 1906.

29. *Ibid.*, November 24, 1906.

30. *Ibid.*, December 1, 1906.

31. *Ibid.*, April 27, 1907.

and council informed company representatives that the company had to act according to the terms of the municipal franchise and place the powerhouse accordingly.[32]

The project would suffer delay after delay and eventually come to nothing, but not because of any kind of obstacle created by local people. In 1907 there had been another nationwide financial crisis that produced a period of "tight" money. More than anything else, the company was having difficulties raising sufficient capital to build the trolley line. Thus, 1907 came to an end without a single section of track being laid. Although H. R. Fine predicted as late as December 28, 1907, that four hundred tons of steel rails would be delivered between mid-January and February 1, 1908, nothing more came of the project, and all enthusiasm for an interurban line once again went into hibernation.[33] A year and a half would pass before someone would again approach the city fathers with a proposal for a streetcar system for New Iberia. On June 23, 1909, Henry A. Mentz of New Orleans petitioned for a franchise to build a trolley system for New Iberia and extend it eastward to Jeanerette. The franchise was granted on the condition that work on the line begin within one year and be completed within two years from the date of the franchise.[34] But a year passed without any activity, and the franchise lapsed.

Waiting in the wings to pick up the franchise was F. W. Crosby of New Orleans, who had just organized the Southwestern Traction and Power Company. Like those who had gone before him, Crosby proposed the construction of an interurban line from Jeanerette to New Iberia. Unlike previous situations, however, there was no mention of a municipal streetcar system nor was there any mention of a franchise.[35]

In December, 1910, Crosby was back in New Iberia with a few individuals to investigate the possibility of building an interurban line between New Iberia and one or more of its neighboring towns.[36] It was not until April, however, that Crosby filed a petition with the municipal authorities of New Iberia and Jeanerette to build and operate a trolley line extending from one town to the other.[37]

---

32. *Ibid.*, July 22, 1907.

33. *Ibid.*, December 28, 1907.

34. *Ibid.*, July 3, 17, 1909.

35. *Ibid.*, July 2, 9, 1910.

36. *Ibid.*, December 31, 1910.

37. *Ibid.*, April 29, 1911.

The Electric Railway

The interurban car at Main and French (above) and at The Shadows (below).

This time, however, the promoters tied the implementation of the project to a two-mill, ten-year tax proposition to the property owners of Jeanerette and New Iberia. The tax revenues would be used to subsidize construction of the streetcar line. If the voters approved the tax measure, work on the line would begin within thirty days thereafter.[38]

The "Trolley Tax," as the proposition came to be called, was put to the voters on July 3. There was widespread support for the measure and when the vote was completed, 255 New Iberians approved and 6 were opposed. The measure was designed to raise $45,000.[39] Thus, by late summer, 1911, it appeared that only a few minor details remained to be handled before construction would begin.

Some of those details had to do with the right-of-way. A black congregation beyond Olivier was paid $200 to defray costs of moving their chapel from the proposed trolley right-of-way. A. G. Barrow, local representative of the Southwestern Traction and Power Company, handled all of the last-minute details.[40]

A fifteen-year-old dream of linking Jeanerette and New Iberia by an interurban electric railway seemingly became reality when, on August 14, 1911, survey work began at Rosedale Plantation, about three miles west of Jeanerette.[41] In September, F. W. Crosby arrived in New Iberia to sell $35,000 in company stock to local residents. In no time at all the stock was sold,[42] and it appeared now that nothing could stop the building of the interurban. But all this activity would prove to be little more than a false start.

In early October the Southern Pacific sought and obtained an injunction to prevent the City of New Iberia from collecting the tax voted to subsidize the Southwestern Traction Co. The railroad company also refused to allow the streetcar company to cross its tracks to establish a municipal streetcar system. The members of the city council denounced these unwarranted tactics of the railroad and called for a mass meeting of New Iberians to condemn the action of the railroad.[43]

38. *Jeanerette Coast Herald*, May 6, 1911.

39. *New Iberia Enterprise*, July 1, 8, 1911.

40. *Ibid.*, August 12, 1911.

41. *Ibid.*, August 19, 1911.

42. *Ibid.*, September 16, 1911.

43. *Ibid.*, October 7, 1911.

The "Indignation Meeting" was held on October 10. Mayor Power called the meeting to order, and addresses were forthcoming from Jules Dreyfus, R. S. McMahon, L. T. Dulany, Edwin Broussard, A. J. Cammack, F. M. Welsh, and others. The theme of these speeches was that it little became the reputation of the great Southern Pacific Railroad to fly in the face of an almost unanimous decision of the voters to tax themselves on behalf of the trolley company. Before the meeting ended, Ventress Smith informed the assemblage that he had just received a telegram stating that there had been an amicable solution to the problem. Nevertheless, a committee composed of W. L. Grant, Jules Dreyfus, Henry L. Smith, R. S. McMahon, and R. D. Southwell was appointed to draw up a series of resolutions to be forwarded to Southern Pacific officials. The main thrust of the resolutions formed a polite indication to the railroad that it should not continue to place obstacles in the way of progress.[44]

The issue existing between the Southern Pacific Railroad, the City of New Iberia, and the Southwestern Traction Company would, however, be settled in the courts. As is usually the case, the matter was slow in coming to a determination, and perhaps the citizens' resolutions proved effective, for early in December the railroad company withdrew its suit.[45] Moreover, the trolley company announced that it had sold its entire stock issue of $6,000,000 to a "French syndicate."[46] Once again, it appeared that nothing stood in the way of the construction of the interurban line.

On January 22, 1912, work on the trolley line began in earnest as thousands of crossties were deposited along Main Street. By the beginning of March, the builders were beginning to lay track; having started at the corner of Railroad Avenue and Main Street, they had reached the corner of Weeks and Main. At the same time, the company announced that it had accepted a site offered by S. C. Sumrall and Henry N. Pharr about three miles below the city limits (now about one mile below) to build the powerhouse for the trolley line. Jerry Taylor and Xavier Herpeche were awarded the contract to build the power plant. Two hundred men were working on the overall project.[47]

---

44. *Ibid.*, October 14, 1911.

45. There is an indication, however, that the railroad and trolley companies compromised on the issue. The trolley line agreed to transport only passengers and express and to leave freight transportation to the railroad. *Ibid.*, December 2, 1911.

46. *Ibid.* The "French syndicate" was headed by Jules Godchaux, the wealthy Louisiana sugar planter. The other investors were also Louisianians.

47. *Ibid.*, March 2, 1912.

Silvio Broussard
from an old newspaper woodcut from the late nineteenth century

By May, Silvio Broussard was busy installing the generators at the power plant, and two streetcars had arrived in New Iberia and were awaiting placement upon the tracks.

Then, the event that all awaited occurred on May 24, 1912. The Traction Company had a trial run of its cars from Olivier to New Iberia. But almost at the very moment that the dream was realized and jubilation reached a crescendo, the first sour note concerning the streetcar line appeared in the local paper:

> A number of vehicles have been broken along Main Street by the rails of the Trolley line since the track has been laid in New Iberia. Almost daily a wheel is broken off some buggy due to the manner the rails have been placed on our Main thoroughfare which is not only a financial injury to the owners of the vehicles, but a great danger to limb. Fortunately, up to the present time none of the animals attached to the buggies broken has run away with the occupants, but such will happen ere long unless a protecting rail is placed along the track. . . . While we have no desire to criticize the Southwestern Traction and Power Co. or the City Fathers for allowing a rail of

The Electric Railway   261

that kind to be placed along our main thoroughfare, still these are serious matters that something should be done about before the City will face several large lawsuits for damage.[48]

Nevertheless, on May 25, 1912, the interurban line between New Iberia and Jeanerette was officially opened. Thousands of New Iberians gathered in front of City Hall and along Main Street for the ceremonies opening the line. The ladies auxiliary of the Civic League[49] had decorated one of the streetcars, and

---

48. *Ibid.*, May 4, 25, 1912.

49. Among the members of the Commission Form of Government League (the Civic League) were A. J. Schexnayder, G. E. LeBlanc, A. Ackal, G. Ackal, Gabriel Abraham, Jake Fisher, M. T. Moss, John Musemache, A. B. Pesson, Emile Gajan, H. J. Smith, Morris Scharff, H. J. Broussard, J. A. Goodwin, A. D. Blanc, Sylvio Broussard, Dr. J. H. White, A. J. Maumus, Alex Bagarry, Sr., Chas. J. Guillot, Albert Courtois, Pierre Jubin, Ed. L. Estorge, A. Daigre, M. W. Fisher, L. Y. Melancon, George W. Dallas, John R. Taylor, John Perry, W. F. Carstens, Samuel H. Hillsman, John Neile, J. F. Breaux, H. O. Miller, H. S. Sealy, J. P. Jennaro, L. P. Bagarry, Homer Dupuy, R. A. Bagarry, Nathan Davis, Alphonse Davis, E. Rister, V. J. Smith, A. A. Dauterive, A. N. Muller, Joseph N. Thibodeaux, E. L. Bernard, Ernest Pete, Arthur Bernard, Daniel C. Boutte, George Cestia, C. F. Seabrough, W. L. Fisher, Y. Arnandez, Paul J. Hebert, A. Delord, W. A. Crews, R. A. Jacob, Francois Guillot, J. G. LeBlanc, Jr., Frank J. Mestayer, M. Arrigo, O. J. Boutte, John Gibblin, O. E. Stansbury, Fred Decuir, H. Gallois, J. P. Suberbielle, Joe Harris, A. J. Suberbielle, Joseph Hayes, Maurice Galiland, R. E. Freeman, Sam Weil, James T. Colgin, A. J. Schrout, H. Blakesley, T. G. Brigham, Jr., J. A. Nereaux, J. A. Decuir, Henry Lopez, R. L. Boudreaux, T. J. Tanner, E. S. Fulton, L. T. Handley, I. T. Rand, E. E. Delhommer, J. H. Kiblinger, Raoul Jacquemoud, R. E. Marin, Charles Perret, Robert E. Daspit, John O'Brian, Alfred Boudreaux, Elie Pesson, Leon M. Lemaire, Felix N. Mestayer, Joe Miguez, W. J. Condon, G. A. Hankin, W. R. Carter, John Holbrook, John Elelock, Alex Broussard, Tom DeBlanc, Fred DeBlanc, L. DeBlanc, Isham Vest, J. J. Lamperez, H. R. McClean, Herman Simon, Edward Pfister, Desire Lissard, Jr., J. C. Robert, W. L. Ruis, H. H. Shadel, J. C. Jacob, St. Martin Fridley, J. M. Angers, H. R. Lunsford, Jewell Dorcey, H. C. Crews, F. Bertram, Roy Hippler, Leon Navarre, Alphe Fontelieu, James F. Hebert, Paul Doerle, R. Winters, C. E. Colgin, Thomas L. Monk, G. J. Hare, G. E. Part, Charles Vest, John A. Pesson, M. Crouchet, L. N. Forsyth, Dr. H. A. King, J. S. Powers, D. A. Dimitry, H. L. Smith, E. F. Millard, Edward T. Weeks, James M. Moran, J. Lejeune, Leon Dreyfus, J. R. Perry, A. Miller, J. T. White, William G. Weeks, H. J. Daigre, Leopold Kling, J. G. LeBlanc, L. V. Jennaro, W. L. Burke, F. G. Blumenthal, X. F. Herpeche, R. S. McMahon, W. J. Miller, Herman Hauser, L. P. Ribbeck, M. P. Moss, Emile Simon, Morris Broussard, Jules Francois, H. Robert, D. Bonin, G. Neile, Albert Neile, Frank Briganti, Sidney C. Laughlin, A. C. Pickett, Morris Rosenzweig, James Carter, Ed. Fisher, Andrew Lassalle, W. J. Eves, S. J. Gautereaux, B. Pavie Breaux, C. H. Lee, W. B. Sharp, P. E. Voorhies, Henry Dorcey, T. E. Conrad, Louis Gajan, C. M. Pickett, Louis Segura, G. H. Stansbury, R. D. Stansbury, L. Delcambre, Henry Patout, Gaston Patout, W. J. Bernard, Frank K. Ribbeck, R. J. Labauve, Phil L. Kramer, W. D. Carter, A. H. French, Louis Hebert, W. O. Hugonin, R. T.

The Interurban
Between New Iberia and Jeanerette

Ribbeck, Henry Meyer, Joseph W. Eckart, W. J. Eckart, George H. Riviere, Charles L. Provost, L. C. Fagot, F. Armentor, F. A. Louviere, Louis Angers, G. A. Blanc, Abe Hirsch, J. L. Perry, W. L. Sonneman, H. T. Hale, J. T. DeValcourt, H. H. Green, J. T. White, Rene LeBlanc, J. M. Perry, Gus T. Weil, J. M. Carlin, Francis J. Voorhies, G. R. Colgin, Aristide Boutte, J. A. Morrow, J. Huval, J. J. Landry, T. B. Rand, Lazard Kling, P. H. Segura, Onesiphore Savoy, Porteus R. Burke, Sidney Hebert, W. C. Segura, W. D. Reynolds, W. L. Grant, F. Davis, A. Helper, Dr. James A. Gibblin, L. V. Barth, E. Taul, H. O. Hebert, Leo H. Reynaud, A. C. Holleman, Golden J. Melancon, W. J. Boutte, Henry Creighton, G. O. Duperier, A. R. Veazey, C. T. Ewing, Cleve B. French, Walter J. Laperouse, J. J.

as all gathered around, Father J. M. Langlois pronounced the invocation. L. T. Dulany followed with a short, but impressive talk on the wonderful spirit of cooperation between the city officials and the trolley company. Jules Dreyfus then followed with a snappy talk on the duties of citizenship. E. T. Weeks then offered resolutions thanking F. W. Crosby and A. G. Barrow for their efforts in making the interurban line a reality. Finally, Waneta Power, daughter of the mayor, christened the rails with a bottle of champagne, and the Reverend R. R. Diggs pronounced the benediction. Following the last "amen," a tide of humanity moved toward the streetcar and soon jammed themselves into it in order to be the first to transit the rails to Jeanerette.[50] All in all, it had been a red-letter day in the history of New Iberia.

The interurban line would operate for the next six years. During that time (in 1913) its track was extended in New Iberia from Railroad Avenue to North Street. During that time, too, the trolley carved a special place in the hearts of Iberians. It served not only the people of New Iberia and Jeanerette, but more importantly, perhaps, it served the country people living between the two towns. Still, the project may have been ahead of its time, for immediately patronage began to drop off. Service was curtailed until only eight trips in each direction were being made per day during the early part of 1918. By then it had become obvious to the stockholders of the Southwestern Traction Company that the enterprise was a failure.

On July 27, 1918, after several months of rumor that the line would be shut down, Robert A. Smith, the company's agent in New Iberia made it official. The last car of the Southwestern Traction and Power Company pulled into the barn a little after 10 p.m., Saturday, July 27, 1918. An era for New Iberia had ended.[51]

Clark, William Lunsford, H. Trappey, John McDavenport, Michel DeBlanc, Walter R. Elmer, Laurence J. Ledet, Carl Carlson, J. P. Russell, F. W. Bauman, Emile Perret, H. L. Fuller, L. J. Dauterive, E. P. Terrell, George Baumgartner, Gracia Huval, Rodney French, Stephen Callin, C. E. Reynolds, C. C. Henshaw, A. C. Boas, F. H. Smith, Gilbert Kahn, Charles Kahn, H. F. Stafford, Nick Muller, J. J. Bonin, L. J. Gautreaux, H. W. Gould, C. M. Aucoin, Hilton Sandoz, Gabriel Ashy, Maron Ashy, Nassin Larkin, Asad Elias, Joseph Doumit, Hatar Haddad, James Campbell, L. C. DeBlanc, J. Bertrand, Joseph O. LeBlanc, Robert C. Taylor, Eddie Dauterive, and George L. Dauterive.

This list of names is taken from the *New Iberia Enterprise,* May 18, 1912. Some names may have been accidentally misspelled by the newspaper.

50. *Ibid.,* June 1, 1912.

51. *Ibid.,* August 3, 1918.

XIV

New Iberia's Steamboat Days

by
Carl A. Brasseaux

From the mid 1770s to the Civil War, the Attakapas region (the former Spanish governmental district encompassing the present parishes of Iberia, St. Martin, Lafayette, Vermilion, and St. Mary) served as an important supplier of beef, vegetables, and agricultural staples to New Orleans. Because many of these products were perishable, it was imperative that they be shipped to the Crescent City as quickly as possible. Thus, shortly after their introduction into the Mississippi Valley, steamboats were employed in steadily increasing numbers on Bayou Teche, and because of its location at the head of sea-going navigation on that waterway, New Iberia derived the benefits of the region's burgeoning commerce.

Steamboats were introduced into the Teche Valley by Francois Duplessis, Jr., and Martin Duralde, Jr., who, through legislation approved by the state's general assembly in mid-February 1818, were authorized to "establish, keep, and maintain a steam boat and ferry . . ." operating between Bayou Portage and Plaquemine.[1] Capitalizing on this opportunity, Duralde and Duplessis ordered con-

---

1. *Acts Passed at the Second Session of the Third Legislature of the State of Louisiana* . . . (New Orleans, 1818), p. 28.

Steamboat Days

The *John D. Grace* was a packet (that is, a scheduled boat) and a "round" boat (that is, with sides so as to travel in open water with possible waves).

struction of the 103-ton steamer *Louisianais* at New Orleans.[2] After the vessel's completion in late 1818, the *Louisianais*, commanded by co-owner Duplessis, briefly engaged in the lower Mississippi trade before launching operations in mid-May 1819 as a cattle ferryboat in the Atchafalaya Basin.[3]

The economic success enjoyed by Duplessis and Duralde prompted William L. Brent, John Duhamel, Alexander Porter, Jr., Thomas B. Brashear, Willis J. Powell, Octave Delahoussaye, John Muggah, J. Merial, Jacob Clements, LePelletier Delahoussaye, William Armstrong, and William Greig to petition the state legislature in early 1819 for permission to operate a steamboat on Bayou Teche.[4] Responding to pressure from this politically powerful interest group,

---

2. *Ship Registers and Enrollments of New Orleans, Louisiana*, 6 vols. (Baton Rouge, 1941), I, 81.

3. The New Orleans *Louisiana Courier*, May 7, 1819.

4. *Acts of the First Session of the Fifth Legislature* . . . (New Orleans, 1819), pp. 32-34.

Bayou front in downtown New Iberia, 1898 (top); 1912 (below). Building with three smokestacks was the Trainor Planing Mill

Bayou front in downtown New Iberia, 1972 (top); 1986 (bottom).

the state legislature passed, and, in late February 1819 Governor Jacques Villeré approved, "An Act to Incorporate the Attakapas Steam Boat Company."[5]

After selling stock at St. Martinville, Franklin, and Opelousas in accordance with the act, and after selecting officers, the company authorized construction of the *Teche*, a 295-ton steamer built at New Orleans in 1820. Upon completion, the *Teche* operated out of New Iberia, regularly carrying Attakapas freight to New Orleans via the Gulf of Mexico. Operating expenses, however, were inordinately high because the steamboat's route along the lower Teche and Mississippi was snag-infested, and, although the Attakapas Steam Boat Company was given a monopoly on steam navigation on Bayou Teche in 1821, the firm failed sometime before 1825.[6]

With the dissolution of the Attakapas Steam Boat Company, the Teche Valley was served only by the *Volcano,* and 217-ton cattle boat operated by Francois Duplessis, Jr., between bayous Cypremort and Plaquemine via Atchafalaya Bay and the Atchafalaya Basin.[7] Capt. Duplessis' vessel, however, was incapable of transporting the area's fast-developing agricultural production to market. Therefore, the region's planters were overjoyed when Capt. Robert W. Curry guided the *Louisville*, a diminutive 48-ton steamer, from the Mississippi River to Franklin via Bayou Plaquemine and the Atchafalaya Basin.[8]

Curry's voyage marked the beginning of a transportation revolution in Attakapas. By successfully navigating Bayou Plaquemine at the height of the Mississippi River's floodstage, a feat hitherto thought impossible because of the tremendous current in the bayou's narrow channel, Capt. Curry demonstrated that direct commerce between the Attakapas and New Orleans was at least possible via the safer internal waterways.

Curry quickly capitalized upon his discovery and from 1825 to 1830 his steamboats enjoyed a virtual monopoly over the waterborne Teche trade. In the 1830s, however, Curry's position was challenged by Mississippi riverboat captains who entered their boats into the Teche trade only in late winter and

5. *Ibid.*

6. *Acts Passed at the Fifth Session of the Fifth Legislature* . . . (New Orleans, 1821), p. 60; William M. Lytle, *Merchant Steam Vessels of the United States, 1807-1868* (Mystic, Conn., 1952), p. 184, 212.

7. Lytle, *Merchant Steam Vessels*, p. 196; The Franklin *Planters' Banner*, April 27, 1848.

8. The St. Martinville *Attakapas Gazette*, April 16, 1825, quoted in the *Planters' Banner*, April 27, 1848.

early spring when the Attakapas sugar production peaked. Not only did sugar production, and hence the volume of Teche cargo, decline in late spring and early summer, but the water level in Bayou Plaquemine customarily became unnavigable as the Mississippi's vernal floodtide abated.

As a consequence, Attakapas planters were compelled to rely upon Gulf steamers as well as sailing vessels during the summer and fall months. Because of this increasing reliance upon ocean-going vessels, New Iberia emerged as a leading local port. According to Alfred Duperier,

> New Iberia being the real terminus of deep water navigation on the Teche, began to assert its commercial importance in the forties [1840s]. The interruption of navigation through Plaquemine during the low stage of water in the Mississippi created a demand for a class of gulf steamers of large carrying capacity. These steamers, not being able to ply above New Iberia, landed their large cargoes, destined for all points south and west on the Vermilion and Calcasieu, at New Iberia. It was then that she became the radiating point for the trade of a large territory, extending some sixty miles in all directions.[9]

The volume of New Iberia's commerce carried aboard steamers increased sharply in the late 1850s, when the New Orleans, Opelousas, and Great Western Railroad laid tracks from Algiers to Brashear City (present-day Morgan City). With the establishment of a rail terminus on the lower Teche, steamboats, at least four of which stopped regularly at New Iberia, could operate on a year-round basis. Moreover, as the steamboats no longer had to ply the snag-infested waters of the Atchafalaya Basin, safe delivery of cargo was virtually assured; hence, the volume of cargo carried by steamers increased. In fact, the volume of merchandise carried by steamboats to Brashear City grew to such an extent that in 1857 forty-five prominent St. Mary Parish planters and merchants petitioned the general assembly to construct a dam across flood-prone Bayou Plaquemine.[10]

The area's growing dependence upon the railroad clearly indicated that the steamboat's days were numbered. The public clearly preferred the safety, con-

---

9. See the essay entitled "A Narrative of Events Connected with the Early Settlement of New Iberia."

10. *Petition of the Citizens of St. Mary's Parish in Relation to the Closing of Bayou Plaquemine* (not given, 1857), pp. 1-2. Microfilm copy on deposit in the Jefferson Caffery Louisiana Room, Dupre Library, University of Southwestern Louisiana.

The *Kurzweg* loading and unloading at New Iberia. The boat was owned by the Consolidated Companies, a wholesale grocery company.

Steamboat Days

Bridge across Bayou Teche at New Iberia, La.

The Bridge Street bridge in 1900 and on a foggy morning in 1978

venience, and regular schedule of the "iron horse." Steamers, on the other hand, rarely maintained their schedules, the captains preferring to lay in at any and all plantation landings along the Teche in order to take on cargo.[11] Moreover, the steamboat clerks were quite unscrupulous about booking passenger accommodations. As one antebellum steamboat passenger lamented, Capt. Curry's clerk had booked "three [passengers] for each bed and four for each plate on the boat."[12] As a consequence, according to Frederick Olmsted, seasoned travelers entrenched themselves in their cabins and warded off all challengers for the vessel's best accommodations with a large caliber pistol. Latecomers were thus forced to sleep under the stars; the stargazers, however, may well have enjoyed the better accommodations, for the Teche steamers' cabins were frequently cramped, dirty, and infested with bedbugs.[13] Moreover, the food served the travelling public was often less than appetizing.[14]

Travel aboard antebellum steamboats was also dangerous. Teche Valley pilots all too frequently whiled away their off-duty hours by drinking and playing cards with the passengers in the bar.[15] Fatigued and often inebriated, the pilots returned to duty frequently to steer their craft over dangerous shoals and snags. In fact, between 1825 and 1860, at least 19 vessels, 89 lives, and thousands of dollars in goods were lost along the Teche and in the Atchafalaya Basin as a result of mishaps. Ocean-going steamers were not much safer, as they were frequently top-heavy and thus were easy prey for the violent thunderstorms for which the Gulf Coast is noted.

Finally, because of the numerous shoals in the Atchafalaya Basin, steamers were accompanied by lighters, very small steamboats to which some of the larger vessels' cargoes were transferred in dangerously shallow waters. This transfer of goods not only produced delays but also substantially raised shipping costs.[16]

Despite the aforementioned liabilities, however, steamboats remained a significant force in local commerce until the 1890s, primarily because of the initiative of the local steamboatmen and the disruptive influence of the Civil War.

11. *Planters' Banner*, February 28, 1850.

12. *Ibid.*

13. *Ibid.*, April 18, 1850.

14. *Ibid.*, April 11, 1850.

15. *Ibid.*, February 28, 1850.

16. *Ibid.*, March 8, 1851.

Although a roadbed had been laid along much of the lower Teche prior to 1861, tracks were not laid to New Iberia by the Great Western's successor, Morgan's Texas and Pacific Railroad, until 1879. From the war's conclusion until 1877, steamboating at New Iberia had been dominated by the Attakapas Mail Transport Line and their successor, Capt. John Newton Pharr's Teche Mail Steamers.

Pharr, a veteran Teche steamboatman who had operated the *Rusk* in the Atchafalaya Basin during the early Civil War years, quickly emerged as the dominant force in the local steamboat business by 1880.[17] Shortly after purchasing two large and luxuriously appointed boats, the *Rene Macready* and the *Mary Lewis*, in 1876, Pharr acquired exclusive rights to transportation of the railroad's freight from Brashear City to New Iberia.[18]

From 1877 to 1879, Pharr's position as leader of the local waterborne freight carriers was challenged, though never seriously threatened, by Capt. Abe Smith. Smith's Teche and Atchafalaya Line enjoyed the unflagging support of the *Louisiana Sugar Bowl*, New Iberia's weekly newspaper which consistently attacked the evils of the Morgan-Pharr line "monopoly."[19] The paper's opposition to the "monopoly" was especially intense during the spring of 1879, when the Pharr line attempted to snuff out its competition by slashing its freight rates by seventy-five percent.[20] Pharr's price war, however, was futile, for not only did Smith's line survive for another year, but also the completion of the railroad to New Iberia in 1879 deprived Capt. Pharr of his mail contract and the bulk of his freight as well. As a consequence, Pharr was forced to retire one of his boats and drastically reduce the number of his employees.[21]

With the reorganization of the Pharr line and the dissolution of its major competitor, Smith's line, New Iberia was served only by Capt. T. R. Muggah's 10-day New Orleans packet, the *John M. Chambers*.[22] In late October 1880, however, Capt. L. T. Belt established the Belt line which operated two packets out of New Iberia.[23] Despite initial success in the Teche trade, the above-

---

17. Carl A. Brasseaux, "The Glory Days: E. T. King Recalls the Civil War Years," *Attakapas Gazette*, XI (1976), 9.

18. See the essay entitled "The Centennial Celebration at New Iberia, 1876."

19. The New Iberia *Louisiana Sugar Bowl*, December 28, 1876; June 12, 1877; May 1, 1879.

20. *Ibid.*, April 3, 1879.

21. *Ibid.*, February 5, 1880.

22. *Ibid.*, February 26, 1880.

23. *Ibid.*, October 28, 1880.

mentioned packets were unable to compete with the more efficient railroad, and the packet disappeared from the Teche by 1915.

The extinction of the packet ushered in the final chapter of steamboat history on Bayou Teche. Unable to compete with the railroad for the agricultural produce market, steamboat captains were compelled to undertake jobs which the railroad was either unwilling or incapable of undertaking. Thus, in the late 1880s and throughout the 1890s, local steamboatmen concentrated exclusively on excursions and "jobbing." By 1900, however, the excursion craze of the late nineteenth century had faded and skippers had begun to provide a variety of charter services. The Chautin Brothers' *Buck Lindsay* and *J. N. Pharr*, which operated on the Teche in the 'teens and twenties, best exemplify the services offered by the early twentieth-century steamboatmen. Not only did the Chautin Brothers' boats carry freight to the plantations along the Teche, but they also transported large rafts of logs from the Atchafalaya Basin to the Teche Valley sawmills.[24]

Though the jobber boats remained on the Teche until the mid-1930s, they were gradually replaced by company-owned, or leased, vessels. For example, from 1907 to 1922, the B. C. Taylor line of steamboats, which were under contract to the Sterling Plantation manager, freighted coal, fertilizer, and cooperage materials to, and rice, sugarcane, and molasses from, plantations along the Teche. Moreover, from 1915 to 1922, the Taylor boats delivered annually approximately 1.5 million barrels of fuel oil to local sugar mills.[25]

The Consolidated Companies of Plaquemine and the Interstate Wholesale Grocery Company of Thibodaux also operated steamboats on the Teche in the early twentieth century. In the twenties, thirties, and early forties, Consolidated's *Carrie B. Schwing* and *Kurzweg*, and the Interstate's *Interstate* regularly delivered groceries to wholesalers along the Teche.

Finally, the *Amy Hewes*, owned and operated by the Hewes Lumber Company of Jeanerette, served as a logging boat on the Teche, transporting huge rafts of cypress logs from the Atchafalaya Basin to local sawmills. After twenty-four years of operation, the *Hewes* last called at New Iberia in 1943.

The final departure of the *Hewes* closed the last chapter on steamboating on the Teche. The vessels had prompted New Iberia's rapid antebellum development, but, dangerous and unreliable, the commercial boats were unable to compete with products of subsequent technological developments--trains and trucks.

24. Interview with Lyman Taylor, July 25, 1976, Franklin, Louisiana.

25. *Ibid.*

Steamboat Days

Nevertheless, the memory of the paddlewheelers remains forever a monument to the daring and individual initiative of the men who opened the Teche Valley to commercial development.[26]

[26]. Paddlewheel boats have returned to New Iberia in the form of the steamboat replica *Teche Queen*. On June 21, 1984, this tourist and excursion boat began plying the Teche on a daily schedule. Owned and operated by Mr. and Mrs. Don Lalande, the *Queen* can comfortably accommodate 150 passengers on a dinner cruise.

The *Teche Queen* comes through the Bridge Street bridge after a Sunday afternoon cruise.

XV

The United Confederate Veterans of New Iberia

by
Glenn R. Conrad

"I wish I was in the land of cotton...." Those familiar lyrics from "Dixie" had a special meaning for the men who served the Confederacy from 1861 to '65. Upon hearing that exciting melody in the years after the Civil War, the veterans' memories sharpened and they easily recalled the friends, the adventures, the victories; occasionally, they remembered the stench, the agony, and the death which characterized that fratricidal conflict. Nevertheless, "The War" had been an experience exclusively their own and it remained so for over thirty years, until another generation of Americans could come home and relate their experiences at San Juan Hill, in Manila, or on Puerto Rico.

Strangely enough, however, the bond of their wartime experiences failed to forge any kind of Confederate association until the formation of the United Confederate Veterans' organization in New Orleans in June 1889. What caused the soldiers in gray to wait so long to form an association has intrigued historians ever since, for the Union counterpart, the Grand Army of the Republic, had been organized as early as 1866.[1]

---

1. For a more detailed account of the activities of the United Confederate Veterans in Louisiana, see Herman Hattaway, "The United Confederate Veterans in Louisiana," *Louisiana History*, XVI (1975), 5-37.

Nevertheless, once the national Confederate organization was established, branches, called camps, sprang up across the South. These UCV units proclaimed their goals to be "strictly social, literary, historical and benevolent."[2] They definitely shunned political ties.

In Louisiana the organization of UCV camps was slow outside of New Orleans. That city boasted UCV Camp No. 2, and Thibodaux, La., had Camp No. 196. By 1910 most of the more than 1,700 camps of the veterans' organization had been formed. New Iberia's Camp No. 1788 had the dubious distinction of being one of the last branches of the UCV formed in Louisiana.

For many years some of the local veterans had attempted to organize a camp in New Iberia, but the response was only lukewarm. Finally, in the fall of 1913, E. J. Carstens and L. G. Williams succeeded in sparking sufficient interest among the old-timers to call for a meeting of the group.[3]

On October 19, 1913, fully fifty years after the Teche Campaign of the Civil War, twenty-four of the old Confederates met at Carstens' seed store at Main and Julia streets. They were E. J. Carstens, J. P. Harrison, Felix Patout, R. D. Stansbury, Gervia Boudreaux, L. A. Pellerin, A. A. Flory, L. G. Williams, L. O. Hacker, P. A. Dupuy, David Hayes, John DeValcourt, Fred Davis, J. B. Winters, A. N. Reggio, C. E. Reggio, B. F. House, John Gonzales, Ovignac Bonin, Auguste Barrilleaux, Adolphe Romero, Paul Darby, Joseph Landry, and Voorhies Derouen. Charter members not present for this meeting were Dudley Avery, Alphonse Boutte, Ovignac Broussard, Sosthen Breaux, Adolphe Broussard, Numa Broussard, John French, H. H. Furr, and Euzebe Gonsoulin.[4]

The assembly quickly conducted its business. Carstens was selected commander; L. G. Williams, first lieutenant; L. A. Pellerin, second lieutenant; and A. A. Flory, adjutant. Following considerable debate, the gentlemen agreed on a twenty-five cent initiation fee and annual dues of ten cents. The meeting was then adjourned until such time as a constitution and set of by-laws for the camp could be drafted and presented.[5]

By mid-December, 1913, the charter and policies were read and adopted and the organization was officially dubbed United Confederate Veterans Camp No. 1788. The main goals of the local group were to assist disabled veterans, their widows and children, and to attend in a body the funeral of a deceased brother.

2. *Ibid.*, 11.

3. *New Iberia Enterprise*, October 11, 1913.

4. *Ibid.*, October 25, 1913.

5. *Ibid.*

The Annual Reunion of UCV Camp No. 1788 in 1914
From left are E. J. Carstens, capt.; L. G. Williams, 1st lieut.; L. A. Pellerin, 2nd lieut.; A. A. Flory, adjutant; J. B. Winters, John A. French; L. O. Hacker; Frederick Davis; Jilson P. Harrison; Gervia Boudreaux; Ovignac Bonin, Paul Darby; Numa Broussard, color guard; R. D. Stansbury, color bearer; Adolphe Romero, color guard; David Hayes; Auguste Barrilleaux, Ovignac Broussard, B. F. House, and John DeValcourt. The photo was taken on the front lawn of the Alma House.

In other business, it was moved that some civic organization or local group should sponsor entertainment for the veterans. This motion passed unanimously.[6]

The veterans met quarterly and held an annual banquet or gathering. Some of these annual events were quite festive occasions, particularly those of 1914, 1915, and 1916.

For about six weeks prior to the 1914 event, a group of ladies planned a banquet and program to honor the old soldiers. Finally, June 18 was set as the date for the affair to be held at the "Alma House." Early on the afternoon of the eighteenth, the veterans gathered at Carsten's store, some sporting new suits,

---

6. *Ibid.*, December 13, 1913.

a few carrying canes, one or two in a cutaway coat, but all in high spirits. They ranged in age from 68 to 84. They proudly lined up in double columns behind the New Iberia Brass Band and at the appointed time the whole group moved up Main Street to the sounds of "Dixie."

Upon the procession's arrival at the Alma House, the veterans were met by their hostesses and friends and were treated to another rendition of "Dixie." The song concluded, young Celeste Dimitry stepped forward and presented a large Confederate flag to the members of the camp and recited an appropriate dedicatory passage.

In the name of the Camp, Capt. Carstens accepted the flag and thanked the young lady for her wonderful tribute. His remarks over, the crowd joined in singing the "Bonnie Blue Flag" before they entered the dining room for the banquet.

The Reverend R. R. Diggs delivered the invocation, and L. G. Williams, famous for his Rebel yells, offered a toast to General Robert E. Lee. After another song, Louis Pellerin toasted the Confederate dead, and this was followed by a violin selection offered by Ello de Blanc. Appropriate remarks were forthcoming from Father J. M. Langlois of St. Peter's Church and the Reverend Lutz of the Methodist Church.

Before the program concluded there was additional entertainment in music and song by Misses Bessie Galiland, Yvonne Arnandez, Mrs. Anna Grant Miller, and a recitation by ten-year-old Gladys Francois.

The ceremonies concluded, the old soldiers rose, formed once again into a double column and returned to their headquarters at Carstens' store. Before returning, however, the group was photographed by I. A. Martin.[7]

Early in 1915, seven veterans joined the Camp to bring the total membership to forty. They were Adrien Conrad, Ernest Bonvillain, Tobias Haines, Octave Louviere, H. F. Stafford, Adrien Louviere, and H. B. Bayard.[8]

The Camp's 1915 annual meeting was held at the Frederic Hotel. About three in the afternoon of October 23, the old Confederates lined up on Main Street for the parade to the hotel. This time, however, they invited guests to march with them. In front of the marchers stood the flagbearers: R. D. Stansbury, late of the Confederate army, held the Stars and Bars, and John T. White, a Union veteran, carried the Stars and Stripes. Following the old soldiers were the veterans of the Spanish-American War. To the sounds of martial music and an occasional Rebel yell, the parade moved up Main Street to the hotel.

During the course of the banquet L. G. Williams recalled for the group some of the more amusing aspects of life in the Confederate army. He was

---

7. *Ibid.*, June 20, 1914.

8. *Ibid.*, January 9, 1915.

Capt. John T. White

followed by Capt. White who spoke about the Blue and Gray with such pathos that many "a dim eye released tears to trickle down the craggy cheeks."

After the banquet the veterans assembled in the lobby of the hotel for a moment of silence to honor their four comrades who had died since their last meeting: Voorhies Derouen, John DeValcourt, David Hayes, and Jilson Harrison. A program of singing and music followed with several young ladies contributing: Ello de Blanc, Mildred Renoudet, Carmen Harry, Elodie Broussard, Edna Walker, and several others.[9]

The 1916 get-together was the one at which the veterans probably had the most fun. In late September the Camp announced that it would stage a typical camp scene (more or less) as it would have been in the days of '61 to '65. The public was invited to attend the mid-October event.

As the appointed day drew near, the veterans perfected their plans. "Lieutenant" L. G. Williams would be the officer of the day. "Sergeant" B. F. House would serve as quartermaster and captain of the mess. The bill of fare would include typical wartime delicacies.

On October 14, at three in the afternoon, Captain Carstens brought the company out from headquarters and marched the "thin grey line" down to the old Holy Cross College grounds "in good old style and splendid form." Before breaking ranks the veterans were welcomed by a chorus of young ladies from Mt. Carmel Convent singing "Tenting on the Old Camp Grounds." After the song, I. A. Martin photographed the scene with the veterans standing in the foreground at "parade rest."

While the old soldiers downed a sumptuous meal prepared by the ladies of the Fair Association, B. F. House prepared to give visitors a taste of wartime fare. He expertly cooked up a watery soup, objects resembling biscuits, items which he termed slapjacks, some parched corn, molasses, corn coffee, and sundry other delicacies. These items were then served in tin cups, tin plates, with pointed

---

9. *Ibid.,* October 23, 1915.

United Confederate Veterans   281

The Annual Reunion of UCV Camp No. 1788 in 1916

wooden sticks for forks, and wooden paddles for spoons. Polite, but somewhat less than enthusiastic, onlookers seemed a bit reluctant to sample Sergeant House's soldiers' menu. Nevertheless, everyone enjoyed the exhibition.

Toward late afternoon the festivities concluded with the old veterans choosing their partners for the Virginia Reel. It had been a beautiful day and a wonderful experience.[10]

It was to be the last such experience, however. While the old veterans continued to have annual meetings, at least until 1922, they never again approached the magnitude of the festive occasions of 1914-1916. The 1917 meeting was held at "Headquarters" in Carstens' store on a Sunday afternoon in December. There is no record of a 1918 or 1919 meeting of unusual interest.

In 1918, however, the veterans joined in the traditional Fourth of July parade. Most of them rode in open cars, the parade route being too long for them to walk. A local observer noted that their "ranks are growing thinner... with each successive public occasion."[11] The observation was accurate, for by

10. *Weekly Iberian,* September 30, October 14, 1916.

11. *New Iberia Enterprise,* July 16, 1918. Deceased members of the Camp at the end of

the end of 1918, one-fourth of Camp 1788's membership had passed away.

In 1920 the Confederate veterans decided to share a banquet at the Frederic Hotel as part of their annual assembly. Promptly at three in the afternoon they moved out of headquarters and marched in a body to the hotel. Commander E. J. Carstens was followed by A. A. Flory, L. G. Williams, Adrien Conrad, P. A. Dupuy, Ben House, O. Bonin, Ernest Bonvillain, J. B. Winters, and H. H. Furr. At the hotel they were joined by Judge L. O. Hacker, who acted as master of ceremonies.

After feasting, the old men swapped tales of their wartime adventures. L. G. Williams then picked up his banjo and everyone joined in singing songs of the Old South. When the singing concluded with "Auld Lang Syne," there was scarcely a dry eye among the handful or old warriors.[12] For some reason, apparently, they all sensed that this would be the last such gathering of the group.

There were, however, occasional gatherings of the old soldiers for other reasons, especially when one of them celebrated an anniversary. For example, on December 12, 1917, Mr. and Mrs. John Winters celebrated their fiftieth wedding anniversary, and Winter's old comrades joined the couple in marking the occasion.[13] In addition, on January 14, 1921, Mr. and Mrs. Frederick Davis were joined by family and friends in celebrating their golden anniversary.[14]

A real treat for the old soldiers, however, was the party honoring the fiftieth wedding anniversary of Mr. and Mrs. L. G. Williams on November 4, 1922. At the outset of the celebration, Mr. Williams was dubbed the "city's youngest old man." Then entertainment followed: Edith Devise played the wedding march; Mrs. Francis Voorhies sang "Oh Promise Me"; Mrs. Donald Burke delivered an appropriate recitation; and Pamela Burke danced gracefully. Most of the surviving Confederate veterans were in attendance and were served during the evening by the tea girls: Genevieve Martin, Aline Minvielle, Mary and Marjorie Sandoz, and Eloise Theriot.[15]

1918 were Dudley Avery, Gervia Boudreaux, Ovignac Broussard, Numa Broussard, John DeValcourt, Voorhies Derouen, David Hayes, J. P. Harrison, Felix Patout, and Octave Louviere.

12. *Ibid.*, April 17, 1920. From January 1919 to April 1920, the Camp lost Paul Darby and H. B. Bayard. John French died a few days after the 1920 meeting, and was followed in death by R. D. Stansbury in September and Judge Hacker in November, 1920.

13. *Ibid.*, December 15, 1917.

14. *Ibid.*, January 15, 1921.

15. *Weekly Iberian*, November 4, 1922.

Col. and Mrs. L. G. Williams on the occasion of their 50th wedding anniversary.

But the end of the old fraternity was fast approaching. On February 16, 1924, Ernest John Carstens, one of the two veterans who had spearheaded the local drive to form a Confederate organization, died at age 82. Eight days later, a few of the surviving thirteen members of Camp 1788 met to elect a new commander. They chose L. G. Williams. A. A. Flory was reelected adjutant, and Adrien Conrad replaced Williams as first lieutenant.[16]

Apparently the group met on only a few occasions before the final tragedy occurred for the Camp. In late October, 1926, while on a Sunday outing, L. G. Williams was riding in a car which was involved in an accident. The old soldier was injured and died two days later. A. A. Flory, Adrien Conrad, and B. F. House eulogized their old friend, saying that "he has passed away to the

---

16. *New Iberia Enterprise*, February 23, March 1, 1924. Between January 1921 and December 1924, the Camp lost Carstens, L. A. Pellerin, John Gonzales, Adolphe Romero, John Winters, and Tobias Haines.

tented field of another world where no bugle will sound the reveille."[17] There is no record of anyone being named Williams' successor, nor is there any indication that Camp No. 1788 every met again.

The last-known survivors of the Camp were Adrien Conrad who died in August, 1932, at age 85; A. A. Flory, died in February, 1935, at age 92; Ernest Bonvillain, of Patoutville, in September, 1935, at age 87. Of the forty members of the Camp, only Flory is known to have passed his ninetieth birthday at the time of his death.[18]

17. *Ibid.*, October 30, 1926. Between January 1925 and January 1929, the following old soldiers died: Williams, Alphonse Boutte, Ovignac Bonin, Adolphe Broussard, C. E. Reggio, and Euzebe Gonsoulin.

18. No death records were located for the following members of Camp No. 1788: Auguste Barrilleaux, Sosthen Breaux, H. H. Furr, B. F. House, Joseph Landry, A. N. Reggio, H. F. Stafford, and Adrien Louviere.

XVI

A Brief Look at the Industry and Commerce of New Iberia

by
Glenn R. Conrad

The Industrial Revolution which transformed parts of the Western world following the invention of the steam engine had little or no impact on the South until the dawn of the twentieth century. Indeed, a factor frequently overlooked by historians in citing long-range causes for the American Civil War is the differing life style being produced in the industrial North as contrasted with that which persisted in the predominantly agricultural South in the years between 1830 and 1860.

Agriculture, as manifested in the plantation system, remained the mainstay of the Southern economy until the beginning of World War II. Tobacco, cotton, and rice held sway as the leading crops of the region, except in Louisiana where sugarcane numbered as one of the big three.

In addition to its broad fields, the South possessed during the nineteenth and early twentieth centuries a seemingly inexhaustible supply of timber. Great pine and hardwood forests enveloped the region. Along the Gulf Coast large stands of oak and cypress competed with pine, gum, tupelo, and other woods for a place in the lumber market.

Thus, after the Civil War, when the shortage of labor crippled the plantation economy, Southern planters and investors turned to industrial pursuits

Downtown New Iberia looking west from Julia St., 1896 (above); 1931 (below)

Industry and Commerce 287

Downtown New Iberia looking west from Julia St., 1938 (above); 1972 (below).

Downtown New Iberia looking west from Julia St., 1978 (above); 1986 (below)

in an effort to supplement their incomes. In Louisiana, where the land and its products were the foremost natural resources of the day, it was only a matter of course that nearly all industrial endeavors would revolve around agriculture and construction, primarily through the lumber industry. Lumbering remained a major industry until the forests were depleted, a result which occurred much sooner than most people anticipated. But Nature has been good to Louisiana, for as the lumber industry declined, large petroleum deposits were discovered and became a mainstay of the economy well into the late twentieth century.

The only industry of the antebellum Teche country worthy of note was that involving the manufacture of raw sugar at the tiny sugar mills dotting the countryside. In addition, a few small foundries along the Teche serviced the primitive mills and the steamboats that plied the bayou. Finally, on Avery Island a nascent salt industry was making itself known.

Before the Civil War, Avery Island salt production, which had its beginnings during the War of 1812, was capable of supplying only local needs, being limited primarily to production by evaporation from salt springs. With the coming of the war, however, the increased need for salt caused shafts to be sunk and, in May 1862, rock salt was discovered. For about a year the mine produced most of the salt used by the Confederacy in the Trans-Mississippi Department. In April, 1863, however, Union troops, advancing through the Teche country, destroyed the salt works, and large-scale production did not resume until 1880 when the American Salt Company leased rights to the mine.

In New Iberia before the war, the only industry worthy of the name was John Stine's tannery. This enterprise, operated in conjunction with Stine's son-in-law, Josiah French, produced leather goods for about forty years before 1830. The tannery was subsequently owned and operated by a man named Fisher, for whom the present downtown street is named.

Probably the first industry to develop after the Civil War did so the year Iberia Parish was created. Returning to Avery Island from Texas in the summer of 1865, Edmund McIlhenny, the husband of Mary Eliza Avery, found that the ebb and flow of war had destroyed the island's sugar crop and salt works. He did discover, however, a few pepper plants growing in Judge Dudley Avery's garden and, being a gourmet, McIlhenny carefully cultivated these peppers to produce a sauce for flavoring food.

By 1868 McIlhenny had perfected the pepper sauce which he called "Tobasco" and which quickly became a popular favorite, not only locally, but nationally and internationally as well. Thus, one of Iberia Parish's major industries was born.

The 1870s were busy years in other aspects of local industry, particularly the construction business. Constricting acres of sugarcane brought on by the postwar labor shortage caused many people to begin harvesting the rich natural resource of timber. A further factor contributing to the development of the lumber industry was the need for housing and commercial expansion for immigrants pouring into America in the three decades following the Civil War.

Two early industries of postwar New Iberia, both on the banks of the Teche, were sawmills. One was established by Jasper Gall, a former New Iberia mayor, and David Riggs on property between Main Street and the bayou just east of Jefferson Street. Gall built three houses facing Main Street and lived in the one on the corner of Main and Jefferson. In time, Captain J. N. Pharr associated with Gall in this business. Although the plant was destroyed by fire in 1884, it was rebuilt and operated successfully for many years thereafter.

Before the Civil War, Ulger Decuir and Jean-Jacques Mistrot had formed a partnership to establish and operate a sawmill in addition to their already successful mercantile business on the corner of Main and Julia streets. The sawmill operation became inactive during the war years. Then, in September, 1870, Decuir and Mistrot closed their mercantile business and the following April formed a partnership with D. U. Broussard to reopen their sawmill. When Decuir died unexpectedly the following month, his place in the partnership was taken by Albert Decuir. The sawmill ultimately produced 50,000 feet of lumber per day. The mill burned in 1880 but was rebuilt and flourished for many years thereafter.

Another early New Iberia industry associated with lumbering was the O. J. Trainor Sash and Blind Factory, established in 1872. Beginning with a work force of five men, this business expanded to the manufacture of mantels, doors, cisterns, and decorative items of wood. Under the name of O. J. Trainor Sons, the firm continued operations until 1920.

The manufacture of sashes and doors in New Iberia was carried on by Edgar P. Folse and Co. at their factory just east of Lewis Avenue between Main and St. Peter streets. This firm, founded in 1912, operated into the 1960s.[1]

Just after the turn of the century, in 1902, the Iberia Cypress Co., also known as the "Big Jim" mill, operated on the banks of the bayou near present-day North Lewis Avenue. Logs for the mill were towed up the bayou by the company's steamboat, the *Sadie Downman*. This mill, under the supervision of George Dallas, operated until 1913.

Another large lumbering enterprise was the Aucoin, Breaux, and Renoudet Cypress Lumber Co. This industry, located on the north side of Jane Street at Chestnut, employed well over 100 men and produced dressed lumber, shingles

---

1. The plant was located in the 1100 block of East Main Street.

Industry and Commerce 291

E. P. Folse & Co.

Iberia Cypress Co. (Big Jim)

and cisterns. Shingle production amounted to 100,000 per day.[2]

But the largest shingle producer was Gebert's Shingle Mill which had a capacity of 200,000 per day. This mill, located on the site now occupied by the Trappey Company on East Main, began operation in the 1890s and continued producing cypress shingles until sold to the Trinity Lumber Company of Houston, Texas, in January, 1902.

Lumbering, however, was not the only construction industry in New Iberia. Brickmaking became a major enterprise in the years after the Civil War. During the 1870s E. T. King operated a brick factory near the bayou just west of Lewis Avenue. This factory had been originally established by King's father-in-law, Jonas Marsh.

A. L. Bergerie, John Emmer, and W. D. Southwell operated brick factories during the 1880s, 1890s, and into the new century. The latter operation was capable of producing 50,000 bricks and 10,000 two-inch tile pipes per day. The output of these brickyards was nevertheless strained after the fire of Octo-

2. At the turn of the century this plant employed 125 men who were turning out 50,000 board feet of rough lumber and 25,000 board feet of dressed lumber per day. At the same time, the company was shipping fifty carloads of lumber and shingles per month.

Gebert Shingle Mill
(after the snowfall of February 14, 1899)

Industry and Commerce

Segura Sugar Mill, built 1897, burned 1912

Iberia Sugar Co-op, 1978

Lutzenberger's, later Simon's, Foundry

ber, 1899, destroyed a large portion of downtown New Iberia. Most of the older buildings on Main Street are constructed with bricks from these kilns.

The successor to these brickyards was the Collins Conrad firm which moved to the Spanish Lake area from Breaux Bridge in 1935. The factory was sold and the equipment moved to Cade at the time the government purchased the property for the New Iberia Naval Air Station. The Conrad Brick Factory produced an unusual brick called the "Conrad Scored" or "Conrad Scratched" brick, which is found in many structures across South Louisiana.

An industry which sprang up in New Iberia after the Civil War to service the many area sugar mills and the steamboats on the Teche was Lutzenberger's Foundry. Established in 1871 by F. S. Lutzenberger on the bank of the bayou at the foot of Swain Street, the business, employing forty to fifty men in its early days, did castings and repairs for steamboats and sugar mills. The foundry burned in 1882 but was immediately rebuilt near the intersection of Jane and Corinne streets. As the years passed, Lutzenberger's descendants, the Simon family, operated the foundry and a supply house until the sale of the business to the Voorhies family.

A machine shop and supply house of considerable proportions is that founded by Paul Voorhies in late 1917. This business continues to the present under

Industry and Commerce 295

the direction of his descendants.

The food-processing industry has been well represented in the parish since the Civil War. In addition to the production of raw sugar, and the McIlhenny "Tobasco" operation, food-processing and packaging has been a major concern of the area. Syrup-making, for example, was once a widespread industry. Today, however, few of the smaller mills remain. A major New Iberia syrup mill, producing 11,000 gallons per day, was Bernard's "Star B" plant which operated on Jane Street between 1930 and 1952.

In the past a large operation was that of the New Iberia Canning Company. Today, Trappey's, Bruce's, and the Frank Tea and Spice Co. are the major food processors of the area. Until the early 1980s, Pelican Creamery, which began operations in March, 1939, was a major dairy-products processor.

Salt, mined in significant quantities at Weeks and Avery islands, is packaged locally and distributed worldwide.[3] Salt was mined at Jefferson Island until the mine disaster of November 20, 1980, at which time the entire mine was flooded and the mining operation abandoned.

Over the years New Iberia has had a number of rice mills. These have been owned and operated by such families as the Conrads, the Halls, the Carvers, Eliases, Burkes, Browns, and Dreyfuses. The only remaining rice mill in New Iberia in the mid-1980s is that founded by Philip Conrad in 1912 and presently owned by Mike Davis.[4]

---

[3]. In 1978 the federal government announced purchase of the Weeks Island mine to be used for crude oil storage as part of the nation's strategic oil reserve.

[4]. The Conrad Rice Mill, Inc., is the oldest privately owned rice mill in the United States.

Conrad Rice Mill, 1915

Conrad Rice Mill, 1986

Industry and Commerce

During the last century New Iberia has had its share of smaller, and sometimes unusual enterprises. In 1875, for example, John Pickett, Jr., began the manufacture of sulphur matches. Said to be of the finest quality, there is little known of the subsequent production.

An industry now exceedingly rare, if not extinct, deals with the manufacture of wooden cisterns. At one time the making of these reservoirs for rainwater was a major part of local industry. Aucoin, Breaux, and Renoudet and O. J. Trainor manufactured cypress cisterns for many years, but the firm of Callahan and Lewis, established in 1880, devoted their entire operation to making cisterns. The plant was capable of producing six per day and these were sold throughout Louisiana and the Plains States. The last remnant of this once sizable industry was the one-man operation of Jim Christian at his home on East St. Peter St.

Icehouses were a part of New Iberia for over a century. The first to serve the town was R. Baggary's, established in 1876 with a capacity of six and one-half tons per day. This enterprise was joined by Victor Erath's New Iberia Ice and Bottling Co. toward the end of the century. The Erath plant was located at the foot of Swain Street. The last ice house in New Iberia, the Daigre facility on Railroad Avenue ceased operations in mid-October, 1985.

The Daigre Ice House at the time it ceased operations in October 1985.

In 1877, A. M. Bernard established on West Main Street the wagon works which produced, for nearly one hundred years, farm wagons and carts made of wood. The present-day successor to this business is the Davis Machine Shop on West St. Peter Street.

The Bernard Wagon Works about 1900

During the 1880s Larkin and Ribbeck, engineers and coppersmiths, began the manufacture in New Iberia of steamboilers, tanks, and iron chimneys.

In 1879, Frederick Gates opened a cottonseed oil mill at the foot of Prairie Avenue. Here was produced cottonseed meal, refined oils and soap. A decade later the mill was producing 1,600 barrels of oil and 900 tons of meal per year. This venture was followed with a similar one undertaken by Maurice Bergerie and Paul Voorhies who operated a cotton gin and cotton oil mill on Frere Street in the 1920s.

One of the most unusual enterprises, at least for the present generation, was Silvio Broussard's New Iberia Electric Light Company. The ancestor of today's large utility companies, this business generated electricity for 650 incandescent lights and forty street lights at the turn of the century.

Another uncommon industry for New Iberia was the Bienville Furniture Manufacturing Company which began local operations in 1934. This company manufactured furniture of all kinds and was for a long time located in the 1100 block of East Main. It subsequently moved to a location along the Abbeville branch line of the Southern Pacific Railroad just off West Admiral Doyle Drive. The operation was destroyed by fire in October 1978.

The Red Fox Companies, Red Fox Machine and Supply Company, Inc., and Red Fox Industries, together comprise what is perhaps New Iberia's largest privately owned industry.

The Red Fox Machine and Supply Company officially came into being on December 1, 1944, when the Jane Street plant was purchased from American Iron and Machine Works by employees Beldon Fox, general manager, and Charles Courmier, who were partners in the new business venture.

The New Iberia shop of American Iron was one of a chain located throughout the oil-producing states. The building and much of the original equipment had been moved to New Iberia from Kilgore, Texas, in 1937. After it became Red Fox, both the size of the shop and the amount of equipment has multiplied several times. Then as now, the business specializies in general oil field repairs.

With Courmier's death in 1969, Fox became sole owner of the company. Since that time his sons, Beldon Fox, Jr., and Robert C. Fox, have become part owners and serve as vice president and secretary-treasurer, respectively.

Red Fox Industries, Inc., is a related company founded by B. E. Fox in 1970, and is located on a waterfront site at the Port of Iberia. Its manufacturing and fabrication operations include the repair and refabrication of drill ships, the construction of new barge workover and drilling rigs, offshore platform rigs, platforms, and other heavy fabrication. The company also manufactures marine and conventional sewage-treatment systems and marine anchor-handling winches.

No discussion of New Iberia industry is complete without some mention of Charles Boldt's Paper Mill.[5] This industry, initially intended to make a fiber board from rice straw, began operations in 1921 with a work force of 250 men. Three years later the company was converted to the manufacture of boxboard, and finally attempted the manufacture of celotex. The factory operated until 1935 when it was sold to a Pensacola firm. The most unusual brick smokestack,

---

5. For more information on the Charles Boldt Paper Mill, see the essay entitled "1920."

The Satterfield Building
Cor. Main and Swain streets
as it appeared about 1896
(left)
and as it appears after
being remodeled in 1982 to
house five offices and two
apartments.

erected by local brick masons and a landmark of New Iberia, remains a constant reminder of what was probably New Iberia's largest industry.

There has been no lack of imagination in promoting industry in New Iberia, whether a century ago along the banks of Bayou Teche or on the channel at the Port of Iberia; a factor which certainly must be reason for the town's steady growth. For example, in 1979 several businessmen, Dailey Berard, Carlos Toca, Robert Angers, and Charles J. Broussard, organized the Agrifuels Corporation to make ethanol, a gasoline additive, from sugarcane molasses. In time the company was sold and was acquired by the Edgington Oil Company of California. On February 8, 1986, the Agrifuels Refining Corporation, a subsidiary of Edgington was dedicated and work began on a $105,000,000 plant near the Cajun Sugar Co-op in Morbihan, just east of New Iberia. When the plant is operational, scheduled for mid-1987, it will produce 35,000,000 gallons of ethanol annually from sweet sorghum and sugarcane molasses. It was estimated at the time of dedication that the plant will employ 100 people when it goes into operation.[6]

New Iberia has always been a commercial center as well as something of a manufacturing town. As transportation and communication have improved, especially in the first half of this century, some forms of local industry have declined or disappeared entirely. Such a fate, however, has not visited the commercial sector. From the initial commercial activity of the town, Murphy's store, at the beginning of the nineteenth century, the commercial development of New Iberia has been steady. Now, nearly two hundred years later, that development has become impressive.

The antebellum businesses of New Iberia are described elsewhere in this volume.[7] The merchants who served New Iberia after the Civil War can be summed up by category. James A. Lee, Julius Koch, and J. G. Mestayer operated drug stores. Grocers were J. C. M. Robertson, L. A. Dupuy, H. Beckman, and S. Boudreaux. Dry goods could be found at the stores of J. H. Wise, Lehman and Taylor, Hayem Gouguenheim, Jacob Davis, David Levy, Max Levy, and Decuir and Mistrot. Jewelry and watchmaking were the interests of Eugene Henry and his brother, and F. Schwab. General stores were operated by Zenon Decuir, W. E. Satterfield, and Pierre LeBron. Burke and Fuller and Hayem Gouguenheim were the local furniture dealers. Finally, E. F. Millard owned a stationery store.

6. *Daily Iberian*, February 9, 1986.

7. See the second and third essays.

To discuss all the successors of these businesses in New Iberia during the past century would be next to impossible and would result in nothing more than a dull recitation. Thus, one way to approach this problem is to look at some of New Iberia's merchants of the past through a sampling of their advertising in New Iberia's newspapers.

The first result of such an investigation reveals some interesting trends in marketing. For example, today's newspapers, virtually on a daily basis, include large-scale advertising by retail grocers, usually supermarkets. Here is a trend which has developed during the past quarter century and has no counterpart in newspaper advertising for the first half of the twentieth century. Indeed, one must go back to the New Iberia papers of over a century ago to find a large part of the advertising dollar given over to food items. Of course, those papers of the past contain nothing comparable, spacewise, to today's one- and two-page ads.

Another example might be found in automobile advertising. One would think that as automobiles became popular in the 1920s there would have been

The Breaux Building
when it housed The Specialty Store about 1912; later housed the Palace Theater

considerable space in newspapers used by local dealers to advertise the horseless carriage. Such, however, was not the case. Examination of New Iberia newspaper advertising in the mid-20s reveals very little space given over to the "raciest runabout" or "the most luxurious landau." But, the fact that the flivvers were on the scene, and occasionally out of the picture, is inescapable when one considers Tom de Blanc's persistent ad: "You wreck 'em, we pick 'em."

What follows is a random selection of New Iberia newpaper advertisers and advertising gimmicks at twenty-five year intervals beginning in 1876. While the selections afford some insight into the various methods employed by advertisers, it is obvious that the purpose of advertising has remained the same: to turn a profit.

In January, 1876, A. Lehman and Co., probably New Iberia's largest "department store," located on Main at Church Alley, took "pleasure in calling the attention of the trade to the very large and complete assorted stock of goods. . . . Particular attention is invited to the blanket and flannel departments." The half-page ad appearing in the *Sugar Bowl* then went on to enumerate the bargains in what amounted to an early-day "white sale."

The same advertiser next informed ladies of the wonderful Domestic Sewing Machine, a machine which "does good work with little skill or rough handling." Mr. Lehman also offered the trade "tooth brushes, pocket combs, ladies back combs, misses side combs, tuck combs, and a wide assortment of satin ribbons."

Because it was good planting time, Sam Cary of Centerville advertised in the New Iberia paper that he had orange trees for sale, ranging in price from ten cents to one dollar. Phil Marquet ran an ad to the effect that his "oyster saloon" business had produced an immense pile of shells and that he was then converting the shells into a fine quality lime, especially good for whitewashing. But, even then, competition was the order of the day, as revealed in Alex Hebert's nearby ad stating that he had quality shell lime "at very low figures."

In the realm of construction, E. T. King announced to newspaper readers that he had rented the lot along the bayou back of the Live Oak Hotel (Alma House) in order to sell split lumber and wood. William Lourd was managing the yard, and together they "confidently expect that our friends, acquaintances, and public generally will give us their patronage. At any rate, call us before purchasing elsewhere."

Anton Karasch notified the public that he was making cisterns and had some really good bargains. Allen Handy, a likely name, advertised that he was a carpenter and cabinetmaker, but could make "plows, wagons, carts, etc." Handy's neighbor in the Escudier Building on Main Street was Frank Hunold, a blacksmith who advertised that he could "iron buggies and wagons," and that all of this work was "faithfully executed."

Stott and Lutzenberger were persistent advertisers during 1876. They offered lift and force pumps, grate bars, furnace mouths, gas and iron pipe, steam whistles, brass and globe valves. They promised the public that "all work done on the shortest notice."

Victor Ruotte, the shoemaker, advertised in June, 1876, that so closely did he attend to his business that "he is rarely seen upon the streets." If industriousness was Ruotte's gimmick, his competitors, Coudron & Whitney of the Rose Bud Shoe Shop, were not at a loss. They noted in their ads that "Ladies not wishing to call at our shop will be waited upon at their residences and measures taken." J. M. Lacarce, whose shoe shop was on Julia Street, was not to be outdone. He advertised that "Screwed shoes are made whenever desired."

For New Iberia housewives, eternally seeking the elusive food bargain, there was a considerable array of grocery stores advertising their wares. Octave Renoudet, who had been clerking in Louis Indest's grocery store, opened his own stand on Main Street in June 1876. But a most fashionable store for milady's marketing was F. Joinville Hebert's emporium on the corner of Bridge and Main streets. Mr. Hebert proudly announced that he had "choice groceries, wines, liquors, tobaccos, segars [sic], crockery, tinware, nails, flour, sugar, coffee, tea, soap, starch--in fact everything to be found in a well-stocked store."

William Kramer also offered a large assortment of items at his food market on the corner of Serret Alley and Main Street. Pierre LeBron, not to be outdone, announced in October, 1876, that he had just returned from a marketing spree in New Orleans, and that his store on the corner of St. Peter and Julia streets would be exceptionally well stocked for the coming holiday season.

Then, if the little woman was tired, depressed, or discouraged slaving over a hot wood-and-coal stove, the loving husband could always take her and the family out to Widow Charles Pointis' "Restaurante Moderne" where meals were served at all times. If it happened to be Thursday evening, after dinner the family could stroll up to Mrs. Jasper Gall's front lawn on the corner of Jefferson and Main to sample some of that lady's delicious ice cream, served to customers while sitting in a swing under the branches of a large oak tree.

Mr. John Lamperez, the baker, advertised in September, 1876, that he had recently occupied the new brick bakery built by John Emmer, and that his bread had to be tasted to be appreciated. Meanwhile, J. G. Johnson notified the public that he was "now making better and cheaper brooms than Mr. Yankee can."

Finally, perhaps a sign of the times, Dr. Colgin ran this notice: "All persons indebted to me are respectfully requested to call and settle their account-- if they desire my services for the coming year." He did not indicate the consequences should his services not be desired.

A generation later, in 1901, the trend in advertising had somewhat shifted. Few ads for food found their way into the newspaper columns. By then, the range of consumer products had greatly increased, and all the gadgets of a technologically advancing society were spread before newspaper readers. Construction interests still held a place as major advertisers, but by 1901 New Iberia newspapers were including real estate and insurance ads.

The new century began with J. W. Eckart, the jeweler, announcing "Cordial Good Wishes for the New Year," and inviting readers to "call and consult us if you have, or think you have, the slightest visual defect. Won't cost you a cent to find out.... See well in 1901 by first seeing us."

Professional people were also getting into the swing of newspaper advertising. Dr. A. G. Emmer, dental surgeon, advertised "Strictly first-class work only." Dr. F. N. Brian, physician and surgeon, notified readers that he was specializing in obstetrics and gynecology. Andrew Thorpe, the lawyer, announced that he gave all cases his closest attention. J. E. Kerrigan and Franz Bernhard, civil engineers, and Voorhies and Voorhies, the lawyers, notified the public of their services. Julius Koch, the druggist and chemist, advertised that he carefully compounded prescriptions from pure, fresh drugs, and that he did this at all hours.

E. W. Phillips, the architect and builder, announced that he was ready to take on any job. J. M. Perry painted houses and signs. T. J. Upton was a drayman. E. B. David would deliver milk twice a day.

Real estate and insurance matters began to appear in newspapers at the turn of the century. Alfred Renoudet and George Robertson were engaged in the sale of both property and insurance. L. A. Pellerin advertised as a notary and a real estate agent. And Burke, Gates and Suberbielle advertised that "A sure anchor against the windward is a policy in a well-established, stable fire insurance company."

Modes of conveyance were attracting more attention from advertisers. Benthall & Horner, horseshoers, blacksmiths, and wheelwrights on Weeks Street, near Main, advertised the construction of wagons and carts. J. Jacquemoud always carried in stock "fine, substantial, home-made buggies." John Broussard, urging readers to be careful when buying a surrey, noted that all surreys are not alike and the unattentive buyer might end up with a lemon. "Buy here and be Safe." Over the months Broussard continued to sing the praises of his Columbus Surreys: "Like riding on a cloud"; "The smoothest running, most comfortable and most stylish"; "To ride in style and comfort too, you need one of our carriages."

If anyone was planning to stay at home and sew, J. G. Arnandez was happy to demonstrate the Singer Sewing Machine, or, if madame preferred, O. B. Ortte

The Erath Building as it appeared in 1986
Built by Auguste Erath about 1885 as a commercial-residential facility

would show her the marvels of the White Sewing Machine.

In still another realm, A. B. Murray advertised that he handled "the best grade Kentucky mules," and Dr. Sheard Moore, the veterinary surgeon, advertised that he bottled "Sure Cure Liniment" for mule ailments.

There were "liniments" for humans, too. One barkeep, for example, advertised eight-year-old bourbon for $3.50 per gallon or ninety cents per bottle, and claret wine sold for sixty cents per gallon for fifteen cents per bottle. Moss' Cafe bottled a variety of wines from Malaga to Sacramento.

E. J. Carstens always had an excellent supply of garden seeds and a seemingly inexhaustible supply of gardening tips. Lee's offered a selection of English, French, and American perfumes, as well as Ramon's Tonic Regulator, " a cure for dyspepsia, weak kidneys, stomach and liver complaints, aches and pains, and all other troubles."

Some of technology's latest miracles were also being advertised in these turn-of-the-century newspapers. Victor Erath regularly advertised his New

Industry and Commerce

The 100 block of West Main as it appeared in November 1985.

Iberia Ice and Bottling Works, "manufacturers of ice, seltzer, soda & mineral waters." The Cumberland Telephone & Telegraph Co., managed by Harry Turner, could put a telephone in a private residence for $1.50 per month, but R. F. Hogsett, manager of the Teche and Vermilion Telephone Co., notified readers of the *New Iberia Enterprise* that his company would install a phone for $1.00 per month.

Twenty-five years later, in 1926, newspaper advertising appealed to a broader cross-section of the merchandising and servicing community. There were also many new names in the retail world of New Iberia.

Davis Brothers, A. B. Murray, and Suberbielle-Derouen, Inc., were advertising as insurance agents. Bertrand Lumber Co. and E. P. Folse were advertising building materials. Estorge Drug Co., Kahn's Pharmacy, and Taylor's advertised the developing emporium of the modern-day drugstore. Dauterive Undertaking Parlors notified the public of free ambulance service to hospitals with prompt service day or night.

Abe Hirsch announced blue serge suits for $22.50 each; flannel shirts for $1.65. The Model Co. "offered the best line of merchandise in every department," and Henry Broussard had opened The Toggery, a men's store, and was offering two suits for $35.

The 100 block of West Main as it appeared in 1937 (above) and 1972 (below).

Industry and Commerce

North side of West Main showing Bouligny Plaza, May 1983.

Banks and savings and loan institutions had begun to advertise. The State Bank notified readers that "checks give you prestige among businessmen and other leaders of the community. Pay by our checks." Iberia Building Association advertised that "the building and loan plan makes dreams come true."

Agricultural products seem to have nearly disappeared from advertising columns in the twenty-five years after the turn of the century. Only L. J. Barrow's ad concerning seed rice for sale could be found. And the farm family could buy pure-bred baby "chix" from William Colgin for $9.90 per hundred. The only grocery advertising during August 1926 was A. Delahoussaye who owned and operated the "Store where Quality Reigns Supreme." He was advertising an assortment of fruit.

It was the new technology which produced new advertising. D. H. Castille offered the marvels of the Atwater Kent Radio for $60. The automobile was beginning to gain some attention. Joseph Davis advertised the 1926 Chevrolet as "the smoothest Chevrolet in Chevrolet History," and asked his readers if they could imagine "rushing from 10 to 30 miles an hour in ten seconds," or could they imagine "driving between 40 and 50 miles an hour, for hour upon hour?" All this quality, all this luxury, all this prestige was available for $765.

Buildings
100 block of West Main
1912 (left) and
May 1983 (below)

Industry and Commerce

North side of West Main, April 1972, before creation of Bouligny Plaza

The 200 block of East Main Street, November 1985.

Homer LaGrange, dealer for Dodge Brothers Motor Cars, advertised the most luxurious car in their line for $795. LeBlanc and Broussard, the Ford dealers, not only sold cars but also the Firestone tires to go with them. To keep all these happy machines merrily spinning along was the responsibility of J. A. Daigre's Oil Co., distributors for Daco Petroleum Products. Of course, if there should occur an untoward incident while out driving, such as bogging running-board deep or not allowing sufficient clearance for a passing car, there was always Tom de Blanc and his "wrecking car service."

Between 1901 and 1926 science produced the motion-picture camera and Cecil B. de Mille produced Hollywood. The two combined gave rise to a major advertiser all across America, the local "picture show." In New Iberia the Elks Theater told newspaper readers that during the week of July 25, 1926, they could see Jack Holt in *Born to the West;* Harry Carey in *Driftin' Thru;* Ramon Novarro in *The Midshipman;* Helene Chadwick and Hedda Hopper in *Pleasures of the Rich.* All of this movie magic *(sans mots)* was available at two bits for adults and a dime for kids.

Not all advertisers were necessarily large corporations or even large businesses. Even then, the small entrepreneur knew the benefits to be derived from advertising. Al Dieudonne advertised his "Al's-No-U" name plates and signs

Industry and Commerce

The Pascal Building (right), 1972, and after renovation, 1983

The Ford agency building (left), now Allain's Jewelry, Inc.

for car, desk, or residence. This indispensable means of identification for the up-and-coming executive was readily available for $1.00.

Jennaro's Taxi Co. advised newspaper readers that their taxis "meet all trains," and that passengers ride in closed cars, day or night. Finally, far ahead of her times, Mrs. O. J. Abadie advertised expert hair styling--for fifteen cents.

A quarter of a century later, in 1951, the list of advertisers in the *Daily Iberian* was largely different from that of twenty-five years before. There was, however, a decided trend toward advertising transportation and entertainment. The auto dealerships in New Iberia: Leonard Buick Co., Gene Fortier, Inc., Patout Nash Motors, Darby-Wattigny Motors, New Iberia Auto Co., LeBlanc and Broussard, Acadian Pontiac, Davis-Delcambre Motors, Mayer Motor Co., and Butaud-Doumit Motors, occupied considerable space in the advertising columns, telling and showing readers the marvels of their products.

The Echo Drive-In, Iberia Drive-In, the Palace, Evangeline, and Essanee theatres were catering to the public in those last years before television foreclosed on so many movie theaters.

Abdalla's and Wormser's were the major advertisers of clothing during October, 1951. Oubre Furniture Co. had a "special sale of felt base linoleum rugs" for $3.95. Minvielle Furniture Co. was advertising the Amana home freezer. Indeed, the home appliance was the center of attention in advertising as mid-century rolled around. D. H. Castille, N. J. Breaux, A & A Home and Auto Supply, United Gas were offering the reading public a wide selection of modern appliances.

One of the few grocery stores to advertise was the Ritz Food Store on the corner of East Main and South Lewis. It offered picnic hams for 44 cents per pound, Blue Plate Salad Oil for $1.98 a gallon, and bananas for 11 cents per pound.

By the late 1970s the trend in advertising had taken new directions, primarily as a result of New Iberia's accelerated growth. There were then many chain and privately owned supermarkets. Food had once again returned to the advertising pages as a major item. A sampling of food store ads in late 1978 revealed that Bodin's Super Market at Bank and Dale was offering Konriko Rice (a local product) for $1.99 a ten-pound bag. Carter's on North Lewis had Luzianne coffee for $2.19 per pound. Delchamps, a supermarket in the Iberia Shopping Plaza on South Lewis, advertised its bargains on a two-page, two-color spread. Menard's Food Store on the corner of Hopkins and West Dale advertised many bargains, one of which was five pounds of bananas for $1.00. Simoneaud and Sons, on Ashton Street, could offer the shopper center-cut pork chops for $1.69 per pound. Winn-Dixie Food Store on West St. Peter Street offered, among other things, a quart of mayonnaise for $1.09. Delicious apples were going for ·49 cents a pound at National Food Store on Center Street. Kroger's on East

Main at Bayard, was selling large eggs for 65 cents a dozen, and Fremin's Food Store, corner of Corinne and Frere streets, was advertising yellow onions at 8 cents per pound. All in all there were nearly ten pages of food bargains in one issue of the local newspaper.

In October, 1985, most of the same food stores were to be found advertising in the local paper. North Lewis IGA offered 5 pounds of flour for 99 cents. Fremin's Food and Furniture, relocated on the corner of Hopkins and West Admiral Doyle, had 10 pounds of Konriko Rice for $2.39. The A & P was selling yellow onions for 23 cents per pound. Kroger advertised a quart of mayonnaise for $1.19 and a dozen large eggs for 43 cents. National was selling Delicious apples for 59 cents per pound, and Simoneaud's Discount Foods had Community Coffee for $2.15 per pound.

Advertisements in New Iberia's newspapers over the past century or more have reflected the changing consumer tastes and the developing commercial market that is New Iberia. As these tastes continue to change and the supply of available goods and services becomes greater, one wonders what will be the story of New Iberia's industry and commerce during the century to come.

A contemporary shopping center in New Iberia

XVII

An Historical Sketch of New Iberia's Banks

by
Glenn R. Conrad

In the years following the Civil War, millions of Americans poured into the vast wilderness beyond the Mississippi River. Some sought the mineral riches of the west, some came to build railroads or to trade, but most came to farm. The railroads, eager to raise money and to develop a clientele of farm customers along the rights-of-way, urged people to move into the new lands.

Side by side with the spread of farming and the railroads was the growth of small towns. The farmers needed a place to trade, and in the days of buggies and muddy roads, the area a town could serve was quite limited. Thus, between 1860 and 1900, the number of towns in the United States with populations of 2,500 to 10,000 grew in number from 300 to 1,300. Such a town was New Iberia.

Typically, the small town, strategically located on a stream or railroad, was a service area for the nearby farms. Spread along any Main Street were the stores which supplied the "country folk" with dry goods, farm implements, feed and seed, kerosene, and furniture. A "progressive" town contained a few doctors, lawyers, and a newspaper or two. If the town happened to be a parish or county seat, it also possessed its fair share of politicians. Finally, the typical American town had a bank--or more likely, two or three banks.

Financial Institutions

The small-town banker was usually a resident who was a promoter or early booster of the town's growth. He was the type of person who combined a profession--such as law, medicine, or merchandising--and finance with an interest in literature and the arts. These were the people who supported America's small towns and who ultimately furnished them with the inevitable opera house, the chautauquas, and the public library.

Often the first small-town banks arose spontaneously to meet the need for deposit facilities. Prior to the formal establishment of a bank, a storekeeper or mercantile company, such as Shute and Taylor in New Iberia, was the depository for surplus wealth. Banks originating in this manner often had no more office space than a corner of the store and no more security than the company safe. But as banking institutions were established, handsome brick or stone, bandit-proof buildings were erected to house them.

Two factors, both at the national level, were responsible for the spectacular increase during the 1860s and 1870s in the number of banks throughout much of America outside of the South. Louisiana was not immediately affected by the first factor, and the second contributed in only a small way to the organization of New Iberia's three original banks within a ten-year span. It was the third, purely regional factor, common to Louisiana which was really responsible for inaugurating New Iberia's banking era.

The first of the national factors was the passage in January 1863 of legislation enabling the establishment of federally chartered national banks. Commercial banking institutions could thereafter be incorporated under federal charter and be subject exclusively to federal control. Minimum capital for these national banks was set at $50,000 for institutions in communities with populations under 6,000; $100,000 for institutions in larger cities. Half the authorized capital had to be paid in before the bank opened for business, the remainder during the succeeding year.

The keystone of the national banking structure was the basis provided for note issue (paper currency). Two purposes were served by the note provisions of the National Banking Act of 1863. First, they provided the United States with a paper currency, uniform throughout the country, and, secondly, the bond collateral requirement for national bank notes assured the federal government a lasting market for its bonds.

Thus, the 1863 act gave birth to the national banking system, but for the first ten years of its existence the system was slow to develop. This sluggishness led to the second factor in the history of American banking, a provision which enabled the system to develop rapidly through the North and East, but only slightly in the South.

In 1873, a financial crisis gripped the country, largely brought on by a scarcity of currency. The act of 1863 had apportioned the number of notes national banks could issue, with the largest portion going to Eastern banks. A decade later, however, there developed such a pronounced shortage of currency that the Act to Remove Limitations on Banking Associations was passed in January 1875. The act removed all apportionment restrictions upon national bank note issue. Any national bank could then issue paper currency in direct relation to its deposit of federal bonds with the Comptroller of the Currency.

The 1875 act was deeply bound up in partisan politics. Northern and Eastern Republicans opposed the liberalization of the Bank Act. Southern and Western Democrats, on the other hand, supported the amendment because of the shortage of currency in their areas. Hence, when a Democratic-controlled Congress was returned by the voters in November 1874, passage of the amendment to the Bank Act was assured.

To small-town leaders and businessmen across much of the country, the Bank Act amendment of 1875 was a clear signal for action. Banking institutions sprang up overnight and multiplied from roughly 2,000 in the late 1860s to 20,000 by 1910. In Louisiana, however, a local factor inhibited the establishment of small-town banking institutions for another decade.

Throughout the state, for roughly twenty years after the Civil War, local politics was dominated by Reconstruction politicians. This unsettled political situation, frequently accompanied by outbreaks of violence, therefore served to further discourage local businessmen, planters, and others from combining their capital reserves to establish banks. The situation changed, however, when, during the mid-1880's, Democrats ousted Republicans from local office. With this political turnover, then, may be dated the return of popular confidence in local institutions and the sudden burst of financial activity and material progress which would characterize Louisiana at the turn of the century. By 1887 New Iberia was ready to join similar-sized towns across the nation as a "typical" American town.

The first national bank in Southwest Louisiana was the New Iberia National Bank, chartered on March 25, 1887, by a group of prominent citizens. The bank's initial board of directors included Joseph A. Breaux, Felix Patout, Charles Gouguenheim, P. L. Renoudet, Auguste Pascal, James Gebert, and Pierre LeBron. The first president was Joseph Breaux, a lawyer-businessman-politician

Financial Institutions 319

New Iberia National Bank headquarters on South Lewis
Under construction, 1982 (above), and as it appeared in November 1985

from New Iberia. Breaux subsequently became state superintendent of education and chief justice of the Louisiana supreme court. He served as president of the bank until September 1924. All of his successors have been associated with the agricultural-commercial interests of Iberia Parish.

The bank's second president was George Labau, the son of French parents, who saw the promise of Louisiana and contributed to its growth. Mr. Labau served as president until his death in September 1937. He was succeeded by Fritz Dietlein, scion of a highly respected Louisiana family. Mr. Dietlein occupied the office of president until his death in June 1939. From that date until March 1940, John Schwing acted as chief executive officer of the bank.

The next president of the parish's oldest bank was J. Paulin Duhe, a well-known planter and oil man. Mr. Duhe and the bank's directors guided the institution through the war years of the forties into the growth years of the fifties and sixties. Mr. Duhe served as president until his death in 1961. He was succeeded as chief executive of New Iberia National Bank by his son, J. Malcolm Duhe, who together with a conscientious board of directors continued to promote the progressive policies of the bank. Mr. Duhe served as president until his death in March 1980. In April of that year Jules B. Schwing was named president and served in that capacity until September 1, 1984; thereafter serving as the first chairman of the board of directors. Later in September 1984 Don Fought became president of the bank.[1]

New Iberia's second oldest financial institution is one which today possesses an outstanding reputation among the state's banking community. At a meeting of the stockholders of the People's National Bank, called by the group's secretary, Leopold Levy, on February 2, 1891, a committee composed of Fred L. Gates, Thomas R. Morse, and George Simon was appointed to select suitable quarters for the bank.

Upon receiving the bank's charter, the stockholders elected a board of directors consisting of S. O. Thomas, Fred L. Gates, W. E. Satterfield, Auguste Erath, Leopold Levy, P. Gouguenheim, Thomas R. Morse, David Laughlin, and George Simon. From these directors, officers were elected: S. O. Thomas, president; Fred L. Gates, vice-president; W. E. Satterfield, cashier.

When Mr. Thomas died in 1898, the directors elected James Gebert as president. Mr. Gebert, who had joined the board in April 1895, served as president

---

1. The following men served, or are serving, as the bank's cashier: P. L. Renoudet (1887-1917), John E. Schwing (1917-1939), George Renoudet (1939-1946), Marcus Shaw (1946-1952), Eldridge Theriot (1952-1983), and Leonard J. Freyou (1983 - present).

Financial Institutions

The State National Bank headquarters
as it appeared in November, 1978

The People's Bank and Trust headquarters
as it appeared in November, 1985

of People's Bank until his death in 1906. He was succeeded by Lazard Kling who, in turn, was succeeded in 1910 by Charles L. Provost. Mr. Provost resigned the office for reasons of health in 1929.

In May 1929 the board of directors elected Leon Minvielle, Sr. Mr. Minvielle remained closely associated with banking circles until his death in February 1974. Upon his father's death, Leon Minvielle, Jr. was elected president and served in that capacity until December 1980. At that time Ron Steed became president and served until late 1984. On March 4, 1985, Don Bordelon became president.

In the late 1970s People's Bank, reflecting the dispersion of commercial activity from Main Street, relocated its main office in a new building on the corner of South Lewis and East Admiral Doyle. The new office opened in February, 1980. Four years later, the Peoples Bank Tower was constructed and was occupied in June, 1984.

New Iberia's third banking institution was put together as the century was drawing to a close. Early in 1897 a group of Iberians headed by L. P. Patout, W. G. Weeks, E. T. Weeks, L. J. Burguieres, J. P. Suberbielle, Alexis Voorhies, Albert Estorge, A. Daigre, Anthony and Nicholas Muller, Emile Gajan, and others, announced their intention to incorporate the State Bank of New Iberia.

In May the stockholders elected the first board: L. P. Patout, R. H. Cage, Lazard Kling, Nicholas Muller, A. Daigre, Albert Estorge, H. S. Sanders, J. P. Subervielle, and W. G. Weeks.

In nearly ninety years of existence, the State Bank, which became a national bank in 1903, has had six executive officers: L. P. Patout (1897-1901), Albert Estorge (1902-1951), Edward Estorge (1951-1954), W. J. Bernard, Sr. (1954-1963), Donald Delcambre (1963-1982), and John H. DeJean (1982-   ).[2]

New Iberia's fourth banking endeavor occurred in 1911 when Charles L. Provost subscribed the necessary $50,000 capital to incorporate the Citizens Bank of New Iberia. In early March the stockholders met and elected a board of directors: P. G. LeBourgeois, Louis Pfister, A. C. Duboin, T. R. Gayle, P. G. DeBlanc, H. Patout, Edward Weeks, Felix Patout, and Charles Provost. Felix Patout was elected president, Edward Weeks, vice-president, Charles Provost, cashier, and Fred Patout, assistant cashier.

---

2. The cashiers of the State National Bank have been J. P. Suberbielle (1897-1905), H. E. Suberbielle (1905-1906), J. Robert Perry (1906-1937), W. C. Segura (1937-1956), Roy G. Delcambre (1957-1976), Ferry P. LeBlanc (1976-1983), and Scott Sutton (1983-present).

Financial Institutions

Emile Gajan

Aristide Daigre

W. E. Satterfield

William G. Weeks

Four of the founding fathers of State National Bank

Perhaps, as time has tended to bear witness, a fourth banking institution was too much for a town the size of New Iberia on the eve of World War I. At any rate, on December 21, 1914, the stockholders of the Citizens Bank gathered, and three-fourths of the stockholders, representing 424 of the 500 shares of stock, voted to dissolve the corporation and cease business on December 31, 1914. The bank's stock was then absorbed by the People's Bank.

It would be forty-four years before another group of Iberians came together to incorporate a bank. Early in 1958 the City Bank and Trust Company was chartered and the stockholders elected as the first directors Leon Minvielle, Sr., John Abdalla, Beldon Fox, Wilfred Begnaud, Cornelius Voorhies, Minos Armentor, J. S. Brown, Jr., J. Allen Daigre, Andrew Romero, Kenneth Ringle, J. L. Duhe, and Francis Voorhies.

Shortly before the bank opened for business in the summer of 1958, Francis Voorhies was elected president. Since then, John Abdalla and Beldon Fox have presided over the bank's board of directors.

City Bank was the first local bank to break with the traditional "downtown" location for banks. Opening its main office on Center Street, the bank has subsequently established branches on the corner of St. Peter and French streets, Duperier Avenue, in Coteau, and on Admiral Doyle.

Branch banks came to New Iberia in the late 1950s. New Iberia National has the distinction of opening the first branch facility, the Center Street Branch, on March 14, 1957. While the State Bank opened its Loreauville branch that same year, it was People's Bank that next opened a branch facility in New Iberia--the Torrido Shopping Village Branch. In the subsequent years all New Iberia banks have spread their facilities throughout the town for the greater convenience of their patrons.

The New Iberia National Bank holds the record for the longest service in the same location. Since its opening nearly one hundred years ago, the bank's main office or a branch has occupied the corner of Main and Julia streets. After the disastrous fire of 1899 destroyed a large portion of downtown New Iberia, the bank rebuilt on its ashes and subsequently acquired additional space. In 1981 construction began on a new headquarters on South Lewis Avenue. The new facility was occupied in December 1982.

All New Iberia banks have consistently given every indication of being sound financial institutions. Perhaps this fact was best demonstrated when, during the Great Depression, the then three banks of New Iberia closed their doors to business for only one day, and that was done at the order of the newly inaugurated president, Franklin Roosevelt.

Financial Institutions

City Bank and Trust headquarters in November 1978 (above) and in the process of being remodeled and enlarged in January 1986 (below).

The Greyhound Bus Depot of the 1940s
has become
City Bank and Trust Co., W. St. Peter St. Branch, of the 1980s

Financial Institutions

Mrs. M. A. Patout

Although banking has been traditionally dominated by males, females, who are usually guardians of the family purse, have not been entirely overlooked in New Iberia's banking circles. In 1896, Mrs. Mary Ann Patout became the first woman to serve as a director of a New Iberia bank. Upon joining the board of the New Iberia National, Mrs. Patout also earned the distinction of being the first woman in the South to sit on the board of a national bank.

No discussion of New Iberia banks could end, however, without some mention, albeit too small, of some of the truly memorable bank cashiers and officials. The person with probably the longest career as a local cashier was Edgar E. Delhommer of the Peoples Bank. He held the position from 1903 until his death in 1942. Also well remembered is J. Robert Perry, long-time cashier for the State Bank until his death in May 1937. Equally memorable in New Iberia banking circles is John E. Schwing, who joined the New Iberia National Bank in 1905. In time he was promoted to assistant cashier under P. L. Renoudet, and in 1929 Mr. Schwing was named cashier. Ten years later he was elected executive vice-president of the bank and held that office until his death in March 1946.

Banks are not the only financial institutions of Iberia Parish; there are also the savings and loan associations. Indeed, the oldest financial institution in

The Bank of Iberia is the town's most recent bank.

New Iberia is the Iberia Savings and Loan Association. This organization was chartered on March 12, 1887, thirteen days before the New Iberia National Bank. The presidents of the Iberia Savings and Loan have been Fred L. Gates (1887-1891), E. A. Pharr (1891-1892), E. F. Millard (1892-1920), Lazard Kling (1920-1924), Max Levy (1924-1941), W. J. Bernard, Sr. (1941-1963), Henry Gallois (1963-1965), R. J. B. Abshire (1965-1967), Louis M. Cyr (1967-1978), John W. Trotter (1978-1981), and Emile J. Plaisance, Jr. (1981 - present).

Until 1978, the president of the Association had acted mainly as chairman of the board. The managing officer of the Association has carried different titles throughout the years: secretary, secretary-treasurer, and executive vice-president. Beginning in 1978, the president assumed the responsibilities of the managing officer.

Financial Institutions

Iberia Savings and Loan Association as it appeared in 1986.

The Association has had five managing officers since its foundation. From organization until April 19, 1887, E. F. Millard managed the Association. W. H. Lewis was manager from April 9, 1887, until July 20, 1888. On July 20, 1888, William G. Weeks became secretary and managing officer and served in that capacity for over fifty-nine years. John W. Trotter became secretary and managing officer in 1947. With the charter changes effected in 1978, Mr. Trotter served the Association as president and managing officer until 1981.

Emile J. Plaisance, Jr., who joined the Association in 1962, now serves as president and managing officer.

The first board meeting of the Association took place on March 18, 1887, in the office of William Robertson, an attorney. After that date, the Association was housed in several downtown buildings, including the Eureka Hotel. In 1924 the Association built the building at 127 West Main Street, and this remained its headquarters until it moved to its present headquarters on the corner of Weeks and St. Peter streets on December 8, 1961. Since then, the Association has opened branches on North Lewis Avenue, East Admiral Doyle Drive, in Jeanerette, Morgan City, and Franklin.

The Iberia Savings and Loan Association is the eighth oldest state-chartered association in Louisiana. Six in New Orleans and one in Monroe are older.

Another financial institution of New Iberia is the First Federal Savings and Loan Association located at 320 East Main Street. First Federal was organized by Frank Simon, F. M. (Pete) Olivier, Arthur Fleming, Ray F. Mestayer, S. Gerald Simon, Harold Wormser, Louis Walet, Clarence Duchamp, and Emile Duchamp. The Association opened on January 26, 1959. The presidents have been Frank Simon, F. M. (Pete) Olivier, and the current president and chairman of the board of directors, Arthur H. Fleming.

The Association has opened branch offices in St. Martinville and Kaplan. Its primary function has been to promote thrift and home ownership; but, in addition, it has invested several million dollars in commercial and industrial development in the Acadiana area.

New Iberia's older financial institutions have had a long and honored history as they move toward completion of their first century of service to the community. The latter-day institutions have proved themselves to be a welcome asset to the community and the region.

First Federal Savings
and Loan Association
November 1985

Financial Institutions 331

The statue of Hadrian, the Roman emperor, sculpted in 127 A. D. has been displayed on the grounds of Iberia Savings and Loan Association since 1961. The Association's sign is reflected in a panel of the glass enclosure.

XVIII

The Discovery of Oil in Iberia Parish: Little Bayou, 1917

by
Glenn R. Conrad

Oil, that magical liquid that presently runs America, is an item which has been relentlessly sought after since the beginning of this century. Perhaps this compulsive search for petroleum is a byproduct of the invention of the internal combustion engine. But, no matter when or where the need for oil in large quantities first arose, today there is little doubt in anyone's mind about the importance of oil in the industrialized world of the late twentieth century.

The search for oil began in earnest in the United States about the beginning of this century. There are many people, therefore, who can recall the "good old days" when exploration amounted to little more than someone reporting seeing gas bubbles in a pool of water, or when the technology of production was strongly akin to waterwell boring. The industry developed swiftly, however, as the internal combustion engine became popular and Americans entered into their love affair with the automobile.

In many ways the coming of World War I was largely responsible for prompting Americans to undertake a widespread search for a petroleum supply which would make the nation self-sufficient. Prior to the European war, a large quantity of oil used in the United States was imported from Rumania and from that portion of the old Austro-Hungarian empire known as Galicia.

Oil, of course, had been discovered in Pennsylvania in the nineteenth century, and the output of that state and other areas sufficed for the production of kerosene and other petroleum products used by Americans until the end of the last century. The coming of the automobile and a rapidly industrializing America, however, required more and more quick, clean energy, and thus the search for oil was launched from coast to coast.

Late in 1901, W. Scott Heywood, a resident of Jennings, Louisiana, and a pioneer oil man noticed certain topographical formations just outside the town which prompted him to begin drilling operations. In August his hunch payed off when Jennings Oil Company No. 1 encountered oil sand at 1,882 feet. Then, in June, 1902, the first commercial producer was completed, and the Jennings (or Evangeline) Field became Louisiana's first producing oil field and the second in the entire Gulf Coast area.

After the events at Jennings, which gave the state an entirely new industry and pointed it in new directions, the search for oil proceeded rapidly across the state. In 1901 the Vinton Field was proved. Then, in 1902, the Hackberry Field in Cameron Parish and the Anse la Butte Field in St. Martin Parish began production. From then on it was a steady process of locating and getting the oil. One clear surface indication of a possible petroleum deposit was the presence of gas seeps and/or paraffin beds.

It was a paraffin bed which prompted the first oil activity in Iberia Parish. In October, 1903, John Emmer and his son-in-law, George Labau, reported that a black substance oozing from the ground appeared to be oil. They therefore decided to sink a test well on Emmer's property on East Main Street, but, hampered by a lack of proper equipment, the attempt was abandoned after reaching a depth of about two hundred feet.[1]

More than a decade would pass before any Iberian would seriously concern himself with the possibility of oil beneath the ground. In the spring of 1916, Solange Sorrel was farming rice, as he had done for years, on land just east of Olivier, about five miles from New Iberia. As he flooded the rice lands, he noticed once again the many bubbles making their way to the surface. This time, however, they seemed to be more numerous and appeared to be produced far faster than ever before. Now, with all the talk of oil, Sorrel decided to take action. He contacted two friends, Dr. George Sabatier and Walter Burke, and convinced them that they should get an expert to investigate the possibility of oil beneath the rice field.[2]

1. *New Iberia Enterprise*, October 24, 1903.

2. *Ibid.*, November 18, 1916.

During the summer and early fall of 1916, experts from the Gulf Refining Co. came into the area and confirmed the fact that there was a strong indication that oil lay beneath the surface of Sorrel's farm on Little Bayou.

By early November rumors were rampant that New Iberia was about to become the site of an oil strike which would make Spindletop look like a drop in a bucket. On November 15 rumors of impending oil activity became confirmed fact when Sabatier, Burke, and Sorrel incorporated their activities as the Little Bayou Oil Co. Simultaneously, another drilling corporation was chartered as the New Iberia Oil Co. The supporters of this venture were Dr. Sabatier, P. A. Landry, J. R. Perry, Julius Scharff, Alphonse Davis, Emile Simon, J. A. Pharr, H. N. Pharr, E. A. Pharr, Joseph Smith, Alfred Renoudet, Solange Sorrel, E. A. McIlhenny, C. C. Henshaw, Robert Martin, the Kling brothers, Ventress Smith, Walter Burke, and others.[3]

Once it was official that the two companies would drill for oil in Iberia Parish, wild speculation was heard in every quarter. Before the first section of pipe hit the ground at the drill site, it was predicted that the discovery of oil would triple New Iberia's population in three years.

By mid-December the Gulf Refining Co. moved in with drilling equipment and selected a site on the Schwing-Goodwin tract in the Little Bayou area. At the same time the New Iberia Oil Co. engaged Edmond Boutte to supervise its drilling operation in the same vicinity. A month later Gulf was down to 130 feet, and Boutte's drill had descended to 800 feet.[4]

Of more concern to New Iberians at the beginning of 1917, however, were indications of oil on the property of Alexis Voorhies. This was the old Emmer tract on East Main where fourteen years before John Emmer had sunk a well in search of oil. A part of the property had been subsequently sold to Voorhies, and now townsmen, including the local editor, tramped out to the place to watch "oil ooze out of the ground and run into the Bayou about one hundred feet distant." Convinced that oil in large quantities must be present, Voorhies and his neighbors, Dr. A. G. Emmer and the Lewis Estate, planned to form a company to drill for oil.[5]

As oil fever rose with each passing day, the plans to drill here, there, everywhere were discussed as casually as one spoke of the weather. The Gulf Oil Co. announced on January 29, 1917, that it had struck oil "in paying quan-

---

3. *Ibid.*

4. *Ibid.*, December 16, 23, 1916; January 13, 1917.

5. *Ibid.*, January 13, 1917.

tities" at a depth of 1,600 feet on the Schwing-Goodwin tract, the well to be known as Schwing No. 1.[6]

A week later, on February 6, Edmond Boutte reported that his operation had been completed at 1,170 feet. Although production was quite limited, these two discoveries in early 1917 were sufficient to bring into New Iberia lease men representing nearly every prominent oil corporation.[7]

Another group of businessmen combined to form the Marston Oil Co., Inc. These were Dr. J. W. Sanders, B. W. Marston (of Shreveport), W. G. Weeks, Robert Jacob, and Edward T. Weeks.[8] Not to be outdone by the New Iberia activity, a group of Loreauville businessmen formed the Loreauville Oil Co., Inc.[9]

By late February the local newspaper commented that "because of the oil boom" New Iberia was overrun by strangers.[10] The paper reported that the companies "seriously engaged" in looking for oil in the area were Little Bayou Oil Co., New Iberia Oil Co., Gulf Refining Co., Sun Oil and Pipe Line Co., Producers' Oil Co., Roxana Co., H. T. Staiti Corp., Jance Bros., Gardiner and Noble, Loreauville Oil Co., Enterprise Oil Co., Marston Oil Co., Nuckolls-Knight Co., and the Henshaw-Duperier-Bernard combine.[11]

By early March the editor commented that "oil fever runs so high in New Iberia that conversations other than upon the oil subject are uninteresting." Apparently speculation also continued to run high, for the local editor reported categorically that the Little Bayou Field "is going to prove one of the largest and best in the world."[12]

Throughout March, however, far more hot air was produced in New Iberia than oil. Indeed, the activity reported from the oil "fields" in the local press

---

6. *Ibid.*, February 3, 1917.

7. *Ibid.*, February 10, 1917.

8. *Ibid.*, February 24, 1917.

9. *Ibid.*

10. *Ibid.* The editor went on to comment that "our hotels and restaurants have never done the business that they are now doing . . . the entire community will propser." *Ibid.*

Two weeks later, the editor wrote: "Every room in different hotels and boarding houses in our little city have been taken, and we feel satisfied within the next thirty days rooms will be at a premium." *Ibid.*, March 10, 1917.

11. *New Iberia Enterprise*, March 3, 1917.

12. *Ibid.*

was negligible as compared with the pep talks which the editor provided his readers on the subject of the great quantities of oil underlying New Iberia. Perhaps it was all this excitement which spurred the Enterprise Oil Co. to begin drilling on the Voorhies property in late March.[13]

As exciting as the oil "boom" was for New Iberia, townspeople nevertheless refocused their attention in early April on the American entry into the European war. Overnight the press was transforming the German kaiser into the Hohenzollern ogre, and everybody was rushing about planning to "make the world safe for democracy."

Throughout April and early May, therefore, little was heard about Iberia's oil "boom" which, in reality, had so far been only a "pop." Perhaps a portent of things to come occurred in early May when the flow ceased on the well completed in February by the New Iberia Oil Co. At the same time, however, it was reported that the Gulf well on the Bernard tract was at 2,800 feet and gave every indication of becoming a success.[14] Enthusiasm was dampened, however, when a week later it was learned that the Gulf well had not struck oil, but rather great quantities of salt water.[15]

Despite many long faces among New Iberia's oil circles, the Gulf Co. decided to continue drilling after the flow of water had been controlled. Then, on Thursday morning, May 24, at 1 o'clock, the strike was made and black gold gushed out of the earth to a distance about thirty feet above the derrick. Iberia's first major producer was on land owned by W. J., A. A., and Edwin Bernard.[16]

May 24, 1917, therefore, is a most important date in the history of the oil industry in Iberia Parish. So important did it seem at the time that Fred Patout, proprietor of the Frederic Hotel, tore the page for that day from the hotel register and framed it. The Bernard brothers sent each of the drillers on the well a new suit of clothing.[17]

With the arrival of Bernard No. 1, rumors, speculation, and oil activity spread across the parish. It was rumored that within a year over one hundred wells

---

13. *Ibid.*, March 24, 1917. With all the "oil talk," few people may have had time to read about a revoltuion in Russia.

14. *Ibid.*, May 5, 1917.

15. *Ibid.*, May 12, 1917.

16. *Ibid.*, May 26, 1917.

17. *Ibid.*

would be producing the liquid gold. Moreover, it was speculated that the value of land in this parish "awash in oil" would increase by five hundred to one thousand percent. Finally, activity was spreading: the Sun Oil Co. had a rig on the Eugene Hebert property; Gulf Oil was drilling on the Pharr and Bussey lands; the Heney Oil Co. had a well on the Gralliano tract, the Paraffin Petroleum Co. was working the Sumrall tract; the New Iberia Oil Co. was putting down Boliver No. 2; the Wilkins Oil Co. was working the Bernard and Grimar tract; the Gulf Oil Co. was establishing sites on the Sabatier-Reynaud-Schwing properties. In New Iberia the Enterprise Co. had descended to 1,300 feet in the well on the Voorhies property.[18]

By June 30 nine wells were being drilled, three or four were producing, but certain signs were beginning to appear which did not augur well for the future. The production of Bernard No. 1 had dropped from an initial 800 barrels per day to 300. Moreover, Gulf had decided to put the well on pump, but sufficient oil was being produced for the company to construct a pipeline from the well to Olivier in order to ship the oil by barge.[19]

During July there was very little oil activity to report in the local press. The editor opined that inclement weather was the culprit. No strikes of any consequence were reported, and it was noted that Bernard No. 1 was producing only 140 barrels per day. A breakdown of equipment and a subsequent cave-in had caused a protracted delay in drilling on the Voorhies well.

As the fall of 1917 rolled around with few new strikes in the Little Bayou Field and with production continuing to decline, everyone came to understand that the oil being tapped here was only in small and shallow deposits. Little Bayou was not going to be another Spindletop or Jennings. On the other hand, it was not going to be a complete failure.

Between 1917 and 1930, thirty wells were put down at Little Bayou. Four of these were completed, twenty-six proved to be dry holes. On January 1, 1931, only one well was producing about 1,500 barrels per year, and there were no active drilling operations. All in all, however, between 1917 and 1939, when better equipment and a market demand resulted in new activity at Little Bayou, the field produced about 80,000 barrels of oil.

The new activity at Little Bayou began in the fall of 1939 when J. J. Hooper No. 1 was completed on November 15. Then, on Christmas Eve of that year, the Texas Co. struck oil at 9,500 feet on the Schwing tract. Slightly over a year later, William Helis No. 3 on the Bernard property was completed at 4,650 feet.

---

18. *Ibid.*

19. *Ibid.*, June 30, 1917.

The Renoudet Cottage

XIX

1920

by
Glenn R. Conrad

On November 11, 1918, the Great War in Europe ended with victory for the Allied Powers. The terrible struggle had finally come to an end. But November 11, 1918, marked something more for the United States than the end of a war-- it marked the beginning of a new era, an era of promise and progress. All America was seemingly caught up in a mood of optimism that was reflected in large cities and small towns throughout the country. The new mood dictated that the old ways of prewar days were outmoded. It emphasized that America on the eve of the 1920s was only then entering the new century. Americans were in a mood for the novel; they were anxious for the material benefits of the new technology which had generated the war and which had been accelerated by it; and they were willing to experiment with new ideas concerning commerce, tourism, and industry. Anyone not exhibiting the current mood was regarded as a "stick in the mud" or a relic of the previous era. The American mood was forever captured by Sinclair Lewis in his two best-known novels, *Main Street* and *Babbitt*.

Within a year after the Armistice, the popular mood sweeping the country found expression in the pages of New Iberia's newspapers. M. W. Fisher, editor of the *New Iberia Enterprise*, reported the transformation taking place in the town: streets were being paved; old business places were being renovated; new businesses were appearing; a sense of civic pride was discernable in the business community. The editor noted, for example, that the Elks had recently sold their building, the Elks Theater, to the Patout family, and that the fraternal order was in the process of remodeling the old Alma House hotel as its new home. Another organization, the Knights of Pythias, had recently lost their "castle" to fire. That organization, in the summer of 1919, was "shaping plans for the erection of a handsome new castle" on the site of the old meeting place. Meanwhile, the Woodmen of the World had recently acquired the old Segura Building on the corner of Main and Julia streets and were in the process of renovating it. In keeping with the times, Editor Fisher noted that the W.O.W. was transforming the building "into a nice, modern structure."

On the east end of the business district, LeBlanc and Broussard, the Ford dealers, were adding a second floor to their building and were completely renovating the ground floor. Fisher's article concluded with the observation that later that year taxpayers were be deciding whether to build a new high school in New Iberia.[1]

It would be an event of late April, 1919, however, that would herald the new wave of progressive thinking. At an informal meeting of several townsmen, it was proposed by Edward Estorge that a chamber of commerce be reorganized.[2] Mayor Sealy agreed that the town was very much in need of such an organization, but he was concerned that the "same old faces" would respond, mainly the lawyers and other professionals. Without those individuals, said the mayor, "there would never be a successful meeting where public matters were to be discussed," but the time had also come for the businessmen of New Iberia to make their appearance. Judge J. S. Power echoed the mayor's concern.

Mr. Joseph Davis of Santa Maria, California, a guest at the meeting, was asked to present his views of New Iberia. Davis responded that while he was proud of New Iberia, the town apparently had not yet "awakened to its possibilities." He pointed to the residential area of East Main Street and noted that there was no "prettier avenue in the United States"; yet, he found the street and yards

---

1. *New Iberia Enterprise,* August 23, 1919.

2. The meeting had been called to deal with several upcoming civic affairs. Attending the meeting were Edward Estorge, Mayor Sealy, Hiram Carver, Judge J. S. Power, Dr. W. S. Gosling, C. M. Compton, Ventress Smith, A. A. DeBlanc, Fred Patout, Jules Dreyfus, Charles Guguenheim, Dr. Walter Carstens, Fred Schwing, Silvio Broussard, Nathan Davis, Robert Jacob, Cyrus de Blanc, Louis Pfister, S. B. DeBellevue, George Dallas, John Buquor, Harvey Hill, John Taylor, E. H. Buffinton, E. Taul, and Joseph Davis, former New Iberian living in California. *Ibid.,* April 26, 1919.

Residential area of East Main Street looking east from between Bank and Prairie avenues (above), and looking west from Prairie Avenue (below).

dirty in many places. While tourists, that new breed of American made possible by the automobile, would probably remember the beautiful oaks along the street, they would undoubtedly also recall the debris beneath them. What New Iberia needed, said Daivis, was "a live chamber of commerce with a hired secretary who had nothing else to do but get out literature and look for big things for the city." The visitor told the gentlemen assembled that almost every California town had a "paid man to do nothing else but boost, and it would pay [New Iberia] to wake up and advertise [its] resources." After Davis' stirring comments, the now enthusiastic group resolved to call a mass meeting of the town's businessmen to form a "live" chamber of commerce.[3]

If enthusiasm reigned supreme among this vanguard, its members were soon to be greeted with disappointment when the "appeal to the advanced thinkers and businessmen of New Iberia" to attend a mass meeting to organize a "real live chamber of commerce" produced only twenty-two individuals.[4] Undaunted, the group decided that if the businessmen would not come to the organizational meeting, a committee would be named to go to the merchants to determine their interest in a chamber of commerce. Moreover, another mass meeting would be called.[5]

The second "mass meeting" produced encouraging results. About seventy-five people turned out to express a willingness to participate in an organization of businessmen and professionals. So enthusiastic was the group that they moved directly to the appointment of a temporary board of directors to serve until the membership drive was completed and a new board elected by the members. The group also sought to raise $5,000 for the forthcoming year's operations.[6]

During the month of May and throughout early June the two weekly newspapers, the *Iberian* and the *Enterprise* lectured readers on the merits of a

---

3. *Ibid.*

4. Attending the "mass meeting" were Ed and Albert Estorge, E. H. Buffinton, Homer Daigre, Charles Outhwaite, Francis Voorhies, C. F. Barnes, A. C. Bernard, Alfred Lewald, Ventress Smith, Leon Bagarry, Frank Dauterive, J. S. Power, A. A. Theriot, Dave Winters, John Taylor, Charles Carstens, J. Suberbielle, A. B. Murray, William Bauman, Leonard Barrow, and Victor Barthe. *New Iberia Enterprise*, May 3, 1919.

5. *Ibid.*

6. *Ibid.*, May 10, 1919. The temporary board was composed of the following individuals: H. W. Carver, Ed Estorge, H. S. Sealy, Fritz Dietlein, Ventress Smith, Alfred Lewald, John Taylor, Luke Bertrand, Robert Jacob, A. C. Barnes, Dr. E. S. Fulton, and Melvin Fisher. *Ibid.*

businessman's organization. Editor Fisher summed up the campaign when he wrote, "New Iberia must have a live Chamber of Commerce if we ever hope to see a changed condition here."[7] Then, on June 17, 1919, organization of the New Iberia Chamber of Commerce was completed. Sufficient funds had been raised to hire a full-time secretary and to fund certain civic projects. The first board of directors was elected.[8] A week later, the board chose its officers: Alfred Lewald, president; E. H. Buffington, vice-president; John Taylor, treasurer; and Melvin Fisher, temporary secretary.[9]

During the remainder of 1919, plans for civic improvements seemed to be popping up in every quarter. There was considerable talk about the paving of Main Street, about the development of the two tourist highways--the Pershing Way and the Old Spanish Trail, which could pass through New Iberia if the builders had the proper incentives, and about the dredging of a canal to connect Bayou Teche and Lake Fausse Pointe. Building and remodeling continued apace as it had in the earlier part of the year. In November, Consolidated Companies of Plaquemine announced the purchase of the Joel Fisher property, in the rear of the Eureka Hotel, for the purpose of building a large wholesale grocery.[10]

As the year was coming to an end, the directors of the Chamber of Commerce announced that Frank Noel of Houston had been employed as secretary of the local organization. It would be his responsibility to keep the Chamber actively engaged in civic improvement. The editor of the *Iberian* opened the new year, 1920, with a stirring editorial which in many ways encapsulates the attitude which prevailed in New Iberia that year and for many years to come. In his article entitled "Hustle or Step Down," the editor wrote that

> communities are like stores; it takes advertising to attract interest and attention. . . . If every community does all it can to help its own men who have new enterprises to start, it lays the foundation for

---

7. *New Iberia Enterprise*, May 10, 1919.

8. The board of directors elected to serve for the year 1919-20 was composed of H. W. Carver, Ed Estorge, Alfred Lewald, George Cousin, Luke Bertrand, John Taylor, Fritz Dietlein, E. H. Buffington, Francis Voorhies, Frank Dauterive, Henry L. Smith, and Melvin Fisher. *New Iberia Enterprise*, June 21, 1919.

9. *Ibid.*, June 28, 1919.

10. *Ibid.*, November 22, 1919. This was the first step in the establishment of Teche Wholesale Grocery.

concerns that will become prosperous and bring people to town....
The old grasping spirit of selfishness has passed into discard. The
time when a man's worth and standing in his community was measured by his bank account passed away when the present idea of
SERVICE was born. Today, he who would be greatest in a community must be the most public spirited, must do the most to promote his hometown, must work the hardest to better the conditions of his fellow citizens. . . . Today, the true measure of a citizen
is his ability and willingness to serve. . . . With a buoyant spirit of
optimism and a strong faith in our future, let us all get together to
work for a NEW NEW IBERIA.[11]

Actually, the *Iberian's* editor was echoing some of the statements made at a "get-together luncheon" of the Chamber of Commerce a few days before. At that time, Ventress Smith reported that there was a new spirit abroad in New Iberia and urged everyone present to "speak a good word for our town whenever occasion presents." Walter Burke detected a "new feeling of optimism and progressiveness" that had taken root in New Iberia. Abe Hirsch, Frank Labit, and Paul Bryant stated that, although natives of other towns, they believed that New Iberia had a "splendid future."[12]

As would become customary during 1920, almost every meeting of the Chamber of Commerce heard a report about new industry moving to town or new improvements being planned or activitated. On this occasion the Frick Brothers and Fritz Dietlein announced that they would be setting up shortly two canneries.[13]

One of the major efforts of the early Chamber was to make certain that one or more of the soon-to-be-tourist-laden transcontinental highways wound its way through New Iberia. Progressive businessmen everywhere knew that the automobile was here to stay. Moreover, they were convinced that the motor car would open travel opportunities to hundreds of thousands of Americans who never before had thought of themselves as tourists. Other communities and other states, notably California and Florida, had recognized the economic bonanza of tourism and were fostering its development through the construction of improved roads and tourist facilities.

11. *Weekly Iberian,* January 31, 1920.

12. *Ibid.*

13. *Ibid.*

Thus, in one of his first activities for the New Iberia Chamber, Frank Noel, the new secretary, invited the route manager of the Pershing Highway to tell the organization something about this "great tourist route." The Pershing Highway was planned to be a north-south transcontinental route, running from Winnipeg, Canada, to New Orleans. Towns along the way were being invited to join the Pershing Way Association, which would be responsible for publishing a monthly magazine extolling the sights and facilities to be found in member towns. For an annual fee, a town could thus expect to receive widespread publicity. Any "forward-looking" town would certainly subscribe the fee to be included in the literature of the Association.[14]

After a round of hearty applause, President Lewald named a "Highway Committee" to canvass the businessmen of New Iberia to get the required fifty-six subscriptions for New Iberia's membership in the Association. Two days later the necessary number of subscribers had been signed up.[15]

At the same time the east-west transcontinental highway from Los Angeles to New Orleans, called the Old Spanish Trail, was nearing completion. H. L. Miller, president of the Old Spanish Trail Association, published the following item in the New Iberia newspapers in anticipation of a subscription campaign.

> In anticipation of the opening of the Los Angeles-New Orleans section, we are putting out magazine and news stories to acquaint the people north and south with the conditions along the highway. The magazines are beginning to ask for stories and the big dailies along the Trail are helping with Sunday illustrated pages. Tourists are extensively reached this way. Travel over the highway will be ready to start when construction is completed.[16]

In March, the Louisiana towns belonging to the Pershing Way Association met in Alexandria to discuss the organization's activities, including the "First Sociability Run." The Run involved parties of motoring tourists from towns in the state joining together in a caravan and converging on one of the member towns. Frank Noel of the local Chamber put in a bid for the motorists to gather in New

---

14. *Ibid.*, January 20, 1920.

15. *Ibid.*, January 24, 1920.

16. *Ibid.*, January 10, 1920.

The Pershing Way-Old Spanish Trail entrance to New Iberia on East Main St. about 1921

Iberia. A majority of members attending agreed, and the event was scheduled for July.[17]

Plans were being made at home for the expected tourists. Noel told the Chamber that the town should provide a "Parking Station" for tourists to camp for as long as they were visiting.[18] In June local motorists discovered that some telephone poles in the area had been painted with a large blue "P" on a white background. They were informed that these were the route markers of the Pershing Way.[19]

Editor Fisher did not fail to comment, nor to speculate. While noting that there had been few results so far from the highway promotional scheme, other than considerable free advertising, the editor felt certain that "it will be only a question of less than one year when [New Iberia] will receive the benefits which was the original intention of the promoter. . . ." Fisher predicted that when the Pershing Way "opens its gates for the influx of tourists the natives in

17. *New Iberia Enterprise*, March 27, 1920. There is no evidence in the newspapers that this "Sociability Run" ever developed.

18. *Ibid.*, April 3, 1920.

19. *Ibid.*, May 22, June 20, 1920.

South Louisiana are going to marvel at the number of sightseeing motorists passing through and stopping en route."[20]

Melvin Fisher was apparently accurate in his appraisal of the amount of publicity New Iberia and Iberia Parish were receiving in magazines with national circulation. What he did not realize, perhaps, was that these articles were beginning to change the focus of the tourist industry from what had been "The Teche Country" to "The Land of Evangeline." This, in turn, may not have been accidental. In 1919 Hollywood produced a version of the Longfellow story that was still vivid in the minds of many feature writers. In interview after interview, feature writers for magazines would preface their remarks with some phrase like, "Of course, having read Longfellow's *Evangeline*...," or "There is probably no story... more widely read... than Longfellow's poem of *Evangeline*."[21]

The result was that feature articles on the area now carried titles such as "In Evangeline Land," "Along the Bayous of the Evangeline Country," and "Deep in Evangeline Country." Once local merchants associated Longfellow's poem with tourism, the name of the poet's heroine began appearing everywhere: "Evangeline Cafe," "Evangeline Theater," "Evangeline Hotel," etc. The Evangeline "phenomena" would climax with the second Hollywood production of that name, starring Dolores Del Rio, and filmed partially in New Iberia in 1929.[22]

Although the development of the tourist trade was important to the Chamber of Commerce, the members were also interested in other civic projects. An interesting one had its origins early in 1920. In February, Chamber of Commerce Manager Noel announced that the organization would sponsor a fifteen-member brass band. Musicians from New Iberia and environs were invited to participate. Spearheading the drive to assemble the band were the members of an ad hoc Chamber committee, J. G. Martin, chairman, L. D. Ribbeck, vice chairman, E. Dieudonne, secretary, and F. L. Broussard, treasurer.[23]

---

20. *Ibid.*, May 22, 1920.

21. Examples of this type of statement can be found in statements by feature writers appearing in the February 7, 1920, and May 22, 1920, numbers of the *New Iberia Enterprise*.

22. In the 1950s the tourist industry began to replace the term "Evangeline" with "Acadiana," a term coined about that time. The 1957 telephone directory for New Iberia listed only two businesses using the name "Acadian," and nine businesses using the term "Evangeline." The 1982 directory listed three firms using the term "Acadia," ten using the term "Acadian" and twenty-three using the term "Acadiana." The number of firms using the term "Evangeline" had declined to six by 1982. Clearly, "Evangeline Country" has become "Acadiana."

23. *Weekly Iberian*, February 14, 21, 1920.

A few days later the prospective musicians gathered for their organizational meeting and chose Yves Arnandez as director. The group planned its first concert to coincide with the opening of baseball season.[24]

The new baseball park, although not a project of the Chamber of Commerce was, nevertheless, an object of civic pride. New Iberia was a baseball town and, at the time, was a club in the Louisiana State League. It was in March that the president of the local club, Julius Scharff, announced the construction of a new ball park, named Myrtis Park, to replace the inadequate Pleasure Park. The new park had a grandstand to seat 700 fans and bleachers offered another 300 seats.[25]

A major project running through 1920 and commanding the attention of most of the town's residents was street improvements. On January 3, the *Enterprise* reported that the successful bidders for New Iberia's paving projects were getting underway with their work. Several New Iberia streets would be curbed and coated with an asphalt composition. This work had already begun when the contractor, Southern Bithuletic Company, began paving West Main between Railroad Avenue and North Street. Main Street from Weeks Street to Railroad Avenue and Railroad Avenue from Main to the Southern Pacific depot were to be bricked. The successful bidders for this project were the Ritchie Bros. By the beginning of the year, brick work had begun on Railroad Avenue.[26]

A month later the paving work had almost come to a halt as a result of bad weather and a shortage of materials, especially the vitrified brick for Main Street. Editor Fisher used the occasion to editorialize that once the Main Street project was completed, the city should undertake to pave St. Peter and Iberia streets. The real problem area of Main Street, however, was the block between Center and Weeks where the graveled roadway was covered with thick mud. The editor reminded city fathers that beneath all that mud was a wooden roadbed. The

---

24. Although the band did make its first public appearance in April at the opening of the baseball season, its "first official public appearance occurred on May 16 when the musicians performed in front of the Elks Home. *Weekly Iberian*, May 15, 1920. The Elks Home at the time was the old Alma House, located on West Main Street on the present-day site of the parking lot for the Bank of Iberia.

25. *Ibid.*, March 13, 1920. Myrtis Park was located on East Main Street in the approximate area of the present-day Town and Country Shopping Center. The opening game of the season was played on April 20 when the New Iberia Sugar Boys met the Abbeville Frogs. After 13 innings the game was called with the score tied at 2 to 2. *New Iberia Enterprise*, April 24, 1920.

26. *Ibid.*, January 3, 1920.

street could therefore be greatly improved if only the mud was scrapped off and the roadbed exposed.[27]

By the beginning of April there was good news and bad news on the paving front. All brick work on Main Street had stopped because of a shortage of materials. The contractors informed the public that the delay might be anywhere from six weeks to three months. On the other hand, the city announced the good news that East Main would be asphalted from Weeks Street to Bank Avenue.[28]

Perhaps the delay in bricking Main Street was providential because, shortly after the delay was announced, Henry Smith, of the Globe Store, proposed to the Chamber of Commerce that the street's merchants purchase lamp standards with subsurface wiring for the purpose of lighting the street.[29]

The idea caught fire immediately and within a week sixty-three merchants and individuals pledged $10 each for the lighting project, now dubbed by the newspapers as the "White Way" project.[30]

Still other projects developed as New Iberians waited for the early spring weather to improve and for materials to become available. Property owners on West Main from Railroad Avenue to North Street discovered that with paving there would be a sizable neutral ground between the street and the sidewalk. Why not plant the area with suitable trees and shrubs? The idea was then suggested to the Women's Council, the female auxillary of the Chamber of Commerce. Since Main Street had become part of the Old Spanish Trail and the Pershing Way, the suggestion was readily adopted by the Council as a means of beautifying the streetscape and making it attractive for tourists.[31]

---

27. *Ibid.*, February 7, 1920.

28. *Ibid.*, April 3, 17, 1920.

29. *Ibid.*, May 1, 1920.

30. *Ibid.*, May 8, 1920. The term "White Way" was appropriated from the "Great White Way," the name applied to Broadway, in New York City, after it was lighted in 1887.

31. *New Iberia Enterprise*, May 8, 15, 1920.

The Women's Council was organized in late 1919, but its constitution and by-laws were not adopted until February, 1920. Mrs. Shaw served as the first president until June of that year when she was followed by Mrs. Walter Burke. *Ibid.*, June 26, 1920.

A major project of the ladies during 1920 was to have a ladies' rest room installed somewhere in the downtown area. By the end of the year, LeBlanc and Broussard, at the request of the Women's Council, agreed to install such a facility. *Ibid.*, May 15, 1920.

West Main Street in the 1930s (above) and in 1978

In mid-May, Mrs. J. W. K. Shaw, president of the Council, appointed a committee to meet with the West End property owners to discuss implementation of their plans. The resulting decision was to plant palms and oleanders along the neutral ground.

As 1920 drew to a close, the new lamp standards had been installed in the business district, the street paving was well underway, and the street beautification project for West Main had been completed.[32]

By summer, 1920, the New Iberia Chamber of Commerce was nearly a year old. During that year the organization had achieved great success in many of its endeavors. With that in mind the directors and members launched a membership drive during the month of June. The campaign was kicked off with a public statement from Hiram Carver on the advantages a town derives from a strong businessmen's association.[33] Mr. Carver's opening salvo was followed by a month of editorial comment in the two papers urging the community to support the Chamber.

The response was not gratifying, however. A major reason for this may have been largely owing to the fact that dues had been raised from $10 to $25 per year. When it became apparent that the dues were too high for a popular response, the directors decided in mid-June to reduce the fee to $10. Moreover, while the directors had first discussed a $10,000 operating budget for 1920-21, they now reduced that amount by half.[34]

By the time that the Chamber's new board of directors was elected, the organization had not met with its anticipated success. The membership drive was therefore continued into July. For the Chamber's leadership, the directors chose Hiram Carver, president, Leon Minvielle, vice-president, and John Taylor, treasurer.[35]

---

32. The street-paving projects would continue on into 1921. A decision was made to brick Bridge Street from Main to the bridge. All other streets paved at the time were covered with asphalt. The streets included were St. Peter, Iberia, Julia, Weeks, French, and Duperier Avenue.

33. *New Iberia Enterprise,* May 29, 1920.

34. *Ibid.,* June 12, 1920.

35. *Ibid.,* July 17, 1920.
The board of directors was composed of Luke Bertrand, Francis Voorhies, John R. Taylor, Alphonse Davis, Clet Gerard, Ralph Frame, A. C. Barnes, Ed Estorge, George Cousin, Alfred Lewald, Robert A. Jacob, W. J. Bernard, and Melvin Fisher. *Ibid.*

The unusual brick smokestack of the Chas. Boldt paper mill in New Iberia shortly after completion in the spring of 1921

The Chas. Boldt Paper Mill at the time it began operations in 1921

If locating new industry in New Iberia was a major goal of the local Chamber of Commerce, that organization encountered outstanding success when Charles Boldt of Ohio announced that he would construct in New Iberia a half-million dollar mill to make paperboard from rice straw. The person intimately involved in the negotiations with Boldt to locate the mill in New Iberia was A.C. Bernard. By late August, 1920, an eighteen-acre tract of land on East Main Street had been purchased for the mill site.[36] Construction of the mill began in October and would take a full year to complete. On October 29, 1921, Mayor Ed LaSalle and Chamber President Albert Estorge were invited by Max Zimmerman, the plant's general manager, to sound the factory's steam whistle announcing the beginning of operations. The mill employed approximately one hundred people for its two work shifts.[37]

As if all the business bustle of 1920 was not enough to excite the people of New Iberia, there were other events taking place which served to mark the be-

36. *Weekly Iberian*, August 21, 1920.

37. *New Iberia Enterprise*, October 29, 1921.
    The papermill, manufacturing cardboard, first from rice straw and then from paper and rag, ceased operation in 1934. Today, a few of the buildings of the large plant are extant. Most obvious, however, is the tall, red brick smokestack with the words in yellow brick "Chas. Boldt Paper Mills" vertically arranged on the Main Street side of the stack, which now has become a New Iberia landmark.

ginning of a new era for the town. One such event had its origins on September 15 when the state of Tennessee ratified the Nineteenth Amendment, thus giving the proposal the necessary three-fourths approval of the states of the Union. With passage of the amendment, women throughout the United States were given equal voting rights with men.

The following morning, J. A. Gonsoulin, clerk of court and ex officio registrar of voters for Iberia Parish, opened the voter registration books to the ladies. The right to register to vote would be available for only several days because Louisiana law provided that registration books be closed sixty days before the national election of November 2.[38]

On September 16, Mrs. Charles Outhwaite, the former Corinne Burgess, the recognized leader of female suffrage in Iberia Parish, presented herself at Gonsoulin's office for the privilege of becoming the parish's first female to register to vote.[39] Within the specified time for registration, more than three hundred ladies had added their names to the voter roles.[40]

Another event important to New Iberia and coming about the same time as approval of female enfranchisement was the election of a New Iberian as United States senator. On September 14, Edwin S. Broussard became the second member of his family to be elected to the United States Senate.[41] A few days later, Broussard returned to his hometown and to a hero's welcome. Debarking from the train in Jeanerette, the new senator joined a motorcade for the trip to New Iberia and welcoming ceremonies at the courthouse. Thousands of people turned out for the event so that Main Street between Iberia and French streets was jammed by the throng.

After introductions and words of welcome, Senator Broussard rose to speak but was delayed for some time by the tumultuous ovation. While the crowd cheered, a delegation of young ladies brought baskets of flowers to the smiling Broussard.[42] Finally, the senator-elect was able to address the crowd. He

---

38. *Weekly Iberian*, September 18, 1920.

39. *Ibid.*

40. *New Iberia Enterprise*, October 2, 1920.

41. Broussard's brother, Robert, had been previously elected to the national House of Representatives and to the Senate.

42. The flowerbearers were Edele Patout, Patricia Burke, Lily Gladys Broussard, Quenta Patout, Rita Arnandez, Ethel May Frame, Celia Dauterive, Marjorie Lyle, Louise Babineaux, Olga Delahoussaye, Hazel Bertrand, Evelyn Colgin, Claudia Laperouse, and Sadie Berard. *Weekly Iberian*, September 25, 1920.

thanked them for their support and promised to do his best to represent them and all Louisianians in Washington.[43]

For the remainder of 1920 the two weekly newspapers continued to report that new industries were looking at New Iberia as a potential site for expansion. J. C. Penny and Co. had inquired through the Chamber of Commerce about available buildings. Quaker Maid Co. of Louisville, Kentucky, also inquired about building sites.

More and more statewide meetings were scheduled for New Iberia. In December, 125 members of the American Institute of Chemical Engineers were visitors to the Queen City. As the year ended, there was increasing talk about further oil exploration in the area, the Teche Transfer Service had begun operating bus service between New Iberia and Franklin, Kahn's Pharmacy opened, and Dr. Henry Dauterive founded Dauterive's Hospital. A group of concerned citizens were talking about acquiring Henshaw's Woods for a city park a project that became a reality in 1921.

All in all, 1920 had been an exciting year in the history of New Iberia. Certainly, there had been a fair share of the routine, but the year became a milestone in the history of the town.

43. *Ibid.*

The Teche Transfer busses at Charenton in 1923.

XX

The Teche Country in the Flood of 1927

by
Glenn R. Conrad

As winter turned to spring in 1927, almost everyone, especially farmers, was well aware of the unusually wet season just passed. Indeed, sugarcane farmers were particularly hard hit by the unfavorable weather conditions and, in the fall of 1926 had succeeded in harvesting only 46,000 tons of cane statewide.

In the train of this unusually wet season, the Mississippi River, by mid-April, 1927, had risen to such a point that a guard system was established by the police juries of the river parishes to maintain a watch on the levees.[1] From New Orleans to New Roads, hundreds of men worked day and night during April to strengthen the dikes in the Lower Mississippi Valley.

Unknown to most people, however, was the fact that the strengthening of these lower Mississippi levees was putting additional pressure on the weaker levees upstream in the Tensas and Atchafalaya basins. Furthermore, although some farsighted individuals understood the problem and argued for a spillway system to relieve pressure on the Mississippi levees, their views were not shared by most politicians and probabaly not by the public at large. John M. Caffery, president of the Atchafalaya Basin Protective Association, had frequently re-

---

1. *New Iberia Enterprise,* April 23, 1927.

ferred to these stubborn opponents of the proposed spillway as "bull headed," "stupid," and "almost criminal."[2] Therefore, as crews built the levees ever higher to contain the Mississippi River in its course between Pointe Coupee and Orleans parishes, a crisis situation was developing further upstream.

In the third week of April, officials of Iberville Parish, just across the Atchafalaya Basin from Iberia Parish, warned persons in low-lying areas to move to higher ground.[3] This had the effect of alarming some Iberians and prompted a committee composed of Police Jury President Clet Girard, Mayor Ed LaSalle, P. A. Landry, Fred Patout, Emile Vuillemot, and Marcus de Blanc to make an inspection tour of the river parishes. Upon the committee's return, M. W. Fisher, editor of the *New Iberia Enterprise,* wrote that "the next thirty days are going to try men's souls in the desperate struggle to hold the levees intact and confine the flood waters to their natural course." He cautioned his townsmen not to become hysterical, but to meet "the situation with clear heads and stout hearts."[4]

In the days that followed, the inevitable rumors spread through New Iberia to the effect that the levees would not hold much longer. It was whispered that the pressure of the flood waters was becoming too great, and any moment the west Mississippi levee might collapse.[5] Should that happen between Torras and Morganza, the additional waters in the Atchafalaya Basin would certainly break the west Atchafalaya levee and flood the Teche country. But old-timers, remembering the "great" flood of 1882, assured everyone that even if the west Atchafalaya levee broke, only the east side of Bayou Teche would flood. It was inconceivable, they maintained, that flood waters would cross the west ridge of Bayou Teche.[6] Most residents of the lower Teche, however, were unaware of the fact that because of the growing pressure from Mississippi backwater several

---

2. *Ibid.,* May 7, 1927. Caffery's statement came after an inspection tour of the levee system between New Orleans and the mouth of the Red River.

3. *Ibid.,* April 23, 1927.

4. *Ibid.*

5. *Ibid.,* May 7, 1927.

6. *Ibid.,* April 30, 1927. The editor of the *Enterprise,* speaking of flood possibility for New Iberia, wrote: "Only that part of the land on the east side of Bayou Teche would overflow. . . . The ridge or banks of the Teche form a natural levee that would withstand a flood, higher by six feet than the greatest flood this country has ever known. . . . That portion lying west of Bayou Teche is perfectly secure from any flood. . . ." *Ibid.*

Bridge Street in the flood of 1927

breaks had already occurred in the levee system along Bayou des Glaises in Avoyelles Parish. Water from that source was spreading southward between the Opelousas-Lafayette ridge (the Lafayette Escarpment) and the west Atchafalaya levee into the Teche Valley.

By May 1, St. Martin residents were becoming alarmed by the continually rising waters in the Atchafalaya Basin, accompanied by rising gauges along the upper Teche. A few days later the water level in the Atchafalaya Basin had risen to the point where it was spilling over the St. Martin Parish levee. A call for help went out and 1,400 volunteers worked for the next few days to strengthen the levee from Port Barre to Butte-la-Rose. For ten days they struggled to raise the levee and may have succeeded in containing the waters had not circumstances elsewhere made their fight hopeless. In mid-May the Atchafalaya levee at Melville broke sending flood waters on a rampage westward and southward in the direction of the overflow from Bayou des Glaises. Thus, it became only a matter of time before the torrent smashed into the hastily constructed levees in St. Martin Parish. Everyone prepared for disaster.

On Monday, May 16, that disaster struck when the levee at Cecelia suddenly crumbled and was followed by another crevasse nearby. Shortly afterward, a 300-foot section of levee gave way at Henderson. A deluge was descending upon the Teche country. Refugees by the hundreds fled the lowlands of St. Martin Parish making their way to safety. Some people carried their children, some brought out the aged and infirm, some sought to save their livestock and furniture, all sought to save their lives.[7] The Southern Pacific railroad drove freight trains to the very rim of the ever-spreading lake and then hurried back to Lafayette laden with people, animals, and personal effects. Trucks and men from neighboring towns, parishes, and even from Houston and Beaumont, moved into the threatened countryside to take residents to safety. Refugee camps opened in Lafayette, Crowley, and Opelousas. The displaced quickly multiplied: 7,000, 12,000, 15,000, over 20,000.

As the flood raced across the flat lands of St. Martin toward the Teche there was a great deal of debate whether the water would be held back by the west ridge of the bayou. Nowhere was the debate more heated than in Breaux Bridge, itself located on the west ridge. Many residents of the town prepared for the onslaught and evacuated. Some businessmen constructed platforms in their stores to elevate their merchandise. Other citizens of the town, however, went about

---

[7]. On May 19, Editor Fisher, Albert Estorge, Charles and Walter Carstens got as far as Nina station in St. Martin Parish in an effort to get a first-hand account of the effects of the disaster. Fisher later reported: "At Breaux Bridge hundreds of trucks were coming out of the flooded area, loaded with furniture, hogs, chickens, and men, women, and children. They were en route to refugee camps in Lafayette." *New Iberia Enterprise*, May 21, 1927.

St. Peter's Church in the flood of 1927

their normal activity assured that the water would never cross the west ridge of the bayou. History was on their side, for never in memory had the town been flooded.[8] Despite the facts of history, however, the New Orleans weather bureau forecast that before long two to four feet of water would inundate the town. All debate ended in the scamper for safety as the flood waters breached the west bayou ridge and poured into Breaux Bridge. The editor of the *Enterprise* commented that there was "probably no human being living this day who can recollect flood waters crossing the West bank of the Teche."[9] This development was an ominous sign for towns farther down the bayou, all of which were located on the west ridge, for now it was known that this flood was capable of invading towns from Breaux Bridge to Patterson.

8. *Ibid.*

9. *Ibid.*, May 28, 1927.

On May 20, 1927, Secretary of Commerce Herbert Hoover, who was directing federal assistance to the stricken area, warned the owners of St. John Plantation, just north of St. Martinville, to begin evacuating their tenants and he cautioned the people of St. Martinville to plan for evacuation.[10] An observer in the Hoover party described the approaching flood; "This mighty wall of water reached the Teche from Port Barre to Arnaudville and went across the ridges of the Teche striking the hills [the escarpment] east of Opelousas, Grand Coteau, Carencro, and Lafayette with such force as to throw it back across the Teche at Cecelia and Parks, filling all the low bottoms between St. Martinville on the east and Broussard on the west, rushing [toward] Spanish Lake."[11]

On May 24 the flood entered St. Martinville, inundated the town and ran swiftly toward Spanish Lake. Some New Iberians hoped that the lake basin would be able to contain the rampaging waters, others prepared themselves for a crisis. All night May 24 the waters poured into the lake and on the twenty-fifth the people of New Iberia waked to learn that the lake basin was filled and about to spill over. Later that morning, the water advanced on the town from two directions: along the Southern Pacific railroad from Segura and along the Missouri Pacific railroad on the north side of town. Indeed, the two railroad beds diverted the waters from their natural courses and served to funnel the flood into the heart of New Iberia. About eight o'clock Thursday morning the torrent struck Jane Street, and within a few minutes Louis Lallande's store was standing in nearly six feet of water.[12] From that point and from the direction of Washington Street, the flood waters entered the town.

Fortunately for the townspeople, before the flooding began some action was taken by a group of farmers in Segura which considerably reduced the water level in New Iberia. Employing their farm laborers, Ulysse and Leon Landry, Theo David, Joseph Segura, Evard Broussard, and Arvillien and Paul Segura dammed culverts leading into the lake (thus preventing the rising waters from backing up through these culverts) and raised small levees across low-lying areas to prevent spillage at those points.[13]

Still, however, the amount of water in and around New Iberia was considerable, rising and falling with astonishing rapidity. In fourteen hours between Thursday afternoon, May 26, and 6 a. m. the next morning, the bayou rose

---

10. *Ibid.*, May 21, 1927.

11. *Ibid.*, May 28, 1927.

12. *Ibid.*

13. *Ibid.*, June 4, 1927.

seven and one-half feet, and during the course of the flood, it rose a total of twenty and one-half feet. This had the effect of putting varying depths of water throughout the town. In the area of Dauterive Hospital (then located at the corner of Marie Street and Duperier Avenue), water stood at about six feet deep.[14] On the west ridge of the bayou, the water's depth was considerably less. In front of St. Peter's Church, for example, water depth was about eighteen inches. Generally speaking, the flood did not move into the area south of the Southern Pacific railroad. Then, once the water level became established in the business district, Councilman Philip Conrad used his farm equipment to erect dams across streets linking Main Street and the bayou. At the same time the city's fire engine pumped water from the town side of these dams to the bayou side so that by Tuesday, May 31, the waters had sufficiently subsided to allow Perry Burke to organize a city clean-up gang and move it into action.[15] By the weekend of June 4, the town was returning to a normal routine--normal, that is, for a town which had just experienced a flood.[16] But normal enough so that a week later, on June 12, St. Peter's College could hold its commencement exercises at the Elks Theater.[17] Claude Babineaux, Lionel Decuir, Alwyn Domingue, Armand Pesson, George Segura, Lloyd Viator, Lawrence Landry, and Henry Louviere graduated from high school on that day in the never-to-be-forgotten flood year of 1927.

14. Since the town's only bridge was inundated and damaged, a ferry service was established between Fisher and Rozier streets, for the convenience of those New Iberians living on the east side of the bayou. The ferry service continued for some time after the waters receded because of the damaged bridge. See *ibid.*, June 18, 1927.

15. *Ibid.*, June 4, 1927.

16. For more on the flood of 1927, see the essay entitled "Reminiscences of the Teens and Twenties."

17. *New Iberia Enterprise*, June 11, 1927.

XXI

Reminiscences of the Teens and Twenties

by
Alice Ann Gates

Among the first things I remember clearly were my school days. In my day young people had to provide for their own recreation and entertainment. There was no public entertainment for children except, later on, one movie on Saturday afternoon. We paid 5¢ to go to the movie. I cannot remember the name of the movie house, but I do remember that we children had an allowance of 10¢ per week, 5¢ for the movie and 5¢ for an ice cream cone after the movie. For the ice cream we went to Lee's Drug Store, located on the corner of Serret Alley and Main Street. Lee's was first on the corner of Iberia and Main streets, but after the fire of 1899 it moved to the corner of Serret Alley and Main. There was a particular drink made at Lee's that we all liked. It was big and tall; I don't remember what it was called, but it seemed to be made of soda water with a citric flavoring added. It was like citronella and was very nice. When Lee's closed, Estorge's took over with a wonderful soda fountain.

The schools offered children most of their organized recreation--they sponsored more activities and entertainments for children than any other agency. Every morning at Central High, when I was in the 8th, 9th, 10th, and 11th grades, we had the morning assembly for one-half hour. During this assembly the 8th grade sat in front, followed by the 9th and 10th grades and then the seniors. There were so few seniors that they sat in chairs in the last row. The assembly hall was on the second floor of the old Central High School. There were sliding doors that opened into a classroom to make the assembly hall larger, if need be.

Every Friday afternoon we had an assembly and loved it because then we debated or engaged in public speaking, recitation and spelling matches. The grades competed against one another and individuals competed against one another. I loved to debate--it was really here that I learned to debate--and when I went to State Normal School in Natchitoches in 1917, as a freshman I debated against two senior men. One was E. B. "Ted" Robert, who later became an important figure in Louisiana education, and I think that the other was named Robertson or Robinson. He also became a leading figure in Louisiana education.

Getting back to Central High School, I recall that some of my teachers were Miss Julia McMahon, Miss Bessie Bauman and Mr. Redmond. Mr. Charles Bahon was principal at the time. The faculty was not very large, but they were all wonderful people. The student body, it seems to me, numbered less than one hundred. There were only seven members of my graduating class: three of us remain, Bernadette Langlois Templet, Sadie Belanger Dupuy (now living in Houma), and myself.

With regard to school activities, as I said, we had the morning assembly and the Friday afternoon assembly. Moreover, the teachers spent a lot of time with the students outside of the classroom. During these non-school hours the teachers would organize much of our recreation and entertainment. There would be hayrides, and we would visit different places. I remember visiting the two nearby sugar mills--the one at Morbihan and the one at Olivier. The boys would bring their pocket knives and, when our visit to the mill was over, they would peel sugarcane for the girls to chew. We consumed quite a bit of sugarcane.

While I was at Central High we were privileged to have a most unusual teacher, Miss Bessie Bauman, later Mrs. J. E. Kyle. She was far ahead of her times in every way. For example, she decided one day that most sporting events were for boys and that there was very little for girls to compete over. So she organized a girl's athletic meet. This event took place on April 8, 1916. The meet was held at the New Iberia racetrack, on Park Street. All of the high school girls participated--grade against grade and individual against individual. The only thing we did not do was put the shot, and we didn't throw the javelin, but we had all the races, up to and including the 440. All I remember about that race is that I ran around the track once and was so winded when I finished that I may have momentarily lost consciousness. Nevertheless, I had won the event and Miss Bessie provided the winners with a medal. I still have mine, it was for best all-around athelete.

For the class which won the most events in the meet, Miss Bessie had a trophy made from a 16-ounce vegetable can. She had trimmed it with black and gold ribbon. Written on the cup, not engraved, was the inscription. Now that I think back, we were so happy with so little.

The only recreation provided on the school grounds was basketball, which we played on a dirt court just to the west of the school. Other activities sponsored by the school were short skits during Friday assembly, but we did not have school plays. There was never anything like the May Day Pageants which were sponsored by Magnolia School later on. Miss Bessie Bauman, then Mrs. Kyle, was involved in the organization of that activity. Edwin Kyle was the first king of the pageant. Those May Day Pageants were in the late 1930s.

We had absolutely no library in the Central High School. We only had one dictionary, and it was practically in pieces. It was kept in a bookcase that had a broken glass door. When I wanted information, I would go to Porteus Burke's law office (he had married my cousin, Mabel Hine). I would go to his office on Main Street and use his library when I wanted to do research.

Outside of school, what was there to do for entertainment and recreation? We did a lot of reading. We had our own books that were given to us at Christmas and for birthdays. This was true not only in my own family but also in other families. We exchanged our books. When I finished reading a book I would exchange it for one someone else had. I particularly remember exchanging books with the Carstens family. Dr. Carstens' children had many books. I would exchange with E. J. and Amy, my sister, would exchange with Amelia and Byrne. We were all contemporaries. On rainy days we would spend the entire day reading.

On good days there were so many things to do. I remember that Steve Terrell taught me to play tennis about 1912. He had his own tennis court in his backyard--he lived on Main Street then, where the Cottage is today (712 West Main St.). After work he'd let me come over and we would play tennis. Not too many girls played tennis in those days. But, eventually, we did have a group of regular tennis players.

There was another tennis court located on the south side of the Aubry home (on Julia Street). I played tennis there many times. It was built by Harold and Rosa Aubry. Mildred, their sister, didn't play tennis. But Amy and

I would play there with Harold and Rosa, and many times Amelia Carstens (Courrege) would join us. I would say that Amelia, Amy and I were about the three best female players around. Once we challenged Mildred Culver, who was then living in Jeanerette and wasn't married at the time, and Maud Trappey, who hadn't yet gone to Washington, D. C. Amelia and I played Mildred and Maud in a terrific doubles match on the Aubry court, and we came away the victors. If memory serves me correctly, this match took place in the early 1930s.

In the 1920s, the Vuillemots, the Lourds, Paul Villermin and the Gates built their own tennis court in Henshaw Woods, just on the east side of present-day Pollard Avenue. We found a place between the trees, scraped it ourselves, and finally got it as hard as a clay court. It was an excellent court. We lined it ourselves, got our own net, and we played there. It was there, in 1928, that I won the local singles' championship. I defeated Ethel David, an excellent player who gave me a hard time winning. I can't remember now who we eliminated before we reached the finals.

Now, there was another tennis court in town, and Amy played on it with the Suberbielle boys, Jimmy and his brother, and George Dupuy. That court was located where the First Baptist Church is today, then across the street from the Central High School. I don't know who built or maintained that court--maybe it was that group of young men.

Bill and Alton (who was nicknamed "Jerry") Lourd lived in the old Indest house, at the present-day entrance to the golf club. Where the first tee is and the clubhouse, and thereabouts, we played as children--the Vuillemots, the Gates, the Lourds, Paul Villermin and others. We played a game called "Red Rover." When sides were chosen, the fastest runners were always chosen first. Each side had a flag (a piece of cloth) and the object of the game was to capture the other team's flag. As best I remember, we were playing "Red Rover" there in the early twenties. The things that amused us were so simple--we had so little, but we were happy.

Another thing we did at the Lourds was learn to swim. This we did in the bayou, right in front of the house. Old man Bill Lourd lived there. We were all there: the Gates, Bill and Alton Lourd, the Vuillemots, Harold, Emile and Bill; Paul Villermin. The Lourds had a skiff and a canoe, and we would paddle endlessly up and down the bayou. We would row the skiff, and when you could row with both hands and then "skip" your oars, that is, just make them dance lightly on the water, you had reached perfection. It was all a lot of fun.

I remember going to plays at the Elks Theater with my sister Marie. One thing in particular I remember seeing which impressed me was the play "Maryland." We had some excellent performances on the stage of the Elks Theater. After a while it became a motion picture theater.

There were parties in the homes, and we played musical chairs. If we were outside, we played "Drop the Handkerchief." Every family seemed to take a turn having a party.

Sunday was a little different then than it is now. Everyone, it seemed, went to church on Sunday morning. In my day, church services were also a little different than they are now. All during the months of May and October, the Catholic church had the May and October devotions. We would all get together and go as a group to church, all of the boys in the group were altar boys. There were between 20 and 30 boys serving as altar boys then. We would sing the litany and then say the rosary. This was followed by Benediction and the devotion was over. We went every evening during the months of May and October.

On Sunday, our day started off with church services, and afterward we would visit. If the weather was bad, we'd come back home and read. When movies came in, we would go to the movie on Sunday afternoon. There were always so many people walking on the streets. We would walk up and down Main Street, looking in the store windows, and visiting with friends who were also walking. When automobiles became popular, everyone then rode up and down Main Street. After awhile it became popular to park the car and watch the people as they passed--but that was much later, that was in the late twenties and early thirties. I didn't own a car, but I would ride with Nina Burke.

New Iberia was always a town that liked horse racing. I remember my father taking me to the racetrack to see the races. Then, I saw Teddy Roosevelt roar into town with his ex-Rough Riders. They came in from the west, probably he was coming from Lake Charles and Lafayette. By the time they rode into New Iberia there seemed to be a multitude of men on horseback, all yelling and whooping it up. Dust was flying on Main Street so thick you could barely see across the street. Main Street was still a dirt street. Mr. Roosevelt then delivered a public address, in the vicinity of the courthouse. This was when he was campaigning on the Bull Moose ticket--I guess that would have been 1914.*

---

*For details of the Roosevelt visit to New Iberia, see Cathi B. Gibbens, "President Roosevelt Visits Acadiana," *Attakapas Gazette*, XX (1985), 123-132.

Roosevelt came before the influenza epidemic. I also remember seeing the flags--not used for influenza, but for smallpox. We had a great deal of smallpox in New Iberia in those early years of the century. Whenever a case was discovered in a household a yellow flag would go up on the house, and no one could go in or out. Since then, science has conquered smallpox and malaria. I had malaria, and I remember Alton Lourd had a terrible case of malaria.

I was in college during the influenza epidemic. We had a lot of cases at the old State Normal, but I seemed to be immune because I would go into the infirmary, with no other protection than a gauze mask over my mouth and nose, and nursed people down with the flu. That was 1918. I wasn't in New Iberia at the time, so I know very little about the effects of the epidemic here.

I forgot to mention the trolley car when I was speaking of our amusements. It was 5¢ to ride the car to Jeanerette. Well, we rode on the trolley car for sheer entertainment. I wish I knew how many trips I made to Jeanerette and back--it was wonderful. On the warm days, the windows would be open and the car would just move across the countryside. It was a wonderful outing-- a form of recreation. Sometimes there were so many people riding the trolley that a second car was hooked on to accommodate all the passengers.

I was in Natchitoches at the time of the Armistice in 1918, so I can't remark on any reactions here in New Iberia. Now that I think about it, I wasn't in New Iberia when World War II ended in 1945.

I remember excursions to New Orleans for a fare of $1.50. The train would leave here in the morning and return in the late afternoon. Sometimes, as a special, the fare was only $1.00. We would go in groups to New Orleans for carnival. It seemed that the whole town of New Iberia would go to New Orleans for Mardi Gras. The automobile changed all that--it has changed our life styles considerably.

That reminds me. The streets of the town were terrible. It was possible, and it frequently happened, that people would get bogged on Main Street. There was a conveyance called a hack, and it was owned by a livery stable-- the places that sold mules and horses. I remember two livery stables--one located on Main Street where the parking lot now exists between Allain's Jewelry Store and Jacob Landry's office, and the other was on Julia Street. Instead of calling for a taxi, as is done today, one called for a cab. My grandmother, mother and aunt would go to church in a cab. They would phone for a cab, or my uncle would arrange to have it sent out. They would go to church and afterward would be picked up and taken back home.

New Iberia City Hall (built 1898) as it appeared about 1912. Buildings to the right are the Emmer Buildings

This hack, as it was called, was just like a bus, but was pulled by a pair of horses. It would go to the depot to meet the trains and pick up those people who wished to go into town or the hotel. There were seats on each side and the aisle down the center. One got in from the back, by way of two or three steps. Many times these hacks would get bogged on Main Street. Buggies would bog on the city streets, too. The drivers would then get down, wade through the mud to the nearest phone and call the livery stable to send out a team of mules to pull out whatever was stuck in the mud. The streets of New Iberia before they were hard surfaced were either all dust or all mud.

The Depression years in New Iberia were personally terrible. My sisters and I were teaching one year when, at the end of seven months, our schools were closed, and our last month's pay was given to us in script. My salary was then about $80 per month and we were told to find someone who would discount the script. It was usually discounted at six or eight percent. I knew that I had to do some kind of work because my father had died in 1921, and we had the family to support.

The federal government was hiring social workers, and I found out they were hiring in Donaldsonville. So I applied and got a job there. I would cross the river every morning and go into Dutch Town and Gonzales and the River Road area. There was a group of people there who had been growing strawberries, but they couldn't sell strawberries to anyone in 1932 and '33. So, they needed help.

Before that I worked around here for awhile because I could understand French, and many people that were called on spoke only French. So the social worker had to understand French in order to take care of their needs. They could get different kinds of help. They could, for example, get immediate help in the form of groceries and medical aid, especially for children. But I really spent most of those years around Donaldsonville, so I don't know a great deal about what went on here. I think people managed to weather the Depression very well. Times weren't easy to begin with, so the Depression was really only a little more of the same. I used to teach summer school and get either 50¢ or $1.00 per week per student for a period of ten weeks.

Another awful experience was the 1927 flood. The water came right up to the sill of my front door--another inch and it would have come into the house. L. G. Porter was a wonderful man. He and I believed that the flood would come to New Iberia, but Walter Kemper and a group of engineers put out leaflets telling the people not to be afraid, there would be no water in New Iberia. Well, I didn't believe that, so Mr. Porter sent men here who raised our sideboard and other dining room furniture about two feet off the floor. The rest of the furniture that could be moved was stored upstairs, so we wouldn't have lost any furniture in the flood. But we lost everything in the yard. I came across the bayou every day to watch the house because there had been a few burglaries.

My mother and sisters went to Lafayette to the home of my sister and her husband, Henry Ortte. Nina and I stayed here and we volunteered our services to the Red Cross. The Red Cross headquarters was located in the building that was on the corner of Main and Iberia streets, where the downtown parking lot is now. It was a large brick building.

I went on the St. Martinville highway and watched water come uphill. There was a large oak tree that parted the road upon what we called the "hill." I stood there and watched the water get higher and higher on the side of that hill. In town, the bridge was out; there was no electricity, no water power. The refugees from the Loreauville and Lake Dauterive area were pouring in-- many of then with nothing more than the clothes on their backs--they had lost everything.

Nina, Eva Landry (Mrs. Joe Broussard), and I helped to register the refugees as they came in. If they had any belongings we would make a record of these, and put the belongings to one side. Once they were registered, the people were taken out to the camp. Now the camp was near the old Segura house--that was where Father John McGlade of St. Edward's Church set up the camps, because the blacks and whites were separated.

The National Guard came in and set up the tent city. The Red Cross then went about feeding the refugees, and caring for them. When I was no longer needed in town, I went out the camp to help out. There was so much to be done. One time we worked straight through forty-eight hours. We would sink down on a pile of sacks or anything and get a couple hours of sleep and then would get back to work. It was really a pitiful sight to see the people pouring in to a completely strange situation. I have no idea how many people were in those camps, but there must have been hundreds. I don't remember how long they stayed, but I do remember the floodwaters entered New Iberia on May 25, 1927, a few days after Lindbergh landed in Paris. I associate the two because the headlines on the newspaper were divided between Lindbergh's triumph and the fact that New Iberia was being flooded.

The flood didn't last too long, the water slowly began to recede. The water was deep from here [corner of Davis Street and Duperier Avenue] to the bayou. I remember that a large Coast Guard boat would tie up to a telephone pole in front of the old Dauterive Hospital [Marie Street and Duperier Avenue]. For more than a month we had to cross the bayou on a ferry--from Weeks Street to wherever the boat could go without getting stuck. I can't remember exactly how long the flood lasted--maybe two weeks--because Nina Burke was working with me in the camp, and Neenal Webster and Nina went away every summer on a trip and she worked only a couple of weeks and then left for her trip.

Miss Julia Decuir and Louise Arnandez were there to fill in. That was where Louise met her future husband. He was the officer in charge of the National Guard, and she was helping with recreation activities at the camp. Now, Miss Julia Decuir was a wonderful lady--a loveable character. She was charitable, unforgettable, an imposing figure.

Whenever I think of the flood, I think of Julia Decuir. I can still see her, tall, straight, with a large straw hat on her head, tied on with a veil. She wore long gloves to protect her arms from the hot sun. She would be out in that hot sun every day, as long as we needed her to help supervise the recreation of the children. She was a member of the Catholic Daughters, and this group took charge of the children, because, at first, the children had nothing to do and were running wild. The kids just weren't used to being confined so much. So the Catholic Daughters purchased some recreation equipment and the National Guard set up the baseball diamond and whatever for the children to use. Anyway, Miss Julia was out there every day getting the children's recreation organized and generally keeping up their morale.

The federal government moved in quickly to protect the health of the community. A hospital train came in and was put on a siding near the depot. This group took care of all the vaccinations. There was a hospital set up by the federal government in the old Harrison home, the same house which was later a night club [The Golden Pheasant]. It was said that babies were born by the dozens there during the flood period. At any rate, the federal people must have done their work well, for we had no epidemic of any kind after the flood.

I have never seen anything that equalled the aftermath of the flood. Everywhere there was debris brought by the waters--dead animals were everywhere. I saw my yard without a blade of grass and with every shrub and bush dead. The only things to survive were the large trees. Everywhere there was slush and mud.

After the flood, the Red Cross stayed in New Iberia for months and months. So many families still needed help after the waters receded. The Red Cross really did a great job during and after the flood. The Red Cross and the federal government were marvelous throughout the disaster, especially for those days.

But it was not only these agencies which responded to our needs. People all over the United States sent things. I especially remember the clothing that was contributed. It was good clothing, not second-hand stuff. A lot of it was right out of the store. There was an incredible number of charitable people throughout the nation.

Herbert Hoover was largely responsible for coordinating the flood relief. No one will ever know how much this man did to alleviate the suffering. We had so much to be thankful for. But that is the wonderful thing about the people of New Iberia. They rebound easily after disaster--as they did following this flood, after smallpox epidemics, malaria epidemics, bad fires, the hurricanes, World War I and II. New Iberia has never gone down, and this, I think, is a tribute to the character of the people who have built this town. I wouldn't live anywhere else. There is a pecular characteristic about the people of New Iberia and that is to take adversity in their stride while marching onward. The people who have built New Iberia are people of hardy stock.

I think some of the town's leaders during the teens, twenties, and thereafter, were people like Charles Bahon and Lloyd G. Porter. Bahon was a wonderful educator. Porter was a classroom teacher who later became superintendent of education in Iberia Parish. This man brought so much good to New Iberia with so little money and so few administrators. In the realm of education it is impossible to forget the dream of Monsignor J. M. Langlois that ultimately became St. Peter's College.

Among the leaders of the legal profession were the Burkes (Walter and Porteus) and the Weekses (Edward and William). These were men of tremendous character.

There were ever so many wonderful doctors in New Iberia during the teens and twenties, but two of them stand out in my mind: Dr. George Sabatier and Dr. Henry Dauterive. Both men possessed the virtues of kindness and charity to a degree seldom found.

Mentioning doctors also brings to mind the Estorge brothers, Albert and Edward. In them was to be found the very essence of Christian concern for their fellow men. To my knowledge no one was ever turned away from their door because there was no money to pay for the needed medicine. In addition, both men were progressives. Edward Estorge was the first president of the Iberia Golf Club.

This also brings to mind two wonderful people: Mrs. Josephine Hitter Sillan and Miss Katherine Avery. Nan Sillan was truly an "angel of mercy" during the 1918 flu epidemic in St. Martinville. Later, in New Iberia, she came to be loved by all who knew her. At present (1978) Mrs. Sillan is 104 years old. Katherine Avery is also a registered nurse and is truly one of our town's civic leaders. She is a founder of the Iberia Tuberculosis Association.

There are other civic leaders of that era who stand out in my mind: Mattie Barnard Shaw was a patriotic citizen and a preservationist long before preservation became the big thing that it is today. She fought a long, hard battle to preserve the old courthouse. Unfortunately, she lost, and we are all the poorer. There was also Bessie Bauman Kyle, a remarkable woman of tremendous energy and genuine civic pride. She has left an indelible mark upon New Iberia. Finally, no discussion of civic leaders during the teens and twenties (and thereafter, for that matter) can be complete without mention of Yvonne Arnandez Southwell. Here is the lady who blazed the trail for businesswomen in New Iberia. She is a civic leader, *par excellence*.

There are two other ladies who deserve special mention. One is Corinne Burgess Outhwaite who, in 1925, organized the Iberia Chapter of the Daughters of the American Revolution. The other person was Louise Taylor Pharr who organized the Louisiana Society of the National Society of the Daughters of Colonial Wars. In addition, she served as Regent of the New Iberia Chapter of the D.A.R. and the Louisiana Society of the D.A.R. She also served as Vice President General of the National Society D.A.R.

I cannot conclude these reminiscences without mentioning something about the filming of *Evangeline* in 1929. Dolores Del Rio played the part of Evengeline. Miss Del Rio was a very beautiful young woman and played the roll with such sensitivity. It was thrilling, I guess, because we were all so young and romantic and here was a story that we could so easily relate to. We were all so excited about the film, about seeing and talking to the stars. They stayed at the Frederic Hotel, but Mrs. Yvonne Southwell can say more about that than I can. At any rate, it was a big thing for New Iberia, to have a movie made here.

Reminiscing about artists brings to mind two New Iberia artists: Weeks Hall and Alphonse Hitter. I accompanied Mr. Hitter many times on visits to Weeks Hall at "The Shadows." Weeks Hall was a very cordial person and made you feel at ease from the moment you met him. Although he was very much a gentleman, he was also very entertaining. One thing about Weeks Hall was always apparent. He had a great sense of pride in "The Shadows," and this feeling caused him to do all in his power to preserve the house for posterity. He often expressed the fear that if he did not do something to protect the house while he was living, after his death it might be demolished and replaced by a hamburger stand. That is an oft-repeated statement. He wanted to be sure that

Dolores Del Rio leaves New Iberia after filming *Evangeline*.

that house would live for New Iberians. Weeks Hall was a fine man, and his dream has come true.

One of the things I think was so characteristic of the teens and twenties was the Chautauqua. We always looked forward to that. My father would buy tickets for all of us every year. We never missed a performance. There were lectures, plays, educational routines, but there was always some sort of entertainment. It was always held under a tent, and the tent was always set up on the corner of Weeks and St. Peter streets, where the First Baptist Church is now.

Also I should mention the city bands. I listened to many a concert by these bands in front of the courthouse on Main Street--that beautiful courthouse beneath those beautiful oaks. These were really good bands. There were also Negro bands that played for dances. These were bands that were organized right here in Freetown [the area of Hortense and Rozier streets north of Henry]. They also played in the pavilion in City Park.

World War I draftees, 1918, on the courthouse steps.

The fire companies would decorate floats and once a year they would parade their floats down Main Street. This had no connection with the Fourth of July parade, which was also an annual event for many years. This is why it seemed so strange to me that New Iberia had no public celebration on July 4, 1976, the bicentennial of American independence. But then, times change.

I have lived through most of the twentieth century and have seen many changes take place in New Iberia. One change that I was deeply involved in and of which I am very proud was being a part of the formation of the Tuberculosis Association. One day, long ago, I received a letter from someone in New Orleans asking me to receive a Mrs. McBride. She arrived on the train and Vida Riggs and I took her to Lake Dauterive to eat a fish dinner. During our meal she asked me to sell the tuberculosis seals in this area. I agreed, and once a year I'd go up and down Main Street putting out my seals, especially at Estorge Drug Company. Then people would drop money in the box. Dr. George Sabatier would always give liberally to the cause.

Once the money was collected, I would mainly use it to buy medicine for the tuberculosis victims. They also frequently needed fuel for their coal oil heaters. I'd buy the coal oil and medicine. Estorge's always provided the medicine at a discount. Ed and Albert Estorge were two good men. I did this work for several years until it became evident that something more had to be done. That was, of course, when the Tuberculosis Association was formed.

Well, these are reminiscences of my life in New Iberia during the teens and twenties. I know other people will remember other things, but it has been a pleasure to share these memories with the reader.

The Masonic Temple Building shortly after it was built in 1911

XXII

The Story of Education in New Iberia, 1848-1983

by
Carl A. Brasseaux

New Iberia, located at the head of navigation on Bayou Teche and at the southern terminus of the heavily used freight portage to St. Maur, emerged by 1850 as the economic hub of the central Teche Valley.[1] The community's burgeoning trade attracted a small corps of professionals and merchants, and, as the typical nineteenth-century mercantile firm was essentially a family business, passing from one generation to the next, merchants had a vital interest in educating their progeny. Thus, New Iberia has had a long tradition of public and private education.

The development of public education in antebellum New Iberia is obscure primarily because of the parochial authorities' refusal to cooperate with state educational surveys. Nevertheless, it is certain that, prior to the establishment of the town's first public school in the late 1840s, a few New Iberia children were educated either by tutors or at boarding schools.[2]

---

1. See the essay entitled "A Narrative of Events Connected with the Early Settlement of New Iberia."

2. See *ibid.*

This reliance upon private schools was necessitated by a dearth of public institutions. Although Eli Riggs had given a one-half arpent school site to St. Martin Parish in mid-July, 1827, the parochial government failed to establish a public school in New Iberia until 1848.[3] According to William R. Burke, a "graduate" of this primary school, the small student body consisted solely of "poor boys and girls." Bully and Gibbs, the faculty members, "ruled with a rod of iron"; in fact, students were disciplined so harshly that "when Bully died ... there was great rejoicing among his pupils."[4] Following the establishment of the first public school, the town's educational system experienced sharp growing pains, especially during the late 1850s, for, by 1861, a second public school and four additional private schools were in operation.[5]

The last school established during the antebellum period, a private institution begun in 1861 by Mrs. Martin Bryant, Mrs. Léonce de la Croix, and Mrs. Emile Soulier, apparently served as the focal point of education in New Iberia during the early Civil War years, for the public school system became moribund from 1862 until 1869.[6] Sometime during the war, however, the Bryant, La Croix, Soulier school closed and was supplanted by a private girls' school, operated by Mrs. De René, Alphonsine De René, Mrs. Bryant, Mrs. Soulier, Henrietta Andrus, and one Professor Müller, a music teacher.[7] This institution prospered until 1867, when a yellow-fever epidemic prompted not only the school's closure, but the dispersal of the faculty as well.[8]

The void created by the demise of the girls' school was filled by five private institutions. Howe Institute, a black private school endowed by Northern

---

3. Eli Riggs' donation is found in St. Martin Parish Conveyance Book 3, p. 169.

4. *New Iberia Enterprise*, February 28, 1931.

5. Felix Goryon and Laurent Plauchin–both French immigrants--listed their occupations as "schoolmaster" in the 1850 census. Ten years later, Englishmen Reed Funt and A. Cook, Louisiana-born Victorin Renoudet, Marylander W. C. White, and French woman Hebe Soulier, composed the ranks of New Iberia educators. U. S. Census for 1850 and 1860; *Report of the Superintendent of Public Education*... (New Orleans, 1858, pp. 50-51.

6. See the essay entitled "Reminiscences of the 60s and 70s."

7. *Ibid.*

8. *Ibid.*

philanthropists, occupied the recently vacated De René building, while in 1868 Mrs. Martin Bryant, a former member of the De René faculty, established a private school for white children, which she operated until 1890.[9] Three white, boys' schools--Professor R. S. Isabel's, first on Main Street and then on Washington Street, Professor P. O. Lyndon's school in the Odd Fellow's Hall on the corner of Weeks and Main streets, and Judge Thomas Balch's school on Main Street--enjoyed a much shorter tenure of operation, all closing their doors by the early 1870s.[10]

The hegemony of the private school in New Iberia during the late 1860s is directly attributable to the economic devastation and political and social turmoil which characterize the early Reconstruction period in Acadiana. New Iberia's postbellum educational development was further retarded by the apathy of the St. Martin Parish officials, who defied state constitutional requirements for the establishment of free public schools.[11] Once freed from the shackles of St. Martin Parish politics by the creation of Iberia Parish in 1868, New Iberians quickly established a public educational system; but, in attempting to fill the void which had existed for so many years, the school system understandably suffered growing pains.

From the establishment of two primary schools[12] at New Iberia in 1870 until the end of Reconstruction in 1877, public education became a political football bitterly contested by the parish's political parties--the Republicans and the Democrats. According to the Democrats, the Republicans, who controlled

---

9. *Ibid.*; Maurine Bergerie, *They Tasted Bayou Water: A Brief History of Iberia Parish* (New Orleans, 1962), p. 84.

10. See the essay entitled "Reminiscences of the 60s and 70s."

11. Francis Newton Thorpe, ed., *The Federal and State Constitutions, Colonial Charters, and Other Organic Laws of the States, Territories, and Colonies* (Washington, 1909), III, 1465; *Annual Report of the State Superintendent of Education for 1869* (New Orleans, 1870), p. 45.

12. The schools, the only public educational facilities in Iberia Parish, were staffed by four teachers who taught 178 pupils. The teachers, two men and two women, were paid $50 per month. *Annual Report of the State Superintendent of Education for 1870* (New Orleans, 1871), p. 82.

Three Early New Iberia Educators

William R. Burke (right),
Parish Superintendent of Education;
R. G. Ferguson (below left) and
C. C. Harris (below right), early
principals of Central High School

the parish board of education until 1877,[13] "seemed bent chiefly on the preservation of the nefarious superiority of their political machine, rather than the

---

13. In mid-May 1877, the newly appointed and overwhelmingly Democratic State Board of Education ousted the Republican parish board and replaced it with Eugene Olivier, W. R. Burke, J. N. Landry, Dr. Alfred Duperier, Adolphe Segura, Dudley Avery, and H. Mobley. The appointed were, in turn, to appoint two "competent colored men." See the *Louisiana Sugar Bowl,* May 24, 1877.

fostering of the public good."[14]

The Democrats' charges appear to have been grounded in fact, for in 1877, parish superintendent of schools W. R. Burke reported that the city's school teachers had been appointed by the outgoing board--most of whom were illiterate--solely on the basis "of the servile offices they might render the party."[15] Moreover, the city's initial schools, the St. Paul and Webster primary schools which were the only public educational facilities in the parish, were supplemented by only two black primary schools during the Republican board's seven-year tenure.[16] Not only did the board fail to establish a sufficient number of schools, but existing facilities were kept in operation only two months per annum.[17] Finally, the outgoing board bequeathed to their successors school properties and equipment valued at $75, while the outstanding debts totalled $5,650.[18]

Despite these significant obstacles, the Democratic board, under the direction of President Eugene P. Olivier and Secretary-Treasurer William R. Burke, quickly placed the school system on a sound financial basis, hired competent teachers, and, in 1882, appropriated $4,000 for the acquisition of property and subsequent construction of white schools on Julia and Madison streets.[19] In

---

14. *Annual Report of the State Superintendent of Public Education, Robert M. Lusher, to the General Assembly of Louisiana, for the Year 1877* (New Orleans, 1878), pp. 94-95.

15. *Ibid.* The Republican school board was composed of R. L. Belden, president; L. C. Allison, secretary-treasurer; Allen Hayes; Paul Schull; Hermogene Daniels; Judge Theodore Fontelieu; P. E. Burke; and Dr. J. J. Lemon. *Louisiana Sugar Bowl*, April 22, 1875.

16. A fifth, short-lived black primary school operated by a person named Wilde closed in 1875. The white schools were segregated by sex and were conducted by J. R. Freeman and Mrs. Slaughter. Misses E. Moore and Rosa Miller taught the black students. Minutes of the Meeting of the Board of School Directors of the Town of New Iberia, La., September 20, 1873. *Louisiana Sugar Bowl*, September 30, 1875.

17. *Annual Report*, 1877, pp. 90-95.

18. *Ibid.*

19. *Sugar Bowl*, April 14, 1881. The New Iberia Ladies' Committee, led by Mrs. C. F. Montagne, assisted the school board in acquiring the necessary funds. The Julia Street School was built by E. W. Phillips. *Weekly Iberian*, December 7, 1895.

Central High School, 1903 (above), and March 1972, just before demolition

addition, in 1884, the board ordered construction of a black school on French Street.[20]

The school board's efforts to expand the New Iberia school system were supplemented by its efforts to improve the quality of instruction within these facilities. For example, beginning in 1877, the school board made every effort to hire teachers with a normal school degree. Moreover, between 1885 and the second decade of the twentieth century, New Iberia teachers were compelled to attend monthly teachers' institutes. These events were public school workshops conducted by local faculty members, and usually consisted of formal papers sandwiched between discussion periods or musical diversions.[21]

Having established a sound primary school system, the Iberia Parish School Board turned its attention to the establishment of a high school. The need for a public high school had become increasingly apparent as growing numbers of primary school graduates were either compelled to attend expensive local private schools or end their educational careers without the business training that the nineteenth-century secondary school afforded. Growing public interest in secondary education was manifested in a meeting of twenty-nine civic-minded New Iberians[22] on June 13, 1885, at Serret's Hall. After organizing themselves into the Iberia Education Society, these citizens, under the leadership of President D. U. Broussard and Vice President W. E. Satterfield, attempted to persuade the parish school board to build a high school. Their pleas, however, fell on deaf ears until mid-July 1887, when Joseph A. Breaux, a member of the Iberia Education Society and newly elected president of the parish school board, persuaded his fellow board members to appropriate $500

20. In 1884 the Iberia Parish School Board consisted of President James A. Lee, Secretary-Treasurer William R. Burke, P. L. Renoudet, J. T. White, Felix Patout, Robert Olivier, Armanco Derouen, Dr. A. Shaw, and A. L. Minnot. *Ibid.*

21. *Weekly Iberian*, September 29, 1895. The parish institutes were begun following the establishment of the high school. They were held on the first Saturday of each month and were presided over by the high school principal.

22. *New Iberia Enterprise*, June 17, 1885. Those attending the meeting were D. U. Broussard, W. E. Satterfield, James A. Lee, Mrs. Carrie Montagne, Miss Amanda Smith, Mrs. C. J. Carstens, J. B. Lawton, Louis Auger, H. Boudreaux, A. M. Escudier, J. G. LeBlanc, L. A. Pellerin, L. B. Delahoussaye, Edmond Broussard, Achille Penniston, Octavia Reggio, N. L. Genares, Frederick Gates, Dr. L. A. Burgess, E. F. Broussard, J. Dupuis, G. Jacob, Achille Patin, Dr. L. G. Blanchet, Mortimer Broussard, P. A. Veazey, Oscar Dupre, C. T. Cade, and J. Emmet Brown.

New Iberia High School, 1922 - 1966

New Iberia Senior High School, 1966 -

for the establishment of a secondary school in New Iberia.[23] In addition, the board appointed President Breaux, C. T. Cade and William R. Burke to a supervisory committee with authority to recruit the assistance of "interested citizens," to provide for the construction of the school, and to hire necessary faculty members.[24]

The committee quickly discharged its responsibilities. During the ensuing months, the committeemen raised approximately $700 from fifty-five individuals for the construction of "a building to be occupied as a High School."[25] Moreover, during the October school board meeting, President Breaux recommended the transformation of Julia Street School, a one-room facility, into a high school and recommended further the appointment of W. R. Harnish as its principal. The school board approved both recommendations and, as the establishment of the high school necessitated the grading of New Iberia's primary schools, the board directed Harnish and Catherine Hawley, a local public school teacher, to "establish six grades beside junior and senior in the high school . . . [and to establish] examinations at the end of each session, February and June."[26]

The opening of the high school on October 10, 1887, signaled the beginning of the end for private schools in New Iberia. Despite the establishment of the New Iberia public school system in 1870, the city's private educational system flourished, and, indeed, expanded. The prosperity of the private schools is directly attributable to the outstanding credentials of the instructors, to a more diversified curriculum, and to secondary and religious instruction. For example, the Attakapas Commercial and Industrial School (founded by Father Beaubien in 1872 and renamed Holy Cross College in the fall of 1873) boasted not only former instructors at domestic and foreign "colleges," but a curriculum which included "arithmetic, algebra, geometry, natural philosophy, chemistry, bookkeeping, commercial law, the theory of accounts, telegraphy, and stenog-

---

23. *Enterprise*, December 28, 1895.

24. Vivien A. Mestayer, "The History of the New Iberia High School" (MA thesis, Louisiana State University, 1951), p. 9.

25. *Weekly Iberian*, December 7, 1895. Joseph Jefferson, the actor-philanthropist, donated $100 to the committee.

26. *Enterprise*, February 21, 1933.

raphy."[27] Moreover, unlike the public schools, which were conducted in English, the Industrial School provided French as well as religious instruction--items of vital interest to the community's significant French-Catholic minority. Other schools offered college preparatory curricula, as well as night classes.[28] Thus, it is hardly surprising that these institutions were well patronized. In 1877, for example, Mount Carmel Convent, a Catholic girls school founded in October 1870, and Holy Cross College boasted a total enrollment of 137--over half of the parish-wide, public school population.[29]

By the late 1880s, however, the public had largely withdrawn its formerly extensive patronage of the city's private schools.[30] The decline of the private school system was the result of the transitory nature of nondenominational private schools and the dramatic improvement in the quality of education afforded by the public schools. By 1891, for example, the high school offered such college-preparatory courses as geography, botany, general history, grammar, algebra, ancient history, physical geography, literature, plane geometry, Latin, and solid geometry.[31] Thus, by 1892 over seventy-five percent of Iberia Parish students attended public schools.[32]

The swelling ranks of students dictated the need for rapid expansion of the public school system. In early January, 1889, Joseph A. Breaux and James A. Lee, trustees of the New Iberia schools, notified the parish school board that:

> The High School class room should be at once enlarged, an addition can be made to it without great expense. The number now is about

---

27. *Sugar Bowl*, April 24, November 6, 1873.

28. *Ibid.*, April 21, 1881; *Enterprise*, September 28, 1885.

29. *Sugar Bowl*, April 19, 1877. *Annual Report*, 1877, pp. 90-95.

30. *Sugar Bowl*, January 27, February 3, March 24, 1881. Tennessean W. W. Hunter, for example, a graduate of Cumberland University, opened a private school in the Odd Fellows' Hall on February 7, 1881, and departed New Iberia approximately three weeks later.

31. Mestayer, "New Iberia High School," p. 11.

32. *Biannual Report of the State Superintendent of Education . . . 1890-1891* (New Orleans, 1892), p. 82.

forty-five average attendance. At least thirty more might be admitted and properly taught, if the room was larger.[33]

Responding to the trustees' recommendations, the school board appropriated $600 for the construction of a wood-frame high school annex and appointed W. L. Brown, Jr., C. T. Cade, and W. R. Burke to supervise the construction.[34]

Construction of the annex was obviously only a stopgap measure for the school system's growing space problem. New Iberians subsequently organized an educational society to secure construction of a new high school. Led by an executive committee composed of Mrs. N. P. Millard, Mrs. P. F. Henry, Mrs. J. A. Pharr, Mrs. J. C. Fuller, and Lizzie DeValcourt, the society "gave entertainments, went begging, and tried by every other means to raise a sufficient amount to start the much desired building." The fund-raising drive, however, generated only $300, far below the amount needed to construct a new high school. As the drive stalled, the parish school board appointed W. R. Burke "to request the ladies' committee to turn over the $300 they had raised so that it might be used in payment of the debt for construction of the wooden building just then built...."[35]

The ladies' executive committee was apparently incensed by Burke's plea for funds, for they adamantly refused to consider his request, which they obviously interpreted as an attempt to subvert their crusade. The committee then submitted a counteroffer, proposing to lend, at the prevailing rate of interest, $300 to the school board on the condition that these funds be utilized solely for construction of a new, *brick* high school.[36] When the ladies' proposal was rejected, the executive committee "invested the amount in bank stock to reserve it for the future brick building."[37] The spark of interest in a new high school thus remained alive.

33. *Weekly Iberian*, December 28, 1895.

34. *Ibid.*

35. *Ibid.*

36. *Ibid.*

37. *Ibid.*

A second high school movement rose from the ashes of its predecessor in 1892. Led by W. M. Howe, who succeeded W. R. Harnish as the high school principal in 1890, New Iberians commited to improving the city's educational system organized the Central High School Association and selected the following board members: James A. Lee, president; L. O. Hacker, vice-president; W. M. Howe, secretary; W. R. Burke, treasurer; Robert S. Perry; Walter J. Burke; E. F. Millard; Dr. H. A. King; and J. B. Lawton.[38] Following their election, the board of directors approved Howe's suggestion that $10 shares be sold to the general public as means of generating the necessary building funds.[39] By this means, as well as other money-making ventures, such as an excursion to Abbeville, the Association raised over $3,600. These funds were supplemented by a $1,000 grant from the parish police jury and $500 from the New Iberia city council. Finally, John Emmer and the Avery family agreed to provide 10,000 bricks and a large shipment of sand necessary for construction of the new high school.[40]

The fund-raising drive having proved to be a monumental success, representatives of the Central High School Association successfully petitioned the parish school board, in early July, 1895 to "combine efforts" with the New Iberia group. Shortly thereafter, the school board met with representatives of the Association to select a joint executive committee, consisting of President John Emmer, Secretary E. F. Millard, Treasurer W. R. Burke, R. S. McMahon, J. B. Lawton, Dr. J. W. K. Shaw, W. R. Farmer, and Jules Dubus, for the purpose of supervising construction of the new high school. Bids were subsequently let and a $10,600 contract was awarded to contractor E. W. Phillips.[41]

The cornerstone of the new high school, christened Central High School, was laid in late January, 1896, and the pressed-brick structure--the only brick school in Louisiana outside of New Orleans--was dedicated nine months later.[42]

---

38. *Ibid.*

39. The stock was initially issued on credit, but forty-four of the 157 persons who agreed to purchase shares subsequently failed to honor their pledges. *Ibid.*

40. *Ibid.*

41. *Ibid.*

42. W. R. Burke presided over the laying of the cornerstone, presenting a lengthy patriotic speech. The cornerstone contained a copy of the October 14, 1895, issue of the New Orleans *Daily Picayune. Ibid.*, February 1, 1896.

St. Peter's College at the time of dedication, May 1919

The following is a contemporary description of the new secondary school, which was located at the corner of St. Peter and Weeks streets on a lot purchased by the Central High School Association in November, 1893:[43]

> It is ... 68 feet by 81 feet, with a 7-foot basement. The first floor is divided into three rooms 30 by 30 feet with a 10 foot hall, library room and tower hall. The second story is an assembly room and can be partitioned off by rolling doors. There is also a tower hall in the upper floor. A neat set of lockers is placed in all halls for the use and accommodation of the pupils. Real slate blackboards are placed all around the walls both on the upper and lower stories. The schoolrooms

---

43. Mestayer, "New Iberia High School," pp. 18-19. The association had purchased a lot for $1,800.

St. Peter's College enlarged, as it appeared in the 1930s

are all supplied with new patent single desks, recitation seats, and all other necessary school furniture.[44]

The establishment of the new high school overtaxed the school board budget, and, as a consequence, all public schools in the parish were closed for one month at mid-term.[45] With the resumption of fiscal stability, however, the quality and quantity of educational services offered by the school board were expanded. For example, in the fall of 1896, a free night school was established.[46] The upgrading of education at the high school was acknowledged in

44. *Ibid.*, p. 19.

45. *Ibid.*, p. 20.

46. The night school was established by the Free Night School Board, directed by Joseph A. Breaux. Mrs. Carrie Montagne taught night classes at Central High School from

the fall of 1906 when the institution was accredited by the state department of education.[47] In addition, in 1909, Dr. O. B. Denwiddie of Tulane University inspected the high school and determined that the secondary school's curriculum was sufficiently advanced to permit its graduates to apply for admission to the New Orleans college.[48]

The high school's educational gains, however, were temporarily overshadowed by a bitter political feud involving the Iberia Parish School Board, the local superintendent of schools, and the Central High School faculty. The dispute arose when the school board, in 1908, appointed A. J. Dupuy to fill J. C. Ellis' unexpired term as superintendent of parish schools, and, prior to expiration of this term, appointed Dupuy to a second, four-year term.[49] Because of the questionable legality of Dupuy's appointment,[50] the succeeding school board named Louis A. Walet superintendent of parish schools. Dupuy, however, not only refused to resign, but sought an injunction to halt implementation of the board's action.[51]

The matter was temporarily resolved when Dupuy and Walet both resigned on the ground that "a third and disinterested party" be selected to fill the resulting vacancy;[52] however, the appointee, A. W. Bittle, quickly resigned, and, in mid-January 1909, Walet applied for his former position.[53] Despite objections that Walet's appointment was in direct contravention of the previous gentleman's agreement, his application was approved, thus igniting a second

---

October 1898 to April 1899. *Weekly Iberian,* May 20, 1899. *Biennial Report . . . for 1896-1897* (Baton Rouge, 1898).

47. Mestayer, "New Iberia High School," p. 23.

48. *Weekly Iberian,* February 6, 1909.

49. *Ibid.,* January 16, 1909.

50. Act 214 of 1902 limited school superintendents' appointments to only four years. Charles G. Gill, ed., *Louisiana Reports* (St. Paul, 1909), CXXIII, 739.

51. *Weekly Iberian,* January 16, 1909.

52. *Ibid.,* January 30, 1909.

53. *Ibid.,* January 16, 1909.

Story of Education

Mt. Carmel Academy as it appeared about 1900 (above), and as it appeared about 1980.

dispute. The smouldering embers of controversy sprang into flame in early May when the Louisiana supreme court, in *State ex rel. Wiley J. Wilson v. John C. Hardin* decision, decreed that:

> When the term of office of a parish superintendent of education expires by limitation, the parish board of school directors ... is authorized to elect his successor.... The board as subsequently constituted is bound by such action so taken, and is without authority to elect another person for such term.[54]

Following the *Wilson* decision, Walet's opponents mounted an intensive campaign to force the controversial superintendent to resign. Their efforts were boosted substantially by Walet's developing feud with the Central High School faculty. The dispute arose in late April at a fund-raising "exercise" for an unidentified high school organization. Walet objected to the presence of an individual on a faculty-appointed committee of judges, alleging that the person was not worthy to sit as a judge.[55] Principal J. L. Cook, who was convinced that the superintendent's action was politically motivated, overruled Walet's objection and, with the backing of the entire faculty, issued an ultimatum: the school board must "accept Mr. Walet's or [their] individual resignations...."[56] After a cursory examination of the incident, the school board accepted faculty's resignations.

Public reaction to the school board's decision was so negative that it drew the attention of Governor Jared Young Sanders. In mid-June, Sanders, acting through the state board of education, ordered wholesale resignations for the Iberia Parish School Board, the parish superintendent of schools, and the appointment of a replacement parish board. The elected board, however, contested their removal in the state courts, and thus until a favorable judicial decision in late September, the Iberia Parish school system was governed by rival boards, both of which lacked operating funds because of the lawsuit.[57]

---

54. *Louisiana Reporter*, CXXIII, 737-38.

55. *Weekly Iberian*, May 1, 8, 1909.

56. *Ibid.*, May 8, 1909.

57. The elected board consisted of Dr. Paul N. Cyr, John D. Walet, L. L. Gonsoulin, Eugene Guillot, H. H. Minvielle, A. C. Duboin, Dr. U. M. Perret, and Edward LeBlanc.

The controversy proved to be only a temporary obstacle to the continued development of New Iberia's schools. By 1920, for example, Central High School, directed by Principal Charles M. Bahon since 1913, had progressed sufficiently to merit accreditation by the Southern Association of Colleges and Secondary Schools. Moreover, in the early 1920s, the high school abandoned the classical curriculum under which it had operated in favor of more flexible modern curricula which permitted students to specialize in college preparatory, commercial, and home economics courses.[58] The trend toward modernization of education in the early twentieth century was also manifested in the establishment of a high school football team in 1904, a horse-drawn bus system in 1907, a school newspaper in 1914, and the construction of a large, modern high school on Center Street in 1922.[59]

The city's primary schools experienced similar growth and modernization. In May, 1903, the *Weekly Iberian* complained that the number of urban students had grown to 820, a number far exceeding the capacity of the existing primary facilities. The editor therefore urged the school board to construct "fitting" schoolhouses. This wish was realized in 1907 when new facilities were constructed on opposite ends of Main Street. Nevertheless, by 1911, the city's primary schools--Magnolia, Julia, Madison, Live Oak, and a black school--were "nearly filled to capacity."[60]

The public's growing interest in education, which manifested itself in the rapid development of New Iberia's school system in the early twentieth century, fostered renewed interest in the town's private schools. At the beginning of the century, for example, the Fasnacht Graded and Mt. Carmel schools--the city's remaining private institutions--witnessed a growth in enrollment. Moreover, in

---

The state-appointed board included C. D. Guidry, Guy A. Shaw, Adolphe Romero, E. T. Weeks, M. Delcambre, Dr. M. B. Tarleton, St. Paul Bourgeois, George L. Fisk, and Dr. H. A. King. *Ibid.*, June 26, August 13, 1909.

58. Mestayer, "New Iberia High School," pp. 26, 27.

59. Construction of the new secondary school was dictated by swelling enrollment after the institution of compulsory education in 1916, as well as stringent building codes adopted by the state board of education in 1921. *Ibid.*, pp. 27-34. When founded, the bus system consisted of two horse-drawn wagons.

60. *Weekly Iberian*, May 2, 1903, May 16, 1911.

Graduating Class, Central High School, 1906
Seated (from left): Gladys Mattes, Eunice Riggs, Lester Cregs, Lily Marin, Standing (from left), Louise Taylor, Richard Eckart, Leon Marie, Eula Taylor, Stella Decuir, Cassie Pollard, Lucy Gebert, and Lizzie Taylor.

early September, 1918,[61] St. Peter's College (present-day Catholic High School) was founded by Mgsr. J. M. Langlois and staffed by a party of Christian Brothers who were refugees from revolutionary Mexico. St. Edward's School for blacks, a coeducational institution founded by the Sisters of the Blessed Sacrament, also opened its doors in 1918. The growth of St. Peter's College was especially dramatic. By 1943, for example, the student body had grown to nearly three hundred students,[62] and the institution boasted a 2,000-volume library and a

---

61. The College, however, was not officially dedicated until May, 1919. *Enterprise*, May 17, 1919.

62. *Ibid.*, September 9, 1943.

bus system which served rural students residing between St. Martinville and New Iberia.[63]

Similar growth was recorded by the public high school. In 1939, for example, two large, two-story additions to the school, the Charles M. Bahon Gymnasium, a band room, and a home economics cottage were constructed on the high school grounds by the Public Works Administration.[64] Ten years later, a 4,400-seat football stadium was built at a cost of $100,000.[65] The growth of the high school's physical plant reflected the expansion of its student body, library and curriculum. The student body, for example, grew from 351 in 1935 to 677 in 1951, and to 1,030 in 1956.[66] A music department was established in 1937, an industrial arts department in 1939, and a physical education department in 1940.[67] Finally, the library, the oldest high school library in Louisiana,[68] grew from "several hundred books" in 1895 to 3,420 volumes in 1950.[69]

New Iberia's drive for educational excellence reached a new plateau in the mid-1960s with the construction of the present high school and the city's attempt to secure the freshman division of the University of Southwestern Louisiana. The roots of New Iberia's interest in higher education can be traced to 1898, when Act 162 of the general assembly created the Southwestern Louisiana Industrial Institute. Under the terms of the measure, the school would be located "in the parish of the 13th Senatorial District which will offer the best inducement therefore to the Board of Trustees, . . . provided that the parish selected for the location of the said Institution shall donate not less than twenty-

---

63. *Ibid.*

64. From 1932 to 1939, the home economics department was housed in the former Nicholas Delcambre home. Mestayer, "New Iberia High School," pp. 40-41.

65. *Daily Iberian*, September 28, 1950.

66. *Ibid.*, September 6, 1951, September 18, 1956. Mestayer, "New Iberia High School," p. 40.

67. Mestayer, "New Iberia High School," pp. 37-38.

68. The library was founded in 1892. *Weekly Iberian*, December 7, 1895. Mestayer, "New Iberia High School," p. 40.

69. *Ibid.*

The First Three Male Graduates of Central High School
As They Appeared in Later Life
From left: Porteus Burke (attorney), Walter Carstens (physician) and Eugene Guillot (architect-builder)

five acres of land and Five Thousand Dollars to said Institution."[70] The campaign to bring the newly established college to New Iberia originated at a public meeting held in early March 1899, at James A. Lee's Drug Store. In a subsequent assembly at city hall, the college proponents established the New Iberia Industrial School Association and elected the following officers: James A. Lee, chairman; P. L. Renoudet, secretary; William R. Burke, treasurer; the Reverend C. C. Kramer, Nicholas Muller, J. B. Lawton, John Broussard, Lazard Kling, and Jules Dreyfus, board members. The meeting concluded with a call for subscriptions which netted $9,000 for the Association.[71]

70. *Acts of the General Assembly of the State of Louisiana* (Baton Rouge, 1898), p. 317.

71. *Weekly Iberia,* March 25, 1899.

The New Iberia meeting launched a bidding war among the rival college sites--St. Martinville, Lafayette, and Scott. Thus, in order to make New Iberia's offer more attractive, fifteen businessmen appointed by the mayor and working in cooperation with the town council and the Industrial School Association recommended in late July "a five-mill tax for the school."[72] The businessmen's decision and the subsequent rally on behalf of the bond proposal were for naught, for no one would donate the necessary acreage, and thus the college was awarded to Lafayette.

Although New Iberia had failed to secure the college, the city retained a high level of interest in the institution, and that spark of interest burst into flame in the spring of 1965 when the United States Navy announced the closure of New Iberia Naval Air Station. As the Navy sought to convert the base to civilian use, New Iberia representatives persuaded President Joel Fletcher of the University of Southwestern Louisiana to use the military facilities, including dormitories and cafeterias, as an "Educational Center," or freshman division. As a means of securing the property, the State Board of Education adopted a resolution establishing a New Iberia branch of the university, and, on the basis of this action, the federal Division of Surplus Property Utilization transferred the 1,400-acre base to the State Board.[73]

The establishment of the Educational Center elicited a tremendous outcry from Lafayette merchants who insisted that the transfer of students would result in declining profits. Eleven businessmen thus sought and secured an injunction in district court, preventing the State Board from establishing the New Iberia branch. The State Board appealed the district court decision, but, in January, 1967, the Louisiana Supreme Court upheld the lower court's ruling on the ground that the Board had violated Article IV, Section 14, of the 1921 state constitution which provided that "no educational . . . institution . . . shall be established by the State, except upon a vote of two-thirds of the members elected to each house of the legislature."[74] As a result of the supreme court decision, on March 24, 1967, Sam G. Wynn, regional representative of the Division of Surplus Property Utilization, notified Dr. Clyde Rougeou, Fletcher's

---

72. *Ibid.*, July 22, 1899.

73. Transcript of *Howard Charles Melancon et al.* vs. *State Board of Education*, USL Papers, Clyde Lee Rougeou Papers, Collection 1A, Box 356, folder h, Southwester Archives, USL. Hereafter cited as Clyde Rougeou Papers.

74. *Ibid.*

successor as president of USL, that the consent agreement permitting the university to use the former New Iberia base was "cancelled."[75]

The loss of the branch campus was partially offset by the construction of the present high school in 1966. New Iberia Senior High School, an impressive brown-brick structure designed by Perry Segura, a local architect, and built by Southern Builders at a cost of $3,500,000,[76] is located on Admiral Doyle Drive at Jefferson Terrace. Senior High houses grades 10 to 12 and boasts an enrollment of 2301 (1983).[77] The student population, which has declined slightly (3 %) in recent years because of the depressed local economy and the resulting emigration of many transient oil workers, is drawn from New Iberia Freshman High School, which served as the black high school from the time of its construction in 1966 until the court-ordered desegregation of the city's public schools in 1969; New Iberia Middle and Anderson Street schools; and ultimately from the thirteen primary schools.[78]

As with Senior High, the student bodies at the Catholic secondary schools--Mt. Carmel and Catholic High (established in 1957)[79]--have remained stable over the past decade as a result of rising tuition costs and the downturn in the oil economy. While the number of students has remained fairly constant, the cost of operating these schools has increased through inflation and the growing dependence of these Catholic facilities upon lay faculties whose salaries have recently become more competitive with their public school counterparts. The resulting fiscal crisis has caused the Catholic school board to suggest the consolidation of the high schools and St. Edward's Elementary School into a unitary system.

The economic realities of the mid-1980s have also caused a reassessment of the value of education by the general population. During the oil boom of the late 1970s and early 1980s, popular appreciation for education reached its

---

75. Sam G. Wynn to Clyde Rougeou, March 24, 1967, Clyde Rougeou Papers.

76. Interview with George Crowson, assistant superintendent of Iberia Parish public schools, October 10, 1978.

77. Interview with Murle McClelland, principal of New Iberia Senior High School, October 10, 1978.

78. *Ibid.*

79. *Daily Iberian,* November 20, 1956.

The Senior and Junior Classes of St. Peter's College, 1922
Bottom row (from left): Walter Walet, George Lambremont, Allen Broussard, James Markey, and Anthony Muller. Middle row (from left): Anthony Landry, Bertrand Robin, Brother Arcenius, FSC, Msgr. J. M. Langlois, Brother Eugene, FSC, Wilfred Conrad, Sr., and J. D. Broussard. Top row (from left), Dick Landry, Alfred Hitter, Sr., Fred Louviere, Paul Minvielle, Carroll Martin, Antoine Moresi, Drilhet Johnstone, Sidney Lassalle, Sr., and Louis Broussard.

nadir, for it was common knowledge that high school dropouts with minimum oil-related skills could earn considerably more than their high school principals. Such employment opportunities have vanished, and the job openings that remained have generally required far greater levels of education. Changing attitudes toward education have resulted not only in a sudden outcry for educational excellence, but also greater parental involvement in, and support of, their local schools. This is seen perhaps most clearly in the vacillating popular attitudes toward the recent (1985) bond proposal (approximately $50 million) for refurbishing existing schools, the renovation of the middle school for use as administrative offices, and construction of a new middle school in New Iberia. In 1984, the proposal was soundly defeated; yet, only months later, in the midst of a severe economic downturn, the same proposal was approved. Though improved physical plants alone will do nothing to improve education in New Iberia, the growing grassroots appreciation of, and demand for, educational reform augur well for the future of the community, for, in the words of Diogenes, "the foundation of every state is the education of its youth."

NINETEENTH-CENTURY SCHOOLS

SCHOOL	LOCATION	FACULTY	YEARS
(Name unknown)	(Unknown)	Gibbs, Bully	1847-(1861?)
(Name unknown)	(Unknown)	Felix Goryon	(1850?)
(Name unknown)	(Unknown)	Laurent Plauchin	(1850?)
(Name unknown)	(Unknown)	Victorin Renoudet	?-1860
(Name unknown)	(Unknown)	W. C. White	?-1860
(Name unknown)	(Unknown)	Hebe Soulier	?-1860
(Name unknown)	(Unknown)	Reed Funt	?-1860
(Name unknown)	(Unknown)	A. Cook	?-1860
Bryant School	Main at Swain	Mrs. Martin Bryant Mrs. Léonce de la Croix Mrs. Emile Soulier	1861-?

80. *Ibid.*, August 22, 26, 1957.

Story of Education   403

School	Location	Teachers	Dates
De René School	Present courthouse site	Mrs. de René Alphonsine de René Mrs. Martin Bryant Mrs. Soulier Henrietta Andrus Professor Müller	(1862?)-1867
Howe Institute	Ditto		1867-1939
Bryant School	(Unknown)	Mrs. Martin Bryant	1868-1890
Isabel School	Courthouse site	R. S. Isabel	(1868?)-?
Lydon School	Odd Fellows? Hall	P.O. Lydon	(1868?)-?
Balch School	Main Street	Judge Thomas Balch	(1868?)-?
Mt. Carmel	Bridge Street		1870-present
St. Paul and Webster schools	West Main and Iberia Street	J. R. Freeman (1875) Mrs. Slaughter (1875) Mollie Hartman L. O. Hacker (1878) Mrs. S. Montagne (1878) Mrs. Rand (1880) Mrs. Hacker (1880)	1870-1882
Attakapas Commercial and Industrial College	East Main Street	Father Bernier Brother Agatho	1872-1873
Holy Cross College (St. Peter's Academy)	East Main St.	Father Beaubien M. Moore (1875) Robert Moise (1875) H. Parmentier (1878) M. Fullon (1878) Blanc Duquesnay (1881)	1873-?
Delacroix School	Main St.	Mrs. T. F. Delacroix	1873
Lagarde School	Washington and Julia streets	Pierre Lagarde	1873-1875
Freeman School	St. Peter Street	J. R. Freeman	1873
Lee School	Live Oak Hotel West Main St.	Althea Lee	1874

SCHOOL	LOCATION	FACULTY	YEARS
White School	(Unknown)	Rev. B. F. White	1874
Black School	(Unknown)	Miss Wakefield	1875-?
Black School	(Unknown)	E. Moore	1875-?
Richardson School	(Unknown)	Mrs. Jos. Caracas	1877
Rand School	Bridge Street	Mrs. I. T. Rand Mary Rand	1877
Blend's Night School	(Unknown)	Wellington Blend	1877-1878
Judice School	E. St. Peter St.	Alcée Judice	1878-1879
Black School	(French St.?)	Laura Mobley Martha Mobley	1878
Judice Night School	Weeks St.	Alcée Judice	1879
New Iberia	Odd Fellows' Hall East Main St.	Wellington Blend Maggie Ker Rev. W. A. Hall Louis Chaubet	1879-1880
Attakapas Male Institute	Odd Fellows' Hall East Main St.	W. W. Hunter	1881
Farley School	(Unknown)	S. A. Farley	1881
Julia Street School	Julia Street	Mrs. C. Montagne	1882-1898
Live Oak School	West Main	Katie Terrell (1905)	1882-?
Maidson School	Madison St.	E. V. Peale (1905) Deborah Doan (1905)	1882-?
Rust School	(Unknown)	F. P. Rust	1885
Pedoussant School	Main St.	Mme Pedoussant	1885
New Iberia High	Julia Street		1887-1926
Central High	St. Peter & Weeks		1892-1926
Fasnacht Institute	St. Peter St.	Mary Louise Fasnacht	1892-1926

NEW IBERIA SCHOOLS
(1983)

Primary Schools

SCHOOL	PRINCIPAL
Bank Avenue	Lloyd Boseman
Center Street	Angus Cobb, Jr.
Dodson Street	Sidney J. Leger
Hopkins Street	Sheldon Landry
Iberia Parish Special Services Center	Ellis Hargrave
Johnston Street	Barbara Boudreaux
Lee Street	Ronald Bienvenu
Live Oak	J. Curley Mouton
Magnolia	Norris Meaux
North Lewis St.	Robert Benoit
North Street	Patrick LeBlanc
Park	James Russell, Jr.
Pesson Addition	Willie Mae Jefferson

Junior High Schools

Anderson Street	Herman James
New Iberia Middle	Edward Broussard, Jr.

Secondary

New Iberia Freshman High	Verge Ausberry
New Iberia Senior High	Murle McClelland

Parochial

Catholic High	Bro. Bernard Boleto
Mt. Carmel High	Sister Rose Marie Penouilh
St. Edward's School	Sister Alice Marie Harkins

XXIII

Retrospections on New Iberia in the Twenties and Thirties

An Interview with
Gertrude C. Taylor and John Holbrook, Jr.

Interviewer's Note: This interview took place on the afternoon of October 26, 1978, at the home of Mr. and Mrs. Paul E. Taylor. Mrs. Taylor and Mr. Holbrook were born and reared in New Iberia and both have a keen faculty for remembering events of the past. Rather than interview them separately, the interviewer felt that a joint interview would probably be more rewarding. His feeling proved to be a fact. The interviewees are recalling, for the most part, events of the 1920s and 1930s. The interviewer was Glenn R. Conrad.

INTERVIEWER: Let's begin our interview this afternoon with some of your earliest recollections.

GERTRUDE: I guess I come from a family of people who have good memories because I can remember things which occurred when I was very young. I remember well the anguish I felt when I learned that my father might have to go to war [World War I]. I was barely four years old at the time, but the thought of him leaving greatly upset me and left an indelible impression upon me.

The Twenties and Thirties

Then, I remember the armistice. In New Iberia on Armistice Day [November 11, 1918] there were bells ringing and whistles blowing. There was a general jubilation which made a distinct impression on me. The popular reaction to the armistice was different from the popular response to the end of World War II. The only way we had any information concerning what was happening with regard to the armistice had to come over the wire [telegraph], and, therefore, there was no preparation, so to speak, for this particular event. On the other hand, in August, 1945, we knew for several days before that the Japanese surrender was imminent.

I think there was much less personal demonstration in 1918 than there was in 1945. I don't think, for example, that as many people left home to go downtown as did in 1945. It was more of a personal thing. But, too, it must be remembered that the armistice came just about the time the horrible influenza epidemic of 1918 was ending.

After the war came Prohibition. I remember the way Prohibition affected some people. It affected others differently. For example, my father, who was not a drinking man but who would occasionally take a drink, came home one day with several large, square, long-necked bottles of whiskey that he stashed away "for medicinal purposes." So, here was my father, a non-drinker, but also an opponent of Prohibition, now bringing home several bottles of whiskey, heretofore a rarity in our home. By the way, that cache sufficed for the era of Prohibition.

Anyway, with Prohibition came the "Roaring Twenties." I can remember the older people remarking about the effect Prohibition would have on the soldiers returning from Europe, and especially France where drinking was a part of life. When they got back, they sparked the changes of the Flapper Era.

JOHNNY: They surely did. I remember that Norma Siebeck was one of the first women in New Iberia to cut her hair in the new fashion. The style of cut was called the "Panjola." Some Hollywood movie star had introduced the fashion on the screen. After that women regularly went to the barber shop to get their hair cut--there were no beauty parlors, of course. Mr. Hebert was one of the best barbers for women in New Iberia.

INTERVIEWER: The twenties and thirties were part of the dance era, do you recall some of the favorite dance spots?

GERTRUDE: The pavilion in City Park was built early in the 20s. That was a real attraction. There was also the pavilion at Charenton. There were dances every weekend in Charenton. The Elks Club also sponsored dances at the Alma House. These were favorites for young men like Harold Dietlein, Dick Landry and Jules Courtois.

JOHNNY: Later in the 1930s the Elks dances were held in the Gouguenheim Building [corner of Iberia and West Main]. The dances were held upstairs, inside and out on the galleries. The young people in those days didn't have automobiles, so whenever there was a dance at the Elks you could see couples walking down Main Street or coming up the side streets. Everyone went formally dressed.

A real tradition that grew up with these dances was to go to the American Cafe--Coleman's--after the dance and get a nickel slice of pie and a glass of milk. They baked their pies during the night, and about 2 a.m. the pies were taken out of the oven and were served piping hot. After this snack, the boy would walk his date home.

Another dance spot of the time was the Evangeline Club on the St. Martinville Road, about one-half mile beyond the parish line.

INTERVIEWER: Tell me about the City Park pavilion.

GERTRUDE: The City Park pavilion had two rows of benches on three sides of the pavilion. The pavilion's sides were made of chicken wire. The roof was supported by tree trunks that had been cut. The bandstand was in one corner.

JOHNNY: Remember, too, that some of the supports for that building were live oak trees. The oaks covered the top of the building.

GERTRUDE: Oh yes, I used to climb atop the building. There were really two roofs. There was a gabled roof and a flat roof. Between the two was a space that we used as a crawl space. Climbing up on the roof of the building was a small town pre-teenager's pastime. On a Saturday we'd pack a lunch (two or three other girls and myself), go to the park, climb onto the roof of the pavilion and spend most of the day up there. What could be simpler entertainment than that? Of course, as I said, I was then only a preteenager.

Later, my tastes in entertainment changed. You know Johnny, many of the trees in the park in those days are now gone.

JOHNNY: Yes, we lost many trees when the pavilion was set afire. Three times in one day it was set ablaze and burned flat. I was in the ninth grade, and we watched the entire fire from St. Peter's College. That must have been about 1933 or 1934.

INTERVIEWER: Tell me about bootlegging.

GERTRUDE: I don't know how much bootlegging was going on, but I can remember people talking about the liquor coming in from boats off the coast. But no one seemed to make a great deal over the fact.

INTERVIEWER: Let's move along to other forms of entertainment. Tell me about the Elks Theater.

GERTRUDE: The Elks Theater was an important factor in my early life. It had a lot of meaning to an impressionistic child. It was there, of course, that I saw my first movie.

JOHNNY: Yes, Mr. Scharff bought the place in 1919 and introduced movies into the building. Prior to that it was strictly a theatrical house.

GERTRUDE: There were some excellent road shows that came to the Elks.

JOHNNY: One of the big things in my mother's life occurred when the Sedgwicks came to New Iberia. Irene Sedgwick became ill, and Mama replaced her for one night. She learned the entire role in one day's time.

GERTRUDE: I remember the Sedgwick players coming to New Iberia. The road shows would come to New Iberia on an irregular basis, and . . .

JOHNNY: But any Broadway road show that played New Orleans usually played the Elks Theater on its way to Texas. Most of the time it was a two-or-three-night stand. They would come into town on a special train. All of the scenery, costumes, props, stage crew, actors, and others would come in on the train.

The Elks Theatre, 1910 (above); 1920 (below).

GERTRUDE: The theater had a double-door opening on Fisher Street, and a truck could back right up and unload scenery, or whatever, right into the stage area.

The dressing rooms were beneath the stage and there were also dressing rooms behind the box seats on either side of the stage. It was really a fascinating building.

JOHNNY: The stage was considered to be the finest in the South with the exception of a theater in Atlanta. There were traps all over the stage. One of the greatest things I saw there was a magician, probably Blackstone, who made a horse disappear on stage. He had this tent that was put up in the center of the stage. He had people from the audience come up on stage and encircle the tent. The magician then brought on stage this large white Arabian, put the horse into the tent, stood off, shot a pistol, opened the tent, and the horse was gone. Two weeks later, I made a point of getting up on that stage to see just where the trap was located. Sure enough, there it was, right in the middle of the stage. The horse had been lowered into the area under the stage. That stage was so fully equipped that any magician would have been happy to perform on it.

There was another popular pastime in New Iberia in the '20s and '30s, and that was prizefighting. This was popular from about 1928 to about 1932. "Ayma" Rodrigue was a promoter. The ring was on Iberia Street in the area where Carroll's Studio is today and Dauterive's Furniture Store was later in the '30s. Vince Palestina refereed most of the fights. Bobby Sage (Baron Gray) and Daniel Mestayer were two of the fighters. The only way I could get to see the fights was to sell popcorn and red pop.

GERTRUDE: Johnny mentioned the dearth of automobiles in New Iberia. Automobiles were something new and daring at the time. Well, my father had a Model T when I was quite small, and Papa would drive that from our home on Duperier Avenue and later Charles Street to his rice mill on Ann Street. But, to give you some idea of the generation gap existing then, his father, who also lived on Duperier Avenue, would go about in a buggy-- never dreaming of owning a car.

By 1924 I finally convinced my father to let me sit on his lap while we were out driving, and in a short time I was driving the car. One day, when I was eleven years old, my mother decided she wanted to go somewhere, but she could not drive. So, I proudly announced that I would drive her wherever she wanted to go. From that day to this I have been driving. My point is that it was relatively safe for an eleven-year-old to drive then, there were so few cars.

Our pastime with the automobile was driving from the old post office to the Episcopal church or to Railroad Avenue. There, we would make a U-turn in the street and go back to the post office, repeating the exercise several times on any given afternoon. This was over the bricked portion of Main Street.

That, incidentally, I also remember. I can remember standing in front of what is Abdalla's today and watching a black mason setting the bricks in place.

JOHNNY: He laid every brick on that street by himself. He said he didn't want help because he wanted to make sure the bricks were properly aligned.

GERTRUDE: The bricks were beautifully laid.

JOHNNY: The brick street is still there and quite usable, if the city would remove all that stuff on top of the bricks.

It seems to me that the bricks were laid about 1918 or 1919. They didn't put the bricks down until the streetcar tracks were pulled up.

INTERVIEWER: Speaking of the twenties, was there any Ku Klux Klan activity in the New Iberia area?

GERTRUDE: The real push for any Klan activity in the New Iberia area, it seems to me, came from the area west of Lafayette. The goals, or objectives, of the Klan then were a lot different from what they are today. At that time, at least in this area, the major thrust of the Klan was religious--that is stirring up religious dissension. That was the first and only time that I was aware of any religious friction in New Iberia. It affected Protestants and Catholics alike and had no place in our community.

The Klan tried to capitalize on this brief period of sectarian misunderstanding and announced that they would stage a parade down Main Street. Well, almost immediately those who strongly opposed the Klan announced that if the group appeared in town there would be confrontation. Well, plans were made by the townspeople. The signal for the approach of the

The Twenties and Thirties

Klan was to be the sounding of the old fire whistle. So everyone was waiting, and early one night, it must have been in the spring of 1922, we were outside when the whistle began to blow.

Everyone seemed to rush into the street. The men began to gather and probably would have headed toward Main Street had not word come that the blast was not a signal of the approaching Klan, but that it was a call for the militia to assemble in order to help fight a break on the levee along the Mississippi River.

That was the first and only brush that New Iberia had with the Klan. After that, religious harmony returned to the town, and I can well remember Protestants and Catholics cooperating thereafter, and down to the present, on various projects.

JOHNNY: Indeed, I can still remember people like James and Alonzo Hall helping out with the church fairs that were staged at St. Peter's College. As for myself, I practically grew up in the Episcopal rectory. I went out with Reverend Digg's daughters, and we all had a great time.

INTERVIEWER: What was shopping like in the twenties and thirties?

JOHNNY: Paÿ's Store on the corner of Weeks and Pershing streets was where we shopped for groceries. I liked to go to the store for Mama because Mr. Paÿ always gave lagniappe--a handful of jelly beans. It was always a fight among us kids to see who would go to the store. No one had to be coaxed to run down the street to the store.

GERTRUDE: We did a lot of shopping at Disch's Store. But the main shopping area of town was, of course, the area between Weeks and Jefferson streets.

JOHNNY: Right, I would regularly hit Main Street at the corner of Julia. The New Iberia National Bank was on the corner. Next to it was The Globe Store, then Estorge Drug Company, State National Bank, Daigre's Store, and finally Dallas Jewelry Store on the corner of Church Alley. On the west side of Church Alley was Jake Weil's store, The Hub. Then came Schwing and Carstens, a marvelous store.

After that was Ackal's. The Model was next and then came Creim's and Bowab's. Before the Bowabs took that building on the corner of

Iberia and Main streets, however, it was a confectionary run by a Greek family. Before that, of course, it was Lee's Drug Store.

GERTRUDE: Ackal's was where it is now back in 1927, and the reason I recall that is because of some research I've recently done on the flood of that year. Ackal's was the only store advertising at that time which is still at the same location. Rivière's was advertising, but they've since moved.

JOHNNY: Across Iberia Street was Hugonin's Pool Hall. Then came my father's barber shop. My summer job for many summers was sweeping my father's barber shop and then I'd go next door to Hugonin's to rack the pool balls and clean the slates. The next business was the New Iberia Hardware Company. There was another building between the hardware and Pfister's Jewelry Co., but I don't remember what was there. Later, during World War II, Ben Franklin's was there. Then came Pfisters' and after that Sidney Harry's store. Beyond Harry's was Theriot's Liquor Store and then People's National Bank.

It was in the next building that the Knights of Pythias met. Then there was another building--Henri Blanchet had a shop there in the early '20s--before you reached Kahn's Pharmacy. Next to Kahn's was Joe Bourg's tailor shop, and then came Dr. Bertrand's office. After that was Abe Hirch's store and the *Enterprise* print shop. Beyond it was the S.O.S. Cafe. Then came the building which for many years was occupied by Handleman's Department Store, but I do not remember what was there before Handleman's. Finally, there was Taylor's Drug Store on the corner of French and Main streets. Crossing French the building on the corner was there a long time before it housed The Specialty Store.

GERTRUDE: Next to The Specialty Store was a divided building with Trahan's Barber Shop and Rivière's Jewlery in it. Then came the driveway leading to the Frederic Hotel parkling lot. Then came the hotel, and for many years the Western Union office was located on the east corner of the first floor of the hotel. Then there was a large vacant lot, with billboards in it. The Plaisance home came next, where the city parking lot is now. Then came

Joe Davis' Chevrolet dealership. Later, Hawley Gary had the Dodge agency there. Then came the King house and you had reached Jefferson Street.

JOHNNY: Across Main Street, on the bayou side, and moving back toward the downtown area was the home of Mary Handley. Then there was a vacant lot before you came to "Crip" Ribbeck's little cottage. He was married to Mildred Malloy. After that were two small places, one a cafe and the other Mr. Sam Cancilla's shoe shop.

Next to Cancilla's was a two-story building (until recently Steinberg's Fur Shop). In the upstairs area was the telephone company and below was the *Weekly Iberian*.

GERTRUDE: Next came the Alma House, or as some knew it, the Olivier Building. Next to it was the Iberia Steam Laundry, and next to the laundry was Jennaro's Printing Shop. Then came the Max Mattes house which was on the corner. It was torn down just before the flood of 1927. The house was built but a few feet from the sidewalk.

Down Swain Street was the ice house and a number of warehouses.

Across Swain Street was an automobile repair shop and then Mc-Mahon's and later Dauterive's Furniture Company. Next to it was a small wooden building that housed Villermin Electric Company. Between Villermin's and Dauterive's were billboards and between Villermin's and the Elks Theatre were billboards. Across Fisher Street from the Elks was the Eureka Hotel. After the Eureka burned in 1931, Walker's Sinclair Station was built there. Then came the courthouse, the city market and the city hall, followed by two two-story buildings. The one nearest the city hall was known as the Emmer Building.

JOHNNY: Yes, and in those days people could do things that can't be done today. In order to get sufficient light for his dental chair, Dr. Emmer built a little room out from the facade of the second story of the building. It was supported by posts that ran down to the sidewalk.

Then, there was the saloon kept by Sam Broody, and on the corner was the Queen City Pool Hall.

GERTRUDE: I don't think that we should continue without mentioning Joe Glorioso's Oyster Palace. That was, for me, one of the truly great places in New Iberia. On Saturday night in the wintertime, my family would often go there for oysters. It was one of the big attractions of the town. The Gloriosos were wonderful people. They had the best oyster loaf made. For a time, I believe, Glorioso had his restaurant on the corner where the pool hall was later. From the corner the restaurant moved to the house further down the block.

There is a legend that there was a tunnel under the bayou, running from the old building that was located where Joe Glorioso's house was later located to the Convent. But the story has never been clear.

On the corner of Iberia and East Main was Octave Renoudet's hardware store. It ran (and still does) the full length of the block. Then there was a succession of small stores, among which were located I. A. Martin's photo studio (in the '30s) and Coleman's Cafe. Jacquemoud's Funeral Home was in that block.

Then came Provost's Cafe and Trahan's Grocery Store on the corner of Main and Bridge. Across Bridge, going eastward, was Kling's Department Store, then The Specialty Store which later became the Palace Theatre. Next to the Palace was Dreyfus' Wholesale, but it went out early in the twenties, before The Specialty Store was there. Later, the remaining part of the Dreyfus Wholesale building became the Evangeline Theater and Sports Center. On the corner was Mrs. Scharff's shop. Then the Masonic Temple Building and the empty lot. Nick Fritella had a shoe shop next and then the New Iberia Plumbing Company. Then came Brooks' Stable.

JOHNNY: Yes, in the thirties Mr. Brooks enclosed a part of the stable and my father had his barber shop there.

GERTRUDE: Next was the Ford garage which was on the corner of Weeks and Main. Across the street, where the People's Bank is now was a vacant lot in the twenties. There was, however, a little house where Charles Street dead-ends into Weeks. This was torn down when the Schwings built their home. There were then billboards that went around the corner of Main and Weeks. We would go downtown from where I lived on Charles Street, use a path that cut through the lot and come out on the side of the little building that was I. A. Martin's studio. Before that it had been Bouligny's studio.

Mama had all our baby pictures and "growing-up" pictures taken in that little room. I remember that he had something like a bay window, or more like a picture window, which was the source of the photographer's light. This was later the site of Drago's Tailor Shop.

The changing face of downtown New Iberia is reflected in the Murray Building and law offices as they appeared in March 1972 (above). Below the enlarged law offices of Landry, Watkins, and Bonin (January 1986).

Next going up Main Street was the Bazus Hotel. On the first floor was Betar's Cafe. Then there was a Piggly Wiggly store. That reminds me, we forgot to mention that the A. & P. store was located in one-half of the first floor of the Masonic Temple Building. It occupied the area where J. Patout Burns' Firestone Store is today. Next to it, on the alley side, was the Railway Express office.

JOHNNY: Getting back to the other side of the street, in that block, probably across the street from the Masonic Temple, was Mrs. Ida Cheatham's haberdashery. The thing I remember most about Mrs. Cheatham was the time she decided to show her hats on live models in the windows of her store. This caused a massive traffic jam on Main Street for two days, maybe a week. Imagine, this was in the twenties, and this lady had the idea of using live models. It was a terrific gimmick because practically everyone in town was in front of her store from 8 o'clock onward to see who would be modeling hats. She asked all her best customers to model. I remember seeing the Burke girls in the window.

The Bazus Building
Probably one of the oldest extant buildings on Main Street

The Twenties and Thirties

GERTRUDE: In that building there was also a drug store for a while. Then Warren Mestayer, Sr., had a pressing shop there.

JOHNNY: Yes, my father's barber shop was also in that building for a time.

GERTRUDE: Also, remember that Mr. Henry Gulotta had a shoe shop there. At one time the Kyle Motor Car Company was on the corner of Main and Julia. That was in the twenties. Then "Lolo" Minvielle opened a grocery store there. That was also in the twenties. Kyle was there until about 1926, and then they moved to Lafayette. After the grocery store, a bar occupied the building.

The building has an interesting legend attached to it. Before Kyle Motors was there, E. J. Carstens (the elder) had a seed business there, and, before that, probably before the turn of the century, the building had housed a saloon. The story goes that when Kyle Motor Car Company moved in, they pulled up the wood flooring and excavated to lay concrete and they found a skeleton. The presumption was that the person had been there since the days of the saloon.

Well, anyway, that completes our circuit of Main Street in the twenties and thirties. I'm sure we've overlooked some businesses because then, as now, businesses started up, lasted a few years, and then closed. It is hard to remember them all.

Before leaving this discussion, however, I do want to mention the Estorge Drug Company's fire which occurred one afternoon in December 1919 or January 1920. It was bitterly cold, and the water that ran off from the firemen's attempt to put out the fire froze, forming large icicles. The fire was mainly on the second floor.

INTERVIEWER: What was on the second floor of that building?

JOHNNY: Mainly doctors' offices. Dr. Sabatier had his office there. So did Dr. Carstens. Drs. Gayle and Shaw also had their offices in that building.

INTERVIEWER: Well, let's move now to your impressions of the flood of 1927.

JOHNNY: Oh, for me as a child, I had so much fun I looked forward to another flood.

GERTRUDE: It was the most awesome thing I've ever seen. My father was extremely curious about the approaching flood, so we went to the levee at Henderson to see the break and the water rushing through it. Each day we would go a shorter distance as the water approached. My father sent trucks to help in the evacuation of people from the Loreauville area.

JOHNNY: The water had risen in the bayou, but had not reached flood stage. Then, one morning we went out and the situation was rapidly changing. In those days we had plank sidewalks and the ditches, about twenty-four inches deep, were lined with boards. They were really wooden gutters. So, we stood there and on this particular morning and watched the water rise in the gutters and then eventually spill over. It was not too long before the wooden sidewalks began to float.

Later, after the flood had arrived, Mama put on her swimming suit, one of those affairs with the skirt on it and her black stockings and swimming shoes and waded through the water to the stores on Main Street. Everything on Main Street stayed open. My father, however, panicked and bought case upon case of pork 'n beans, boxes of crackers and that sort of food, which we then had to eat for eons afterward.

GERTRUDE: Well, we ate chicken stew for a comparable time. We had to evacuate my aunt and uncle from their home at the end of Duperier Avenue. We went in a motor boat to get them. The boat was parked at St. Peter's College and we got to it by flatboat. I still have a picture of William Conrad, Wilfred Conrad, Uncle John, Wilfred's father, taken in the flatboat in front of Maurice Lemaire's house on Bank Avenue. We had a boat tied at the front steps of the Brothers' home. We'd board there and then go out the back, get into the regular channel of the bayou and go wherever we wanted. This time we followed the bayou all the way around to near the end of Duperier Avenue. Well, we brought the flatboat to evacuate their furniture and clothing. So we get them all loaded up and are about to leave when my aunt appears with a coup of chickens. Well, here we were at our home in mid-town, water all around us; where were we going to put the chickens? We couldn't do with the chickens what Dr. Emmer had done with his cow, which was to put it on his front porch. Our front porch was already cluttered with yard items and other things that had to be kept out of the water. So, my aunt decided the chickens had to go--their necks were wrung, they were plucked, and a cauldron of chicken stew resulted. It seemed to me like that pot was bottomless.

At the time of the flood, my father was on the town council, and one night he received a phone call and was told that Spanish Lake had filled and was beginning to overflow; that the water was entering town from behind Lallande's Store on Jane Street. From there it flowed approximately between La Salle and North streets until it hit the Southern Pacific railroad bed. That effectively blocked its passage further south, so the water turned eastward and began to flow into town from the west side.

The water came so swiftly that many people had not evacuated from the area of Jane, North and Fulton streets, and the fire department and members of the town council had to go out during the night and help these people get out.

My father returned home about 6:30 that morning and told us that the water was approaching along St. Peter Street. I ran out and stood on the edge of the street. Looking west, I could see the sun reflecting on the approaching water. Soon a trickle of water reached where I was standing, and within a few minutes the gutter filled, the street flooded and water began to enter the yards. We ended up with about eighteen inches of water at our home on Charles Street.

JOHNNY: One of the most unforgettable experiences connected with the flood was being taken to the big oak tree that stood in the middle of the St. Martinville road to see the Ahspeaks, a large mud snake that is jet black except for its red underside. It is really a harmless, but nevertheless big, snake. These snakes had all congregated on this oak tree to get out of the water. That tree trunk was covered with snakes.

Another thing I remember is that once the water went down and the yards began to reappear, everyone had to cover their yard with lime. Once we did that, we left town for a week. We stayed at the Bouttes. We didn't leave during the flood, but we had to leave afterward because of the terrible odor.

I remember seeing the trains pass with refugees. There were boxcars filled with people going to higher ground to the west. I don't recall seeing anything like that again until Hurricane Hilda came along in 1964, and people were again evacuated from the east in boxcars.

But during the flood, there was very little water on Main Street. For example, the sidewalk on the south side of the street was completely out of water. The economic impact on New Iberia was not great.

GERTRUDE: That's right. Few people in New Iberia were hurt by the flood. But the only person I know who benefitted from the flood was my father. That year, even though he lost the use of his pumping plant along the bayou to water his rice crop, he made the cheapest rice crop of his career. As his pump became inoperative because of the flood, he simply provided an opening under the Southern Pacific tracks and the water flowed through, over his rice lands all the way to Peebles Plantation. It resulted in a beautiful rice crop. He had watered his crop for nothing.

INTERVIEWER: We've talked about the automobile, but what are your recollections of the early days of the airplane?

JOHNNY: My first plane ride was in 1929. That was with Captain Smith. He had a plane that he had put together from the parts of World War I planes. He was going around the country barnstorming. One Saturday afternoon he picked up my brother Warren, myself, Johnny Marin and George Minvielle and asked us to pass out handbills around town. He promised to take us up in his plane the next day if we did a good job. Well, the next day George's mother absolutely refused to let him get in a plane. John Marin's mother refused to let him leave the house, so Warren and I went and we flew over the town. That afternoon the plane had a mishap while Clegg Labauve was aboard and later the plane did fall apart in New Orleans; fortunately, no one was hurt.

INTERVIEWER: Tell me something about the old racetrack off Park Street.

GERTRUDE: Horse racing was a very popular thing in New Iberia.

JOHNNY: What I remember most about the racetrack is that it was completely surrounded by Cherokee briars. This is how Cherokee Street got its name. When the Cherokees bloomed, it was an embankment of flowers.

GERTRUDE: The grandstand was wooden and typical of so many grandstands built at that time.

JOHNNY: The Fourth of July was the big day for the races. It seemed that everybody went to the races on that day.

GERTRUDE: I think that the popularity of the racetrack began to cool down around the late twenties.

Before we go on to another subject, I want to return for a moment to the subject of the Elks Theatre.

After Mr. Scharff brought movies to the Elks, there was a regular routine of subjects. The drama of the week was on Wednesday and Thursday. Friday was usually the serials. Saturday was a western; Sunday there was a light drama. On Saturday, children were admitted for six cents and on Sunday for ten cents. So I got a weekly allowance of sixteen cents plus a nickel to buy candy or ice cream.

JOHNNY: Remember, though, if someone had something to present on the stage, Mr. Scharff would cancel the movie so the stage could be used. I remember once that Dorothy Mitchell put on a big musical. The Elks was completely equipped for stage presentations, and this musical turned out to be terrific. Irene Belanger was studying with Dorothy Mitchell and she was in the show. The stage was set as a garden scene, typically Victorian, and Irene came out in a completely green costume and did some sort of a frog dance. The dance was mostly acrobatic. Then Hawley Gary walked out on stage and the chorus girls, in antebellum dresses, entered and a beautiful waltz scene followed. Hawley then sang "Can't You Hear Me Callin', Caroline?" Carolyn Carstens was in the chorus line, and everytime Hawley would say "Caroline," Carolyn would start giggling and eventuallly the situation nearly stopped the show. It was really a big musical with a cast made up entirely of local people.

GERTRUDE: I don't remember that particular number, but I do remember two other people who were in the show: Patricia Burke and Juliette Levy.

JOHNNY: Well, Patricia Burke inherited her talent from her mother, Mrs. Donald Burke. That reminds me, when the Little Theatre was organized by Mrs. Walter Burke in the 1920s, they used the Elks Theatre. I have a picture of E. J. Carstens, Celeste Burke, Donald Burke and Annie Archer in one of Mrs. Burke's shows at the Elks Theater.

GERTRUDE: The schools would put on shows there and would hold their graduation exercises there because, until the high school was built on Center Street, the old Central High had no auditorium.

I remember one show that the high school put on. It was called "A Spanish Cantata" and was directed by Mary Briganti. She was quite talented. Vince Drago had one of the leads.

JOHNNY: Speaking of Mary Briganti reminds me that she and Inez Hebert would alternate as the piano player for the silent pictures. Before that was Camilla Perraro, and before her was Mrs. De Generes.

GERTRUDE: Yes, they were fantastic. They could switch from one tune to another without any difficulty, depending on the mood being portrayed on the screen.

JOHNNY: I'll never forget that the music always accompanying a running horse was the "William Tell Overture." For the love scenes it was always "Love's Old Sweet Song."

INTERVIEWER: Why not recall some of the people of New Iberia who impressed you for one reason or another.

JOHNNY: Well, I remember someone called "Ahoogah." I don't remember her real name. But I cite her as an example of how, in years past, children would find ways to torment certain townspeople. The Lord only knows that the adults involved were perfectly harmless, good people, and the kids were only up to childish mischief, but, nevertheless, there were these situations. I don't see anything like them anymore, and that's why I want to mention this case.

"Ahoogah" was a small, elderly woman, always dressed in mourning black, and, I guess, being unaccustomed to automobiles she crossed the street one day without looking for traffic. Well, it so happened that someone driving a Model T nearly hit her, and, as is common, the driver hit the horn. Everyone knows that a Model T horn said: "Ahoogah." Well, when the horn sounded, this poor little lady jumped sky high and rattled on at great length in French.

Today, such an incident would be scarcely noticed, but not then, it was a big thing. Almost immediately this lady, who was on Main Street nearly every day, became known to the kids as "Ahoogah." They tormented her to the point where she began to carry rocks in her large black purse. Whenever the children called out, she would throw rocks at them, but I don't think that she ever intended to hit one of them.

GERTRUDE: I remember another case similar to that. I think the lady was called Madame Fadeuille. Poor soul, she would go crawfishing and then try to sell her catch in town. In those days people had to find many different ways to support themselves. There was nothing like old-age assistance, welfare, or social security.

JOHNNY: Indeed not, in those days no one looked down upon the livelihood of anyone, even someone who might be picking trash to find things to sell. Everyone knew everyone else in town, and even though a person might be in reduced circumstances, they were still respected.

GERTRUDE: Yes, that's right. Well, Madame Fadeuille was apparently a widow and had no real means of support except selling crawfish. Well, one day Madame Fadeuille was selling crawfish when a minor disturbance occurred. A policeman came on the scene, there was something of a scuffle, and some of Madame Fadeuille's "unmentionables" loosened and fell to the sidewalk. Well, ever after, as in the case of "Ahoogah," Madame Fadeuille was known by the whole town.

JOHNNY: Then, there was a constant collection of old men who would sit on the benches in front of the courthouse. Someone later complained about the men's comments to passersby, and the benches were removed.

GERTRUDE: But now I want to mention someone who should never be forgotten in New Iberia, and that was Miss Julia Decuir. Julia Decuir was a fine, charitable woman, loved by everyone who knew her. She was always helping someone in need. Frankly, I think that if monuments are ever erected to New Iberians of the past, no one could ever overlook this noble woman. The fact is, however, that her deeds became her monument. She had so little to give away, but she would have gladly given her last crust of bread to someone in need. She was quite an outspoken woman whenever she saw injustice. She had her causes and defended them.

A person who should also be remembered in New Iberia for generations to come was Dr. George Sabatier. He was probably the most highly revered person in the community. He may well have given away a fortune in medical practice, always saying "Pay me whenever you have the money."

JOHNNY: Dr. Sabatier was a great diagnostician. Another thing about him, if a person was ill, he would just drop by the house every day or every other day to see how the person was getting along. He and Dr. Dauterive pulled me through a very serious illness.

GERTRUDE: Dr. Sabatier had many long years of practice. He was truly a loveable person, a person never to be forgotten.

INTERVIEW: Let's turn now to the end of Prohibition and night life afterward.

GERTRUDE: I do not recall any speakeasies in New Iberia before Prohibition was repealed. There were some, however, in the nearby towns.

After Prohibition, the Evangeline Club opened. Then, too, there was Deare's. Deare's was primarily an eating place, a real good eating place.

Now, for the big dances, we went to Opelousas, Lafayette and Abbeville. But that was probably before Prohibition ended.

JOHNNY: There were so many good dances. And when you'd go to these, there would be tag dancing. That is something that is gone entirely today. But, back then dancing was an art--maybe it still is, but its not obviously the art that it was.

I went with a girl for six years, Grace Delcambre, primarily because we loved to dance and were good dancers, and I'm not bragging. But we would dance only the first and last dances. Between we danced with everyone else. Sometimes a girl would dance with four or five different partners before the number was over. That was tag dancing.

The band would play medleys that might go on for twenty minutes. There would be a waltz followed by a tango, followed by a samba, then a rumba and a two-step. There was a different step for every dance. It is not like today where there appears to be one step for any tempo of music. We danced to the melody rather than to the rhythm--today they dance to the beat of the drums and that never changes.

GERTRUDE: I would say that dancing then was an art.

JOHNNY: Yes, when a Fred Astaire-Ginger Rogers picture would come to town, we'd sit in the theater for maybe as many as five features, and in that way learn every step of the dance. Then, later, we'd get out on the dance floor and break it in on the rest of the crowd. The "Carioca" came out, and Grace and I sat in the Evangeline Theater through five features. At the end of the week, there was a big dance in St. Berchman's Hall at Mt. Carmel. One of the chaperons was Mrs. John Schwing. We asked Al Dieudonne to play the "Carioca," and when Grace and I started dancing, everyone cleared the floor. About midway through the number, Mrs. Schwing came onto the floor and hauled us off. I guess it was because to dance the "Carioca" the partners' heads were together and their hands on one another's hips. Well, the rest of the group had been infected. Al continued to play the "Carioca," and everyone joined in.

GERTRUDE: There were many other good bands--the Banner Band, Claiborne Williams, the Schriever Band. It was a dance era. The Schriever Band was a terrific jazz band.

JOHNNY: I think that there are about four members of the Banner Band still living. I also knew Bunk Johnson. Not long ago, J. B. Henderson and I were reminiscing about Bunk.

GERTRUDE: There was the Banner Band from Lafayette which was quite good. During the 1930s the Jonas Henderson High School sponsored the appearance of several of the big-name bands.

Paul, my husband, Lester Kahn and I went to hear Duke Ellington. Louis Armstrong also played New Iberia.

I don't suppose we should overlook the Showboat. It was at the foot of Evangeline Street. I think it was first a restaurant. I think Charlie Moore had it when it was a restaurant.

JOHNNY: Don't forget "Co" Leleux's place. It was a real old-fashioned dance hall. There was also the Green Lantern on the corner of West Main and North streets. They set up a small dance hall.

GERTRUDE: There was also the Jungle Club that had big bands, and then Leo Etie had a place on West Main that featured dancing.

Well, I suppose we've covered most of the topics dealing with the era. It's impossible to remember it all, but it was a romantic era, even though such things as Prohibition and the Depression were around. We all lived through it and I don't think we're any the worse for it.

INTERVIEWER: Thank you both for sharing these memories of the twenties and thirties with us.

The Essanee Theatre
New Iberia's last downtown theatre opened in November 1937 and closed on Thanksgiving Day, 1985

XXIV

An Historical Overview of Afro-Americans in New Iberia, 1865-1960

by Sandra E. Egland

with an introduction by
Glenn R. Conrad

This essay might have been the opening essay of this book, it could have appeared midway the essays, or it could be last in this history of New Iberia. The fact is it should not have to be written at all because Afro-Americans, like other racial and ethnic groups discussed in these essays, have been an integral part of New Iberia's history since 1779.

Black people helped build the houses of New Iberia's Spanish settlers. More than likely Afro-Americans helped construct The Shadows, the Alma House, and Mintmere. For a certainty, a black woman, known only as Félicité, did so much to assist the New Iberia yellow-fever victims of 1839 that her name has been immortalized in the annals of the town. Black men, women, and children harvested the cane, rice, and cotton crops that were so much a part of the nineteenth-century economy. Indeed, the plantation system of antebellum and postbellum Louisiana, as was true across the South, was structured upon the free and cheap labor provided by Afro-Americans. In addition, black people helped move the commerce of the region, be it by steamboat, railroad, or truck.

Many of the "gandy dancers" who helped bring the railroad to New Iberia were Afro-Americans. Black people were on the streets of downtown New Iberia on the awful night of October 10, 1899, when fire ravaged the town.

They helped their white neighbors pass the buckets of water that ultimately quenched the flames. On the morrow of that disaster, New Iberia's Afro-American community helped the Creole, Acadian, Anglo, German, French, and Jewish merchants to rebuild their stores and warehouses; in fact, to rebuild much of downtown New Iberia.

As the twentieth century dawned, black people helped build the post office, and the trolley line between New Iberia and Jeanerette. Afro-Americans were largely responsible for laying the bricks that paved Main Street from the railroad depot to the old post office. Black women have traditionally helped white women with domestic chores, and in doing so made the black contribution to "Creole" and "Cajun" cuisine as important as the fabled South Louisiana roux. Finally, throughout this century, the black community has sent out its sons and daughters to help "make the world safe for democracy."

But these and other contributions and achievements of New Iberia's Afro-Americans are scarcely, if ever, mentioned in these essays. The reason being that the contributions and achievements of American blacks are only rarely documented during the more than three centuries that the race has been in North America. Until recently, black Americans have been treated by other Americans as an invisible people. A contemporary researcher in Asia, Africa, or Europe, for example, poring over microfilm copies of official American documentation or even popular literature of the nineteenth century and first half of the twentieth century could easily arrive at the conclusion that there were few people of African descent in the United States and that Afro-Americans as a group produced an unusually high percentage of legal offenders in relation to the apparent size of the community. Such a conclusion is not fantastic after one has researched archives for records of the Afro-American contributions to, and achievements in, American society.

Indeed, it has taken longer for Afro-Americans to gain entry into the American mainstream than any other racial or ethnic group, with the possible exception of Native Americans. The black exclusion from recognized means of fulfilling the American dream was systematically contrived from colonial times down to living memory. As in the case of New Iberia's history, black Americans, until recently, have always been allowed to "help" others develop the American political and economic systems that have led to the fulfillment of individual aspirations. Afro-Americans seldom have had the opportunity, until recently, to emerge from the mass of "helpers" to become "the achiever," "the director," "the founder," or any other label which designates original thinking that has been brought to fruition.

Afro-Americans

The causes for the lengthy exclusion from the pathways of American success are easily discerned. To begin, there were 250 years of bondage that cast the black American into the role of machine of production rather than that of aspiring human being; a system which stigmatized all blacks as "helpers," never allowing for the talented or skillful to emerge as innovators. Then, there was denial of access to the fruits of the early American cornucopia. For example, few blacks, and then usually only those of mixed racial parentage, were allowed to become landowners or shopkeepers. Finally, once the shackles of bondage were thrown off, a mass of largely ignorant, generally poverty-stricken humanity was left drifting without direct links to the existing American educational, political, and economic systems.

Thus, Afro-Americans encountered segregation, discrimination, and denigration to a degree never experienced by another ethnic or racial group in America. It is therefore easy to understand that black Americans have sometimes found it difficult to identify with what are generally termed "American values." Their role in America in the 125 years or so since emancipation has been largely the role of helper, and history seldom records the thoughts and deeds of helpers, be they black or white. Nevertheless, whenever and wherever American society has allowed Afro-Americans to develop leadership roles, albeit among their own community, blacks have acquitted themselves well. This becomes more impressive when one takes into consideration the fact that blacks in leadership roles have had few resources to draw upon and have had to be wary constantly that their leadership did not meet with marked success, for a consequence of that was to be "run out of town."

What follows then is a brief discussion of the areas where black leadership in New Iberia was allowed to develop and blossom. As will be seen, the initial area for black leadership was in the community's arts, crafts, professions, and commerce. Recently, it emerged in the political realm. Today, Afro-Americans are no longer drifting aimlessly on the periphery of American society; they are slowly but inexorably moving into the mainstream.

It may be that in the future another history of New Iberia will be written and that the author will deem it unnecessary to develop a chapter on New Iberia's black community because there will have existed for such a long time only one New Iberia community.

THE OVERVIEW

History is the record of people, it is the story of humankind. Theoretically it is complete, it cannot be flawed by omission or distortion. But, as we all know, that occurs and when it does it is usually the fault of the recorder of history, the historian, who consciously or unconsciously chooses between what will be remembered or recorded and what will become the chaff of history. Too often, however, hidden in the chaff are grains of a people's heritage which, if one takes the time to discover, reveal the potential for a rich harvest. Such a potential should never be mistakenly underrated; nevertheless, that has been true among American historians who, until recently, have overlooked, disregarded, or generally ignored the Afro-American experience since emancipation.

To suggest that people of African descent have not had a significant history in America is to admit an ignorance of the story of the race and of our country. From the beginning, blacks have been integral to the American cavalcade; they are not incidental to American history; they are not intruders; they are Americans. Nevertheless, throughout most of the Afro-American experience, blacks have sometimes been pushed and shoved by people who chose not to see the African descendant as a partner in the evolution of the American dream. History, however, provides a means for anyone who has it in his heart to see and to understand the black experience. History gives everyone a chance to judge wisely the past; to properly focus on the present, and to correctly plan for the future.

The historical tapestry of the United States is woven of many threads of different fibers. Louisianians have long contributed to the national skein, and the Louisiana contribution is itself a multiplicity of human endeavor. Part of that endeavor is found in the historical tapestry of New Iberia, a fabric of many colored threads. Unfortunately for the history of the town, some threads have long been overlooked, thus detracting from the fullness and richness of our past. What follows is an account of one overlooked thread--an attempt to weave it into the story of New Iberia.

Religion

Because religion has always been important to most African-Americans and because the black church is and has been a significant institution, this overview of black life in New Iberia will begin with a look at a few of the older African-American churches.[1]

Most of the African-American churches in the major cities north and south were organized in the 1770s. Blacks frequently took the iniative in bringing about separation, especially when it became obvious that they were not welcome in the white churches. Most of the African-American churches in New Iberia were organized shortly after the Civil War, with the exception of St. Edward's.

The role of the non-Catholic African-American church was not limited to Sunday services. The black's church was a highly socialized institution with many functions and responsibilities, a community center where one could find recreation and release. It was a welfare agency, dispensing help to sick and poor members. It was a training school in self-government, in handling money, in doing business, and it was a newspaper. It was the black man's very own, allowing him to make decisions for himself which was seldom possible elsewhere.

St. James United Methodist Church, formerly called St. James Methodist Episcopal Church and St. James Methodist Church, is the oldest black congregation in New Iberia. As the Civil War was drawing to a close, a few black New Iberians gathered together out of concern for a place to worship God and serve mankind through fellowship, service, and mission. On April 9, 1865, they organized St. James Methodist Church. Their first pastor was the Reverend William Davis who toiled and struggled with the congregation to provide a place of worship. Beginning as a mission church, the congregation grew to the point where a new church was constructed in 1893 under the pastorate of the Rev. A. H. Banks. The Rev. S. E. H. Morant, presiding elder, and Bishop J. M. Fitzgerald were of great help in making this dream a reality. Pastors who have subsequently served the congregation are the Rev. W. Davis, Rev. C. D. Bryant, Rev. C. Shallonhorm, Rev. M. J. Dyer, Rev. W. B. Anderson, Rev. H. J. Wright, Rev. Valco Chatman, and Rev. J. F. Johnson.

St. James congregation is proud to record in the pages of its history the fact that it has supported and inspired several persons to further their education and become Christian ministers. They were J. D. Richard, Q. W. Obee, Ed Richard, Travic Larkins, J. J. Obee, Eugene Johnson, Robert Wilkins, William

---

1. These histories of the churches were obtained from the Rev. C. V. Jackson, Rev. Larry Norbert, Rev. Burnell Robinson, Rev. Alvin Dixon, the *Daily Iberian*, church programs, commemorative brochures, and other reference materials. Also supplying information were Mr. Edran Auguster, Mrs. Ruth Sophus, Mrs. Ruby Egland, Mrs. Ruth Bolden, Mr. and Mrs. Borie Stinson, and Mr. Leander Viltz.

and Russell Jones. These men have served the Louisiana conference with pride and dignity. The Jonses continue to serve the conference.

A great highlight in the history of St. James occurred in 1918 when the annual statewide conference was held at the church. The Rev. Henry Taylor served as the Host Pastor, and the late Bishop Thirkield presided.

For 121 years, and with twenty-nine ministers serving as spiritual leaders, the St. James congregation has stood as a beacon in the community.

This establishment of the separate houses of worship for blacks, as inconsistent as it may seem with the teachings of their religion, gave to blacks an unusual opportunity to develop leadership. In New Iberia, one such leader was the Rev. Jessie Giles, who, in 1869, with only a small group of dedicated Christians, among whom were Joe Morris, Ann Levy, Sylvian Thorton, Ben Ramey, Sally Butler, and Louis Randolph, pulled together to form the Old Ironside Church. Ten years later the church's name became Star Pilgrim Baptist Church. Rev. Giles served this community until his death twenty-eight years later.

Thereafter, the Rev. A. J. Horton continued the mission of service and leadership. He was followed to the pastorate of Star Pilgrim by the Rev. Prince Albert (1916-1931), the Rev. William Bowers (1931-1932), the Rev. John Parker

St. James United Methodist Church

(1932-1956), and the Rev. Cyrus V. Jackson (1956-   ). Assistant pastors have been the Rev. James Simmons and the Rev. McKinley Smith. The Rev. Jackson and many members of his congregation have long been associated with civic and community activities, and the church is used for numerous civic programs.

Another church established in New Iberia shortly after the Civil War was St. Paul's United Church of Christ. St. Paul's began as a Congregational Church sometime between 1866 and 1868, several years after the freed slaves had held religious services in houses on the Gall Plantation. The church was organized by William Butler, a missionary of the American Missionary Association of the Congregational Church. The first church built by the congregation was on Washington Street near the railroad depot. After that edifice burned, the American Missionary Association assisted in the building of a new church on the corner of

Star Pilgrim Baptist Church

French and West Pershing streets. In 1891 the church was renovated and enlarged.

Although St. Paul's began as a Congregationalist church, it became St. Paul's Congregational Christian Church in 1931, when the Congregational and Christian churches were united. In 1957 there occurred the merger of the Congregational-Christian churches and the evangelical and reformed churches. The merger gave birth to the United Church of Christ and the name of St. Paul's became St. Paul United Church of Christ.

A never-to-be-forgotten pastor of St. Paul's was the Rev. R. V. Sims who served as shepherd to his congregation from 1897 to 1940. The Rev. B. J. Robertson, the current pastor, came to his flock in 1956.

St. Paul's United Church of Christ

Afro-Americans

Mt. Calvary Baptist Church was organized in 1875, with a membership of eighteen, under the leadership of Rev. J. B. Livingston who served as pastor until 1922. Other pastors to serve the congregation were the Rev. F. M. Boley, 1922-1949; Rev. H. M. Jones, 1949-1972, under whose leadership the present edifice was built. The Rev. L. M. Norbert, the fourth pastor of Mt. Cavalry, has served since January, 1973. He was baptized and grew up as a youth in Mt. Calvary.

Property acquired with God's help include four houses: two 2-story houses and one single-story house located on Julia Street to the rear of the church and another one adjacent to the church. Next to this property was another single-story house on Weeks Street. The site of this house is now the church's parking lot.

Through the Bus Ministry, needed transportation is provided by bus and van for persons who are able to get out to enjoy and participate in worship service and Christian fellowship.

For the sick and shut-in, there is available the Radio Ministry which includes a broadcast of the regular Sunday morning services. In addition to the church site and property adjoining it, the Mt. Calvary congregation owns an

Mt. Calvary Baptist Church

eight-and-one-half-acre tract of land in rural New Iberia which is the site of Mt. Calvary Memorial Park, a cemetery under development.

Classrooms for Sunday School, the Summer Tutorial Program and the annual Winter and Summer Institutes are located at 419 Julia Street. At 425 Julia Street is housed Operation Sharing Center which provides food and clothing on regular bases and financial assistance (when feasible). Mt. Calvary's general membership exceeds 575.

The churches were places of real release for a people who worked long hours, usually in the full sunshine of an open field, and who had few material pleasures. More than that, however, the church was a place where black people could get recognition for achievement, sympathy for sorrow, and the strength and love of brotherhood. The church was a place for maintaining community and family values--it was a place for hope.

During the 1920s, and '30s, and '40s, these and other black Protestant churches served as centers of social life as well as places of worship. Fairs and other social fund raisers were held to promote the work of the churches. Many of the great cooks of the town showed off their culinary skills, producing sweet-potatoe pies, peach pies, coconut delights, blackberry cobbler, ice cream, pralines, fudge, and a host of other good foods to delight the palate. To raise money there were Friday night fish fries, Saturday fairs, and Sunday services with lemonade and fried chicken dinners interspersed between religious teachings.

Churchgoing was an extended family affair. Women and girls wore dresses starched stiff as cardboard and carried lace handkerchiefs and fans with funeral home advertisements. Every Sister (as all women were called and all men were addressed as Brother), wore a hat, but if they were deaconesses and/or missionaries they wore a specially made headdress. The men and boys, of course, always donned their Sunday best for church services.

In those days of no air-conditioning, fainting was as commonplace in Baptist and Holiness churches as Hollywood's conception of swooning among antebellum white women. Shouting was also common. Baptisms by Baptists were done in Bayou Teche until the 1940s and 1950s. Ladies who were to be baptized wore long white dresses that tied at their feet in order that their dress would not float when they were emersed. Beginning in the 1940s and 1950s, pools were constructed in the church for the purpose of baptism.

A social function performed by the black churches was to provide a place for courtship. Young men would go to church to meet their sweethearts, or they would walk with them to church. If those who were courting walked to church, they did so always a few feet ahead of the accompanying chaperons. In church and on the church grounds the young couple was permitted to hold hands only.

The development of separate black Catholic churches across South Louisiana, including the one in New Iberia, was the result of complex political, sociological, and religious factors.[2] From colonial days to the time of the Civil War, black and white Catholics had worshipped together, even though they did so from segregated seating. Such an arrangement held sway even after the Civil War and emancipation. But change was in the wind. With emancipation, black Protestants established black churches, conducted worship services, and participated in the social activities of their community. Many black Catholics yearned for a similar religious life. In politics, once Reconstruction ended and whites regained political domination, tensions developed between the races at all levels, even the religious; hence, black Catholics came to understand that their presence in the mixed congregations was embarrassing for many whites. Numerous black Catholics therefore began to drift away from their lifetime relgious experience. Also, between 1890 and 1900, the Louisiana legislature passed a series of laws designed to separate the races at certain points of contact and to deprive the blacks of the franchise. Official segregation therefore fueled racial tensions that finally burst into violence. Between 1882 and 1903, for example, there were 285 confirmed lynchings in the state. A combination of these political, sociological and religious factors, therefore, began to impact upon the black population of Louisiana and especially black Catholics.

The Catholic hierarchy was aware of deteriorating race relationships and was deeply concerned about the consequences. The official response to this multifaceted problem came when, in 1888, Francis Janssens was appointed archbishop of New Orleans. After consultation with clergy and laity, the archbishop found a possible solution to the many problems facing black Catholics in the concept of the national church. National churches for various ethnic groups, Irish, Italian, German, for example, were common in most American urban centers. The national churches were designed to accommodate the immigrant family until it sought integration into the American social system. No member of any ethnic group was compelled to belong to a national church, he

---

2. An excellent account of the establishment of black Catholic parishes can be found in Dolores Egger Labbe's *Jim Crow Comes to Church: The Establishment of Segregated Catholic Parishes in South Louisiana* (Lafayette, Louisiana: University of Southwestern Louisiana, 1971).

could belong to his territorial church. The national church thus provided the model from which Janssens drew his plan for Louisiana's black Catholics. The archbishop "was certain that blacks were leaving the church and he was just as certain that the attraction of an active parish life would serve as a strong reason for remaining in the church and perhaps persuade some who had left to return."[3]

Janssens' plan was gradually put into practice during the archbishop's tenure, and continued at a slow pace during the episcopacy of Archbishop Louis Placide Chapelle. When, however, James Herbert Blenk became archbishop of New Orleans in 1909, the program of separate parishes accelerated as a result of the archbishop's appreciation of two facts: the rapid decline in the black Catholic population of the archdiocese and the mounting racial tensions.

3. Labbe, *Jim Crow Comes to Church*, pp. 38-39.

St. Edward's Roman Catholic Church

Thus, when Monsignor J. M. Langlois, pastor of St. Peter's Church in New Iberia, petitioned the archbishop in 1916 (the Diocese of Lafayette had not yet been created) to establish a black parish in New Iberia, Blenk moved swiftly to act upon the request. In February 1917 the archbishop received agreement from the Holy Ghost Fathers to staff the new parish. In the meantime Mother Katharine Drexel, founder of the Sisters of the Blessed Sacrament and heiress to a large fortune which she had used to fund many missionary activities of the Holy Ghost Fathers, agreed to fund the purchase of land and the construction of buildings for the new black parish in New Iberia. The actual donation came from Mother Drexel's sister, Mrs. Louise D. Morrell, who asked that the new parish be named St. Edward's as a memorial to her husband Edward Morrell.

Fr. F. Xavier Lichtenberger, the first pastor, arrived in New Iberia on October 1, 1917. He moved into his new house on January 1, 1918, and celebrated the first Mass in St. Edward's Church on November 10, 1918. In May 1919, St. Edward's was the first church to be blessed by the bishop of the new Diocese of Lafayette, the Most Reverend Jules B. Jeanmard. St. Edward's is therefore considered by many people to be the mother church of all churches in the diocese that were founded as national parishes for black Catholics.

Fr. Lichtenberger faced an enormous task. His congregation was scattered over a large geographical area; more importantly, many members of the flock strayed from the Catholic church. He therefore spent his pastorate in the work of gathering the flock. His two successors continued this work with success thereby making it possible for Fr. John McGlade, after he became pastor in 1924, to begin the work of conversion.

The Holy Ghost Fathers continued to minister to this congregation until 1977 when personnel problems necessitated the order's withdrawal from the parish. After a brief transition period, priests of the Society of the Divine Word have taken up the work of shepherding the flock.[4]

In 1933 St. Edward's School was accredited by the state board of education. The school had seven grammar grades and four grades of high school.

---

4. Pastors of St. Edward's: F. X. Lichtenberger, 1917-19; T. A. Wrenn, 1919-21; J. A. Pobleschek, 1921-24; John C. McGlade, 1924-35; Anthony Walsh, 1935-36; J. P. Lonergan, 1936-45; J. E. Stegman, 1945; James McCaffrey, 1945; Herbert Frederick, 1945-49; Clement Roach, 1949-58; Eugene Monroney, 1958-66; Martin Kirschbaum, 1966-68; John Schlicht, 1968-71; John Burns, 1971-76; William Havenar, 1976-83; J. Gus Johnson, 1983-84; Alvin Dixon, 1984 -

Thousands of children have graduated from this school to continue their education and assume responsible positions in society. The school is now part of a unitary system serving all Catholic children of New Iberia from kindergarten through third grade.

Today, St. Edward's is a thriving complete parish unit with church, school, and rectory built largely through the generosity of the parishoners. The convent is the only remaining original structure. This parish and its mission, St. Jude's in Olivier, stand as monuments to the dedicated black men and women who kept their faith.

The Benevolent Societies

There were other organizations established in the late nineteenth and early twentieth centuries to care for the more material needs of the black community. These groups tended to serve as a bridge between the charitable activities of the churches and the purely secular functions of the latter-day insurance companies. These organizations were called benevolent societies. Among the best known benevolent societies of New Iberia were True Friends, Young Union, Lincoln, St. Matthew's, and Solid Rock. Basically speaking, the purpose of the societies was the care for the sick and to bury the dead. In addition, the societies usually had a monthly meeting that was largely a social gathering. Then, once a year, some societies would sponsor a "turn out." For this event, members of the society would dress in white and parade as a group to a local black church. Every year a different church was selected. Once in the church, the society members would hear a sermon by the pastor and, before leaving, deposit a small contribution in thanksgiving to God and to help the church with its various programs.

Benevolent societies served the black community in much the same way as their white counterparts, particularly in the first half of the twentieth century. The True Friends Society was founded in 1915 by Joseph Bush. In addition to performing the usual functions of such societies, True Friends gave vouchers to its members to redeem for such items as food and fuel.

Another society, formed in 1931, during the depth of the Great Depression, was the Lincoln Benevolent Society. The organizing directors were Samuel Bowles (president), James Thompson (vice-president), James J. Perry (financial secretary), Daniel Lewis (recording secretary), Mary Robertson (treasurer), Bernie Lewis (marshal), Betsy Bowles (chaplain), Lucy Green (juvenile

Afro-Americans

president), and Louise Gardner (juvenile secretary). This corporation was dissolved in 1985.

Although a few of the societies have survived into the 1980s, they are for the most part inactive. Their decline was largely brought about by the formation of black-owned insurance companies.

When established insurance companies refused to write policies for blacks, Afro-Americans came together to form small, locally owned insurance companies. As time has passed some companies, such as Golden State of California, North Carolina Mutual, and Atlanta Life, have become, through growth and consolidation, nationwide in scope and activity.

New Iberia's contribution to the black insurance industry was the People's Insurance Company. Among Iberians closely associated with this company were Octave Lilly, Sr., Octave Lilly, Jr., Mattye Lilly Stinson, Myrtle Lilly Vallot, Mr. Tibbs, Lizzie Mack, Louis Robertson, and Borie Stinson, the latter a former district manager.

Also assisting the New Iberia black community in financial matters is the Iberia Parish Federal Credit Union. Founded in 1941, this credit union has

People's Insurance Company staff and spouses about 1945

provided loans for home building and remodeling, for automobile purchases, and for other worthy purposes. Charter members of the Credit Union still residing in New Iberia are Ruby Robertson Egland and Ruth Robertson Sophus. The current board of directors includes Matthew Polk, J. B. Henderson, Velma Jackson, and C. D. Byrd. Melvina P. Durall and Harriet Hill are the most recent additions to the board.

Schools

No history of the community is complete without some discussion of education. An earlier essay in this volume outlines the story of white, and to a degree, black education in New Iberia. Some of the older members of the black community recall some of the educational institutions dating from the turn of the century.

Louis Robertson operated a small school in his home on the outskirts of New Iberia. It was there that many youngsters as well as adults learned to read and write. There were no grades as such; the schooling was not formal; nevertheless, it offered the rudiments of learning. Robertson did not charge a fee for his services, but students were required to attend regularly.

A more structured educational facility was that operated by Ms. Lorance Adams. Here children were offered the basics in a primer and a first-grade. The school was located on West Washington near West Avenue. A well-known graduate of the Adams school is Edran Auguster, the former principal of Park Street Elementary School.

Daisy and Mamie Robertson operated a small private school on Iberia Street.

Another early school for New Iberia's black community was the Douglass Institute, named for the great abolitionist Frederick Douglass. The school, opened at the turn of the century, was located in the 400 block of French Street. It offered graded classes from first to high school.

Probably the best-known private black school in New Iberia was the Howe Institute, located on the block that is now the site of the Iberia Parish Court Building. The Howe Institute operated from just after the Civil War until the 1930s. It was supported by the Howe family of Chicago and the Union Sixth District Missionary Baptist Association.

Howe Institute, founded in 1887, was unique because it was the only school of its kind for black students between Beaumont and New Orleans. Opportunities for Afro-American Youth were few and far between, but thanks to the Rosenwalds and of course the Howe's, some few people were able to become formally educated.

Afro-Americans

Ruby Robertson Egland (left), a pioneer black teacher and principal looks out from the doorway of Morbihan School (below).

A school for blacks at Morbihan in the 1920s

Approximately forty students boarded at the school at a time. The ratio was usually about 60% female and 40% male. The girls lived in one building and the boys another. At the peak of the school's operation, there were 150 students, boarders and day students.

The faculty consisted of five or six teachers with the principal also serving as a teacher. All of the teachers were certified by the State of Louisiana, but most of the teachers were from outside of New Iberia because it was difficult to find local people who were certified to fill the teaching positions. One of Howe's teachers from New Iberia was Ruth Robertson Sophus, who taught J. B. Henderson, the son of Jonas Henderson, and Matthew Polk, former principal of Jeanerette High School, during the last year as students.

A. B. Simon School faculty, 1954

Seated from left: Katie Sims Powers, Marguerite Spencer, Ruby Egland, Ethel Hill, Myrtle Williams Butler, Willie Mae Davis Manuel, Franzella Volter, and Joseph Kelly. Standing from left: Mae H. McDonald, Esther Bernard Heard, Lillian Johnny, Telitha Duchane, Avian Jeanlouis James, Lottie Amos Jones, Eloise Jeanlouis Jefferson, Melda Dominique, Hazel Simmons Hector, Mattye Lilly Stinson, Ethel Simon Byrd, and Cora Joseph Conway.

Howe Institute consisted of two three-story buildings. The Henderson family lived in one building. The girls lived on the second and third floors of the original building and the boys lived on the second and third floors of the newer building. The school did not start with two buildings, only with one; later, a second building was added. The kitchen and dining room was on the first floor of the original building. The newer structure was known as the instructional building of the institute. On the first floor were classrooms, an auditorium, and the principal's office.

Jonas Henderson, Sr., was principal of Howe Institute from the late 1800s until the school closed in 1933. He had a M. A. in Education from Leland College in Baker, La., and taught mathematics and history both at Howe and in the parish school system after the Institute closed. Jonas Henderson worked throughout the city and state promoting educational opportunities for blacks. He served as president of the Louisiana Education Association. Mrs. Henderson was also a teacher. She retired with the closing of the Institute, but her husband continued to teach at IPTS for about five years before he retired.

The Iberia Parish Training School opened its doors in the late 1920s with A. B. Simon as principal. Later, when the school was rebuilt, it was named for Simon. Local black residents raised the necessary money to buy the land for the school. Spearheading this effort were Louis and Mary Robertson. Lee Bowles, John Boutte, and the Bates, Ford, Ledbetter, and Guillet families worked hard for the success of this project.

IPTS was at one time the only high school for blacks in Iberia Parish. Children from Jeanerette and outlying areas had to come to New Iberia to school. Ruby Egland bought a bus to transport the children and Herbert Vital drove it. Charles Robertson also operated a private bus that brought children from Jeanerette, Olivier, Belle Place, and Morbihan. Some children would room and board in New Iberia in order to go to school. Many times teachers also made arrangements to stay in town during the school week. Some of the teachers who taught at IPTS are Ethel Simon Byrd (A. B. Simon's daughter), Lillian Johnny, Ruby Egland, Hazel Hector, Ruth Sophus, Lottie Amose Jones, Mattye Lilly Stinson, Willie Mae Davis Manuel, Taletha Duchane, Mary Ruth Thomas Rogers, Eloise Jefferson, Katie Sims Powers, Ethel Hill, Cyrus Jackson, Melda Dominique, Cora Joseph Conway, Marguerite Spencer, Bessie King, Frenzella Volter, Avian James, and Mae H. McDonald.

The schools, like the churches, were social centers for the black community. When, during the 1930s and 1940s, the big bands came to New Iberia, they usually performed at the IPTS. Outstanding artists such as Count Basie, Ella Fitzgerald, Cab Calloway, The Inkspots, the International Sweethearts of

Rhythm, and Louis Armstrong entertained New Iberia audiences. When these artists performed, people danced. They danced not for style, but because they enjoyed dancing. Parents and children rubbed shoulders on the dancefloor. Shoes were shined, faces were painted, and there was not a single wallflower in the place. They danced until their straightened hair again became curly, until their starched dresses became limp, until their shirts stuck to their backs with perspration. It was a wonderful means of emotional release in trying times.

There were also annual dances called "The Grand March." These dances, resembling a high-school prom, were held at IPTS and at Henderson High School. This was an event for juniors and seniors and their dates. The students began the evening by marching around the gym floor to the wonderful rhythms of the band. They would form the school letters and other designs. Afterward, the young men, always dressed in dark suits, and the young ladies, in evening dresses accented with a corsage, danced the evening away. Parents frequently joined in the dancing, and the prom became an event for taking family pictures.

Another family event sponsored by the schools was the school fair. These were always fun-filled events that involved sack races, egg rolling, relays, grab bags, and other competitive games. There was always hot dogs, popcorn balls, delicious fudge, and pralines. Fairs were held on Saturdays and were well attended by adults and children.

A second grade class at Iberia Training School
Teachers are Ruth Robertson Sophus (left) and Lillian P. Johnny (right)

Craftsmen and Artisans

The schools, be they the formal kind like Howe Institute or the informal classroom of human experience, turned out men and women who had a contribution to make to our town. Many people exhibited publicly and privately their artistic talents, their craftsmanship, their ability to create beauty. Artemas King, for example, apprenticed in his father's cabinet shop in the 1920s and thereafter operated a furniture repair shop. From 1941 to 1974, he operated King's Antique and Cabinet Shop. As time passed, Mr. King instructed others in his knowledge of antique furniture and cabinetry.

Sylvester Rochon was the first black New Iberian to earn a plumber's license. It was former State Representative, now Mayor J. Allen Daigre who made it possible for Rochon to take the state test at Delgado school in New Orleans in the late 1940s. Although Mr. Rochon installed plumbing in many New Iberia subdivisions, he was never allowed to join a trade union.

Preston Egland, although a full-time employee of Southern Pacific Railroad, was a first-rate carpenter and cabinetmaker. His skill was developed as he worked alongside his father and was then perfected with additional training in the army. Egland constructed many residences, but he specialized in crafting picket fences and cabinets. In addition to these interests, Egland and his brother-in-law, Gordy Sophus, opened the first black-owned service station in town.

The Miller and Bryant familes produced outstanding brick masons. A New Iberia landmark, the smokestack of the Charles Boldt Paper Mill on East Main Street, was built by the Bryants. The Bryants also constructed the entry gate at Avery Island. Taylor and Lloyd Miller's father, Romoul Miller, was a skilled brick mason and was called upon to do restoration work at The Shadows. Four generations of the family have maintained the tradition of masonry work.

Artists, Writers, and Musicians

Octave Lilly, Jr., a native of New Iberia, the son of Octave Lilly, Sr., and Emma Hayes, was a widely known writer, poet, and businessman. In addition to his already-mentioned connection with the People's Insurance Company, Mr. Lilly, a graduate of Dillard University, worked closely with Lyle Saxon and the Federal Writers' Project. He is the author of "Cathedral in the Ghetto" and other poems published in black journals. While still in grammar school, he published an article in *Screenland Magazine*. Mr. Lilly died in New Orleans in 1975.

Another published New Iberia author is Elaine Polk Campbell, the daughter of the late Washington Polk, Sr., and Virginia Porter Polk. Head of the English Department at New Iberia Senior High School, Mrs. Campbell's works include *Dreams at Twilight: A Book of Religious Prose and Poetry*, three plays, and *Tales from the Other Side of Bayou Teche*, a collection of short stories. Mrs. Campbell is also responsible for the publication of a black newspaper for Acadiana, *The Acadiana Ebony Journal*.

Musicians and singers abound in New Iberia's black community. There are, for example, piano players like Ethel Atlas Sparrow who holds an M. A. degree from Northwestern University. Other accomplished pianists, who studied at Dillard University and Southern University, are Eleanor Egland Mitchell and Kathleen Foreman Hutchingson. Among talented singers are Thomas A. Bolden and Rose Landry Joseph. These contemporary musicians follow in the footsteps of great trailblazers such as Gus Fontenette and Bunk Johnson.

In the world of art, William Lenord Jones teaches art at Dillard University; Eleanor Egland Mitchell, a fashion designer in San Francisco, won the Designer of the Year (1965) Award at the San Francisco School of Fashion Design; Ruby Robertson Egland is a specialist in the art of papercrafts and dollmaking; and Helen Johnson has received acclaim as a primitive painter.

The black business community of New Iberia has a history of long standing. Early in the twentieth century Afro-Americans opened shops and stores of every kind. Sam Cooper had People's Drug Store. Other drug stores were operated by the Bouttes and Pemiltons. Mr. and Mrs. Booker T. Mathis owned and operated three food stores. The Dauphine brothers had a grocery and also operated a nightclub. Tom Bolden and Wilbert Fletcher were funeral-home directors. T. B. Harrison operated a dry-cleaning shop. There were innumerable barbers and beauticians. Louis and Mary Robertson owned and operated the Robertson Cafe on Hopkins Street from the mid-1930s into the 1950s. The cafe was a gathering place for the black community, where professional and business people met for coffee, a snack, or a meal. This long-established tradition of businesses in New Iberia continues in the present.

Physicians and Dentists

Black physicians and dentists have long served the needs of the New Iberia Afro-American community. It may be that black doctors were caring for their patients before the turn of the century; unfortunately, however, their names and deeds remain to be discovered. Since 1900 some of New Iberia's black physicians and dentists are Drs. B. Easter, _____ Pickett, J. F. Garrett, H. C.

Scroggins, Linus Williams, E. L. Dorsey, Ima Pierson, _____ Chatters, George W. Diggs, James Henderson, Neville Anthony, Brunette King Blue and Donald R. Blue. New Iberia's black community has also produced members of the medical profession. Among these are Drs. Viola Coleman, Richard Sims, J. B. Barnes, Earl Washington, Jr., and Judy Destouet.

West End Division
Louisiana Sugar Cane Festival and Fair Association

This organization, also called the Negro Division of the Louisiana Sugar Cane Festival, was organized in 1950. The Robert Green Post of the American Legion was the initial sponsor. In the beginning, a young lady became queen of the Division's festival by raising the most money. The king was chosen from among farmers producing the largest tonnage of sugarcane. Later, queens were selected by regulations established by the Festival Association and kings were chosen by the queen.

The annual Miss Iberia and Queen Brown Sugar pageants were held at the West End Park. The contestants were often judged by music and drama teachers, and other civic-minded people. Contestants usually displayed their talents by singing, playing the piano, dramatic interpretations. Later, they were also judged on appearance, poise, and personality and tested on current events and general intelligence. The winners were given scholarships.

The chairman in 1957 and 1958 was Sam W. Cooper. Other chairpersons were Sylvester Rochon, Dr. James Henderson, and Joseph Kelly. Some women involved were Maude JeanBatiste, Delores Rochon, Fannie Simon, Lillian Manuel, Ruby Egland, Iris Williams Alexander, and Bessie Decuir. There were others. Some of the men involved were T. B. Harrison, "Poppa" Joe Rochon, George Ledbetter, Clarence Alex, Watkins Livingston, Renoudet Green, Toney Tauriac, Jake "Sonny" Durall, and John B. Brooks. The homemaking committee in 1958 included Ruby Egland, Rhona Cooper, Lois Spencer, Cora Lee Conway, Althea Rochon, and Lea Sigue. The agricultural committee: Louise Hadnot, Mrs. J. L. Lewis, Sylvester Rochon, Joseph Rochon, Lawrence Broussard, and Junius Francis.

The black businesses that supported the Festival were Rochon's Plumbing, Rochon's Club DeHut, Fletcher's Funeral Home, Egland's Servicenter and Auto Repair, Leo's Rendezvous, Dr. James H. Henderson, Harrison's Cleaners, Journet & Bolden Funeral Home, Green's Cash Grocery, Dauphine's Food Mart, Bastain's Barber Ship. Victor Jackson's Barber Shop, Stop Inn Cafe, Tauriac's Grocery and Market, People's Drug Store, Club Mid Day, Pemilton's Drug Store, McDonald's Barber Shop, Auguster's Studio, and People's Life Insurance Company. These businesses usually took ads in the Festival Book and/or supported floats for the parade. The Afro-American schools entered floats annually.

All of the parades had themes, sometimes there were songs, children's songs, nursery rhymes, etc. The floats were designed by local black people. Decorating the floats was in itself a festive event. There were always refreshments and music and the children and the adults worked together.

The girl and boy scouts paraded, high school and college bands played, the American Legion paraded, and black queens from other towns rode in convertable cars. There were black men and women on horses parading also. They paraded from Bank Ave., down Main Street, turning on Hopkins and turning again west onto Field Street to the West End Park.

Henderson High Band parades on Main Street during the 1958 Sugar Festival

Afro-Americans

There was a block dance on the Friday night of the three-day holiday in the 500 block of Hopkins St. in front of Sam Cooper's drug store. Everyone wore blue jeans, overalls, plaid shirts, etc., the farmer look was in for the block dance. Everyone went to the block dances, children and adults. There was live music.

Two of the Brown Sugar Queens were Rita Grace Collins of Baton Rouge and Barabara Miller of New Iberia. Some Miss Iberia's were Rhona Dauphine, Brenda Manuel, and Mary Alice Fontenette. Girls could participate more than once. Eleanor Victoria Egland was first runner-up to Queen Brown Sugar Barbara Miller in 1958, and First Runner up to Miss Iberia in 1959. Ms. Valerie Rochon and Delores Smith and Phyllis Polk were the three runners up in the 1962 Miss Iberia Pageant.

Whatever happened to the Queen Brown Sugar or West End Division? According to former presidents Sylvester Rochon and Dr. James Henderson there were several reasons for the death of this organization.

One problem arose when some newer members pushed for the Brown Sugar Queen to ride in the "white" Sugar Sunday Parade along with the other queens such as the Dairy Queen and Yam and Shrimp queens. A second problem was that the black organization was getting only $500.00 to sponsor their activities, while whites were getting much more money. There were times when the members of the black community used their own money to pay for festival activities. Those persons interested in the organization then realized that without a fair share of Sugar Festival funding, their efforts were becoming personally costly. They therefore decided to dissolve the organization in the mid-1960s.

Conclusion

As stated in the beginning of this essay, this is an overview of some of the activities of New Iberia's black community between 1865 and approximately 1960. It does not pretend to cover the story in detail, particularly the momentous events that have swept across black America since school desegregation and the Civil Rights Acts of the mid-1960s. This essay is only intended to guide the reader to some of the highlights of the local black experience; it omits any detailed discussion of the personal and group hardships suffered by Afro-Americans in New Iberia. To tell the full story of black success and adversity in New Iberia a much larger volume, based on much more extensive research, will be required. It is hoped that this essay will spark the interest of some person or group to undertake the larger work. This thread has been spun, it only needs now to be woven into the historical tapestry of New Iberia.

XXV

A History of the New Iberia Library

by
Ruth Lefkovits
and
Carla Klapper

The first library in New Iberia was established by the women of the First Methodist Church and was intended for the use of church members. The original collection of books was given by Mrs. Henry Pharr, Miss Lucy Gebert, and Miss Louise Taylor; these ladies, together with Henry Pharr, comprised the first library committee. This Sunday School library officially opened in 1918, housed in a building which had been the Methodist parsonage. When the first educational building was erected, the library was moved into it.

At a later date the ladies then served on the library committee, Mrs. Robert Perry, Miss Hilda Roberts, and Miss Katherine Winters, together with the Reverend and Mrs. H. W. Brown organized themselves into a board of directors. Soon the library opened to the neighborhood children and later the public.

Women of other religious denominations were added to the board, bringing total membership to twelve. Various ladies served as volunteer librarians until 1921, when Miss Alma Sharp became the first paid staff member. Thereafter, Miss Florence Trotter was appointed and dedicated herself to the task for many years.

In order to supply the demand for books, a yearly drive was held with board members serving as collectors. In 1927 the seemingly enormous sum of $266.25

The Library

New Iberia Community Library and Iberia Parish Library, 1940-1966

was collected; some years later the collected amount rose to $698.75. The Methodist Church, during the twenty-two years it housed the library, provided heat, light, and janitorial services.

The board, realizing that to serve the public adequately more funds and a suitable building had to be provided, began to raise money to erect a library building. The Iberia Parish School Board, through its superintendent, Lloyd G. Porter, Sr., donated a lot at 214 Weeks Street for the construction of a library building. The Young Men's Progressive Association, which had concerned itself with the industrial progress of the community, was then disbanding. Through the good offices of Carlos J. Bodin, Maurice Bergerie, and Judge S. O. Landry, the Association donated the surplus of its treasury, $2,300, to the Library Building Fund. This marked the first substantial contribution.

On March 31, 1940, the Iberia Community Library moved its 8,000 books into the new building designed by Architect Owen J. Southwell. Mrs. C. Arthur Provost was then serving as president of the board.

After several years of operation, the board realized that a more adequate, parishwide service was needed. The Louisiana State Library was requested to provide a demonstration library for the parish. With the help of that agency, the governing body of the community library aroused parishwide interest in the project. The result was the passage of the necessary ordinance by the Iberia Parish Police Jury. In turn, the State Library sent into the parish a field worker who made a survey of parish needs, and, with the help of local citizens, worked out a plan of service with branches in communities and a bookmobile to serve the rural areas. The independent libraries in Jeanerette and at Weeks Island also agreed to join the parish system.

The Iberia Parish Police Jury appropriated $7,000.00 to cover overhead expenses and the payment of the salaries of necessary local workers during the demonstration year.

On September 1, 1947, Miss Elizabeth Cammack, a graduate librarian, and field worker Miss Sallie Farrell, who later became the Louisiana State Librarian, were sent to initiate the project, assisted by Mrs. Walter Carstens of the Community Library staff. They brought in a new bookmobile and nine thousand books which had been catalogued ready for use. Two other trained librarians were added--Miss Ruth Lefkovits, later second Parish Librarian, and Miss Louise Risley (later Mrs. Frederick Fisher), Branch Librarian, who became assistant librarian.

The formal opening of the Iberia Parish Library, the twenty-sixth parish library in the state, was on October 24, 1947. Ceremonies were held in the old courthouse building on Main Street, where the headquarters operation was located. The New Iberia Branch occupied the Community Library Building on Weeks Street. Members of the Demonstration Library Board were Jacob S. Landry, president; Dr. L. M. Villien; L. G. Porter, Sr.; George Lallande; Howard Olivier; Paul Hebert, ex officio.

The State Library provided the staff and a bookmobile and 12,000 books during the demonstration year and use of the library increased significantly. Meanwhile, work was going on throughout the parish to locate and equip branch libraries in Jeanerette, Loreauville, Weeks Island, and the Booker T. Washington Branch in New Iberia. A campaign of less than one year's duration was carried on to demonstrate to the people of the parish the significance of a parish library. On July 13, 1948, a two-mill tax was voted to continue the project with local financing. One hundred sixty-two people voted $1,103,162 in valuation for, twenty-six persons voted $74,231 against. From the beginning, members of each Parish Police Jury and Parish Council have been most helpful and cooperative in working with the library.

The board which assumed control of parish library operations on November 1, 1948, was composed of Jacob S. Landry, president; George Lallande; Lloyd Porter, Sr.; Dr. L. M. Villien; W. D. Reynolds; and Howard Olivier, ex officio (police jury president). On November 10, John Darnell was appointed to replace Reynolds as a board member. Mary Collins joined the staff as cataloger in 1948.

In 1949 the old courthouse was sold, and W. J. Quick, who bid $25,895 was award the contract to build an annex designed by Hayes Town to the New Iberia Branch library building. Construction started in mid-June. Meanwhile, the Library Board and the School Board jointly donated to the police jury all library property and assets to be used for library purposes. The headquarters was occupied by the staff in late 1949 and a formal opening was held on January 12, 1950.

For having made the greatest progress in the public-library field in 1949, the Iberia Parish Library received the Modisette Memorial Award of the Louisiana Library Association.

In July 1953 the New Iberia Community Library Board presented to the parish library a check for $2,051.41 to help pay to air condition the New Iberia Branch and headquarters building. This closed out the treasury and the Community Library board dissolved.

Miss Elizabeth Cammack, who was appointed in September 1947 to conduct the demonstration library and remained as Iberia Parish Librarian, resigned effective June 15, 1954. Ruth Lefkovits, assistant parish librarian since the demonstration began, was appointed to succeed Miss Cammack.

The Booker T. Washington Branch Library that served the black community was erected in 1954, designed also by Hayes Town. F. & F. Material and Construction was awarded the bid for $14,875. The lot on the corner of Frere and Walton streets was bought for $2,200. The building was dedicated on February 6, 1966, and replaced the original branch on the grounds of Iberia Training School. This branch was discontinued in July 1976 because of lack of use.

On March 11, 1958, the two-mill tax was renewed for another ten years. The proposition passed with a majority of 281 votes and $1,041,449.50 in assessed valuations. Three hundred seventeen voters went to the polls, where the commissioners served without pay.

In May 1959 the library purchased the Archie Campbell property adjoining its property on Weeks Street. The house was sold and moved, and the site became a parking lot. In July 1959 the City Park Branch opened in the New Iberia Recreation Center.

Iberia Parish Library, 1966 -

In 1961 a campaign was initiated to construct a new library building on the grounds of the proposed Civic Center. Owing largely to the efforts of Mayor P. Armand Viator, this eventually resulted in the construction of the present building, which opened for use June 27, 1966. The city gave a ninety-nine year lease on the site, a $300,000 bond issue (with no increase in taxes) financed construction. Three hundred fifty ballots were cast in the April 21 election, three hundred thirteen for the proposition. With a bid of $293,628, E. E. Rabalais and Sons became contractors. The firms of Perry Segura & Associates and Perry Brown were the architects.

The library sponsored the work of Maurine Bergerie in preparing a history of New Iberia and Iberia Parish based upon her M. A. thesis. On March 20, 1963, the library held a reception and autograph party for the author of the first published history of the parish, *They Tasted Bayou Water*. Several organizations and individuals participated in the event with Mrs. A. C. Bernard as chairman. The response nearly overwhelmed the facilities as fellow Iberians came to honor Miss Bergerie.

The Library

The first trust fund donated to the library was dedicated on May 14, 1964, in memory of Rear Admiral Kenneth D. Ringle by his family. Funds from the trust have established a special collection of naval history books. In 1970, Mr. and Mrs. Jacob S. Landry endowed the Avery-Contonio-Dietlein-Landry memorial collection of classic literature. The large-print book collection for those with poor vision was started with a $200 gift made by the New Iberia Lions Club. This collection was later endowed by Vincent G. and Katherine Bowman-Brigante in honor of their parents and is now known as the Bowman-Brigante Large Print Collection. Other library trusts include the Karl James Bigler III fund for the purchase of books on wildlife and the Eugene Morrow Boudreaux trust established in memory of this library trustee in 1981.

In 1967 the parish began opening the Theda Ewing (now Hopkins Street) School library once a week during the summer, and neighborhood children came in great numbers. This summer program resulted in the establishment of a 3,000 volume branch being opened in the West End Recreation Center located in Martin Luther King, Jr., Park on Field Street at the request of citizens of the area. Working closely with the city Parks and Recreation Board, the Library Board dedicated the new library on May 30, 1985.

George J. Lallande, president of the Iberia Parish Library Board and local business and civic leader, was named recipient of the 1967 Modisette Trustee Award for "his firm support and guidance which had been felt from the laying out of the first bookmobile routes in 1947 to the completion of a new $350,000 headquarters and main library branch in June 1966." The presentation was made at the Louisiana Library Association convention in Shreveport in March 1968.

Jacob S. Landry received the Modisette Memorial Trustee Award in 1977 for his long and outstanding service to libraries in Louisiana.

On April 16, 1968, the parish library tax was again renewed for two mills for a ten-year period. The vote was three hundred ninety-seven and $1,717,193 in favor, and seventy-five votes representing $195,850 against.

A tax election in December 1977 doubled the library millage. Following this show of support from the community, a bond issue was passed in 1980, to allow the renovation of the twenty-year-old main library. The second floor was opened to house offices, the processing department, and storage, while the first floor stack area was greatly enlarged and an expanded public meeting room and bookmobile department added.

Ruth Lefkovits retired after thirty-five years of service, twenty-eight of them as Parish Librarian, in 1982. During her term, the library outgrew three buildings and expanded its parish-wide system of operation. She left the library on firm financial footing with a newly renovated building and a book collection now exceeding 100,000 volumes. Her many years of effort were commended by the Police Jury upon her retirement. Carla S. Klapper, formerly director of the Bayouland Library System, was appointed in her place.

Mrs. Klapper continued the policy of improvement and expansion by overseeing the full automation of the library beginning in 1984. Offering computerized cataloguing, circulation control, and on-line public access, the Iberia Parish Library was the second library in the state to become fully automated.

Renewed emphasis was also put on public services. Three new professional positions: acquisitions, reference, and children's librarians, were added to the staff. Under first children's librarian, Karen Wallace, a year-round program of children's activities were implemented and a separate Children's Room created on the first floor of the library.

The reference department now headed by Christopher Brown coordinates interlibrary loan services through the Bayouland Library System, and interlibrary loan network of twelve parishes and three academic libraries which the library joined in 1974 after many years of cooperative efforts with surrounding parishes.

Shelby Jung in acquisitions has overseen the purchase of 7,000 new books annually since starting in her position in 1983.

Under Susan Edmunds, public relations assistant, the library continues a strong program of community activities. Art exhibits begun in 1964 with Leo Louviere have continued to feature Louisiana artists and photographers such as George Rodrigue, Bob Gordy, and Elemore Morgan. Creative writing and dramatics programs begun under Mrs. Diane Moore in 1971 have evolved into a full summer program of activities for youth now sponsored by the New Iberia Optimists Club where young people can attend workshops on computers, nature study, needlework, video-taping, and a variety of other topics.

Displays and lectures continue on a monthly basis and have included such diverse subjects as Leonardo da Vinci, Louisiana archaeology, antique clothing, and mules. Of special interest are a series of photo exhibits featuring the work of I. A. and Carroll Martin, New Iberia photographers. Copies of over eight hundred Martin pictures showing life in the area from 1895 to 1958 are now a permanent part of the library collection.

Current members of the Library Board are George Lallande, president, Jacob S. Landry, Evans LeMaire, John Rogers, David Degeyter, Mrs. Rosetta

The Library   461

Diggs, and the chairman of the Iberia Parish Council serves as ex-officio member.

As of 1986, the Iberia Parish Public Library operates a bookmobile and seven branches, New Iberia, City Park, Martin Luther King, Jr., Park, Jeanerette, Loreauville, the Morton Branch of Lydia, and the Delcambre Branch jointly operated with Vermilion Parish, and working toward further growth and service.

City Hall in the Civic Center complex, January 1986.

XXVI

Entertainment, Sports, and Recreation in New Iberia, 1830-1978

by
Carl A. Brasseaux

The recreational pursuits of New Iberians have experienced a remarkable evolutionary process during the past 130 years, for the media of public entertainment are molded by the technology and taste of each successive generation. One thing, however, has remained static; as in small towns throughout the country, recreational and cultural events in New Iberia have consistently been organized and promoted by a small corps of well-educated, middle and upper-middle class citizens. It is indeed a tribute to this cadre of public-spirited individuals that, with the exception of the Civil War and early Reconstruction years, the town has traditionally been blessed with a broad variety of public entertainment.

DEBATING SOCIETIES

The roots of cultural entertainment in New Iberia can be traced to the organization of the New Iberia Friendly Association by nineteen prominent local residents in early June 1847.[1] A debating society, the Association pro-

---

1. The organization included Jerome Mudd, president; J. B. Hacker, vice-president; A. Duperier, secretary; S. R. Singleton, censor; B. M. Amsden, treasurer; J. W. Richardson;

moted "sociability and intimacy, as well as . . . the mutual improvement of the members and their friends."[2] Under the organization's by-laws, the meetings, held at the Methodist Church,[3] consisted of a formal address "on some subject relating to science,"[4] a subsequent debate over a previously selected, and frequently controversial, topic, and, finally, dinner.[5] The meetings were well attended, and audiences of approximately 100 men and women were not uncommon, especially at debates featuring such topics as "Is it to [sic] the interest of the Government of the United States to Colonize Liberia?"[6] The society, however, reached the apogee of its short-lived existence when Charles Gayarré, the noted Louisiana historian and politician, participated in a debate.

Despite its manifest popularity, the Association collapsed sometime prior to the beginning of the Civil War, and, with its dissolution, debating lay dormant in New Iberia until 1880 when the Phihistorians' Society was established. Interest in debating, however, seems to have died with the Society in early 1881, only to rise from its ashes in New Iberia's early twentieth-century secondary schools.

Debating's checkered career in New Iberia was due principally to its limited appeal. The early debating societies' ranks, for example, were consistently filled by local professionals, usually lawyers, and the topics of discussion usually held little interest for the masses. Other recreational pursuits, such as horse racing, suffered no such liability.

Samuel J. Denyer; Alfred Delahoussaye; E. M. Richardson; Alcibiades de Blanc; D. D. Richardson; G. Gonsoulin; Francis Richardson; A. C. Works; B. Hunter; J. G. Richardson; Alexandre Olivier; and Henry Delahoussaye. In their initial meeting, the debaters elected the following persons as honorary members: John Moore, Judge C. Voorhies, Col. Charles Olivier, Dr. W. Brashear, Rev. Jenkins, and Alexandre DeClouet. The Franklin *Planter's Banner*, June 10, 1847.

2. *Ibid.*, July 22, 1847.

3. In the 1840s, the Methodist Church was located on the corner of French and Washington streets. See the essay entitled "A Narrative of Events Connected with the Early Settlement of New Iberia."

4. *Planter's Banner*, June 10, 1847.

5. *Ibid.*, July 22, 1847.

6. *Ibid.*, August 5, 1848.

HORSE RACES

John Fitz Miller, David Weeks, and seven New Orleans area planters brought horse racing to New Iberia in the early 1830s through the establishment of the Attakapas Association for the Improvement of the Breed of Horses.[7] Horse racing had truly been the "sport of kings" in the Atlantic seaboard states in which most of the Association members had been born and reared--an expensive hobby involving the best available blooded stock. It is hardly surprising, therefore, that the Association attempted to continue this tradition in Attakapas through the importation of "George Martin" and "Sorrow," two fine English thoroughbreds, in 1835.[8] Through the acquisition of the initial blooded stock as well as the subsequent purchases of Kentucky, South Carolina, and Mississippi thoroughbreds, the Attakapas planter aristocracy could boast some of the finest turf competition in the South. Thus, it is hardly surprising that the Association's New Iberia track attracted racing fans from New Orleans and the river parishes.[9]

The early antebellum races were clearly dominated by David Weeks and John Fitz Miller. At the 1834 spring races, for example, horses owned by these men either won or finished second in each of the three featured races. Moreover, at the conclusion of the three-day turf extravaganza, Miller's bay filly "May Daigre" and Weeks' "Iberia" were matched in a $100 challenge race.[10]

Purses, however, as well as distances varied tremendously in the early New Iberia meets. In the 1834 spring races, for example, amounts varied from $150 to $300, and the featured races were of three miles, two miles, and the best "three of five" heats of undetermined distance.[11] It is apparent, however, that these meets were seasonal at best, and that the bulk of the antebellum horse fancier's time was devoted to improving his stock's blood lines.

7. St. Martinville *Attakapas Gazette*, July 12, 1834.

8. See the essay entitled, "The Obituary of William F. Weeks."

9. *Attakapas Gazette*, May 3, 1834.

10. *Ibid*.

11. *Ibid*.

The Civil War temporarily disrupted horse racing in and around New Iberia, for not only were most prominent local horsemen in the Confederate army, but practically all horseflesh in the city and its environs had been expropriated by the Confederate or Union armies. Local horse racing was revived, however, with the restoration of peace. In fact, by 1873, racing had become a sport of the masses in the New Iberia area. No longer was "the kind of sports" reserved for the wealthy, and, although the feature races, usually held on Sunday afternoons, included substantial purses ranging from $100 to $250, as well as Kentucky-bred stock, the featured races were clearly eclipsed by the number of challenge races involving work animals owned by small farmers.[12] Moreover, attendance figures at the local tracks indicate that local horses had their followings. For example, in early June, 1873, Bernard Suberbielle, L. Fontelieu, Theogène Viator, Martial Bonin, T. A. Babin, Louis Miguez, Derelle Romero, Sylvester Romero, and Lacroix Hebert travelled to Breaux Bridge to watch a challenge race between horses owned by Louis Delcambre, a New Iberian, and Emile Babin of Pont Breaux.[13] Moreover, in April 1880, approximately 1,200 local racing fans viewed a $400 match race between horses owned by John Raymond of St. John the Baptist Parish and O. Leleux of New Iberia.[14] Thus, whether a New Iberia horse ran at Smith's track, about one mile below New Iberia's southern boundary, or at Breaux Bridge, Broussard, or Lafayette, there were sure to be New Iberians on hand.[15]

Interest in local racing remained intense in New Iberia until the closure of the local track in the 1930s; now racing fans are compelled to follow the "sport of kings" from either the rural track at nearby Coteau or in the tinseled showcase of Evangeline Downs.

BALLS AND DANCING

Music and dancing have long been popular in New Iberia. Little is known of dancing in New Iberia prior to the Civil War, but it is certain that dances

---

12. New Iberia *Louisiana Sugar Bowl*, May 1, 1873.

13. *Ibid.*, June 12, 1873.

14. *Ibid.*, April 28, 1880.

15. *Ibid.*, June 12, 1873; February 17, May 20, 1876; April 28, 1880.

were highly caste oriented, attended by members of one social stratum. The musicians, however, appeared to have been Acadian fiddlers.

The most conspicuous of the antebellum town dances were given by the local planter aristocracy. One such ball, held in January, 1861, was described by a participant as "charmant, les demoiselles ont beaucoup danser et se sont bien amusée."[16]

Such "charming" outings, however, were soon suspended by the outbreak of hostilities. Moreover, the ravages of war as well as the emancipation of the slaves decimated the planters' fortunes, thus dictating the necessity of pursuing a more modest lifestyle and, concomitantly, less opulent social gatherings. According to Louis Paul Bryant, the early postbellum social events were held at Mrs. Gugueche Boutte's dance hall, the only public hall in New Iberia.[17]

In the 1870s, however, public dances largely lost the joyous informality of the early postwar years, especially after the rise of the New Iberia temperence movement in 1874. After 1874, balls were usually held specifically as fund-raisers in halls recently erected by local civic, fraternal, and temperence organizations.[18] Moreover, by 1880, the brass band had replaced the Cajun fiddler at the town balls. These fund raisers, which remained the principal source of revenues for many civic and charitable organizations until World War I, took many forms, but the local favorite was masquerade balls given in early spring.[19]

MARDI GRAS

The masquerade balls were the forerunners of the New Iberia Mardi Gras carnival. The first *bal-masque*, held in late March, 1875 for the benefit of the

---

16. Louise DeClouet to Paul DeClouet, January 12, 1861. DeClouet Family Papers, Collection 22, Box 1, folio ee, Southwestern Archives, University of Southwestern Louisiana.

17. See the essay entitled "Reminiscences of the 60's and 70's."

18. The earliest recorded fund raising ball was held in September 1873 for the benefit of America Fire Co. No. 2, an event which quickly evolved into an annual affair. *Sugar Bowl*, March 25, 1875; March 2, 1876; February 1, 1877.

19. For more on dancing, particularly in the 1920s and '30s, see the essay entitled "Retrospections on New Iberia in the Twenties and Thirties."

The Mardi Gras parade of 1896 moves along Main Street

Iberia Brass Band, was very well attended and its popularity provided the impetus for larger celebrations in the Crescent City mold.[20]

Beginning in the mid-1870s, hundreds of New Iberia residents made an annual pilgrimage to New Orleans for Mardi Gras, and New Iberia merchants loudly lamented the fact that large sums of local money were being spent in the Crescent City.[21] Profits thus provided the motive for, and the successful masquerade balls the means of, keeping these funds at home. In 1877, therefore, New Iberia merchants organized the town's first carnival parade, and the America Fire Company No. 2 held its annual masked ball on Mardi Gras evening for the first time.[22]

The city's first carnival celebration, however, proved to be a monumental disappointment, for not only was the weather uncooperative, but at least 315

20. *Ibid.*, March 25, 1875.

21. *Ibid.*, February 15, 1877.

22. *Ibid.*, February 1, 15, 1877.

New Iberians boarded steamers bound for the Crescent City.[23] Thus snubbed by the citizenry, the city fathers washed their hands of the fledgling carnival celebration, and, until 1895, Mardi Gras was again celebrated privately in New Iberia. For example, in February, 1880, the New Iberia Musical Society paradoxically "celebrated" Fat Tuesday at "Temperance Hall."[24] Moreover, in the early 1890s, the Order of the Kronick Kickers organized a series of private Mardi Gras balls.

Interest in a public carnival celebration thus remained dormant until early April, 1895, when the Iberia Carnival Association was organized for the expressed purpose of sponsoring "a street parade and ball annually on Mardi Gras or thereabouts."[25] During the months which followed, large numbers of the New Iberia citizenry were recruited as workers by the Association.[26] The result was the "most magnificent spectacle ever witnessed in New Iberia"[27]-- the 1896 Mardi Gras parade.

Highlighting the celebration was a half-mile-long parade featuring eight impressive floats. The first float, entitled "The Ship of Progress," represented America's rapid growth and development. In the wake of this landbound craft came the second parade float--"A Fool for Luck, and a Poor Man for Children." On this elaborately decorated, horse-drawn wagon sat a "titled fool" beneath a hexagonal, silken canopy, as well as an enormous shoe stuffed with children-- à la Mother Goose.[28] Float number three, "Evangeline Sits Before a Log Cabin Dreaming of Gabriel," was followed by a caricature of future generations, entitled "Anno Domini 2000." In this "humorous," though ironically prophetic, depiction of the distant future, men have become effiminate, "doing the household work such as nursing the baby and doing the family washing."[29]

23. *Ibid.*, February 15, 1877.

24. *Ibid.*

25. *Weekly Iberian*, April 6, 1895.

26. *Ibid.*, November 23, 1895.

27. *Ibid.*, February 22, 1896.

28. *Ibid.*

29. *Ibid.*

Women, on the other hand, have not only become breadwinners, but have violated the most sacred social taboo by becoming politicians as well. In order to convey this image to the public, the float featured a man rocking a child to sleep, while the woman stood at their side wearing pants. The fifth float, "Louisiana Sweetness for Which We Ask No Bounty"--a title reflecting the Iberia Parish sugar planters' position on the sugar bounty issue, featured a young girl representing New Iberia seated next to "Mother Louisiana, whose right arm is placed in an affectionate rather than a protecting manner on New Iberia's shoulder."[30] The remaining floats honored the region's bounteous agricultural production and featured caricatures of the local black population.

The floats, however, were not the parade's sole attraction. The 10,000 spectators lining Main Street for the 7:30 p.m. procession saw, in the eerie light of the 1,000 torches lining the roadway, the costumed splendor of "His Royal Highness, Le Roi des Cypres," attired in a red velvet costume "of the time of Louis XIII." His Majesty's approach was announced by a mounted platoon of costumed "household guards," the king's jester, the New Iberia Brass Band, the royal herald and his escort, and, finally, the King's bodyguard--the Knights of Pythias, Division No. 10.[31]

The tremendous success of the 1896 carnival gave impetus to even more impressive Mardi Gras celebrations. The foundation for these future extravaganzas was laid during the summer of 1896, when the Carnival Association constructed a large, wood-framed warehouse on the corner of St. Peter and Vine streets and collected over $3,000 for the 1897 carnival and ball.[32]

The growth of New Iberia's Mardi Gras celebration was also due, in part, to the efforts of a rival carnival association. Shortly after the organization of the Iberia Carnival Association, the Kronick Kickers--whose members, by this time, had become an endangered species--founded their own carnival association, the Phrisky Phunny Phellows. Lacking funds, the Phunny Phellows nevertheless sponsored a modest, and therefore poorly attended, parade in February 1896. Nevertheless, according to the *Weekly Iberian*, "their display was fully up to their motto 'We are out for Phun.'"[33] Despite the disappointing debut of their

30. *Ibid.*

31. *Ibid.*

32. *Ibid.*, September 19, 1896.

33. *Ibid.*

initial parade, however, the Phellows managed not only to acquire a modest warehouse during the summer of 1896, but to raise over $1,000 for their war chest as well.[34] These initial gains were subsequently offset by a loss of membership, and, as a consequence, the organization disappeared from the scene by 1905.

The Iberia Carnival Association, however, survived and sponsored successful Mardi Gras carnival parades and balls until the Great Depression. With the demise of the parish's original carnival association, Fat Tuesday was not celebrated on a grand scale in New Iberia until 1948, when the newly organized Krewe of Iberians held a street parade and masquerade ball. Although the street parade was discontinued after its debut, the Krewe has continued to sponsor annual Mardi Gras balls, as has the rival Krewe of Andalusia since 1957.

SUGAR CANE FESTIVAL

With the discontinuation of the Mardi Gras celebration in the early Depression years, New Iberia was left without a major festival. This void was filled in 1937, when Charles Stevenson, a native Californian, organized the Sugar Cane Festival as a means of promoting the area's major industry. Participation in the celebration was initially limited to New Iberians, but, following the establishment of the Louisiana Sugar Cane Festival and Fair Association in 1940, all of the state's twenty-two sugar parishes were invited to participate.[35]

The expansion of the festival's base of support fostered a concomitant growth in the celebration itself. For example, in 1940, an agricultural fair was established and the first pageant, the Cavalcade of Cane, was presented. The pageant, or coronation of the festival royalty, has, in fact, become the focal point of the festival itself. The coronation of Queen Sugar highlights one of Louisiana's most notable beauty contests, while the crowning of King Sucrose acknowledges outstanding service to the state's sugar industry.[36]

---

34. *Ibid.*

35. The number of participating sugar parishes has fallen to seventeen in recent years. Mrs. E. A. Dauterive, Jr., "History of the Louisiana Sugar Cane Festival," *Louisiana Sugar Cane Festival and Fair* (New Iberia, La., 1972), non-paginated.

36. Alberta Mestayer was crowned as the first Queen Sugar, while Earl K. Long reigned as King Sucrose I. *Ibid.*

The 1974 Queen's Parade of the Louisiana Sugar Festival moves along Main Street

The coronation ceremonies, and indeed the festival, were suspended during the Second World War, but from the cessation of hostilities until the mid-1970s, the celebration grew in size and importance. Thousands of spectators from throughout Louisiana flocked to New Iberia in late September for the opening ceremonies, coronation, agricultural fair, and the three major parades: the farmers' parade on Friday afternoon, the children's parade on Saturday morning, and the Queen's parade on Sunday afternoon. A fourth parade, organized by the black community and held on Saturday afternoon, was discontinued in the mid-1960s.

The growth and long-term success of the festival was due principally to the efforts of Robert J. "Bobby" Miranda, Sr. Miranda, a former King Sucrose, served as festival president from 1956 to 1984. An excellent organizer and promoter, he annually dispatched the reigning queen to the New York Ad. Club to speak on behalf of the festival and the Louisiana sugar industry, and also organized goodwill tours into other parts of the country.[37] He is succeeded by Miriam Krepper.

PATRIOTIC CELEBRATIONS

Festivals, such as the Sugar Cane Festival, have long filled the void occupied by the Fourth of July celebrations in the North and Midwest. Local neglect of Independence Day stems largely from the Civil War, for the firing of guns and fireworks, as well as lengthy patriotic speeches typified the town's antebellum observances.[38] The scars produced by the war, however, festered until July 4, 1876, when the town celebrated the country's centennial anniversary in grand style.[39]

The euphoria permeating New Iberia's Centennial celebration was due principally to the national upwelling of patriotism on the hundredth anniver-

---

37. Janice Dugas, "Salute to Robert J. Miranda, Sr.," *33rd Annual Louisiana Sugar Cane Festival and Fair* (New Iberia, La., 1974).

38. James H. Dormon, "Aspects of Acadiana Plantation Life in the Mid-Nineteenth Century: A Microcosmic View," *Louisiana History*, XVI (1975), 368.

39. For a detailed discussion of the 1876 celebration in New Iberia, see the essay entitled "The Centennial Celebration at New Iberia, 1876."

sary of the Declaration of Independence and did not reflect a local *rapprochement* with the federal government. In 1879, for example, the Fourth of July was marked by "a few discharges of powder."[40] In fact, only at the turn of the century had the wounds created by the Civil War healed sufficiently to permit a truly significant, annual observance of the nation's birthday.

In 1899, Capt. Anthony N. Muller of the local militia unit, the Attakapas Rifles, organized a Fourth of July celebration at Iberia Park, featuring a military parade, clay pigeon shoot, mock battle, tournament and ball at the city hall.[41] In subsequent years, the celebration was sponsored by America Fire Co. No. 2 and, as a consequence, emphasis was shifted from the martial arts to field sports and horse racing. The tournament instituted by the Rifles, however, remained, and the "successful knights" consistently crowned the "queen and maids of honor" at the balls which traditionally concluded the celebration.[42]

Independence Day celebrations persisted as a local social institution until the Great Depression. As with the Mardi Gras celebration, the economic dislocation stemming from the Depression compelled local sponsors to curtail and, by 1939, to discontinue local observance of the national holiday. Moreover, following the Depression and subsequent war years, no attempt was made to revive the traditional celebration; therefore, only the occasional crackle of firecrackers distinguishes the nation's anniversary from the unhallowed days surrounding it.

Even at their zenith, however, the Fourth of July observances could not match the intensity of the spontaneous celebrations precipitated by the state's redemption in 1877 and the conclusion of the First and Second World Wars. The end of carpetbagger rule in Louisiana in early May 1877 resulted in wild rejoicing in the streets of New Iberia. According to J. Y. Gilmore, editor of the *Louisiana Sugar Bowl*:

> Our hearts are filled with joy at being once again a free people, allowed to govern ourselves in our own way, and hence the thousands of people who on this occasion paraded our streets in procession, both

---

40. *Sugar Bowl*, July 10, 1879.

41. *Weekly Iberian*, July 8, 1899.

42. *New Iberia Enterprise*, June 16, 1899; June 16, 1900; July 5, 1905.

day and night, and hear the public speaking at Weeks' Grove, all bore joyous faces. . . . Many colored people participated in the processions, some with appropriate banners, and many were interested listeners at the speaking. United States flags, for the first time since the war, were displayed from almost every house. We feel the Union is now fully restored, since we have resumed our place as a sovereign State, and all will pray, 'Long live the Union.'[43]

The intensity of emotion reflected in Gilmore's statements pale by comparison to that displayed by New Iberians on Armistice Day 1918. At four a.m. on Monday, November 11, the suspension of hostilities was announced by the tolling of bells and incessant blasts of steam whistles. The men of the community assembled on Main Street, and, upon hearing the glad tidings, were so overwhelmed by a spontaneous outpouring of joy that they remained in the thoroughfare. At dawn, the crowd grew rapidly as women, children, and residents of the outlying areas descended upon Main Street to determine the cause of the uproar. They, too, became enraptured and remained. Thus,

> The laborer, the artisan, the merchant and clerk, the banker and professional man, the house wife, all by common consent, abandoned the day's tasks, all with hearts laden with happiness and countenances beaming with joy, joining the crushing; surging mass on the street where dynamite stocks, horns, trumpets, hand bells, and all manner of noise making devices created a turmoil which was enhanced to pandemonium by the incessant tolling of bells, blowing of whistles and discharge of an improvised cannon in front of the Court House.[44]

Pandemonium reigned on Main Street until two p.m., when a parade was organized by the local Red Cross chapter. Leading the procession was "a line of automobiles." The cars were followed by delegations representing local organizations, the most noteworthy of which was the local Italian-American club, the Christofo Columbo Society. Bringing up the rear were the local black school children. After "Marching up Main Street," the parade participants and spec-

---

43. *Sugar Bowl*, July 10, 1879.

44. *Enterprise*, November 16, 1918.

tators formed ranks on the public square in anticipation of patriotic speeches. Upon conclusion of the addresses, however, the revelry resumed and continued until long after dark.[45]

The outpouring of emotion which characterized Armistice Day also typified V-J Day. The announcement of Japan's surrender on August 14, 1945 elicited

> ... tears, laughter, hysteria and prayers. ... New Iberia flung off its wartime restraint and exploded in the greatest wildest celebration of all time. Boisterous, happy crowds sang, danced and cheered into the early morning. The main streets were jammed with cars, all with horns sounding, until late.[46]

The package liquor stores and bars did a heavy business before closing. The churches were crowded throughout the afternoon, and large crowds attended special V-J Day services the next day.[47]

BASTILLE DAY

Patriotism and Americanism in New Iberia have not always been synonymous. Throughout the late antebellum period, New Iberia boasted a substantial and prosperous French immigrant minority; though separated from the motherland by over 4,000 miles, the immigrants' bonds to French soil remained strong. As a consequence, in 1877, the Frenchmen organized the Société de Bienfaisance et d'Assistance Mutuelle, a social organization which held regular meetings--or, more precisely, drinking bouts--until World War I.[48]

Information regarding the Société is fragmentary, but the organization annually held elaborate banquets to commemorate Bastille Day. On July 14, 1904, for example, the immigrants gathered at Pierre Cornière's restaurant, which was bedecked with French tri-colors. "A most pleasing program was carried out of toasts, responses, songs, especially the 'Marseillaise' by Mr. A. J.

---

45. *Ibid.*

46. Contributing to the din was a plantation bell beaten with a hammer and mounted on a large truck. *Ibid.*, August 17, 1945.

47. *Enterprise*, August 17, 1945.

48. Pierre Jubin served as president of the organization from 1888 to 1910. *Ibid.*

Maumus and Chas. A. Badon, which thrilled the entire company and called up all the martial ardor and patriotic pride of those present."[49]

BRASS BANDS

The depth of feeling at the patriotic and political gatherings was frequently intensified by martial airs played by local brass bands. New Iberia's first brass band was organized in the early 1870s and, under the direction of Homer Segura, was reorganized in August 1874.[50] In their debut, these musicians, who styled themselves the Original Iberia Brass Band, "played at the White League meeting and acquitted themselves well."[51] The band's initial performance was a harbinger of things to come, for, from 1874 until its dissolution during the Great Depression, the Original Iberia Brass Band remained the community's premier musical organization.[52]

Apparently prompted by the success of Segura's band, a host of imitators soon sprang into existence. In the spring of 1875, for example, Dick Palmer, former leader of the Hyperion Brass Band of Vermilionville (present-day Lafayette), moved to New Iberia, and, shortly thereafter, organized the Iberia Brass Band (thus forcing Segura's musicians to assume the name Original Iberia Brass Band). In order to generate funds for the acquisition of new instruments for the Iberia band, Palmer persuaded his former Vermilionville band students to perform at a charity, masquerade ball.[53] The proceeds from the ball were indeed gratifying, for the members of the Iberia Brass Band subsequently purchased "the best instruments which ever came to Western Louisiana."[54] The formid-

---

49. *Ibid.*, July 16, 1904; July 20, 1907; October 16, 1910.

50. *Sugar Bowl*, June 25, 1874.

51. *Ibid.*

52. The band underwent at least two reorganizations during the first quarter-century of its existence. In 1879 the band was reorganized by Prof. G. Sontag, a former European music instructor, while two years later, Prof. J. E. Martin directed a second reorganization. *Ibid.*, September 4, 1879; June 30, 1881.

53. *Ibid.*, March 25, 1875.

54. *Ibid.*, April 29, 1875.

able combination of fine instruments and a seasoned director, however, did not ensure longevity, and the band appears to have dissolved by 1876.

Other pretenders to the Original Iberia Brass Band's title as the best musical organization in New Iberia were the following: an unnamed string band organized in 1874; a colored brass band, 1875; the Excelsior Brass Band, 1875; Holy Cross College Brass Band, 1876; and the Emma Warren Band, 1896.

CIRCUSES

New Iberia music lovers could also hear brass bands at the numerous circuses which performed frequently at the community. Blessed with excellent steamboat connections with New Orleans, New Iberia was visited by a surprisingly large number of circuses. For example, in the spring of 1855, a menagerie and a "grand Circus" performed in the community. The performances, always preceded by a circus parade down Main Street, were apparently well patronized, for Eliza Robertson noted that "a circus company have just arrived and the town is in the greatest excitement. there [sic] is a perfect crowd of people."[55]

The Civil War disrupted the traditional circus schedules in the South, and no circus performed at New Iberia from 1861 until early December 1876, when Dan Rice's Circus, Menagerie, and Trained Animal Exhibitions staged the "largest and best river show seen for 20 years. . . ."[56] From 1876 to 1920, however, entertainment-seeking New Iberians thrilled to the exploits of at least one touring circus per year.

Circuses touring Southwest Louisiana prior to the advent of the iron horse had to charter at least two steamboats; however, the circuses calling upon New Iberia in the late 1870s were rather unspectacular side shows, but, with the completion of the Morgan line to New Iberia in 1879, the quality of the circus acts gradually improved. In fact, by the mid-1890s, some of the best circuses in the country stopped at New Iberia. For example, the Great Wallace Show, which called itself "The Eighth Wonder of the World," performed at New Iberia in 1895 and 1896. Like most contemporary circuses, the Wallace Show featured a menagerie, a hippodrome, and a small theatre, featuring pantomime artists. But the show clearly overshadowed its contemporaries in sheer bulk of

---

55. Eliza Robertson Diary, quoted in Dormon, "Aspects of Plantation Life," 368.

56. *Sugar Bowl*, December 7, 1876.

THREE GENERATIONS OF CIVIC BANDS

Civic bands were for a long time a New Iberia tradition. That fact is emphasized in the pictures here. Three generations of the Martin family have been closely associated with these civic endeavors. In the photograph above, seated center, front row (with mustache) is Jacob Martin who settled in New Iberia in 1876. In the photograph on the opposite page (above), Jacob's son, Guy Martin, Sr (far right) is seen with the Chamber of Commerce Band in 1921. Below (opposite page), Guy Martin, Jr., stands at far left in this 1951 photograph of the New Iberia City Band.

Entertainment, Sports, and Recreation 479

talent. For example, the show, transported by *four* trains, was housed in "ten acres of canvas" and was capable of seating 20,000 persons. Moreover, the circus featured internationally famous circus performers, such as Ralston, "whose feat of leaping from the Washington Monument 555 feet is unparalleled."[57]

The real attraction for local circus fans, however, was the traditional circus parade.

> At about half past ten o'clock A. M. the great [Wallace] street parade started from the tents, and passed through on both St. Peter and Main streets, with its four brass bands, and from ten to twelve cages. Some of the cages contained lions, tigers and one with a lady with snakes around her neck, also a new calliope with its sweet songs, and we must say that they had five elephants, two of the largest that ever set foot in New Iberia. Mr. Wallace also had four large camels. In the parade was a clown in a cart, representing a large bottle which was the ad of a firm. The hour of the parade was about to start, crowds gathered at the tent and at nearly every corner. There were but two performances and each proved to be very successful. The first performance was 2 o'clock P. M. and a very large crowd witnessed it. The night performance was a very good one and was witnessed by from four to five thousand people.[58]

WILD WEST SHOWS

New Iberia not only attracted such fine circuses as the Wallace and Ringling Brothers[59] shows in the 1890s and early twentieth century, but the two greatest wild west shows in American history. Pawnee Bill's Wild West Show the "Greatest WILD WEST in the World," came to town in early October, 1895, with a remarkable array of horsemen and cowgirls, including "Australian Aborigines, Genuine Carnival Bush Men, Famous Black Trackers"; Indian chiefs of renown;

---

57. *Weekly Iberian*, November 7, 1896.

58. *Ibid.*, October 25, 1902.

59. *Ibid.*, November 30, 1895.

Entertainment, Sports, and Recreation

Evangeline Theatre, June 1933

dozens of Sioux, Cheyenne, and Arapahoe warriors; a Mexican band; two brass bands; an "army" of cowboys; and a troupe of Japanese "lancers, fighters, and fencers."[60] Also featured was "Miss May Hollie, the only lady who can shoot unerringly with a rifle from Horseback."[61] This bevy of talent was employed in a variety of acts ranging from boomerang exhibitions, and reenactments of Indian battles, to horse and chariot races, to lariat exhibitions, to rodeo contests.

Pawnee Bill's show was rivaled only by that of "The King of Them All," Col. W. F. "Buffalo Bill" Cody. Buffalo Bill's show came to New Iberia in late October 1902, with more "peerless Riders, Warlike pageants, Chivalrous Charac-

---

60. *Ibid.*, October 5, 1895.

61. *Ibid.*

ters, [and] Strange People Than ever before presented...."[62] In addition to a street parade, the wild west show staged one afternoon performance at New Iberia, and for the price of fifty cents (twenty-five for children) one could attend "A Veritable Kindergarten of History"--epic reenactments of Indian battles, rescues at sea, and the "thrilling military spectacle of the capture of Pekin."[63]

EXCURSIONS

If the show, however, did not come to town, the New Iberian could, following the establishment of rail connections with New Orleans in 1879, go to the show. The most popular means of attending "big-name" performances in New Orleans was by rail excursion, sponsored by the Texas and Pacific Railroad. The railroad also offered promotional excurstion from New Iberia to New Orleans for the Mardi Gras carnival. The most popular excursions, however, involved trips by rail to neighboring communities for fairs, balls, or picnics, sponsored by civic and fraternal organizations. In the first recorded rail excursion from New Iberia in July 1880, for example, 450 townsmen attended a "grand affair" sponsored by the Thibodaux Benevolent Association.

As excursions proved an economic boon for the hosting community, New Iberia merchants encouraged city sponsorship of these "affairs." This call for action was taken up by New Iberia's civic organization and the black community, and, as a consequence, black and white excursionists visited New Iberia in the 1880s and 1890s.

TOURNAMENTS

A principal, late-nineteenth-century New Iberia attraction for the local traveling public was the tournament sponsored annually by the Episcopal Church of the Epiphany. The tournament, traditionally held in May or early June, usually featured three-legged races, pigeon shoots, women's rifle competition, bicycle races, a tug of war, and a mule race. In the late 1890s, the mule race was replaced by the *tournoi*. In either contest, however, participants

---

62. *Enterprise*, October 25, 1895.

63. *Ibid*.

Entertainment, Sports, and Recreation

"The Louisiana Six"
A popular New Iberia dance band of the 1930s. From left: Leo Girouard, Coosoon Girouard, Noah Hebert, Cap Hebert, Viola Hebert Landry and Wilton Hebert

dressed in colorful costumes, and, for the day, assumed the title of knight. The three best riders always crowned the queen of the ball which traditionally closed the tournament.

PICNICS AND PROMENADES

The Episcopal tournaments, which endured from the 1870s through the 1890s, were simply large-scale versions of the town's favorite weekend pastime-- the picnic. According to Louis Paul Bryant, "All-day picnics and fishing parties were very popular and were generally arranged for weeks in advance."[64] By

---

64. See Bryant, "Reminiscences of the 60's and 70's."

1915, in fact, picnics had "become the order of the day, more especially on Sunday our young people have time to get a days [sic] recreation in some lovely spot in the Parish."[65] In addition, by 1915, fishing had become an integral part of picnics organized by local businessmen; these outings, however, generally netted as many empty bottles as fish.[66]

Another popular weekend pursuit was the promenade.

> It was also the custom for young people to attend vesper services at the Catholic church on Sunday afternoon, and thereafter the boys and girls would pair off and walk down East Main Street, which was known as Lover's Lane. The walks would extend no further than to a bridge which spanned a large canal at a point where Ann Street now intersects East Main and this bridge was called 'Lover's Bridge.' The walks did not extend any further because it was an unwritten law that the young ladies had to be back at their homes by sundown.[67]

BASEBALL

Though Cupid reigned over Sunday afternoons, Abner Doubleday ruled for a good portion of the weekend. Local newspapers suggest that New Iberians regularly participated in the sport, both in sandlot and in intercity games. The first recorded intercity contest, a "dread encounter" between the New Iberia Quicksteps and the St. Martinville Attakapas Club, initiated a long-standing rivalry between these neighboring communities.[68]

Games such as those between the New Iberia and St. Martinville teams were not merely athletic contests, but significant local social events as well. For example, after the game between the Quicksteps and the St. Martin Mutuals in

---

65. *Enterprise*, July 10, 1915.

66. *Ibid.*, June 11, 1904.

67. Bryant, "Reminiscences of the 60's and 70's."

68. Maurine Bergerie, *They Tasted Bayou Water: A Brief History of Iberia Parish* (New Orleans, 1962), pp. 89-90.

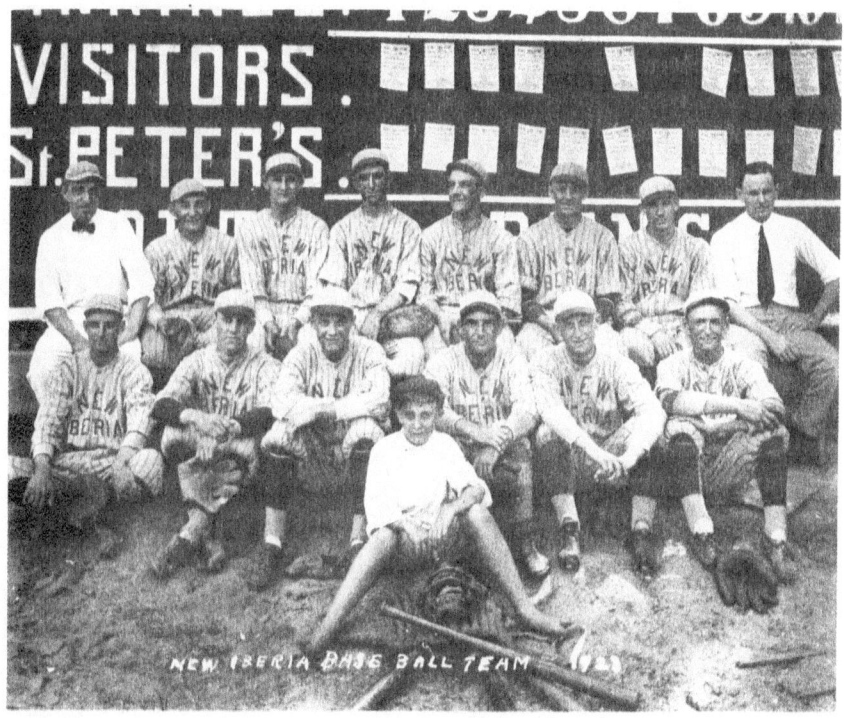

The 1923 New Iberia Baseball Team
Top row, from left: Luca Jennaro, Chummy Trappey, Alfred Hitter, Sr., Fisher Koch, Lawrence Dietlein, Oswald Mestayer, Wilfred Conrad, Sr., and James Hall. Seated, from left: Val Pourciau, _____ Lemmon, Bernard Tabony, _____ Gonsoulin, C. C. Gunn, Herby Pourciau. Batboy, Joe Dimarco

May 1874, the players and many of the spectators attended a ball at Boutte's Hall.[69] Moreover, in July 1878, a game between the Quicksteps and a Franklin team attracted a boatload of spectators from St. Mary Parish.[70]

The interest displayed by the St. Mary residents typifies the intensity of baseball fever in the New Iberia area. This local interest and support of the Quicksteps is also reflected in the remarkable amount of news coverage given to the team by the local newspaper. Thus, the outcome of the games was a source of public rejoicing or lamentations.

69. *Sugar Bowl*, May 28, 1874.

70. *Ibid.*, July 25, 1878.

The 1940 New Iberia Cardinals of the Evangeline League

The intense local interest in baseball was due in part to the Quicksteps' proficiency on the field. Between 1875 and 1879, for example, the Quicksteps No. 2, successors to the original New Iberia nine, compiled a record of thirteen wins and only three losses in intercity competition.[71]

The Quicksteps' season ranged from May to October and their games were played at the Holy Cross College campus. The contests ranged in length from four to nine innings, but, regardless of the length, fans were sure of seeing plenty of scoring. For example, in May 1874, the Quicksteps scored 39 runs against the St. Martin Mutuals *in a losing cause.*[72] Moreover, in 1879, the Quicksteps and Jeanerette Pelicans scored a total of thirty-one runs in a four-inning game.[73]

71. *Ibid.*, May 1, 1879. The Quicksteps disbanded for two weeks in May 1879.

72. *Ibid.*, May 28, 1879.

73. In 1879, the Quicksteps were composed of Albert Escudier, G. Gardemal, S.

The Quicksteps' dominance of the local baseball circuit began to wane by the mid-1880s. In 1885, for instance, the Quicksteps were trounced in three consecutive games by their St. Martinville rivals. Interest in the club seems to have fallen with its fortunes, and the team apparently disbanded sometime prior to 1895.

Interest in baseball was revived in 1899 with the organization of the New Iberia Iberians.[74] The club was mediocre at best, and it apparently disbanded by the turn of the century. In 1902, however, local interest in the national pastime was temporarily revived through the establishment of the "Iberia Jr. and Iberia Sr." teams;[75] the former club consisted of teenagers and was the prototype of the present American Legion team (which was organized in 1947), while the latter club consisted of adults, thus serving as the forerunner of the minor league, professional and semi-professional clubs that played at New Iberia.

Semi-professional baseball first appeared at New Iberia in 1903, when the town acquired a franchise in the Sugar Belt League. The league, however, disbanded long before the beginning of the First World War. From the conclusion of the Great War until the early 1920s, St. Peter's College students manned a team which played for gate receipts. The play of the collegians, however, was clearly overshadowed by that of a semi-professional, Texas League club organized in 1920 by Julius Scharff. The team, which was composed of "discards" from Southern minor league clubs, especially the New Orleans Pelicans and the Houston Buffaloes, performed before large crowds at Myrtis Park, an open field owned by Scharff (the present site of Town and Country Shopping Center), until the club's dissolution in 1924.

Professional baseball was introduced into New Iberia in 1934, when the Evangeline League was established. New Iberia was an original member of the D-class league, and served as a farm club for the St. Louis Cardinals. According to Rayford Mullins, former league president, the Evangeline League furnished more players to major league teams than any comparable farm system in the

---

Migues, G. Doerle, H. Gankendorff, T. Blake, A. Escudier, A. Wiltz, and J. Emmer. *Ibid.,* October 23, 1879.

74. At the time of its organization, the Iberians included Gabriel Conrad, Willie Lourd, Alfred Duperier, Joe Davis, Armand Daspit, L. S. Lemaire, Paul Voorhies, Frank Ledger, John Mason, Nemour Bergerie and Gabriel LeBlanc. *Weekly Iberian*, August 5, 1899.

75. *Enterprise*, August 2, 1902.

country. Prior to its dissolution in 1957, the New Iberia franchise, for example, furnished a host of players to St. Louis, including pitchers Mel Parnel, Red Monger and Terry Fox.

The passing of the Evangeline League in 1957 did not spell the end of baseball in New Iberia. On the contrary, from the late 1950s to the present, New Iberia has consistently fielded some of the most outstanding high school and American Legion teams in Southwest Louisiana.

TENNIS, GOLF, ROLLER SKATING, AND FOOTBALL

Tennis is a relative newcomer to the realm of sports in New Iberia. Local interest in tennis apparently dates from the founding of the New Iberia Tennis Club in 1909.[76] In addition, in 1914, a tennis team was organized at Central High School.[77] The sport, however, was enjoyed only by the upper and upper-middle classes until the tennis craze of the late 1960s and 1970s.

Golf, like tennis, dates from the formation of a local country club, the Iberia Golf Club. Founded in the 1920s by Rev. John McGlade,[78] the club has served as the focal point of local interest in the sport to the present.

Roller skating has enjoyed a rather checkered career in New Iberia. Local interest in the sport dates from the construction of a roller rink on Iberia Street in 1906.[79] In fact, local interest in skating was sufficiently intense in December 1906 to justify the booking of Professor Albert C. Waltz, "the champion roller skater of the world."[80] The skating "craze," however, soon died out, and local participation in the sport was confined to school yards and city sidewalks until recent years.

Football was introduced into New Iberia in 1904, when the Central High

---

76. *Ibid.*, September 14, 1912.

77. Vivien A. Mestayer, "The History of the New Iberia High School, 1887 Through 1950" (MA thesis, Louisiana State University, 1951), p. 31.

78. The Iberia Golf Club's initial officers were Edward Estorge, president; Charles Henshaw, vice-president; E. H. Buffington, treasurer; and Alice Gates, secretary.

79. *Enterprise,* September 29, 1906.

80. *Ibid.*, December 22, 1906.

New Iberia High School's Yellow Jackets of 1921
Seated in front: George Dupuy. First row, from left: Milton Herpeche, _____ Soileau, Chris Memtsas, Frank Guillot, Clarence Delcambre, James Suberbielle, Jacob Landry, Walter Gosling, Knox Broussard. Second row, from left: Carroll Romero, Leroy Sumrall, Leon Pennison, Abraham Hebert, Roland Lejeune, Wofford Sanders, Vaughan Taylor, Walter Carstens. Third row, from left: Vernon Belanger, Alton Lourd, Jules Landry, Charles Sullivan, Mervin Daniels, Ulysse Landry, George Cousin, Walter W. Teekel, Franklin von Yeutter. In rear: Charles M. Bahon, principal.

School team was organized under the tutelage of Coach E. S. Jenkins.[81] Unlike modern teams, the eleven-man New Iberia squad played the entire game without substitutes.[82] The early Central High teams, whose colors were orange and black, were noted for their successful campaigns on the gridiron. The 1904 eleven, for example, defeated squads representing Franklin, St. Martinville

---

81. Mestayer, "New Iberia High School," p. 29.

82. *Ibid.*, pp. 29-30.

The 1923 St. Peter's College Basketball Team
Front row, from left: Walter Angers, Jr., Val Pourciau, Herb Pourciau, and Albert Landry. Back row, from left: J. S. Brown, Jr., Tony Landry, and Ed. Landry.

and Jennings high schools, as well as the Southwestern Louisiana Industrial Institute team.[83]

St. Peter's College (present-day Catholic High School) sponsored six-man football squads in the 1940s, and, like most small southwestern Louisiana high schools, switched to eleven-man football in the early 1950s.

THEATRICALS

Sports were the principal outdoor diversion for New Iberians, but theatricals were the undisputed king of indoor entertainment in the late nineteenth and early twentieth centuries. Local theatrical interest dates from the establishment of the Iberia Dramatic Association in late September 1874.[84] The Association staged amateur, dramatic productions, such as the temperance play, "Ten Nights in a Barroom," at Thespian Hall until the mid-1880s.

The organization of the Iberia Dramatic Association precipitated, in 1875, the establishment of the Iberia Glee Club, which staged comedies, farces, and vaudeville tableaux, such as "Le Fin Mot," "Une Chambre a Deux Lits," and "Handy Andy," at Fourcade's Hall.[85] Despite these initial successes, the Glee Club apparently disbanded in 1876.

The dissolution of the Iberia Dramatic Association and the disbanding of the Glee Club, however, were eclipsed by the advent of touring professional troupes. The first touring company to perform at New Iberia was the Helen D'Este Dramatic Company which staged "Two Orphans" at Pickwick Hall in mid-February 1877.[86] The D'Este troupe was followed in succeeding months by an unidentified "company of mutes," and the Stuttz Dramatic Company.[87]

The Stuttz Company, billed as "the best Company that has ever visited New Iberia," was so well patronized, in fact, that they played the town for

---

83. *Ibid.*

84. *Sugar Bowl*, September 10, October 1, 1874.

85. *Ibid.*, June 17, 1875.

86. *Ibid.*, February 15, 1877.

87. *Ibid.*, March 22, 1877; May 10, 1877.

twenty weeks; the bi-weekly performances following the initial Pickwick Hall attraction, however, were open only to subscribers who had purchased season tickets at "Dr. Mestayer's drug store."[88] Acquisition of a season ticket was apparently a wise investment, for the troupe's predominantly female audiences witnessed performances of the most current theatrical successes, including "Rip Van Winkle" and "Camille."[89]

Following the Stuttz Dramatic Company's departure in September 1877, Pickwick Hall featured performances by combination companies (comedy and dramatic troupes) as well as magicians on an irregular basis;[90] but, for unknown reasons, the Pickwick abruptly ceased sponsoring traveling shows in mid-1878.

From 1878 until the early 1890s, professional theatricals lay dormant in New Iberia. With the opening of the Iberia Opera House and Veazey's Opera House in the early 1890s, the Golden Age of Entertainment in New Iberia began. The Iberia theatrical season extended from mid-September to early May and each opera house normally offered thirty to forty attractions, including vaudeville teams, black and white minstrels, and theatricals. Because the town's direct rail communications with New Orleans, the New Iberia opera houses could attract several famous theatrical companies which were touring the South. For example, Mrs. Tom Thumb and her internationally famous Company of Lilliputians, James J. "Gentleman Jim" Corbett, "the champion pugilist of the world," the Iowa State Band, and the New Orleans French Opera Company performed at the Iberia Opera House, New Iberia's premier theatre.[91]

Heavyweight campion Corbett, however, delivered the death blow to big name performances at New Iberia. Upon arrival at New Iberia, "Gentleman Jim," the flamboyant prototype of Mohammed Ali, made a grand entrance into town aboard "one of the finest livery turn-outs in town." The hundreds of fans who greeted the champ at the station and subsequently filled the Iberia Opera House soon dropped their cheers for boos when Corbett failed to appear for the play's finale, a sparring match ostensibly re-creating conditions at the fighter's "training quarters." As the "boys" armed themselves with "hen fruit,"

---

88. *Ibid.*, May 10, 1877.

89. *Ibid.*, May 17, 1877.

90. *Ibid.*, December 6, 1877; February 28, 1878.

91. *Weekly Iberian*, December 8, 15, 1894; January 5, 1895.

Mr. [Max] Mattes, the Opera House manager, then went to Gentleman Jack and demanded that he should render the play in full or the admission would be returned to the audience. Hot arguments and compliments were in order. The Sheriff and other officers appeared upon the scene, when the 'gentleman' yielded.[92]

It soon became common knowledge that Corbett's sudden incapacitation resulted from the fact that the Southern Pacific Railroad Company would "hold" the champion's special train only until ten p.m.

It is hardly surprising, therefore, that the Iberia Opera House failed to book such prima donnas thereafter. In subsequent years, the Iberia Opera House, like modern television, geared its programming to the lowest denominator of public taste. For example, when asked why his theatre did not schedule "three or four first class companies every season," Max Mattes replied: "every winter some plays which are far above the average . . . come here, but they are no better patronized than the poorer plays, and only one-tenth of the troupes which come here make money."[93] The actor thus gave way to the vaudevillian and minstrel.

The Veazey Opera House was replaced by the Vendome in 1901, and the latter served as the center of public entertainment in New Iberia until its destruction by fire in May 1905. In such theatres, and the movie houses that succeeded them in the teens, such popular performers as Al. H. Wilson, the "German dialect" comedian and singer who was a perennial favorite at New Iberia, were forced to contend with "the masses" attracted by the light format and modest admission fee. As the *Weekly Iberian* lamented in 1897:

> The boys of New Iberia seem to feel that the opera house was built to be a playhouse for them, a large building where they can yell, whistle, stamp their feet to certain time all over the house, and especially in the galleries, jeer at performers, throw vegetables on the stage, clap their hands in and out of season [whenever] they can make life miserable for those who come to enjoy the entertainments.[94]

92. *Ibid.*, January 5, 1895.

93. *Ibid.*, December 19, 1896.

94. *Ibid.*, June 4, 1897.

The burning of the Vendome Opera House in mid-May 1905 permanently altered not only the theatrical atmosphere, but the variety of entertainment as well. Built in 1906 by the Elks Club, the Elks Theatre became the arbiter of public taste from November 1907 until the 1930s. Under the management of Julius Scharff and his partner, David A. Wise, the theatre shifted its emphasis to a new entertainment medium--silent movies.[95]

Silent movies had been introduced into New Iberia by the Vendome Opera House. In mid-January 1905, Archie L. Shepard, a touring cinematographer, presented not only *The Great Train Robbery*, to which he held exclusive exhibition rights, but *Fairyland, The Life of Marie Antoinette, An English Stag Hunt,* and *The Baltimore Fire*. Scharff recognized the potential of the motion picture and geared the Elks Theatre's programming accordingly; this foresight paid off and by 1910 movies had become the dominant entertainment medium in New Iberia. In fact, by 1914, the town boasted three movie theatres--the Elks, the Alamo, and the Pastime. The Elks, however, remained the premier movie house, showing on a nightly basis movies starring early cinema's outstanding stars. In 1917, for example, the Elks featured movies starring Mary Pickford, Alla Nazimova, Sessue Hayakawa, George M. Cohan, Marguerite Clark and Charlie Chaplin. Moreover, unlike live performances whose admission fee usually ranged from thirty-five to seventy-five cents, children could spend an entire afternoon at the movies for a nickel (adults were admitted for a dime).

With the onset of American involvement in World War I, the standard movie fare was supplemented by propagada films. One of the most notorious of the War Department movies viewed at New Iberia was *The Kaiser: The Beast of Berlin*, a jingoistic film billed as "the picture that will make your blood boil with rage."[96] The patriotic ferver generated by the propaganda films was reinforced by such militaristic films as Charlie Chaplin's *Shoulder Arms*.[97]

Changing with the times enhanced the movies' popularity. In fact, by 1920, motion pictures so completely dominated local entertainment that vaudevillian acts had become virtually extinct.[98]

95. *Enterprise*, September 21, 1907.

96. *Ibid.*, May 18, 1918.

97. *Ibid.*

98. In fact, between 1917 and 1920, only one vaudeville troupe, Hila Morgan's tent show, performed at New Iberia. *Ibid.*, December 29, 1919.

Entertainment, Sports, and Recreation

The void created by the demise of professional theatricals was filled by the now-defunct New Iberia Little Theatre. The first little theatre organization was founded in the spring of 1923 by a group of New Iberians, headed by Mrs. Walter Burke, who felt the need to express their latent dramatic talent and thereby enrich the community's cultural life.[99] During its two-year existence, the local players staged five plays; following the production of "The Maker of Dreams" in February 1924, however, the little theatre organization disbanded for twenty-five years.

As in the case of the initial movement, the second little theatre organization was established during the aftermath of a world war. From its organization until its dissolution in 1952, the Iberia Little Theatre staged "excellent performances of well-known plays, perhaps the most memorable being the local rendition of 'Outward Bound.'"[100]

A third modern, amateur theatrical organization was established at New Iberia in 1960. The association's initial productions--"The Glass Menagerie," "Biography," and "The Great Big Doorstep"--were staged at the Sugar Cane Festival Building.[101] Subsequent productions were presented at "The Carriage House," a former drug warehouse acquired by the little theatre association in 1961. The association, however, was compelled to disband in 1972 when the playhouse was demolished to make way for a structure which would further enrich the town's cultural atmosphere--a parking lot.[102]

CONCLUSION

New Iberia's long history of public entertainment accurately reflects national trends in recreation pursuits. Picnics, excursions, baseball, circuses, vaudeville, silent movies, "talkies," football, and fishing have been forced to keep pace with continuously improving technology and public taste; recreational pursuits which were unable to change with the times perished. What does

---

99. Glenn R. Conrad, "The New Iberia Little Theatre, 1923-1973," *Attakapas Gazette*, XII (1977), 102.

100. *Ibid.*, 103.

101. *Ibid.*

102. *Ibid.*, 104.

the future hold? Since the introduction of movies, public entertainment has been geared increasingly to visually oriented productions. While such productions are a feast for the eye, they are all too often a famine for the mind. Mesmerized by television or the blaring notes of a stereo system, the individual is incapable of interacting socially with fellow family members; hence the growing unpopularity of such traditional family outings as picnics. The day of the insular individual is at hand.

XXVII

Some Recollections of New Iberia

by
Yvonne Arnandez Southwell

I was born in 1895, in a small cottage on St. Peter Street, in the vicinity of the present Maumus home [209 East St. Peter Street]. A few months after my birth, my father and mother decided to move into the home of my grandparents on Julia Street. The house was a large frame building, and at the time my grandparents rented some of the extra rooms to friends who did not wish to live alone. Among these were the Leon Minvielles and his mother.

The elder Mrs. Minvielle was a well-proportioned lady, and I remember that she would wear a jet-black shawl, embroidered with jet beads. These beads sparkled like diamonds, and I was fascinated by the shawl.

Another older lady was Mrs. Henry Gallois, mother of Henry Gallois, Jr., who was for many years manager of the Southern [now South Central] Bell Telephone Co. office in New Iberia. She was an interesting person.

The first event that I can recall from early childhood was the great snowfall of February 14, 1899. I remember my mother lifting the sash and letting me feel the snow and play with this wonderful white substance that had fallen out of the sky.

I also remember the terrible fire that took place about the same time [the fire occurred October 10, 1899] which began in the Estorge Drug Company. A great part of the business district of the town burned as a result of that fire.

My grandparents had one of the first telephones installed in New Iberia. It was installed at the end of a long hall which divided the house. It was quite exciting to talk over the telephone, and everybody in the neighborhood would occasionally drop in to try the telephone. The caller had to crank the handle which called the operator. Once she was on, you gave her a number, waited a few seconds and soon you heard the voice of the person being called. It was most exciting.

Dr. J. W. K. Shaw operated upon my grandmother in the house on Julia Street. He had my mother and aunts remove all of the furniture from the "operating room." The floor and walls were scrubbed, and then the room was fumigated so that it would be as sterile as possible. Only a hospital bed was in the room. This was the first time I remember being frightened and sad. My grandmother recovered from this breast operation and lived to make Edele's baby trousseau.

A short time after that my father bought a home on Duperier Avenue. I was about six or seven. In those days this house was in "the country." The dirt road and the wooden banquette were our only connection with the town. Our home was comfortable except for the fact we had no bathroom. It was a happy day when the bathroom and fixtures for it were installed and we could indulge in running hot and cold water.

During the early years when summer rains came down in torrents, Duperier Avenue was a canal. The wooden bridges were dislodged from their moorings and all of us children had a wonderful time--each now had a raft which we pushed with a long pole. So long as there was water deep enough to float the raft, we'd float up and down the avenue. When the street was paved our good times came to an end.

Our home life was a happy one. My brother, then only one, two sisters and two cousins, who had come to live with us, had all the love and devotion my parents could give us. But, we had our duties to perform. One that I detested was dusting the dining room, and especially the china closet, every Saturday morning before I could do anything else.

Then came the convent and all the dear sisters. I loved all of them, and my years at Mt. Carmel were really golden years. There were many, many sisters

Residences of East Main Street about 1910 (above)
and seventy-five years later

who did many good and kind things. One person at the convent stands out in my memory more than anyone else. She was Jane, the old cook. Jane, every afternoon at 3:30 recess would hand out to us through the kitchen window a great nose of French bread filled with syrup. This, for us, was the best thing we had ever eaten.

Then came the commencement exercises, and this was the event of the year at the convent. The stage for these exercises had to be built on the porch, and, of course, we had the weather to contend with. Every year, it seemed, at commencement time it would rain and rain. I can remember the fine curtain and the paper dresses fading all over the place. The purple dresses fading on the red, the red on the blue, etc. It just went on and on. So many of the commencement exercises were completely wiped out.

Then came St. Berchman's Hall with seating and a stage, and the boys at Mt. Carmel. I graduated from Mt. Carmel with many long-time friends: Ello, Bertha Mae, Harriet and myself. Since my father was not a rich man, my choice of colleges was rather limited. When the *Enterprise*, our local newspaper, announced that the police jury was offering a scholarship to the student who would make the highest mark in the examination to be given, I was the only applicant, so for two years I attended S.L.I.I. Since I did not realize that the scholarship was good for four years, and feeling that I should get as much out of the two years as possible, I took the commercial course. When I went to thank Mr. Willie Burke, then secretary of the police jury, he said, "Well, aren't you going to complete the next two years?" This came as a surprise because I did not know that I would be allowed to take any course offered, and that if I made good grades. the police jury would allow me to remain until the degree was awarded, whether two or four years.

Southwestern was a young educational institution at that time. There were only four girls in the domestic science department: Estelle de la Loire, Margaret Smith, Caladonia Wilder, and one whose name I can't remember. We had the business department on the top floor of the old Martin Hall. The business department was on one end of the floor and the domestic department on the other. Each day we waited expectantly for the goodies that came out of the domestic science class. Sometimes the samples were real good--sometimes not so good.

I played tennis at S.L.I.I., joined the dramatics club and played on the first and only all-girl football team. Poor Mr. Mac [McNaspy], who loved athletics, was struggling to get the boys out for his games. When the games were scheduled no one would show up, so something had to be done. In des-

Some Recollections 501

peration he decided to form an all-girl team so that we could at least learn the fundamentals of the game. He organized the first all-girl team, and we played back of the girls' dormitory in bloomers that looked like tents. We learned the game, and soon Mr. Mac's dream became reality. The teachers at Southwestern were truly dedicated, and many men and women today can be grateful for the interest and devotion given to them at Southwestern.

My first job was with the New Iberia and Northern Railroad. Mr. Bryan Snyder was the traffic manager and I was his secretary. The arrangement did not last too long, for Fred Patout was anxious to be married. So, on April 7, 1915, I became his wife. He died on July 5, 1942.

Now, with regard to entertainment in New Iberia in those days, I must go back a bit. There were two very active fire departments at that time: No. 1 and No. 2. No. 2 was located somewhere out Julia or Weeks Street. They had a huge hall there, and they would have entertainments of all kinds, dances and parties and all that. The two stations vied with each other to be the most outstanding, so there was always something going on with the fire stations. Once, when I was very young, I recited for one of their entertainments a piece called "Nobody's Child." I was about six years old then.

Through these early years of my life, I was called upon to do a part on the different programs, either to sing or to do a recitation. Some of the pieces recited were: "The Night Before Christmas," "St. Peter at the Gate," "Old Glory," "A Calmer Sea," "Gunga Din" and many others.

One of my mother's good friends was Weeks Hall's mother. She and my mother would visit often, and Weeks often joined his mother in the visit. He and I and the neighborhood children would play together. Among our friends were Nick and "Frotcha" Muller, and the Walets. Henrietta Dauterive would play the piano for us, as we played children's games. Several times for the Unsectarian Aide Society, Weeks and I would perform some sort of act. We did a cake walk once, another time we sang "When I Was 21, And You Were Sweet 16," I was decked out in Miss Patty Weeks' (later Mrs. Torian) finery. Dot Smith taught us all the intricate music and dance steps.

Across the street from our home, we had a very interesting family--the Hulls. Mrs. Hull had at one time been quite an actress. Her stage name was Jenny Coleman. We became great friends. Her husband, J. B. Hull, wrote music. He and Harold Henshaw wrote a number of songs, one of which I premiered from the convent stage. It was entitled "A Southern Lullaby."

The first movies in New Iberia were nickel and dime shows.

The first automobile I remember seeing in New Iberia was owned by Dr. J. W. K. Shaw.

We had the chautauqua come to New Iberia every year, and everyone looked forward to its arrival. It was a change from the routine of our lives. There was nothing of this sort permanently located here, so it was greeted with enthusiasm.

Then we had the Van Dreet Woodland Players. They were Shakespearian actors who did their work outside. I can remember seeing "A Mid-Summer Night's Dream," and Puck jumping from the branches of the oaks as he did his part.

Then we had a very wonderful woman come to New Iberia. She sang in the Elks Theatre in April 1911. Her name was Ellen Beach Yaw. She was a lyric soprano and sang beautifully. Later, of course, we had community concerts.

Now, I would like to move to another subject--the Fortnightly Club. The Senior Fortnightly is 52 or 53 years old [in 1978]. Well, a long time ago a group of young mothers, Bessie Bauman Kyle, Lillian Barrow, Roberta Voorhies, Henrietta Courts and myself, met while out strolling with the babies, and we asked ourselves what could we do that would be intellectually stimulating while still caring for the young ones. Thus, we decided to form a literary club. Celeste Dimitry Burke also joined us. She had the first program. We had decided to study short stories the first year, and her subject was *The Necklace* by Guy de Maupassant. From there we branched out in all directions. Thus, the club grew to a membership of twenty--the maximum number. The idea of a literary club caught on and today [1978] there are six Fortnightly Clubs, including one in Franklin and one in Abbeville. The Senior Fortnightly still meets, but our ranks are thinning.

I'd like also to mention the New Iberia Garden Club. The organization of this club was largely the work of Mrs. Wofford Sanders, and Mrs. Morsie Pharr Lemaire. The club has met in the homes but also in the old Central High School. The garden clubs of New Iberia have worked hard in New Iberia, they have tried to instill in the community a love for plants and trees. The idea has taken hold in the community and there are now several garden clubs.

I remember that we used to have a camellia show in the hotel every year. It was an outstanding show. Many people had beautiful specimen trees. We've also had shows in connection with the Sugar Cane Festival. Gust Catsulis has been a mainstay of horticulture in New Iberia. Now Guy Patout has come along with some outstanding dahlias.

Mintmere Plantation House before restoration

The Little Theatre was organized back in the twenties by Mrs. Walter J. Burke. I played in several of her plays. When she became ill, the activity stopped. Then, Jeanette Ackal revived Little Theatre in the forties. Mrs. Beldon Fox performed in many of the plays of this second Little Theatre era. May Holbrook and Herman Hauser were also strong backers of Little Theatre. I remember once that we did "The Cradle Song" for Our Lady of Perpetual Help Church. May Holbrook, E. J. Carstens, Mrs. Ernest Nereaux, Sr., Madeline Ackal and myself were in the play. My husband, Owen, did the scenery for the presentation. It was a nice play.

Another organization that worked tirelessly was the St. Peter's College Mothers' Club. The purpose of the club was to finance the maintenance of the Brothers' home and supply some of their needs. At one time the Brothers' situation was very bad. I remember one Brother whose robe was full of holes and there was no money for him to buy another. It probably was because of that situation that some of us believed there should be an auxiliary.

Mrs. Albert Emmer became the first president of the St. Peter's College Mothers' Club. Mrs. Edgar Folse was the next president, and then I became

Mintmere after restoration

Some Recollections

president for many years thereafter. But it wasn't good for the club to have the same president year in and year out, so I retired but stayed active. After that, I remember some of our presidents were Mrs. Clarence Louvière, Mrs. Allen Conrad, Mrs. J. S. Brown, Jr., Mrs. Julian Conrad, Mrs. Dessard Broussard, Mrs. T. E. Mixon, and several others.

The club did good work. For instance, the Brothers needed blankets and quilts for their beds--they had no heat in the building--the old Henshaw house. So the club adopted as a project getting blankets, etc., for them. So we got the material, and some of the older members of the club made the quilts. Mrs. Nini and her friends made quilts. Then, we asked all the children in the school to bring us Octagon soap wrappers because Octagon soap was offering money in return for so many coupons. So we began gathering coupons, and in this way we made enough money to get sheets, pillow cases and blankets for the Brothers.

Then, we asked Father Langlois if we could put in a heater. He said "We have no money." But we replied that we just wanted to put in the heater, whether there was any money or not. He responded, "Well, I don't know who is going to pay for it." We sold cakes and candy and that's how we paid for the heater.

Then we wanted to make a study for the Brothers, and the Mothers' Club did achieve this end. The club put in more bathrooms. But, when you stop to think about it, everyone helped to keep the school going. The Brothers were men who understood children and could work with them. They were wonderful teachers.

Let me recall, now, a few things about the Frederic Hotel. One thing that most Iberians know or can recall is that Dolores Del Rio made the movie *Evangeline* in this area. She was a lovely young woman. Even with everyone clamoring to see her and talk with her, she remained very composed and very kind. Many of the movie crew stayed at the hotel. Extras for the movie came from New Iberia.

My husband, Fred, took the director out into the countryside to select locations for filming. Then, when the movie was finished and Dolores Del Rio boarded the train to leave New Iberia, some of the townspeople gave her a large bouquet of flowers. She had been a nice person to work with.

Lyle Saxon also stayed at the hotel. Teddy Roosevelt stopped briefly for a drink when he passed through New Iberia.

After Fred's death, I was astonished by the amount of work in the day-to-day routine of running the hotel, but I enjoyed the work most of the time. During World War II the hotel posed a real challenge to keep open. Everything, including sheets, was so hard to get. We were trying to run the dining room and, just two weeks after Fred died, the man that he had hired as chef decided to leave. So, there I was, really at my wits' end. To make matters worse, I had to constantly beg the O.P.A. (Office of Price Administration) people for supplies for the dining room. If Clara Roy hadn't been so kind to us during those difficult days, I don't know what our patrons would have done. She, somehow, saw to it that we had enough to keep going.

But it was meat that was the real problem. Gaston, my brother-in-law, realizing my predicament, said that I could slaughter some of his cattle to supply the hotel dining room. Well, the O.P.A. people heard about this and came rushing to the hotel to confiscate all that meat--our own beef. They told us we had no business killing our own cattle. They even took some ducks that the boys had shot on a weekend hunt. It was terrible, and I don't know how I stayed out of jail in those days. But we kept the hotel open. Indeed, there were more people at the hotel during World War II than at any other time. It was an exciting, sometimes perplexing, never-to-be-forgotten time.

Over the years I have come to know many people who have stood out in the community, and while it is impossible for me to name all of them here, I would like to mention a few. Certainly, in my mind, there were no two finer men than Doctors J. W. K. Shaw and George Sabatier. In connection with the doctors and babies I should also mention Louisa Hayes, a midwife, who was always helping everyone. The Burke brothers were outstanding men. Felix Patout was a wonderful gentleman. The Renoudets and the Dietleins were staunch supporters of the town. A person never to be forgotten was Mrs. Jules Mestayer--a most charitable woman. She made First Communion clothes for children whose parents couldn't afford to buy the outfits. Katherine Avery and Julia Decuir should also be remembered for their charities. Another remarkable person is Bertha Courrege. She has been administrator of St. Peter's cemetery for so many years--a task that is not very rewarding. Blanche Sagrera is also a hard worker in this cause. Alaska Bernard was a really fine person. She was always interested in so many things. She always helped people, especially children. She was a talented teacher. And there are so many people who should be mentioned.

New Iberia has certainly changed since I first knew it, and I think that the two greatest instruments of change have been the automobile and television. The change which they have wrought has not always meant progress. Cars, in many instances, have become the modern-day Vandals. They sweep everything before them. Lovely old buildings--many with outstanding architecture--have been demolished to make way for an acre or two of sterile concrete parking area. Pleasant front lawns of a generation ago are now scarred with the ruts of the Vandal. Our majestic trees are toppled senselessly to make way for the automobile, or the trees die a slow death as the concrete of parking lots is pushed up to the trunk to get the last inch of parking space. I know the automobile is a virtual necessity in modern society, but must we pay such a high price to have it? Do we have to mortgage the beauty of the land for future generations in order to carry on our love affair with the automobile?

Well, these are some of my recollections of New Iberia in the twentieth century. There has been tremendous change--the little sleepy town of eighty years ago has now become a bustling commercial-industrial center.

Maison Marceline
circa 1890
Restored by Ernest Nereaux, Jr.

Appendix

HISTORICAL ORIGINS OF SOME NEW IBERIA STREET NAMES

Adrian	Named for J. Adrian Conrad, grandson of Philip A. Conrad, developer of Caroline Subdivision
Albert	Named for Albert LeMaire
Alice	Named for Alice Gonsoulin
Aline	Named for Aline Voorhies Segura
Allen	Named for J. Allen Daigre
Alvin	Named for Alvin Badeau
Angers	Name for the family
Angie	Named for Angie Cartimeglia Ariola
Ann	Named for Ann Lewis, member of the Lewis family that owned before and after the Civil War the area between Bank Avenue and Evangeline Street
Arlene	Named for Arlene Broussard Defelice
Armentor	Named for the family
Ashton	Named for Ashton Broussard
Babb	Named for the family
Bahon	Named for the family
Bank	Named for Citizens' Bank of New Orleans which owned the property after the Civil War
Barrow	Named for the family
Bayard	Named for the family
Berard	Named for the family
Blaise	Named for Blaise Plaisance
Boas	Named for the family

Bond	Named for the family
Bonnet	Named for the family
Bourgeois	Named for the family
Breaux	Named for the family
Broussard	Named for the Edwin Broussard family
Bruner	Named for the family
Burke	Named for the family
Calhoun	Named for Floyd Calhoun
Carmen	Named for Carmen Harry Daigre
Carol	Named for Carol Cartimiglia Henderson
Caroline	Named for Susan Caroline Taylor Pellerin, grand daughter of Philip Conrad, developer of Caroline Subdivision
Carstens	Named for the family
Carter	Named adopted as a shorted form of Cartimiglia
Celeste	Named for Celeste Henry
Center	So named because it bisects the Weeks Subdivision
Charles	Named for Charles Weeks, son of David Weeks
Chris	Named for Chris Bayard
Cobb	Named for the family
Compton	Named for the family
Corinne	Named by Harvey Hopkins, possibly for a member of his family
Courrege	Named for the family
Craig	Named for Craig Rutten
Curtis	Named for the family
Dalton	Named for Dalton Babineaux, Sr.

Appendix 511

Dan	Named for Dan Polk
Danny	Named for Danny Bayard
Darby	Named for the family
Darcey	Named for Darcey Burke
Daspit	Named for the family
David	Named for David Broussard
Davis	Named for Judge John (Jack) Davis
De La Salle	Named for St. Jean-Baptiste de La Salle, founder of the Christian Brothers order of teachers
Deare	Named for Clarence Deare
Decuir	Named for the family
Dehart	Named for the family
Daigre	Named for the family
Dodson	Named for Dr. William Dodson
Donald	Named for Donald Voorhies
Dore	Named for the family
Eckart	Named for the family
Elliot	Named for Elliot D. Taylor, grandson of Philip Conrad, developer of Caroline Subdivision
Emma	Named for Emma Reynolds
Fisher	Named for the family
Florence	Named for Florence Gonsoulin
Fontelieu	Named for Alphe Fontelieu, a mayor of New Iberia
Francis	Named for Dale Francis Cartimiglia (named Francis because of an existing Dale Street
Frederick	Named for Frederick Decuir
Fremin	Named for the family

French	Named for Josiah French, a early New Iberia settler
Frere	Named for Alexander Frere
Frisby	Named for the family
Fulton	Named by Harvey Hopkins in honor of Robert Fulton, inventor of the steamboat
Gajan	Named for the family
Girouard	Named for the family
Glenn	Named for Glenn R. Conrad, grandson of Philip Conrad, developer of Caroline Subdivision
Hacker	Named for Judge L. O. Hacker. The section of this street between Weeks and Henshaw Alley was originally named Alfred Street, for the son of David Weeks.
Halphen	Named for the family
Harriet	Named for Harriet Weeks, daughter of David Weeks
Hebert	Named for the family
Helm	Named for the family
Henry	Named for Henry Frederick Duperier, son of Frederick Henry Duperier, the incorporator of New Iberia
Henshaw	Named for the family
Higdon	Named for the family
Hilliard	Named for the family
Hine	Named for Olga Hine
Hopkins	Named for Harvey Hopkins, an antebellum planter who subdivided the area between Jefferson and North streets.
Hortense	Named for Hortense Berard, wife of Frederick Henry Duperier
Howard	Named for Howard Fenstermaker
Iberia	Named for the town and parish; formerly known as Petite Anse Road
Indest	Named for the family

Appendix

Ivan	Named for Ivan Polk
James	Named for James Kilchrist
Jefferson	Named by Harvey Hopkins in honor of President Thomas Jefferson
Jefferson Terrace	Named for the actor Joseph Jefferson who at one time owned property in the area. Before being renamed Jefferson Terrace, the street was known as Peebles Avenue, named for Dudley Peebles.
Johnson	Named for Thomas Johnson, son-in-law of John Stine, an early New Iberia settler
Jules	Named for Jules Schwing
Julia	Named for Julia Bourriaque
Kathryn	Named for Kathryn Fenstermaker
Kristi	Named for Kristi Hamilton
Lafayette	Named for the marquis de Lafayette
Landry	Named for the family
Lanza	Named for the family
LaSalle	Named for the family
Lawrence	Named for Lawrence Villermin
LeBlanc	Named for the family
Lee	Named for James A. Lee; not named for the Confederate general
LeMaire	Named for the family
Leonard	Named for Leonard Solomon
Lewis	Named for Cordelia Wheeler Lewis who at one time owned the area between Bank Avenue and Evangeline Street
Lietmyer	Named for the family
Lombard	Named for Capt. Lombard, a steamboat captain
Louise	Named for Louise Mixon
Mabel	Named for Mabel Delahoussaye

Main	Before being called Main Street this thoroughfare was called "the Main Road between Franklin and St. Martinville."
Margaret	Named for Margaret Mixon
Marie	Named for Marie Appoline Duperier, daughter of Frederick Henry Duperier, incorporator of New Iberia
Marie Elise	Named for Marie Elise Daigre
Marjie	Named for Marjie Pecot
Maumus	Named for A. J. Maumus, deputy clerk of court, Iberia Parish
McIlhenny	Named for the family
Mississippi	Named by T. E. Mixon for his native state
Mixon	Named for the family
Montagne	Named for the family
Mullins	Named for the family
Myra	Named for Myra Decuir
Myrtis	Named for Myrtis Mixon
Nancy	Named for Nancy Mixon
Napoleon	Named for the emperor
Nelson Canal Rd.	Named for Stephen O. Nelson, an antebellum planter
Nita	Named for Nita Villermin
North	So named because it formed the northern boundary of the Hopkins plantation
Oswald	Named for Senator Oswald Decuir
Pamaleen	Named for Priscilla and Kathleen Mullins
Park	Named for the horseracing track and fair grounds that is today the Broussard Subdivsion
Parkview	So named because it forms in part a boundary of City Park
Patrick	Named for St. Patrick

Appendix 515

Perry	Named for Perry Burke
Pershing	Named for General John Pershing. Formerly named Madison Street; named for President James Madison by Harvey Hopkins
Pesson	Named for the family
Philip	Named for Philip Lee
Pollard	Named for J. M. Pollard of Norton, Ohio, who bought the surrounding land subdivided it about 1898
Pratt	Named for Pratt Munson
Prioux	Named for Vicknair Prioux, a developer of the area
Pullen	Named for the family
Reynolds	Named for the family
Rex	Named for Rex Champagne
Rita	Named for Rita Comeaux Bayard
Robert S.	Named for Robert S. Pesson
Robertson	Named for the family
Rosier	Named for the family
Rouly	Named for the family
Russell	Named for Russell Bourgeois
Sam	Named for Sam Cartimiglia
Sarah	Named for Sarah Helm
School	Named for the Julia Street School which was on the corner of Julia and School streets
Sofas	Named for the family
Spell	Named for the family
St. Peter	Named for the church parish
Stephanie	Named for Stephanie Mixon

Swain	Named for John D. Swaim, a New Iberia businessman before and after the Civil War
Sydney	Named for Sydney Pesson
Terry	Named for Terry Pecot
Thompson	Named for the family
Trotter	Named for the family
Viator	Named for the family
Vicknair	Named for Vicknair Prioux
Washington	Named by Harvey Hopkins for President George Washington
Webre	Named for the family
Weeks	Named for the family
Wicklow	Named by Ray Mullins for a town in Ireland
Weldon	Named for Weldon deBlanc, Sr.
Worthy	Named for Worthy Quereau

Index

A & A Home and Auto Supply, 314
A & P Store, 315, 418
A. B. Simon School faculty, 446
A. Lehman & Co., 144
Abadie, Dr., 161
Abadie, Mrs. O. J., 314
Abbeville Frogs, 348n
Abbeville, La., 42, 111, 115n, 175, 426
Abbey, S. F. R., 97
Abdalla, John, 324
Abdalla's Dept. Store, 314, 412
Aborn, Joseph, 70, 74, 94n, 123n, 133, 245
Abraham, Gabriel, 261
Abshire, John, 118n
Abshire, R. J. B., 328
Acadiana, 347n
Acadiana Ebony Journal, 450
Acadiana Motor Lodge, 169n
Acadiana Pontiac, 314
Acadians, 8, 17, 115n
   agreement with D'Hauterive, 18n
   arrive in New Orleans, 18n
   assist in construction of New Iberia, 8
   refugees from Santo Domingo, 1, 18n
Achinard, P. E., 187
Ackal, A., 261
Ackal, G., 261
Ackal, Jeanette, 503
Ackal, Madeline, 503
Ackal's Dept. Store, 413, 414
Acklen, J. H., 216
Adams, Lorance, 444
Adler, Sol., 220, 225, 228
Agatho, Brother, 403
Agrifuels Refining Corp., 301
"Ahoogah," 424
Albert, Rev. Prince, 434
Albrizo fresco, 195
Albrizo, Conrad, 200
Aldrich, K. P., 229n
Alex, Clarence, 451

Alexander, Iris Williams, 451
Alexander family, 135
Alexandria, La., 345
Algiers, La., 209, 214, 215, 269
Alicante, Spain, 5
Allain's Jewelry Co., 313, 368
Allison, L. C., 328n
Alma House, 26, 27, 31, 88, 88n, 96, 124, 133, 134n, 278, 279, 303, 340, 348n, 408, 415, 429
America Fire Co. No. 2, 203, 211, 466n, 467, 473
American Cafe, 408
American Institute of Chemical Engineers, 355
American Iron and Machine Works, 299
American Missionary Association, Congregational, 435
American Salt Co., 289
Amtrak depot, 213
Amy Hewes, The, 274
Anderson Street Middle School, 400
Anderson Street School, 405
Anderson, Rev. W. B., 433
Anderson, Texas, 107n
Andre, Jules, 183
Andrus, Henrietta (Mrs. John N. Pharr), 154, 154n, 379, 403
Andrus, Louis, 154n
Andry, Louis, 1, 18n
Angers, J. M., 261
Angers, Louis, 262
Angers, Robert, 301
Angers, Walter, Jr., 490
Anglo-American merchants
   in New Iberia, 118n
Anglo-Saxons
   as early settlers on Teche, 115n
Anse la Butte Oil Field, 333
Anthony, Neville, 451
Aponte, Bernard, 23
   purchases Prevost land, 23
Aponte family, 13

Arcenius, Brother, 401
Archer, Annie, 423
Arial, Manna, 70
Armentor, F., 262
Armentor, Minos, 324
Armistice Day, 407, 474
Armstrong, Louis, 427
Armstrong, William, 265
Arnandez, J. G., 305
Arnandez, Louise, 372
Arnandez, Rita, 354n
Arnandez, Yves, 261, 348
Arnandez, Yvonne (Mrs. Frederic Patout; Mrs. Owen Southwell), 169n, 279, 374
Arnaudville, La., 361
Arrigo, M., 261
Artacho, Josef, 23, 37, 72, 93n
  resettles in New Orleans, 12
Artigue, Pierre, 143
Astaire, Fred, 426
Atchafalaya Basin, 2, 6, 359
Atchafalaya Basin Protective Association, 356
Atchafalaya River, 102, 110, 209, 215
Atchafalaya River Railroad Ferry, 215
Atlanta, Ga., 242
Atlanta Life Insurance Co., 443
Attakapas Association for Improving Breed of Horses, 464
Attakapas Baseball Team (St. Martinville), 484
Attakapas Canal, 103
Attakapas Commercial & Industrial School, 386, 387, 403
Attakapas country, 73
Attakapas, County of, 130n
Attakapas Debating Society, 87
Attakapas District, 2, 3, 10, 115n
  Acadians in the, 18n
  census of the, 19n
  population of the, in 1774, 2
Attakapas Jockey Club Association, 135
Attakapas Mail Transportation Co., 177, 273
Attakapas Male Institute, 404
Attakapas Rifles, 473
Attakapas Sanatorium, 219

Attakapas Steam Boat Co., 268
Attakapas Turf Association, 104
Aubry, Charles-Philippe, 18
Aubry, Harold, 365, 366
Aubry, Mildred, 365
Aubry, Rosa, 365, 366
Aubry, Victor, 219, 228, 237
Aucoin, C. M., 263n
Aucoin, Victor, 164n
Aucoin, Breaux, & Renoudet Cypress Lumber Co., 290, 297
Auger, Louis, 384n
Augur, F. A., 245, 255
Auguster, Edran, 433n, 444
Auguster's Studio, 452
Aurora Lodge of Free and Accepted Masons, 144
Ausberry, Verge, 405
Automobile, first in New Iberia, 502
Avery, Daniel Dudley, 66, 107, 131, 146, 191, 197, 289
Avery, Mrs. Daniel Dudley, see Marsh, Sarah
Avery, Dudley, 128n, 159n, 277, 282n, 381n
Avery, John M., 43
Avery, Katherine, 373, 374, 506
Avery, Mary Eliza (Mrs. Edmund McIlhenny), 289
Avery family, 31, 103, 389
Avery Island, La., 57n, 102, 109, 449
  salt production on, 295
Avery salt mine, 103, 152
Avery-Contonio-Dietlein-Landry Memorial Collection, 459
Avoyelles, Parish, La., 359
Azor, 87n

B. F. Trappey and Sons, 295
Babin, Alcide, 31
Babin, Emile, 465
Babin, T. A., 465
Babineaux, Rev. Albert, 78n
Babineaux, Claude, 362
Babineaux, Louise, 354n
Bacquet, Rev. Albert, 78n
Badon, Charles A., 476
Bagarry, Alex., Sr., 261
Bagarry, L. P., 261

Index 519

Bagarry, Leon, 342n
Bagarry, R. A., 261
Bagarry's Ice Factory, 143, 150, 297
Bahon, Charles M., 364, 373, 395, 489
Bahon Gymnasium, 397
Baker, Joshua, 50n
Baker family, 115
Baker, La., 447
Balch, Sarah (Mrs. L. O. Hacker), 155, 160
Balch, Thomas, 155, 380, 403
Balch's School, 403
Baldwin, Eliza Ann (Mrs. John C. Marsh) 128n
Baltimore, Md., 53, 103, 115, 118n, 165
Bands, city, 375
Bank Avenue, named for Citizens' Bank of New Orleans, 129n
Bank Avenue School, 405
Bank of Iberia, 328
Banks, Rev. A. H., 433
Banks, branch, 324
Banks, Iberia Parish, 151-52
Banks, Nathaniel P., 31, 129n
Banner Band, 427
Banquettes, wooden, 498
Bar, Charles, 183
Barnard, Alfred G., 146, 163, 164, 195
Barnard, Mattie (Mrs. J. W. K. Shaw), 349n, 351, 374
Barnes, A. C., 342n, 351n
Barnes, C. F., 342n
Barnes, J. B., 451
Barnes, Mr., 176
Barrilleaux, Auguste, 227, 278, 284n
Barrow, A. G., 258, 263
Barrow, Leonard J., 308, 342n
Barrow, Lillian (Mrs. Leonard J.), 502
Barth, L. V., 262
Barthe, Victor, 342n
Baseball, 484
Bastian's Barber Shop, 451-52
Bates family, 447
Baton Rouge, La., 3, 119n, 145
  Gálvez's siege of, 3
Bauman, Bessie (Mrs. J. E. Kyle), 364, 365
Bauman, F. W., 263n
Bauman, William, 342n

Bauman family, 31
Baumgartner, George, 263n
Bayard, Alfred, 45, 46
Bayard, Baron, Jr., 45, 46, 51n
Bayard, Benoit Baron, 45, 97n
Bayard, Mrs. Baron, see Boutté, Hortense
Bayard, Hipolite, 43, 45, 46, 279, 282n
Bayard plantation, 138
Bayard property, 255
Bayou des Glaises, 359
Bayou Goula, La., 108n
Bayou Lafourche, 3, 103
Bayou Parcperdue, 7n, 118n
Bayou Plaquemine, 6, 95, 102
Bayou Portage, 17, 19n, 95, 264
Bayou Salé, 210
Bayou Sara, La., 118n
Bayou Teche, 3, 7, 17, 17n, 20, 33, 39, 51, 101, 102, 103, 110, 119n
  compromise site for establishment of Malagueños, 6
  Creole settlers along, 19
  development of New Iberia on west bank of, 20n
  drainage canals to, 33n
  early Anglo-American settlers along, 115n
  French and Spanish land grants along 16
Bayou Teche Railway Co., 255
Bayou Tortue, 17-18, 18n
Bayou Vermilion (see also Vermilion River), 17, 18, 115n, 138n
Bayouland Library System, 460
Bayside Plantation, 138, 144n
Bazus, Laurent, 217n, 226, 228
Bazus, Mrs. Laurent, 185
Bazus Hotel, 165n, 233, 418
Beard, Thomas, 118n
Beau Sejour Motel, 169n
Beaubien, Father, 386, 403
Beaulieu & Bourgeois, 151
Beaumont, Texas, 444
Beauvais, Jean-Baptiste, 89n
Beauvais, Mrs. Jean-Baptiste, see Ozenne, Suzanne
Beauvais, Marie Marguerite Irma, 89n
Beckman, H., 301

Begnaud, Wilfred, 324
Belanger, Irene, 423
Belden, Robert, 164, 382n
Bell, R., 145n
Bell, Richard, 121n, 122
Bell, Mrs. Richard, see Swayze, Rachel
Bell, municipal fire, 221
Belle Place, La., 447
Bellocq, S. B., 98
Belmont Plantation, 163
Belmonti, Louis, 59n
Beln, Rev., 77n
Belt, L. T., 273
Belt Line, 273
Ben Franklin Store, 414
Benedict, Rev., 78n
Benevolent Association of Army of Northern Virginia, 211, 214, 215, 216
Benjamin, Judah P., 121n
Benoit, Robert, 405
Benthall & Horner Blacksmith Shop, 228, 233, 305
Bérard, Achille, 45, 97n, 245
Bérard, Mrs. Achille, see Boutté, Hortense
Bérard, Achille, Jr., 45, 46
Bérard, Camille, 45, 46
Bérard, Dailey, 301
Bérard, Ernest, 45, 46
Bérard, Hortense (Mrs. Frederick Henry Duperier, Sr.), 45, 46, 48, 77n, 92n, 144
Bérard, Jean, 92n
Bérard, Jean-Baptiste, 45
Bérard, Mrs. Jean-Baptiste, see Huval, Marie-Aurelie
Bérard, Marie-Mathilde (Mrs. Frederick Henry Duperier, Jr.), 91, 239
Bérard, Mathilde, 45, 46
Bérard, Sadie, 354n
Bérard estate, 92n
Bérard family, 2
Bérard plantation, 138
Bergerie, A. L., 292
Bergerie, Augustin, 41, 41n
Bergerie, Mrs. Augustin, Jr., see Fontelieu, Pauline
Bergerie, Mrs. Augustin, Sr., see Migues, Anna Carmelite

Bergerie, Jean, 41n
Bergerie, Maurice, 298, 455
Bergerie, Maurine, 458
Bergerie, Nemour, 487n
Bergerie family, 177
Berkeley County, Va. (W. Va.), 54n
Bernard, A. A., 336
Bernard, A. C., 342n, 353
Bernard, Mrs. A. C., 458
Bernard, A. M., 298
Bernard, Alaska, 506
Bernard, Arthur, 261
Bernard, Bertha (Mrs. George Dallas), 150n
Bernard, E. L., 261
Bernard, Edwin, 32, 336
Bernard, W. J., Sr., 261, 322, 328, 336, 351n
Bernard & Grimar lands, 337
Bernard lands, 336
Bernard Wagon Works, 298
Bernard's Syrup Mill, 295
Bernhard, Franz, 305
Bernier, Rev., 403
Berry, Albert, 236
Bertram, F., 261
Bertrand, Dr., 414
Bertrand, Hazel, 354n
Bertrand, J., 263n
Bertrand, Luke, 342n, 343n, 351n
Bertrand Lumber Co., 309
Berwick Bay, 115n, 215
Berwick, La., 210, 211, 215, 247, 248, 252
Berwick, Thomas, 118n
Bessan, Mayo, 169n
Best Western Motel, 169n
Betar's Cafe, 418
Bewely, Lonnie, 64
Bicentennial Celebration, New Iberia, 1979, 204-08
Bienvenu, Ronald, 405
Bienvenu family, 177
Bienvenue, Joseph, 41n
Bienvenue's Bakery, 41n
Bienville Furniture Mfgr. Co., 299
Big Jim Sawmill, 150n, 290
Bigler, Karl James, 111, 459
Bisland, Battle of, 174

Index 521

Bittle, A. W., 392
Blackstone, 411
Blake, T., 486n
Blakesley, H., 261
Blanc, A. D., 183, 261
Blanc, Frank, 118
Blanc. G. A., 262
Blanchet, Gustave, 161
Blanchet, Henri, 414
Blanchet, Jules, 176, 184
Blanchet, L. G., 384n
Blanchet, Louise, 169n
Blanchet, Mrs. Octavia, 185
Blend, Wellington, 67, 404
Blend's Night School, 404
Blenk, Archibishop James Herbert, 440, 441
Blue, Donald R., 451
Blumenthal, F. G., 261
B'nai B'rith Hall, 184
Boas, A. C., 163n
Boas, A. L., 239
Bodin, Carlos J., 455
Bodin's Super Market, 314
Bolden, Ruth, 433n
Bolden, Thomas A., 450
Boldt, Charles, 353
Boleto, Brother Bernard, 405
Boley, Rev. F. M., 437
Bonaparte, Napoleon, 101
Bonaton & Vivien, 98
Bonin, D., 261
Bonin, Dominic, 169n
Bonin, Genevieve, 20n
Bonin, J. J., 263n
Bonin, Martial, 465
Bonin, O., 282
Bonin, Ovignac, 277, 278, 284n
Bonner, Prudence (Mrs. William Smith), 123n
Bonvillain, Ernest, 279, 282, 284
Booker T. Washington Branch Library, 456
Booth, William, 98n
Bordeaux, France, 42, 118n
Bordelon, Louis, 106n
Borel, Joseph, 23
Boseman, Lloyd, 405
Bossier, Pierre, 54n

Boston, Mass., 110, 125
Boucvalt, Roy, 131n
Boudreaux, Alfred, 261
Boudreaux, Barbara, 405
Boudreaux, Eugene Morrow, 459
Boudreaux, Gervia, 277, 278, 282n
Boudreaux, H., 384n
Boudreaux, R. L., 261
Boudreaux, S., 211
Boudreaux, Rev. Warren, 78n
Bouligny, Francisco, 4, 5, 8, 10, 25, 73, 76n, 115n
  account of founding of New Iberia, 7n
  buys land from Prévost for settlement of New Iberia, 7
  death of, 8
  favors settling Malagueños on Ouachita River, 6
  leaves New Iberia, 8
  presents emigration plan for Spaniards, 5
  purchase agreement with Prévost for land at New Iberia, 7
  role in the establishment of New Iberia, 7n
Bouligny Plaza, 73, 308
Bouligny's studio, 416
Bourda, Jean, 89n
Bourg, Joe, 414
Bourgeois, St. Paul, 395n
Bourriaque, Joseph, 183
Boutté, Alphonse, 277, 284n
Boutté, André-Claude, 19, 43, 45
Boutté, Antoine, 45n
Boutté, Aristide, 262
Boutté, Daniel C., 261
Boutté, Edmond, 334, 335
Boutté, François Cézar, 43, 44, 45, 97n, 131n
  land grant, 46
Boutté, Mrs. Gugueche, 157, 158, 466
Boutté, Hortense, 45, 46, 48, 97
  partition of estate among children, 46
Boutté, John, 447
Boutté, Marie, 98n
Boutté, Marie-Thérèse (Mrs. Samuel C. Meyer), 45

Boutté, O. J., 261
Boutté, Mrs. Octave, 157
Boutté, Philippe, 52, 53
Boutté, W. J., 262
Boutté & Gonsoulin Livery Stable, 217n
Boutté family, 2, 118n, 421
Boutté land grand, map of, 44
Boutté property, 133
Boutté's Drug Store, 450
Boutté's Hall, 485
Bowab's Dept. Store, 413
Bowers, Rev. William, 434
Bowles, Betsy, 442
Bowles, Lee, 447
Bowles, Samuel, 442
Bowman-Brigante Large Print Collection, 459
Bowman-Brigante, Katherine, 459
Boyer home, 133
Brandon, John, 118n
Brandt & Co., 242
Brantley, Robert, 245
Brashear, Thomas B., 265
Brasher, W., 463n
Brasher City, La. (see also Morgan City, La.), 209, 269, 273
Brass band, black, 477
Brass bands, 476
Breaud, B. Pavie, 261
Breaux, J. F., 261
Breaux, John B., 108n
Breaux, Mrs. John B., see Walsh, Margaret
Breaux, Joseph A., 43, 108, 108n-109n, 142, 151, 164, 164n, 225, 228, 318, 320, 384, 386, 387, 391n
Breaux, Mrs. Joseph A., see Mille Eugénie
Breaux, Sosthen, 277, 284n
Breaux & Renoudet, 151
Breaux Bridge, La., 465
Breaux Building, 302
Breaux family, 110
Breaux, Renoudet, & Broughton Sawmill, 149
Brent, William L., 71, 101, 123n, 265
Brent family, 115, 134n
Brewer, Billy Ray, 245
Brian, F. N., 305

Briant, Paul, 101, 154n
Briant family, 115
Bridge Street bridge, 271
Bridge Street in flood of 1927, 358
Brigante, Vincent, 459
Briganti, Frank, 261
Briganti, Mary, 424
Brigham, T. G., 261
Bristol, England., 118n
Brittain, James F., 252
Broody, Sam, 415
Brooks, John B., 451
Brooks' Stable, 416
Broussard, Adolphe, 277, 284n
Broussard, Alex, 261
Broussard, Allen, 401
Broussard, Anne, 92n
Broussard, Charles, 301
Broussard, Mrs. Dessiard, 505
Broussard, Dominique Ulger, 28, 36n, 60, 146, 162, 169, 184, 186, 193, 194, 201, 290, 384
  accomplishments of, 29
  Confederate soldier, 29
  memorial to, 200
Broussard, E. F., 384n
Broussard, Edmond, 384n
Broussard, Edward, Jr., 405
Broussard, Edwin S., 259, 354
Broussard, Elodie, 280
Broussard, Evard, 361
Broussard, F. L., 347
Broussard, Felonise, (Mrs. Don Louis Broussard), 97n
Broussard, H. J., 261
Broussard, Henry, 309
Broussard, J. D., 401
Broussard, Mrs. Joe, see Landry, Eva
Broussard, John, 217n, 218, 219, 221, 241, 305, 398
Broussard, Knox, 489
Broussard, La., 361, 465
Broussard, Lawrence, 451
Broussard, Leontine (Mrs. Dubuc Etie), 106n
Broussard, Lily Gladys, 354n
Broussard, Louis, 401
Broussard, Morris, 261
Broussard, Mortimer, 384n

Index

Broussard, Numa, 277, 278, 282n
Broussard, Ovignac, 277, 278, 272n
Broussard, Robert F., 43, 146, 147, 230, 231, 232, 236, 237, 241, 243, 354
   becomes district attorney, 149
   elected to Congress, 149
Broussard, Mrs. Robert F., 237
Broussard, Silvio, 146, 245, 260, 261, 298, 340n
Broussard, Suzanne (Mrs. Maximilien Decuir), 97, 97n
Broussard, Tertule, 176
Broussard & Decuir Sawmill, 28, 150, 169
Broussard family, 110
Broussard's Livery Stable, 220, 222, 228
Brown, Christopher, 460
Brown, J. Emmet, 384n
Brown, J. S. Jr., 324, 490
Brown, Mrs. J. S., Jr., see Sandoz, Mary
Brown, James, 130n
Brown, John, 125
Brown, Rev. H. W., 454
Brown, Mrs. H. W., 454
Brown, Perry, 458
Brown, Robert, 150
Brown, W. L., Jr., 388
Brown, William H., 158, 159, 159n
Brown's rice mill, 295
Brownson, John, 57n, 70, 101
Brownson, Mrs. John, see Stelle, Caroline
Brownson, Sarah, 155n
Brownson family, 115
Bruce's Food Products, 295
Bruno, Mr., 101, 101n

Bruns, J. Dickson, 176
Bryant, Rev. C. D., 433
Bryant, Louis Paul, 142, 153, 154n, 344, 466, 483
Bryant, Mrs. Martin (see also De Lauréal, Hermance), 153, 379, 380, 402, 403
Bryant, William, 154n
Bryant, Mrs. William, see Eicher, Minerva
Bryant family, 449
Bryant School, 402, 403
Buck Sindsay, The, 274

Buffington, E. H., 340n, 342n, 343, 343n, 488n
Bully, Mr., 379, 402
Bundick, William, 118n
Buquor, John, 340n
Burbridge, S. G., 32n
Burd, Edward, 49n
Burgess, Charles, 145-46
Burgess, Corinne (Mrs. Charles Outhwaite), 354, 374
Burgess, L. A., 146, 384n
Burguières, L. J., 322
Burke, Celeste, see Dimitry, Celeste
Burke, Donald, 423
Burke, Mrs. Donald, see Dimitry, Celeste
Burke, James L., 52, 52n, 160, 162, 170, 182
Burke, La., 110
Burke, Nina, 367, 372
Burke, Pamela, 282
Burke, Patricia, 354n, 423
Burke, Patrick E., 107, 160, 169n, 184, 193, 382n
Burke, Perry, 362
Burke, Porteus R., 112n, 255, 262, 365, 373, 398
Burke, Mrs. Porteus, see Hine, Mabel
Burke, Roberta (Mrs. Francis Voorhies), 282, 502
Burke, Walter J., 43, 52, 147, 261, 333, , 334, 344, 373, 389
Burke, Mrs. Walter, see Perry, Bertha
Burke, William R., 33n, 97, 160, 163, 183, 186, 194, 237, 379, 381, 381n, 382, 384n, 386, 388, 389, 398, 500
Burke & Fuller, 301
Burke's rice mill, 295
Burkhart, A. C., 146
Burkhart, Casimir, 245
Burns, J. Patout, 418
Burns, Mrs. J. Patout, 49
Burns, Rev. John, 441n
Burns, Robert, 158
Burns home, 55
Burns property, 418
Burr, Aaron, 129n
Bush, Joseph, 442
Bussey plantation, 138, 210
Bussey's sugar mill, 151

Butaud-Doumit Motors, 314
Butler, Myrtle Williams, 446
Butler, Sally, 434
Butler, William, 435
Butte à Peigneur, 57n
Butte la Rose, La., 53, 359
Byrd, Ethel Simon, 446, 447

Cable, George Washington, 59
Cade, C. T., 142, 146, 155, 164, 194, 384n, 486, 388
Cade, Mrs. C. T., see Ker, Elizabeth
Cade, La., 110, 151, 202, 221
Cade, Overton, 142, 185
Cade, Robert, 155n
Cade, Sarah (Mrs. E. B. Smedes), 48, 131n, 155
Cade, William, 142
Cadiz, Spain, 5
Caffery, Donelson, 203
Caffery, John M., 356
Cage, R. H., 322
Calcasieu River, 111
Caldwell Parish, La., 107n
California, 154
Callahan, J. W., 152
Callahan & Lewis, 150, 297
Callin, Stephen, 263n
Calloway, Cab, 447
Cameron, Mr., 188n
Cameron Parish, La., 333
Cammack, A. J., 248, 259
Cammack, Elizabeth, 456, 457
Camors, Dominique Henri, 89n
Camors, Mrs. Dominique H., see Beauvais, Marie
Camors, Irma, 98n
Camors, Jean-Marie, 89n
Camors' store, 89
Campbell, Archie, 457
Campbell, Beverly, 157
Campbell, James, 263n
Canada, 32, 165n
Canary Islands, emigrants from, 5
Canby, Joseph, 56n, 130n
Canby, Mrs. Joseph, see Canby, Mrs. Sarah
Canby, Mrs. Sarah, 49, 54, 55, 56n, 59n, 130n

Cancilla, Sam, 415
Caracas, Mrs. Jos., 404
Cardinals, New Iberia baseball team, 1940, 486
Cardinals, St. Louis baseball team, 487
Carencro, La., 361
Carlin, J. M., 262
Carlin, Joseph, 19, 20, 66n, 68
  land grant of, 52, 53, 66
  land grant map, 22
Carlson, Carl, 263n
Carmelites, Order of, 144n
Carondelet, Baron de, refuses permission for Malagueños to leave New Iberia, 12
Carr, Joseph, 118n
Carriage House, The, 495
Carrie B. Schwing, The, 274
Carroll's Studio, 411
Carstens, Amelia (Mrs Errol Courregé), 365, 366
Carstens, Byrne, 365
Carstens, Mrs. C. J., 384n
Carstens, Caroline, 423
Carstens, Charles, 342n, 359n
Carstens, E. J., 219, 283, 283n, 306, 365, 419, 423, 503
Carstens, Ernest John (E. J.), 277, 278, 279, 280, 282
Carstens, Walter F., 261, 240n, 359n, 365, 398, 419, 489
Carstens, Mrs. Walter, 456
Carstens family, 365
Carstens' store, 278, 279, 281
Carter's Superette, 314
Carter, James, 261
Carter, Jimmy, 121n
Carter, W. D., 261
Carter, W. R., 261
Carver, Hiram W., 340n, 342n, 343n, 351
Carver's rice mill, 295
Cary, Sam, 303
Casa Mena, marqués de, 204, 205
Casa Mena, marquésa de, 205
Castille, D. H., 308
Castille, P. F., 183
Cathcart, James Leander, 78n
Cathedral in the Ghetto, 449

Index 525

Catholic Daughters, 372
Catholic High School, 396, 400, 405, 491
Catholic Knights of America, 228
Catholic Relief Association, 186
Catsulis, Gust, 502
Cattle ranching, Attakapas, 95
Caulking family, 131n
Cecelia, La., 359, 361
Cecil, Martha (Mrs. Henry Stubinger), 32n
Celotex factory, 149
Census
    Attakapas, 1774, 2
    Attakapas and Opelousas districts, 19n
    Malagueños, 14
Centennial Celebration, 1876, 143, 144, 201-204
    black parade during, 203
Centennial Committee, 202
Center Street School, 405
Centerville, La., 210, 303
Central High School, 363, 364, 365, 366, 381, 383, 392, 394, 395, 404, 423, 502
    cornerstone laid, 389n
    first male graduates of, 398
    football teams of, 488-89
    graduating class, 1906, 396
    opens, 368
    tennis team of, 488
Central High School Association, 389, 390
Central sugar factories, 150-51
Cestia, A., 183
Cestia, Alexander, 184, 245
Cestia, Alphé, 42
Cestia, Mrs. Alphé, see Fontelieu, Zulme
Cestia, George, 261
Chaignon, Mrs. Louisa, 185
Chamber of Commerce
    band, 478
    formation of, 1919, 341
Chapelle, Archbishop Louis Placide, 440
Chaplin, Charlie, 494
Chapman, Morris, 169n
Charenton, La., 254, 408
    settlement of Malagueños at, 6

charivari, 41
Charles Boldt Paper Mill, 51, 149, 299, 353, 449
    smokestack, 352
Chassaignac, Charles, 187
Chasse, Rev., 77n
Chatman, Rev. Valco, 433
Chatters, Dr., 451
Chaubet, Louis, 404
Chautauqua, 375, 502
Chautin brothers, 274
Cheatham, Mrs. Ida, 418
Chew, Mr., 49n
Chicago, Ill., 57, 126, 242, 444
Chitimatcha Indians, 6
Christian Brothers, 396, 503, 505
Christian, Jim, 297
Christofo Columbo Society, 474
Church of the Epiphany, 31, 112n, 159n
    cornerstone laid, 31n
Church, Cecilia (Mrs. John Nicholls), 130n
Cincinnati, Ohio, 54n, 130n, 185
Circuses, 477
Cistern manufacturing, 297
Citizens' Bank of New Iberia, 322, 324
Citizens' Bank of New Orleans, 57, 60, 62, 63, 65n, 92, 129n
City Bank & Trust Co., 324, 325
    W. St. Peter St. branch, 326
City Hall, 461
    old, 415
City Market, 415
    described, 40
City Park, 355, 375
    branch library, 457
    pavilion, 408, 409
Civic Center, 52, 58n, 65, 66, 458
Civic League, 261-62
Civil War, 173-74
    aftermath of in New Iberia, 173-74
Claiborne, William C. C., 53, 103n
Clark, Daniel, 48, 49, 51n, 104, 131n
Clark, Elizabeth (Mrs. John Stine, Sr.), 36n, 37n, 40n, 90n
Clark, J. J., 263n
Clark, Marguerite, 494
Clark, Patrick Francis, 37n

Clark, Mrs. Patrick Francis, see Malone, Rachel
Clay, Henry, 105
Clements, Jacob, 265
Clerc, Charles, 51n, 52n, 202
Clerc, Mrs. Charles, 185
Clerc, Ilma, 203
Clerc home, 242
Clerc property, 183
Club Mid Day, 452
Cobb, Angus, Jr., 405
Cobb, Mary E. (Mrs. Jacob Schriener), 41
Cody, W. F., "Buffalo Bill," 481
Cohan, George M., 494
Coleman's Cafe, 408, 416
Coleman, Viola, 451
Colet, see Prévost
Colgin, A. J., 183, 211
Colgin, C. E., 261
Colgin, Dr., 159n, 304
Colgin, Evelyn, 354n
Colgin, G. R., 262
Colgin, George, 60, 161
Colgin, Jackson, 142, 157, 160
Colgin, James T., 261
Colgin, Rufus, 157, 160
Colgin, William, 308
Colgin's School, 35n
Collège Louis le Grand, 153
Collie family, 131n
Collins, John, 69
Collins, Mary, 457
Collins, Rita Grace, 453
Collins, Thomas W., 38, 72, 93n
Collins brothers, 118n
Colonial Motel, 169n
Colonists
    Acadian, 3
    French, 3
    German, 3
Color, Jack, 169n
Comeaux, Mrs. Antoine, 185
Commandant, colonial
    duties of, 2
Commencement exercises, early, 500
Commercial Canal, 105n
Commission Form of Government League (see also Civic League), 261-62

Compton, C. M., 340n
Conbrough, William, 70
Condon, W. J., 261
Conery, W. P., 255
Confederate breastworks, 31
Confederate veterans, 276-84
Congregation Gates of Prayer, 112n
Congressional Construction Co., 242
Conrad, Adrien, 279, 282, 283, 284
Conrad, Alfred, 119, 119n
Conrad, Mrs. Allen, see De La Loire, Estelle, 503
Conrad, Ann Alexander (Mrs. John Towles), 118n, 121n
Conrad, Charles M., 119, 119n, 120, 120n, 121n
Conrad, Mrs. Charles M., see Lewis, Mary Eliza Angela
Conrad, Collins, 294
Conrad, Elizabeth Frances, 119n
Conrad, Frances Elizabeth (Mrs. Winthrop Sargent Harding), 119n, 121n
Conrad, Frank, 119n
Conrad, Frederick, Sr., 119n
Conrad, Mrs. Frederick, Sr., see Thruston, Frances
Conrad, Frederick D., 99, 118n, 119, 119n, 120
Conrad, Mrs. Frederick D., see Duncan, Fanny
Conrad, Gabriel, 487n
Conrad, Henry, 119n
Conrad, John, 420
Conrad, Mrs. Julian (Margaret Corcoran) 505
Conrad, Mary Clara (l. Mrs. David Weeks; 2. Mrs. John Moore), 54n, 67, 100, 118, 119, 120, 126n, 128n
Conrad, Philip A., 295, 362
Conrad, Sydney Ann (Mrs. William T. Palfrey), 119n, 121n
Conrad, Sylvia (Mrs. Glenn R. Conrad), 205
Conrad, T. E., 261
Conrad, Wilfred Sr., 401, 420, 485
Conrad, William, 420
Conrad Brick Factory, 294
Conrad family, 115
Conrad Point, 119n
Conrad Rice Mill, 295, 296

Index 527

Consolidated Association Bank, 92
Consolidated Companies, 270, 274, 343
Constitution, U. S.
  19th Amendment, 354
Convent, colored, 225
Convent Ste-Clothilde, 153
Conway, Cora Joseph, 446, 447
Conway, Cora Lee, 451
Cook, A., 397n, 402
Cooper, Rhona, 451
Cooper, Sam W., 450, 451, 453
Corbett, James J. "Gentleman Jim," 492, 493
Corniere, Pierre, 475
Cornwall, Engalnd, 130n
Costa Rica, 154
Côte Blanche Bay, 189, 191
Côte Gelée, La., 102
Coteau, La., 202, 465
Cottage Plantation, 120n
Cotton oil mill, 163
Coudron & Whitney, 304
Couget, Mrs. Leon, 185
Count Basie, 447
Courmier, Charles, 299
Courregé, Bertha, 506
Courtableau family, 19
Courthouse, 146, 146n
  earliest, 191
  early, 189, 192
  in Veazey Building, 192
  new, 194
    additions of 1976, 197
    additions of 1985-86, 198
    Albrizo fresco, 195
    courtroom fresco, 200
    plan to build, 199
    statue of Justice, 196
  old, 151, 161, 170, 190, 193, 375, 415
    on site of old Stine home, 40
    plan to remodel, 1922, 199
    property purchased from Taylor and Devalcourt, 29n
  site, 133
Courtois, Albert, 261
Courtois, Jules, 408
Courts, Frank, 58
Courts, Mrs. Frank, see Russell, Henrietta

Courts, Henrietta (Mrs. Frank), 502
Cousin, George, 343n, 351n, 489
Coxe, Daniel, 49n, 50n, 54n, 56n, 74, 131n
Craig, Euphemie (Mrs. John C. Marsh), 128n
Craig, J. J., 228
Craufurd, Martha (Mrs. Robert Hamilton), 130n
Cregs, Lester, 396
Creighton, Henry, 262
Creim, Mrs. Percy, 112n
Creim's store, 413
Crene (Crane), Ebenezer, 118n
Creoles Baseball Club, 115n, 184
Crews, H. C., 261
Crews, W. A., 261
Crowson, George, 400
Culver, Mildred (Mrs. William), 366
Cumberland Telephone & Telegraph Co. 309
Cumberland University, 387n
Curry, Robert W., 268, 272
Cyr, Louis M., 328
Cyr, Paul N., 151, 394n

D.H. Castile, 314
Daigle, Clarence, 147n
Daigre, A., 261, 322
Daigre, Aristide, 323
Daigre, H. J., 261
Daigre, Homer, 228
Daigre, J. A., 312
Daigre, J. Allen, 205, 324, 449
Daigre, Mrs. Joseph A., see Harry, Carmen
Daigre's Ice House, 297
Daigre's Oil Co., 312
Daigre's store, 133, 413
Daily Iberian, 149, 314, 433n
Dallas, George W., 261, 290, 340n
  biographical sketch of, 149
  death of, 150n
  home of, 150
Dallas, Mrs. George W, see Bernard, Bertha
Dallas & Bertram Hardware Co., 150n
Dallas Jewelry Store, 413
Dance hall
  Mrs Octave Boutté's, 157

Daniels, Hermogene, 382n
Daniels, Mervin, 489
Darby, Ernest, 157
Darby, Ezelda, 185
Darby, François Optat, 105n
Darby, François St-Marc, 26, 35n, 77n, 87n, 153, 154
Darby, Mrs. François St-Marc, see De Blanc, Constance
Darby, Jean-Baptiste St-Marc, 12, 13, 76n, 78
   commandant at New Iberia, 10
   commission as commandant, 10n
   death of, 13n
Darby, Mrs. Jean-Baptiste St-Marc, see Pellerin, Françoise Hélène
Darby, Marie Celeste (Mrs. Joseph Dautrive Dubuclet), 26, 154
   sells Alma House to Robert Hilliard, 27
Darby, Marie Ladoiska (Mrs. Leonard Smith), 26, 134n
Darby, Paul, 277, 278, 282n
Darby estate, 133
Darby family, 98, 154
Darby House, 136
Darby plantation, 156
Darby-Wattigny Motors, 314
Dariet, Eugene, 217n
Darnell, John, 457
Daspit, Armand, 487n
Daspit, Robert E., 261
Daughters of the American Revolution, 374
Daunoy, A. F., 239
Daunt, William G., 245
Dauphine, Rhona, 453
Dauphine brothers, 450
Dauphine's Food Mart, 451
Dauterive, A. A., 261
Dauterive, A. B., 176
Dauterive, Celia, 354n
Dauterive, Eddie, 263n
Dauterive, Fernand, 219
Dauterive, Frank, 342n, 343
Dauterive, George, L., 263n
Dauterive, Henry, Sr., 137, 355, 373
Dauterive, Mrs. Henry J., Sr., 118n, 137, 229n

Dauterive, Henrietta, 501
Dauterive (D'Hauterive), Jean-Antoine-Bernard, 17, 19
Dauterive, L. J., 263n
Dauterive family, 98, 177
Dauterive Furniture Co., 411, 415
Dauterive Hospital, 144, 362, 372
   founded, 355
   new, 179
   old, 179
Dauterive Undertaking Parlors, 309
Dauterive vacherie, 18
David, Dave, 112n
David, Ethel, 366
David, Mrs. E., 169n
David, Theo., 361
Davis, Alphonse, 245, 261, 334, 351n
Davis, Elizabeth (Mrs. Ramus), 138n
Davis, Frederick, 262, 277, 278, 282
Davis, Mrs. Frederick, 282
Davis, Jacob, 301, 308
Davis, Mrs. John R., see Winters, Margaret
Davis, Joseph, 308, 340, 340n, 342, 415, 487n
Davis, Mike, 295
Davis, Nathan, 261, 340n
Davis, Ramus, 138n
Davis, Rev. W., 433
Davis, W. B., 232
Davis, Rev. William, 433
Davis brothers, 309
Davis Furniture Store, 133n
Davis Machine Shop, 298
Davis property, 65
Davis' oak grove, 214
Davis-Delcambre Motors, 314
Dayton House, 41
De Blanc, A. A., 340n
De Blanc, Alcibiades, 169, 170, 203, 210, 216, 463n
De Blanc, Constance (Mrs. François St-Marc Darby), 26, 35n
De Blanc, Cyrus, 340n
De Blanc, Elisabeth Marcelite, 26
De Blanc, Ello, 279, 280
De Blanc, Fred, 261
De Blanc, George Thomas, 26
De Blanc, Jean-Baptiste Dorsinos, 26